TRANSFORMATIVE JUSTICE AND TIBETAN BUDDHISM

PRINCIPLES FOR RESTORATIVE OFFENDER REHABILITATION & MODERN CRIMINOLOGY

ISHAAN D. JOSHI

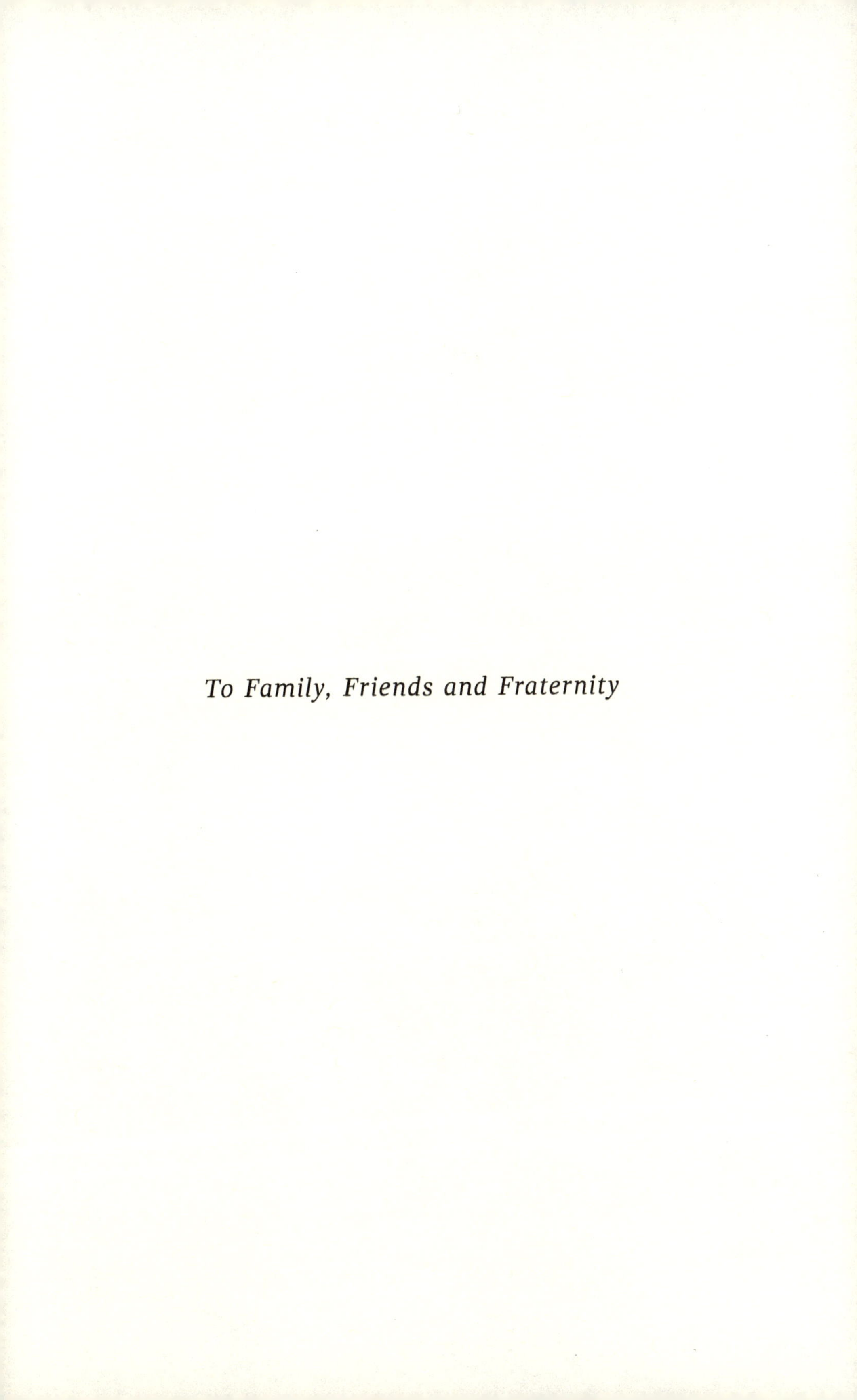

To Family, Friends and Fraternity

Contents

Contents

Foreword

Ven. Geshe Lhakdor
Director - LTWA,
Honorary Professor - University of British Columbia & University of
Delhi, Department of Psychology

Transformative Justice & Tibetan Buddhism: Principles for Restorative Offender Rehabilitation & Modern Criminology, by Ishaan D. Joshi is a very timely analysis. This book provides a comprehensive framework for applying ancient wisdom to contemporary justice systems and the potential for personal transformation. Its primary goal is to reshape the justice system by incorporating the ethical, philosophical, and practical aspects of Tibetan Buddhism into offender rehabilitation. Joshi's dedication to advancing knowledge extends beyond national borders, reflecting a deep-seated commitment to holistic learning, which also goes very well with the Buddhist philosophy of taking care of the wellbeing of all sentient beings.

I have always asserted that Buddhism is a perennial philosophy and has the capacity to transform the individual and the society at large, irrespective of time and period. Many of the problems that we see today are clear indications of the starvation of the human mind. It is easy to run after ephemeral pleasures and get bogged down there. We have become slaves to the dictates of the senses while the main controller, the mind, is left untouched. As goes our mental state, so goes the person and the society at large. This entire earth is today mad with unchecked greed. Unchecked greed leads to lack of contentment which, in turn, leads to the disastrous behaviour of destroying the whole planet.

Look at the big cities everywhere in the world, where most of the so-called educated and intelligent people and the leaders of the world are living. Air is polluted, water is polluted and the whole environment is not so suitable for healthy life. We are quite efficient in destroying others with ballistic missiles and many other clever inventions designed to kill but not so efficient iri dealing with pandemics, pollution and epidemics. This is all aresult of minds deluded by negative emotions and deprived of basic, good human qualities like love and compassion.

So, in dealing with any human problems, the solution also should be human and not animalistic. We cannot solve problems by being unkind, exploitative and authoritative. Just as a sick person is treated with medicine and kindness, similarly criminal activities are also a kind of sickness and hence should be treated with kindness and wisdom.

One of the great counsels given in the Buddhist texts is to make a distinction between the wrongdoing and the wrongdoer. The wrongdoing should be pointed out and identified, and corrective measures should be taken, but the wrongdoer should be given the opportunity to transform and remain as a member of the community. Transgressors should not be ostracized and should not be treated as black sheep among society. After all, who is there who does not make a mistake and engage in wrongdoing? Nagarjuna in his Precious Garland, chapter 4, "Compassion and Wisdom in Public Policy," says that criminals are to be treated like one's own children with a compassionate wish to reform them:

Just as deficient children are punished
Out of a wish to make them competent,
So punishment should be carried out with compassion,
Not through hatred nor desire for wealth.

Even when ministers have jailed criminals, those rulers should be concerned for those they incarcerate. Offenders who have committed particularly awful crimes are to be treated with special compassion. Weaker prisoners are to be freed after brief incarceration, and all others eventually. While incarcerated, prisoners should be treated humanely.

If, upon analysis, some prisoners are determined to be particularly dangerous, they should be exiled. It is clear that for Nagarjuna there are no limits to the compassion required for a religious or civilised government.

What is really missing in today's human affairs and day-to-day activities are love, compassion and concern for others. The main concern is unfortunately how to make money and increase material affluence. A society where the basic human good qualities are missing can never be happy and harmonious.

It doesn't really matter how many grand buildings and other shiny gadgets we accumulate. It is high time we become sensible and good human beings - Homo sapiens - the wise human.

I much appreciate that Ishaan D. Joshi has written this book, a well-timed disquisition. It is definite that his fresh insights contain valuable advice for making the right decisions when punishing wrongdoers and criminals. Tashi delek- may all have the auspiciousness of current wellbeing and long-term goodness.

Geshe Lhakdor
Director
LTWA
27 October 2024

"Benevolence is the choice of the strong; true virtue lies in the voluntary restraint of power."

Ishaan D. Joshi

Acknowledgements

Gurukul Fellows 2023' with His Holiness The Dalai Lama

This book is the culmination of an extraordinary journey, one that has been enriched by the diverse perspectives each of you have shared with me. It is your unique insights that have sparked my curiosity, brought vibrancy to my life, fortified my faith, and imbued my writing with purpose.

I extend my heartfelt gratitude to all of you: **Akashleena, Hrnoor, Sonam, Yogeshwar, Ashmeet, Kalyan, Dhanuja, Dinu, Isar, Jaishree, Kapeesh, Afaan, Soham, Penpa, Aditi, Aparajita, Lobsang, Namdol, Akshaya, Zehra, Tanvi, Abhiraj, and Sarah.** Your contributions have been invaluable.

I also wish to thank **Shilpi, Yash, and Norzom,** as well as the entire team at **FURHHDL.** A special note of appreciation to **Mr. Rajiv**

Mehrotra, not only for the life-changing opportunity but also for his guidance on the technical aspects of this work. My sincere thanks go to **Meenakshi Gopinath Ma'am, Seema Kakran Ma'am, and Anukriti** for their unwavering support.

A profound thanks to the **Central Tibetan Administration, the Library of Tibetan Works and Archives, and Director Ven. Geshe Lhakdor la** for their invaluable insights. I am deeply grateful to Head Abbot Sonam la of Dip Tse Chok Ling Monastery for his wisdom and guidance.

I extend my deepest gratitude to **my mentors, guides, and professors** in law, criminology, forensics, psychology, and conflict resolution. Your mentorship has been a cornerstone of this endeavor.

Above all, my utmost gratitude goes to **His Holiness The Dalai Lama,** whose teachings and guidance have been the beacon illuminating this journey.

བྱམས་པ་ན་ས་ན་ཅང་ད་ེ་ན་ད་ུ་གཟ་་་བ།

About The Author

Ishaan D. Joshi is a dedicated Consulting Forensic Detective, Forensic Psychology and Medico-Legal Expert, Criminology Research Author, ADR Expert and Coach, whose work brings a distinctive, holistic approach to the fields of criminology, forensic psychology, and criminal justice. His expertise spans various aspects of the justice system, including behavioral analysis, criminal intelligence, abnormal psychology, forensic medicine, cyberforensics, and counterterrorism, which he integrates into a nuanced understanding of the complexities within each case he handles.

As an author, Joshi has written several books on forensic psychology, cyberpsychology, and predictive policing, contributing thoughtful insights to these ever-evolving disciplines. With over 70 published articles in national and international journals, he continues to build a respected body of work that enriches discussions on ethics, law, criminology, and forensic science. His role as an Editorial Assistant at the Psychreg Journal of Psychology in London and his work as an academic reviewer for notable journals reflect his commitment to advancing research and encouraging high standards in academic publication.

During his time at NALSAR University of Law, Joshi developed the HOPE Model (Holistic Observation and Prisoner Enhancement Model), an AI-driven system for offender rehabilitation that embodies his forward-thinking approach to criminal justice. This model underscores his belief in the power of technology to enhance rehabilitation efforts, aiming to create a justice system that is not only effective but also empathetic and reformative.

Currently, Joshi is pursuing an LLM in Criminal Law and Criminal Justice at Edinburgh Law School in Scotland, where he serves as the Programme Representative. His academic journey reflects a continuous commitment to professional and personal growth. His book Kantian Ethics in Indian Legal Education, housed in the Supreme Court Judges Library, offers a unique perspective on the intersection of ethics and legal education, demonstrating his dedication to philosophical inquiry alongside his forensic expertise.

A former Gurukul Fellow of the Foundation of Universal Responsibility of His Holiness The Dalai Lama, Joshi's experiences reflect a profound commitment to ethical responsibility and societal betterment. In all his work, Ishaan D. Joshi exemplifies the drive to seek truth and justice, leaving an indelible impact on the fields he touches, and inspiring those around him to pursue a more just and informed world.

Preface

With Ven. Geshe Lhakdor (LTWA, Dharamshala, June 2023)

In the tranquil heights of Dharamshala, where the whispers of ancient wisdom float on the crisp mountain air, I embarked on a journey that would forever change the trajectory of my professional and personal life. Selected as a Gurukul Fellow in 2023 through the prestigious Foundation of Universal Responsibility of His Holiness The Dalai Lama (FURHHDL), I joined a diverse cohort of students and scholars, each one carrying the torch of knowledge from a different realm of human inquiry. Philosophy, Buddhism, history, psychology, sociology, neuroscience, political science, journalism, law, linguistics, tantric studies, zoology, design, and cinematography—each discipline converged in this sacred space, fostering a rich tapestry of dialogue and discovery. Previously, I was on the committee of The Dalai Lama Chair at MIT Pune.

Nestled within the serene confines of the Dip Tse Chok Ling Monastery, our days were punctuated by moments of deep reflection and vigorous debate. Over Butter Tea, Tsampa, and Balep, we shared our insights and challenged each other's perspectives. These discussions often stretched into the late hours of chilly nights, illuminated by the soft glow of moonlight in my modest cottage at the edge of the forest. It was in these moments of intellectual camaraderie and spiritual introspection that the seeds of this book were sown. The integration of Buddhist principles with the field of crime and forensics began to take shape in my mind, driven by the realization of the potential these teachings held for transformative justice.

During my time there, I attended the lecture series by Ven. Geshe Lhakdor at the Library of Tibetan Works and Archives (LTWA). His talks on Nagarjuna and the Middle Way were particularly illuminating, providing a philosophical foundation that resonated with my quest for a more humane approach to justice. This culminated in me publishing a paper titled *Pratītyasamutpāda, Social Comprehension & Accountability In The Framework Of Restorative Justice*, which explored the intricate connections between Buddhist concepts of interconnectedness and modern restorative justice practices. This work was not merely an academic exercise but an exploration of how ancient wisdom could address the complexities of contemporary justice systems. One of the most transformative moments of this journey was meeting His Holiness The Dalai Lama. His serene presence and insights left an indelible mark on me. His teachings on compassion, ethics, and the importance of doing what is right resonated deeply with my belief in the potential for transformation within every individual.

My professional path has always been intertwined with the pursuit of justice. As a researcher, author, forensic detective and mediator, my work has often confronted the darker aspects of human behavior. The cynical postmodern world views benevolence, justice, and morality with suspicion, often dismissing these virtues as naive. Yet, my engagement with Buddhist philosophy offered a glimmer of hope—a vision of justice that was not solely punitive but deeply restorative. The story of Angulimala, a tale of redemption and potential, became a beacon of possibility. It challenged me to envision a system that recognizes the inherent worth and capacity for change in every individual.

The pivotal moment was a phone call from Justice Mridula Bhatkar (Retd.) of the Bombay High Court, Chairperson of the Maharashtra Administrative Tribunal and the Indian Law Society. She was visiting Dharamshala on a vacation, and had visited my monastery. This encounter, months after my stay at Dip Tse Chok Ling, was a symbolic reminder of the intersection between justice and compassion. It was then, that I began to envision a comprehensive framework that could integrate Buddhist principles with modern criminological practices.

In 2024, this vision took a concrete form during my time at NALSAR with the creation of the *HOPE Model—Holistic Observation and Prisoner Enhancement*—an AI-integrated rehabilitation software designed to facilitate restorative offender rehabilitation. It synthesizes my extensive knowledge into a practical tool for the future of Correctional Sciences. The development of this software was a pivotal step in my journey, marking the transition from theoretical exploration to practical application.

'Transformative Justice & Tibetan Buddhism: Principles for Restorative Offender Rehabilitation & Modern Criminology' is the culmination of this journey. This book is structured to provide a comprehensive exploration of how Tibetan Buddhist principles can inform and transform modern justice systems. It begins with an in-depth examination of the foundational teachings of Buddhism, exploring concepts such as the Middle Way, Dependent Origination, and the Four Noble Truths. These chapters lay the groundwork for understanding how these ancient principles can be applied to contemporary issues in rehabilitation.

The book then delves into the practical applications of the Eightfold Path in rehabilitation, offering detailed strategies for developing ethical perspectives, promoting honest communication, supporting ethical employment, and fostering mindfulness among offenders. Each chapter is enriched with case studies and practical examples, illustrating the transformative potential of these practices. The exploration of the Bodhisattva Ideal in justice further expands on these themes, highlighting the importance of compassion, altruism, and ethical leadership.

In the subsequent sections, the book focuses on the integration of mindfulness and meditation in rehabilitation, emphasizing their benefits for stress reduction, emotional regulation, and long-term mental health. The chapters on ethical precepts and personal responsibility explore how Buddhist ethical principles can guide offenders towards accountability and transformation. Restorative practices inspired by Buddhism, such as restorative justice and mediation techniques, are examined in detail, providing a comprehensive guide for practitioners.

The final part of the book bridges Buddhist philosophy with modern criminology, offering insights into the development of comprehensive rehabilitation programs and policy recommendations for reforms. It also outlines future directions and research opportunities, encouraging continued exploration and innovation in this field.

This book is dedicated to all those who believe in the power of hope. It is a testament to the potential for transformation that lies within every individual and a call to create a justice system that honors this potential. I invite you, dear reader, to join me on this journey towards a more compassionate and just world.

Ishaan D. Joshi

Part I: Foundations of Tibetan Buddhist Principles

—

CHAPTER ONE

Introduction to Tibetan Buddhist Principles

Contents

- Historical Evolution and Key Figures
- Fundamental Concepts: Dharma, Samsara, Nirvana
- The Three Pillars: Ethical Conduct, Wisdom, Mental Discipline
- Relevance to Modern Justice Systems
- Case Studies of Buddhist Principles in Justice

———••⧜••———

1.1: Historical Evolution and Key Figures

Tibetan Buddhism, a rich and intricate tradition, traces its origins to the 7th century, marking the arrival of Buddhism in Tibet from India. This profound journey began under the reign of King Songtsen Gampo, who is credited with introducing Buddhist teachings to the Tibetan people. The king's marriage to Princess Wencheng of China and Princess Bhrikuti of Nepal played a significant role in this cultural and religious transmission, as both princesses were devout Buddhists and brought sacred texts, relics, and statues to Tibet. These early introductions laid the groundwork for what would become a deeply rooted spiritual tradition. The development of Tibetan Buddhism was further solidified by the work of Padmasambhava, also known as Guru Rinpoche, in the 8th century.

Invited by King Trisong Detsen, Padmasambhava is often revered as the "Second Buddha" for his foundational role in establishing Buddhism in Tibet. His teachings and tantric practices, along with those of his consort Yeshe Tsogyal, were instrumental in overcoming local resistance and integrating Buddhist philosophy with indigenous Bon traditions. Padmasambhava's legacy includes the establishment of the first monastery at Samye, a significant milestone in the institutionalization of Buddhism in Tibet. Tsongkhapa, a 14th-century scholar and yogi, further shaped Tibetan Buddhism through his extensive writings and reformative efforts. He founded the Gelug school, known for its emphasis on monastic discipline and scholarly rigor. Tsongkhapa's works, including the Lamrim Chenmo (The Great Treatise on the Stages of the Path to Enlightenment), remain central to Tibetan Buddhist study and practice. His synthesis of Madhyamaka philosophy and Vajrayana practice provided a comprehensive framework that continues to guide practitioners.

The Dalai Lamas, spiritual leaders of the Gelug school, have played a pivotal role in the evolution and preservation of Tibetan Buddhism. The institution of the Dalai Lama began with Gendun Drup, posthumously recognized as the first Dalai Lama, but it was the third Dalai Lama, Sonam Gyatso, who was granted the title "Dalai Lama" by the Mongolian ruler Altan Khan. The current Dalai Lama, His Holiness, Tenzin Gyatso, is the 14th in this lineage and has been instrumental in promoting Tibetan Buddhism globally, especially following his exile from Tibet in 1959 after the Chinese invasion. His efforts in spreading the message of compassion, non-violence, and universal responsibility have earned him international acclaim, including the Nobel Peace Prize.

Significant texts and scriptures form the bedrock of Tibetan Buddhist practice and philosophy. The Kangyur, a collection of the Buddha's teachings, and the Tengyur, commentaries by Indian and Tibetan scholars, are the primary canonical texts. These scriptures cover a vast array of topics, including ethics, meditation, philosophy, and ritual practices. The Kangyur consists of over 100 volumes, while the Tengyur comprises more than 200 volumes, reflecting the extensive nature of Tibetan Buddhist literature. These texts are not merely studied but are also recited, memorized, and ritually performed, embedding their teachings deeply into the spiritual lives of practitioners. In addition to these canonical texts, terma (hidden treasures) discovered by tertons (treasure revealers) play a unique role in Tibetan Buddhism. These teachings, said to be hidden by Padmasambhava and his consort Yeshe Tsogyal for future generations, are revealed at auspicious times to guide and inspire practitioners. The discovery of terma continues to be a dynamic aspect of Tibetan Buddhism, contributing to its adaptability and evolution.

The integration of these teachings into the daily lives of Tibetan Buddhists is evident in various aspects of their culture, from art and architecture to festivals and rituals. Monasteries and stupas, adorned with intricate murals and statues, serve as centers of learning and spiritual practice. Festivals such as Losar (Tibetan New Year) and Monlam (Great Prayer Festival) are significant cultural events that embody the community's devotion and reverence for the Buddha's teachings. Understanding the historical evolution and key figures of Tibetan Buddhism provides a profound context for exploring its doctrines and their relevance to modern justice systems. The tradition's emphasis on compassion, ethical conduct, and mental discipline offers valuable insights for addressing the root causes of criminal behavior and fostering personal transformation. By delving into the rich tapestry of Tibetan Buddhism, we can uncover the potential for creating a more compassionate and effective justice system that aligns with the core principles of this ancient wisdom.

1.2: Fundamental Concepts: Dharma, Samsara, Nirvana

In the vast expanse of Buddhist thought, three core concepts stand out as the bedrock of the philosophy and practice in Tibetan Buddhism: Dharma, Samsara, and Nirvana. These principles not only shape the spiritual lives of adherents but also offer profound insights into ethical behavior and personal transformation. Understanding these concepts is crucial for grasping how they can influence modern justice systems and rehabilitation practices. Dharma, often translated as "the teachings of the Buddha" or "cosmic law and order," is a multifaceted concept in Buddhism. It encompasses the path to enlightenment, the moral and ethical guidelines for living, and the fundamental truths about the nature of reality. In Tibetan Buddhism, Dharma is not merely a set of doctrines to be intellectually understood but a lived experience that permeates every aspect of life. Practitioners engage with Dharma through study, meditation, and ethical conduct, striving to align their actions with the teachings of the Buddha. This alignment fosters personal growth, ethical integrity, and a deeper understanding of one's place in the interconnected web of life.

The concept of Samsara, the cycle of birth, death, and rebirth, is a central tenet in Buddhist philosophy. Samsara is characterized by suffering (dukkha) and driven by karma, the law of cause and effect. According to Buddhist teachings, beings are trapped in Samsara due to ignorance and attachment, continually experiencing various forms of suffering. In Tibetan Buddhism, the goal is to break free from this cycle and attain liberation (moksha) or Nirvana. Understanding Samsara involves recognizing the impermanent and unsatisfactory nature of worldly existence and cultivating a sense of detachment and equanimity. This understanding is pivotal for developing compassion towards all sentient beings, as it highlights the shared plight of suffering and the potential for liberation.

Nirvana, the ultimate goal of Buddhist practice, represents the cessation of suffering and the end of the cycle of Samsara. It is a state of perfect peace, wisdom, and freedom from all defilements and afflictive emotions. In Tibetan Buddhism, attaining Nirvana is not seen as an escape from the world but as the culmination of a transformative journey that involves profound inner change and the realization of one's true nature. Nirvana is described as beyond ordinary human comprehension, a state where dualities such as pleasure and pain, existence and non-existence, cease to exist. Achieving Nirvana requires rigorous practice, including ethical living, meditation, and the cultivation of wisdom and compassion. These fundamental concepts—Dharma, Samsara, and Nirvana—form the foundation of Tibetan Buddhist practice and philosophy. They provide a framework for understanding the nature of existence, the causes of suffering, and the path to liberation. In the context of modern justice systems and rehabilitation practices, these principles offer valuable insights into addressing the root causes of criminal behavior and fostering personal transformation.

The concept of Dharma emphasizes the importance of ethical conduct and moral responsibility. In a justice system, this translates to policies and practices that uphold fairness, integrity, and compassion. By aligning with Dharma, justice practitioners can create an environment that encourages ethical behavior and personal growth in offenders. This approach goes beyond punitive measures, focusing instead on rehabilitation and the potential for positive change. Samsara, with its emphasis on the cyclical nature of existence and the pervasive presence of suffering, underscores the importance of addressing the underlying causes of criminal behavior. Rather than viewing crime as a simple act of wrongdoing, Samsara invites us to consider the complex web of factors—social, psychological, economic—that contribute to such behavior. This holistic perspective can inform more effective rehabilitation programs that seek to break the cycle of reoffending by addressing these root causes.

Nirvana, representing the ultimate goal of liberation and inner peace, provides a vision of what is possible when individuals undergo profound personal transformation. In the context of rehabilitation, this vision translates to helping offenders achieve a state of psychological and emotional well-being, free from the afflictive emotions and negative behaviors that led to their criminal actions. By incorporating practices that promote mindfulness, compassion, and wisdom, rehabilitation programs can support offenders in their journey towards personal transformation and reintegration into society. Understanding these concepts also highlights the importance of compassion and empathy in justice practices. Recognizing the shared suffering of all beings, as emphasized in the teachings on Samsara, can foster a more humane and compassionate approach to justice. This perspective encourages justice practitioners to see offenders not merely as wrongdoers but as individuals caught in a cycle of suffering, deserving of support and opportunities for rehabilitation.

Furthermore, the principles of Dharma, Samsara, and Nirvana underscore the interconnectedness of all beings and the impact of individual actions on the broader community. This interconnectedness calls for a justice system that not only addresses individual behavior but also considers the broader social context and seeks to create conditions for collective well-being. By promoting ethical conduct, addressing the root causes of criminal behavior, and supporting personal transformation, a justice system informed by these Buddhist principles can contribute to a more just and compassionate society. The core concepts of Dharma, Samsara, and Nirvana provide a profound framework for understanding and addressing criminal behavior. They emphasize the importance of ethical conduct, the interconnected nature of existence, and the potential for personal transformation. By integrating these principles into modern justice systems and rehabilitation practices, we can create a more compassionate and effective approach to justice that aligns with the deepest aspirations of Tibetan Buddhist philosophy.

1.3: The Three Pillars: Ethical Conduct, Wisdom, Mental Discipline

The Three Pillars of Tibetan Buddhism—Ethical Conduct (Sila), Wisdom (Prajna), and Mental Discipline (Samadhi)—form the foundation of Buddhist practice and provide a comprehensive framework for personal transformation. These pillars are not merely abstract concepts; they are practical guidelines that shape the behavior, thoughts, and spiritual development of practitioners. Understanding these pillars and their interconnections is essential for appreciating their potential impact on modern justice systems and rehabilitation practices. Ethical Conduct, or Sila, is the cornerstone of Buddhist practice. It encompasses the moral and ethical guidelines that govern behavior, promoting actions that are beneficial to oneself and others while avoiding harm.

In Tibetan Buddhism, ethical conduct is often codified in the form of precepts or vows, which practitioners commit to uphold. These precepts include refraining from killing, stealing, lying, sexual misconduct, and intoxication. The practice of ethical conduct is seen as essential for creating a stable and harmonious mind, which is necessary for the development of wisdom and mental discipline. The emphasis on ethical conduct in Tibetan Buddhism aligns with the concept of karma, the law of cause and effect. According to this principle, actions have consequences, and ethical behavior leads to positive outcomes while unethical behavior leads to suffering. This understanding of karma reinforces the importance of ethical conduct in creating a just and compassionate society. In the context of justice systems, the principle of Sila can inform policies and practices that promote ethical behavior and accountability, both among offenders and within the broader community.

Wisdom, or Prajna, is the second pillar of Tibetan Buddhism. It involves the cultivation of deep understanding and insight into the true nature of reality. This wisdom is not merely intellectual knowledge but a profound experiential realization that transcends ordinary perceptions. In Tibetan Buddhism, wisdom is often associated with the understanding of emptiness (Shunyata), the recognition that all phenomena are interdependent and lack inherent existence. This insight into emptiness is seen as crucial for overcoming ignorance, attachment, and suffering. The development of wisdom in Tibetan Buddhism involves both study and meditation. Practitioners engage in the study of Buddhist scriptures and philosophical texts to gain a conceptual understanding of key teachings. This study is complemented by meditation practices that help deepen and internalize this understanding. Wisdom is also cultivated through the practice of ethical conduct and mental discipline, as a stable and harmonious mind is essential for the development of insight. In the context of justice systems, the principle of Prajna can inform approaches that emphasize understanding the root causes of criminal behavior and fostering insight and self-awareness among offenders.

Mental Discipline, or Samadhi, is the third pillar of Tibetan Buddhism. It refers to the cultivation of concentration and mental clarity through meditation and other contemplative practices. The practice of Samadhi involves training the mind to remain focused and stable, free from distraction and agitation. This mental discipline is seen as essential for the development of wisdom and ethical conduct, as a calm and focused mind is better able to understand the true nature of reality and act in accordance with ethical principles. In Tibetan Buddhism, mental discipline is cultivated through various forms of meditation, including shamatha (calm abiding) and vipashyana (insight) meditation. Shamatha meditation involves focusing the mind on a single object, such as the breath, to develop concentration and tranquility. Vipashyana meditation involves using this concentrated mind to investigate the nature of phenomena, leading to the development of insight and wisdom. The practice of Samadhi also includes other contemplative techniques, such as visualization and mantra recitation, which are used to train the mind and cultivate positive qualities.

The cultivation of mental discipline has numerous benefits, both for individuals and for society as a whole. A mind that is calm, focused, and free from distraction is better able to make wise and ethical decisions. In the context of justice systems, the principle of Samadhi can inform practices that promote mental well-being and self-regulation among offenders. Meditation and other contemplative practices can be integrated into rehabilitation programs to help offenders develop greater self-awareness, emotional regulation, and resilience. The interconnection between these three pillars—ethical conduct, wisdom, and mental discipline—is a central theme in Tibetan Buddhism. Ethical conduct provides the foundation for mental discipline, as a mind that is free from the agitation of unethical behavior is better able to develop concentration and clarity. Mental discipline, in turn, supports the development of wisdom, as a calm and focused mind is better able to understand the true nature of reality. Wisdom reinforces ethical conduct, as a deep understanding of the interdependent nature of phenomena fosters compassion and ethical behavior. This interdependence highlights the holistic nature of Tibetan Buddhist practice, where each pillar supports and enhances the others.

In the context of modern justice systems, the integration of these three pillars offers a comprehensive approach to addressing criminal behavior and promoting rehabilitation. Ethical conduct can inform policies and practices that promote accountability and ethical behavior. Wisdom can inform approaches that emphasize understanding the root causes of criminal behavior and fostering insight and self-awareness among offenders. Mental discipline can inform practices that promote mental well-being and self-regulation through meditation and other contemplative techniques. The application of these principles in justice systems is not merely theoretical but has practical implications for creating a more compassionate and effective approach to justice.

For example, rehabilitation programs that incorporate meditation and mindfulness practices have been shown to reduce stress, improve emotional regulation, and promote positive behavior change among offenders. Ethical training programs can help offenders develop a sense of responsibility and accountability for their actions. Educational programs that emphasize the development of wisdom and understanding can help offenders gain insight into the root causes of their behavior and develop the skills needed for positive change.

Furthermore, the integration of these principles can also benefit justice practitioners, including judges, lawyers, and correctional officers. The practice of ethical conduct can promote integrity and fairness in the administration of justice. The cultivation of wisdom can enhance decision-making and promote a deeper understanding of the complexities of criminal behavior. The development of mental discipline can improve focus, resilience, and emotional well-being, reducing burnout and promoting a more compassionate approach to justice. The Three Pillars of Tibetan Buddhism—Ethical Conduct, Wisdom, and Mental Discipline—provide a comprehensive framework for personal transformation and ethical living. These principles are not only relevant to individual practitioners but also offer valuable insights for creating a more compassionate and effective justice system. By integrating these pillars into modern justice systems and rehabilitation practices, we can address the root causes of criminal behavior, promote ethical transformation, and foster a more just and compassionate society.

1.4: Relevance to Modern Justice Systems

Tibetan Buddhist doctrines offer profound insights that are highly relevant to modern justice systems. These teachings provide a comprehensive framework for understanding human behavior, addressing the root causes of crime, and promoting ethical transformation and rehabilitation. The relevance of these doctrines to justice systems lies in their potential to create a more compassionate, effective, and holistic approach to addressing criminal behavior. Tibetan Buddhism emphasizes the interconnectedness of all beings and the importance of compassion and ethical conduct. This perspective is crucial for creating a justice system that not only addresses the actions of offenders but also considers the broader social, psychological, and environmental factors that contribute to criminal behavior. By understanding the interdependent nature of existence, we can develop more effective interventions that address the root causes of crime rather than merely treating its symptoms.

One of the key principles in Tibetan Buddhism is the concept of karma, the law of cause and effect. According to this principle, actions have consequences, and ethical behavior leads to positive outcomes while unethical behavior leads to suffering. This understanding of karma reinforces the importance of ethical conduct and personal responsibility in creating a just society. In the context of justice systems, the principle of karma can inform policies and practices that promote accountability and ethical behavior among offenders. By helping offenders understand the consequences of their actions and encouraging them to take responsibility for their behavior, we can foster a sense of accountability and promote ethical transformation.

Another fundamental concept in Tibetan Buddhism is the Four Noble Truths, which provide a framework for understanding and addressing suffering. The first Noble Truth acknowledges the existence of suffering (dukkha), which is an inherent part of human life. The second Noble Truth identifies the causes of suffering, which include attachment, ignorance, and aversion. The third Noble Truth asserts that it is possible to end suffering by eliminating its causes, and the fourth Noble Truth outlines the path to the cessation of suffering, known as the Eightfold Path. This framework is highly relevant to justice systems, as it emphasizes the importance of addressing the underlying causes of criminal behavior and promoting healing and reconciliation.

The Eightfold Path, which is the practical aspect of the Four Noble Truths, provides a comprehensive guide to ethical living and personal transformation. It includes eight interrelated practices: Right View, Right Intention, Right Speech, Right Action, Right Livelihood, Right Effort, Right Mindfulness, and Right Concentration. Each of these practices contributes to the development of ethical conduct, wisdom, and mental discipline. In the context of justice systems, the Eightfold Path can inform rehabilitation programs that promote ethical behavior, self-awareness, and personal growth among offenders. For example, the practice of Right View involves understanding the true nature of reality and recognizing the interdependent nature of all phenomena. This perspective can help offenders develop a deeper understanding of the impact of their actions on others and foster a sense of compassion and empathy. The practice of Right Intention involves cultivating positive motivations and intentions, such as the desire to help others and alleviate suffering. By encouraging offenders to develop positive intentions, we can promote ethical behavior and reduce the likelihood of reoffending.

The practice of Right Speech involves speaking truthfully, kindly, and respectfully. In the context of justice systems, this practice can promote honest and compassionate communication among offenders, victims, and justice practitioners. By fostering open and respectful dialogue, we can facilitate healing and reconciliation and create a more supportive environment for rehabilitation. The practice of Right Action involves behaving ethically and avoiding harmful actions. In rehabilitation programs, this practice can be promoted through activities that encourage positive behavior and discourage actions that cause harm to oneself or others. By helping offenders develop ethical conduct, we can support their personal transformation and reintegration into society.

The practice of Right Livelihood involves choosing work that is ethical and beneficial to others. In the context of offender rehabilitation, this practice can inform vocational training programs that help offenders develop skills and find employment opportunities that are aligned with ethical principles. By supporting offenders in finding meaningful and ethical work, we can promote their successful reintegration into society and reduce the likelihood of reoffending. The practice of Right Effort involves making a consistent and diligent effort to cultivate positive qualities and eliminate negative ones. In rehabilitation programs, this practice can be promoted through activities that encourage self-discipline, perseverance, and personal growth. By helping offenders develop a strong work ethic and a commitment to positive change, we can support their rehabilitation and transformation.

The practice of Right Mindfulness involves being fully present and aware of one's thoughts, feelings, and actions. In the context of justice systems, mindfulness practices can be integrated into rehabilitation programs to help offenders develop greater self-awareness and emotional regulation. By teaching mindfulness techniques, we can support offenders in managing stress, reducing impulsivity, and making more thoughtful decisions. The practice of Right Concentration involves developing the ability to focus and maintain mental clarity. Meditation practices that cultivate concentration can be incorporated into rehabilitation programs to help offenders develop mental discipline and resilience. By supporting offenders in developing a focused and calm mind, we can promote their psychological well-being and support their journey towards personal transformation.

The Bodhisattva ideal, another central concept in Tibetan Buddhism, emphasizes the cultivation of compassion and the commitment to helping others achieve liberation from suffering. Bodhisattvas are beings who, out of compassion, choose to remain in the cycle of Samsara to assist others on their path to enlightenment. This ideal of selfless service and compassion is highly relevant to justice systems, as it promotes an approach to justice that prioritizes healing and reconciliation over punishment. Incorporating the Bodhisattva ideal into justice systems involves encouraging justice practitioners to cultivate compassion and adopt a service-oriented approach to their work. This can be achieved through training programs that emphasize the importance of empathy, compassion, and ethical conduct. By fostering a culture of compassion within justice systems, we can create an environment that supports healing and rehabilitation for both offenders and victims.

The principle of interdependence, or Dependent Origination (Pratityasamutpada), further reinforces the interconnected nature of all phenomena. According to this principle, all things arise in dependence upon multiple causes and conditions, and nothing exists independently. This understanding of interdependence highlights the complex web of factors that contribute to criminal behavior, including social, economic, psychological, and environmental influences. By recognizing the interdependent nature of criminal behavior, we can develop more holistic approaches to rehabilitation that address these multiple factors. For example, rehabilitation programs can include components that address the social and economic conditions that contribute to criminal behavior, such as poverty, lack of education, and unemployment. By providing offenders with access to education, vocational training, and employment opportunities, we can address some of the root causes of criminal behavior and support their successful reintegration into society.

Additionally, programs that address psychological factors, such as trauma, mental health issues, and substance abuse, can help offenders develop the emotional and psychological resilience needed for lasting change.

The integration of Tibetan Buddhist principles into justice systems also has the potential to benefit justice practitioners, including judges, lawyers, and correctional officers. By incorporating practices that promote ethical conduct, wisdom, and mental discipline, justice practitioners can enhance their ability to make fair and compassionate decisions. Meditation and mindfulness practices can support the well-being of justice practitioners by reducing stress, improving focus, and promoting emotional regulation. This, in turn, can contribute to a more compassionate and effective administration of justice.

The relevance of Tibetan Buddhist doctrines to modern justice systems lies in their potential to create a more compassionate, effective, and holistic approach to addressing criminal behavior. By incorporating principles such as karma, the Four Noble Truths, the Eightfold Path, the Bodhisattva ideal, and Dependent Origination, we can develop justice practices that promote ethical conduct, personal transformation, and healing. These principles provide a comprehensive framework for understanding human behavior and addressing the root causes of crime, offering valuable insights for creating a justice system that aligns with the deepest aspirations of Tibetan Buddhist philosophy.

1.5: Case Studies of Buddhist Principles in Justice

The application of Buddhist principles in justice settings offers a profound and transformative approach to addressing criminal behavior and fostering rehabilitation. By examining case studies where these principles have been implemented, we can gain valuable insights into their practical implications and effectiveness. These case studies illustrate how Buddhist teachings can create a more compassionate and effective justice system, emphasizing healing, reconciliation, and personal transformation over punishment. One notable case study is the application of Buddhist principles in the rehabilitation program at Tihar Jail in New Delhi, India.

Tihar Jail is one of the largest prison complexes in South Asia and has faced significant challenges related to overcrowding, violence, and recidivism. In the early 1990s, Kiran Bedi, the first female Indian Police Service officer, became the Inspector General of Prisons and initiated several reforms based on Buddhist principles, particularly focusing on Vipassana meditation. Vipassana, an ancient meditation technique rediscovered by the Buddha, involves observing the sensations in the body to develop self-awareness and insight into the nature of suffering. The practice aims to purify the mind and cultivate inner peace and wisdom. Bedi introduced Vipassana courses in Tihar Jail, making it the first prison in the world to offer such programs.

The impact of Vipassana meditation on inmates at Tihar Jail has been profound. Inmates who participated in the courses reported significant reductions in stress, anger, and aggression. Many experienced a deep sense of inner peace and clarity, which led to improved behavior and relationships with fellow inmates and staff. The practice also helped inmates develop greater self-awareness and emotional regulation, contributing to their personal transformation and rehabilitation. A study conducted by the Indian National Institute of Mental Health and Neurosciences evaluated the impact of Vipassana meditation on Tihar inmates. The study found that participants exhibited marked improvements in psychological well-being, including reduced anxiety, depression, and hostility. Additionally, the study reported that inmates who practiced Vipassana were less likely to reoffend after their release, indicating a positive long-term impact on recidivism rates.

Another compelling case study involves the use of mindfulness-based interventions in juvenile detention centers in the United States. The Mind Body Awareness (MBA) Project, a non-profit organization, has implemented mindfulness programs in several juvenile facilities across California. These programs aim to teach young offenders mindfulness and emotional regulation skills to help them cope with stress, make better decisions, and reduce violent behavior. The MBA Project's curriculum includes mindfulness meditation, body awareness exercises, and discussions on topics such as anger management, empathy, and self-compassion. The programs are designed to be trauma-informed, acknowledging the high prevalence of traumatic experiences among juvenile offenders and the impact of trauma on their behavior. Evaluations of the MBA Project's programs have shown promising results. Participants reported reductions in stress, anxiety, and anger, as well as improvements in emotional regulation and impulse control. Staff members also noted positive changes in the behavior and attitudes of the youth, including increased cooperation, respect, and empathy. The success of these programs highlights the potential of mindfulness-based interventions to support the rehabilitation and personal growth of young offenders.

In Thailand, the Dhammayatra program provides another illustrative example of the application of Buddhist principles in justice settings. The Dhammayatra, or "Peace Walk," is a rehabilitation program for incarcerated youth inspired by the teachings of the Thai forest monk Ajahn Chah. The program combines meditation, ethical training, and community service to foster personal transformation and social reintegration. Participants in the Dhammayatra program engage in daily meditation and mindfulness practices, learn about Buddhist ethics and principles, and participate in community service projects. The program aims to help youth develop a sense of responsibility, compassion, and connection to their community. By cultivating inner peace and ethical conduct, participants are encouraged to make positive changes in their lives and avoid reoffending.

The Dhammayatra program has been praised for its holistic approach to rehabilitation. Participants have reported significant improvements in their mental and emotional well-being, as well as a stronger sense of purpose and direction in life. Community members have also expressed support for the program, noting the positive impact on both the participants and the broader community. The program's success underscores the potential of Buddhist-inspired rehabilitation programs to promote healing, ethical transformation, and social reintegration. In the United States, the Engaged Buddhism movement, led by figures such as Thich Nhat Hanh and Joan Halifax, has also made significant contributions to the application of Buddhist principles in justice settings. Engaged Buddhism emphasizes the application of Buddhist teachings to social, political, and environmental issues, including criminal justice reform. Practitioners of Engaged Buddhism have initiated various programs that integrate mindfulness, compassion, and restorative justice practices in prisons and other justice settings.

One such initiative is the Prison Dharma Network (PDN), founded by Fleet Maull, a Buddhist teacher and former inmate. PDN offers meditation and mindfulness programs to inmates, as well as training for correctional staff. The network aims to provide support and resources for individuals and organizations working to bring Buddhist practices into prisons and promote a more compassionate approach to justice. PDN's programs have been implemented in numerous prisons across the United States, with positive results. Inmates who participate in the programs report reduced stress, increased self-awareness, and improved emotional regulation. Many also experience a shift in their attitudes and behavior, becoming more compassionate and responsible. PDN's work demonstrates the potential of Buddhist practices to support the personal transformation and rehabilitation of inmates.

In addition to these specific programs, Buddhist principles have been integrated into broader restorative justice initiatives. Restorative justice, which focuses on repairing the harm caused by crime and fostering reconciliation between offenders and victims, aligns closely with Buddhist teachings on compassion, interdependence, and ethical conduct. Restorative justice practices, such as victim-offender mediation, circle processes, and community conferencing, aim to address the needs of all parties involved and promote healing and accountability. Case studies of restorative justice programs that incorporate Buddhist principles highlight their effectiveness in promoting healing and reconciliation. For example, the Centre for Peacebuilding and Conflict Management in Sri Lanka has implemented restorative justice programs inspired by Buddhist teachings. These programs focus on facilitating dialogue between offenders and victims, fostering understanding and empathy, and promoting collective healing.

Evaluations of these programs have shown positive outcomes, including reduced recidivism rates, increased victim satisfaction, and improved community relations. Participants report that the programs help them develop a deeper understanding of the impact of their actions, take responsibility for their behavior, and make amends to those they have harmed. These findings underscore the potential of Buddhist-inspired restorative justice practices to create a more compassionate and effective approach to justice. Case studies of the application of Buddhist principles in justice settings demonstrate their profound potential to transform the way we address criminal behavior and promote rehabilitation. Programs that incorporate mindfulness, meditation, ethical training, and restorative justice practices have shown significant benefits for offenders, victims, and communities. These case studies illustrate how Buddhist teachings can create a more compassionate and holistic approach to justice, emphasizing healing, reconciliation, and personal transformation over punishment.

CHAPTER TWO

Madhyamaka - The Middle Way

Contents

- Nagarjuna's Philosophy of the Middle Way

- Balancing Retribution and Rehabilitation

- Practical Applications in Criminal Justice

- Case Studies of Balanced Approaches

- Policy Implications and Recommendations

2.1: Nagarjuna's Philosophy of the Middle Way

Nagarjuna's philosophy of the Middle Way, or Madhyamaka, is a cornerstone of Mahayana Buddhism, representing a profound and intricate understanding of reality that transcends conventional dualistic thinking. Central to this philosophy is the rejection of extremes—both eternalism, the belief in an unchanging, eternal essence, and nihilism, the belief in the total nonexistence of things. Nagarjuna's Middle Way posits that phenomena exist in a state of dependent origination, meaning they arise in dependence upon causes and conditions, lacking any inherent, independent existence.

This view is encapsulated in his seminal work, the Mūlamadhyamakakārikā, or "Fundamental Verses on the Middle Way," where he meticulously deconstructs all philosophical positions that assert intrinsic existence. The Middle Way's foundational principle is sunyata, or emptiness. Emptiness does not imply nonexistence but rather the absence of inherent existence. Nagarjuna argues that all things are empty of intrinsic essence because they are interdependent and constantly changing. This perspective is not a denial of the world but a deep affirmation of its fluid and dynamic nature. By understanding emptiness, one can avoid the extremes of asserting an eternal essence or denying existence altogether, thus embracing a balanced and realistic view of the world.

In the context of justice, the Middle Way offers a framework that transcends rigid punitive measures and permissive leniency, advocating for a balanced approach that addresses the root causes of criminal behavior while promoting rehabilitation and reintegration. This balanced approach acknowledges the interdependence of individuals and their environments, recognizing that criminal behavior is often the result of a complex interplay of factors including social, economic, psychological, and environmental influences. Nagarjuna's philosophy encourages a justice system that is neither harshly retributive nor naively lenient but one that seeks to understand and address the underlying causes of crime. This approach aligns with modern criminological theories that emphasize the importance of addressing systemic issues such as poverty, education, and mental health, which contribute to criminal behavior. By focusing on these root causes, a justice system inspired by the Middle Way can promote healing and transformation rather than merely punishing wrongdoing.

The practical implications of the Middle Way in justice are vast. For instance, in sentencing, it advocates for measures that are proportionate to the crime and consider the broader context of the offender's life. This might include community service, restorative justice practices, and rehabilitation programs that focus on mental health and addiction treatment. By avoiding the extremes of excessively harsh sentences or inadequate responses, the Middle Way promotes a fair and balanced approach that seeks to restore harmony and prevent future harm. Nagarjuna's emphasis on dependent origination also has profound implications for understanding criminal behavior. It suggests that individuals are not inherently criminal but are shaped by a web of interrelated factors. This perspective encourages a more compassionate and empathetic approach to offenders, viewing them as products of their circumstances rather than inherently evil. By addressing these circumstances through social support, education, and community engagement, the justice system can help individuals break free from cycles of crime and reintegrate into society as productive members.

Moreover, the Middle Way's rejection of intrinsic existence challenges the notion of fixed identities. In a justice context, this means recognizing that offenders are not defined by their crimes but have the potential for change and growth. This view supports rehabilitation efforts that focus on personal development, skill-building, and creating opportunities for positive transformation. By fostering an environment that encourages growth and change, the justice system can help individuals rebuild their lives and contribute positively to society. Nagarjuna's Middle Way also underscores the importance of wisdom and compassion in justice. Wisdom, in this context, involves understanding the true nature of reality and the complex causes of suffering, while compassion involves responding to suffering with kindness and a desire to help. A justice system informed by these principles would prioritize restorative practices that seek to heal and restore rather than punish and exclude. This could include victim-offender mediation, community conferencing, and other practices that promote reconciliation and understanding.

The Middle Way's balanced approach is not limited to individual cases but extends to broader policy implications. It calls for policies that address systemic issues and promote social justice, recognizing that true justice involves creating conditions that prevent crime and support healthy, thriving communities. This might include investments in education, healthcare, housing, and other social services that address the root causes of crime and support overall well-being. Nagarjuna's philosophy of the Middle Way offers a profound and transformative framework for justice. By rejecting extremes and embracing a balanced approach that acknowledges the interdependence of all things, the Middle

Way promotes a justice system that is compassionate, fair, and effective. It encourages us to look beyond punitive measures and consider the broader context of criminal behavior, addressing root causes and supporting rehabilitation and transformation. By integrating these principles into modern justice systems, we can create a more just and compassionate society that upholds the dignity and potential of all individuals.

2.2: Balancing Retribution and Rehabilitation

Balancing retribution and rehabilitation within the justice system is a delicate and complex endeavor that requires a nuanced understanding of human behavior, societal norms, and the principles of justice. The Middle Way, as articulated by Nagarjuna, provides a philosophical foundation for navigating this balance, advocating for an approach that avoids the extremes of harsh punishment and unchecked leniency. This balanced perspective is particularly relevant in contemporary discussions about the effectiveness and ethics of criminal justice practices. Retribution, a concept rooted in the notion of just deserts, holds that offenders deserve to be punished in proportion to the severity of their crimes. It is grounded in the belief that punishment serves as a moral response to wrongdoing, providing a sense of justice to victims and society. However, retribution alone often fails to address the underlying causes of criminal behavior or contribute to the rehabilitation of offenders.

In many cases, purely retributive measures can exacerbate issues such as recidivism, social alienation, and mental health problems. Rehabilitation, on the other hand, focuses on transforming offenders into law-abiding citizens through various forms of treatment, education, and support. This approach is based on the belief that individuals can change and that providing the right resources and opportunities can facilitate their reintegration into society. While rehabilitation aims to address the root causes of criminal behavior, it can sometimes be perceived as overly lenient or insufficiently punitive, particularly in cases involving severe or violent crimes.

The Middle Way philosophy offers a framework for integrating retribution and rehabilitation, promoting a justice system that holds offenders accountable while also providing opportunities for personal growth and societal reintegration. This balanced approach recognizes that justice should not only respond to the harm caused by crime but also seek to prevent future harm by addressing the conditions that lead to criminal behavior. One practical application of the Middle Way in balancing retribution and rehabilitation is the implementation of restorative justice practices. Restorative justice emphasizes repairing the harm caused by criminal behavior through processes that involve victims, offenders, and the community. These practices aim to hold offenders accountable, encourage them to take responsibility for their actions, and provide opportunities for making amends. By focusing on the needs of all parties involved, restorative justice seeks to create a sense of closure and healing, which is often missing in traditional retributive approaches.

Restorative justice practices can include victim-offender mediation, where offenders and victims meet in a controlled and supportive environment to discuss the impact of the crime and agree on steps the offender can take to make amends. This process allows victims to express their feelings and needs, while offenders gain a deeper understanding of the consequences of their actions. By facilitating direct communication and mutual understanding, restorative justice can foster empathy and remorse in offenders, contributing to their rehabilitation and reducing the likelihood of reoffending. Another example of balancing retribution and rehabilitation is the use of alternative sentencing programs that combine punitive measures with rehabilitative support.

For instance, drug courts offer an alternative to traditional incarceration for individuals with substance use disorders. Participants in drug court programs are required to undergo treatment, attend regular court sessions, and comply with strict supervision and drug testing. While these programs hold participants accountable for their actions, they also provide the support and resources needed to address the underlying issues contributing to criminal behavior. Studies have shown that drug courts are effective in reducing recidivism and promoting long-term recovery, demonstrating the potential of a balanced approach to justice.

The principles of the Middle Way can also inform sentencing policies that take into account both the severity of the offense and the individual circumstances of the offender. Sentencing guidelines can be designed to provide judges with the flexibility to impose sentences that are proportionate to the crime while also considering factors such as the offender's background, mental health, and potential for rehabilitation. This approach allows for a more tailored response to criminal behavior, ensuring that justice is served while also addressing the unique needs of each offender. In addition to individual sentencing, the Middle Way philosophy can guide broader criminal justice policies that aim to create a more equitable and effective system. For example, policies that prioritize prevention and early intervention can address the root causes of criminal behavior before they escalate into more serious offenses. This might include investing in education, mental health services, and community programs that provide support and resources to at-risk individuals. By addressing the social and economic factors that contribute to crime, these policies can help prevent criminal behavior and reduce the need for retributive measures.

Community-based programs that offer support and supervision for offenders as they reintegrate into society are another example of the Middle Way in action. These programs provide a structured environment where offenders can receive vocational training, education, and counseling while being held accountable for their progress. By combining elements of retribution, such as supervision and accountability, with rehabilitative support, these programs can help offenders transition back into the community and reduce the risk of recidivism. The integration of retribution and rehabilitation also has significant implications for the treatment of juvenile offenders.

Adolescents are at a critical stage of development, and their behavior is often influenced by a range of social, psychological, and environmental factors. A justice system that balances retribution and rehabilitation recognizes the potential for growth and change in young people and seeks to provide the support and guidance they need to make positive choices. This might include diversion programs that steer young offenders away from the formal justice system and into community-based services, as well as restorative justice practices that involve the family and community in the rehabilitation process.

In the context of the Middle Way, it is also essential to consider the role of compassion in the justice system. Compassion involves understanding the suffering of others and responding with kindness and a desire to alleviate that suffering. A justice system that embodies the principles of the Middle Way integrates compassion into its policies and practices, ensuring that offenders are treated with dignity and respect and that their needs are addressed alongside those of victims and the community. This compassionate approach can be seen in programs that provide mental health treatment and support for offenders with mental health issues. Rather than punishing individuals for behavior that may be driven by underlying mental health conditions, these programs seek to provide the care and treatment needed to address those conditions. By focusing on healing and support, rather than punishment, these programs can help offenders achieve stability and reduce the likelihood of reoffending.

The Middle Way also emphasizes the importance of wisdom in the administration of justice. Wisdom involves a deep understanding of the complexities of human behavior and the ability to make decisions that are fair, compassionate, and effective. In the context of justice, wisdom means recognizing that there are no simple solutions to the challenges of crime and punishment and that a balanced approach requires careful consideration of all factors involved. For justice practitioners, cultivating wisdom involves ongoing education and training, as well as a commitment to self-reflection and personal growth.

By developing a deeper understanding of the principles of the Middle Way and their application to justice, practitioners can make more informed and compassionate decisions that promote the well-being of all parties involved. Balancing retribution and rehabilitation within the justice system is a complex and nuanced endeavor that can be guided by the principles of the Middle Way. By avoiding the extremes of harsh punishment and unchecked leniency, and instead integrating elements of accountability, support, and compassion, we can create a justice system that is both fair and effective.

2.3: Practical Applications in Criminal Justice

The practical applications of the Middle Way in criminal justice settings are vast and multifaceted, offering a transformative approach that balances retributive and rehabilitative elements to foster a more humane and effective justice system. By integrating the principles of the Middle Way, justice practitioners can develop policies and practices that address the root causes of criminal behavior, promote personal transformation, and support the reintegration of offenders into society. One of the key areas where the Middle Way can be applied is in sentencing and correctional practices. Traditional sentencing often leans heavily towards retribution, focusing on punishment as a response to crime. However, this approach can fail to address the underlying issues that contribute to criminal behavior and may lead to high recidivism rates.

By contrast, a Middle Way approach to sentencing considers both the need for accountability and the potential for rehabilitation, seeking to impose sentences that are fair, proportionate, and conducive to personal growth. Judges, informed by the principles of the Middle Way, can utilize alternative sentencing options that combine punitive and rehabilitative elements. These options might include community service, probation, and restorative justice programs that encourage offenders to take responsibility for their actions and make amends to their victims and communities. For example, in cases involving non-violent offenses, judges can order offenders to participate in community service projects that benefit society while also providing a form of reparation for the harm caused by their actions.

Restorative justice practices are a particularly powerful application of the Middle Way in criminal justice settings. These practices focus on repairing the harm caused by criminal behavior through processes that involve victims, offenders, and the community. Restorative justice aims to create a sense of closure and healing for all parties involved by fostering dialogue, mutual understanding, and empathy. This approach can take various forms, including victim-offender mediation, family group conferencing, and community circles. In victim-offender mediation, offenders and victims meet in a controlled and supportive environment to discuss the impact of the crime and agree on steps the offender can take to make amends. This process allows victims to express their feelings and needs, which can be a crucial step in their healing journey. Offenders, in turn, gain a deeper understanding of the consequences of their actions, fostering a sense of empathy and remorse. By facilitating direct communication and mutual understanding, restorative justice can help offenders develop a sense of responsibility and a commitment to making positive changes in their lives.

Family group conferencing is another restorative practice that brings together offenders, victims, and their respective families and supporters to discuss the harm caused by the crime and develop a plan for making amends. This approach recognizes the broader social and familial context in which criminal behavior occurs and seeks to engage the offender's support network in the rehabilitation process. By involving families and communities in the justice process, family group conferencing can strengthen social bonds and support networks, which are essential for successful reintegration. Community circles, or peacemaking circles, are restorative practices that involve a broader cross-section of the community in the justice process. Participants, including offenders, victims, community members, and justice practitioners, come together in a circle to discuss the impact of the crime and identify ways to address the harm and prevent future offenses. This approach fosters a sense of collective responsibility and community cohesion, promoting a culture of mutual support and accountability.

The principles of the Middle Way can also inform the design and implementation of rehabilitation programs within correctional facilities. Traditional correctional practices often focus on punishment and containment, with limited opportunities for personal growth and transformation. By contrast, a Middle Way approach to rehabilitation emphasizes the importance of addressing the underlying causes of criminal behavior and supporting offenders in their journey towards positive change. Rehabilitation programs that incorporate mindfulness and meditation practices are an effective way to apply the Middle Way in correctional settings. Mindfulness and meditation can help offenders develop greater self-awareness, emotional regulation, and resilience, which are essential for personal transformation. For example, mindfulness-based stress reduction (MBSR) programs teach participants techniques for managing stress, reducing impulsivity, and cultivating a sense of inner peace. These programs have been shown to improve mental health outcomes and reduce recidivism rates among offenders.

Cognitive-behavioral therapy (CBT) is another rehabilitative approach that aligns with the principles of the Middle Way. CBT focuses on identifying and changing negative thought patterns and behaviors, helping offenders develop healthier coping mechanisms and decision-making skills. By addressing the cognitive and emotional factors that contribute to criminal behavior, CBT can support offenders in making lasting positive changes. Programs that integrate CBT with mindfulness and meditation practices can provide a comprehensive approach to rehabilitation that addresses both the psychological and emotional aspects of criminal behavior.

Vocational training and education programs are also critical components of a Middle Way approach to rehabilitation. These programs provide offenders with the skills and knowledge needed to secure employment and reintegrate into society successfully. By offering opportunities for personal and professional development, vocational training and education can help offenders build a sense of purpose and self-worth, which are essential for preventing recidivism. Programs that emphasize ethical employment and align with the principles of Right Livelihood, as outlined in the Eightfold Path, can further support offenders in making positive contributions to society.

In addition to individual rehabilitation programs, the principles of the Middle Way can inform broader systemic reforms in the criminal justice system. Policymakers can develop policies that prioritize prevention and early intervention, addressing the social and economic factors that contribute to criminal behavior. For example, investing in education, mental health services, and community support programs can help prevent crime by addressing the root causes of criminal behavior. By creating conditions that support overall well-being and reduce the risk of offending, these policies can contribute to a more just and compassionate society. The principles of the Middle Way also emphasize the importance of compassion and empathy in the administration of justice. Justice practitioners, including judges, lawyers, and correctional officers, can benefit from training programs that promote emotional intelligence, empathy, and ethical decision-making. By cultivating these qualities, practitioners can create a more supportive and humane justice system that prioritizes healing and rehabilitation over punishment.

Furthermore, the Middle Way encourages a holistic approach to justice that recognizes the interconnectedness of all individuals and the broader social context in which crime occurs. This perspective calls for a justice system that not only addresses individual behavior but also considers the impact of systemic issues such as poverty, discrimination, and inequality. By addressing these broader social issues, the justice system can create conditions that support overall well-being and reduce the likelihood of criminal behavior. The practical applications of the Middle Way in criminal justice settings offer a transformative approach that balances retributive and rehabilitative elements. By integrating the principles of the Middle Way, justice practitioners can develop policies and practices that address the root causes of criminal behavior, promote personal transformation, and support the reintegration of offenders into society. Restorative justice practices, alternative sentencing programs, mindfulness and meditation-based rehabilitation, and systemic reforms are all examples of how the Middle Way can be applied to create a more compassionate and effective justice system.

2.4: Case Studies of Balanced Approaches

Examining case studies of justice systems or programs that have successfully implemented a balanced approach is crucial for understanding the practical application of the Middle Way in modern criminology. These case studies provide valuable insights into how principles of balance, compassion, and wisdom can transform justice practices, reduce recidivism, and promote healing and reconciliation. By analyzing these real-world examples, we can identify best practices, challenges, and potential for broader application. One notable case study is the implementation of restorative justice practices in New Zealand's juvenile justice system. New Zealand has been at the forefront of incorporating restorative justice into its legal framework, particularly for young offenders.

The country's approach is guided by the belief that addressing the harm caused by crime and involving the community in the justice process can lead to better outcomes for victims, offenders, and society as a whole. The New Zealand model includes family group conferences (FGCs), which bring together the offender, victim, their families, and community representatives to discuss the impact of the crime and agree on a plan for making amends. This process emphasizes accountability, reparation, and support for the offender's rehabilitation. Research has shown that FGCs in New Zealand have led to high levels of victim satisfaction, reduced reoffending rates, and positive behavioral changes in offenders. The success of this approach highlights the potential of restorative justice to create a more balanced and effective justice system.

Another compelling example is the Community Justice Center (CJC) model in the United States, particularly the Red Hook Community Justice Center in Brooklyn, New York. The Red Hook CJC operates on the principle that justice should be community-based and restorative, rather than solely punitive. The center addresses low-level offenses through a combination of social services, community engagement, and restorative practices. At the Red Hook CJC, offenders are given the opportunity to participate in programs that address underlying issues such as substance abuse, mental health problems, and unemployment. The center also facilitates restorative justice circles, where offenders and victims can discuss the impact of the crime and agree on steps to repair the harm. This approach has led to significant reductions in recidivism and improvements in community trust and cohesion. The Red Hook CJC demonstrates how integrating restorative and rehabilitative practices within the justice system can promote healing and community well-being.

In Norway, the country's correctional system provides another powerful example of a balanced approach to justice. Norway's prison system is renowned for its focus on rehabilitation and humane treatment of offenders. The country's approach is guided by the principles of normality, which dictate that life inside prison should resemble life outside as much as possible, and that the primary goal of imprisonment is to prepare inmates for successful reintegration into society. Norwegian prisons, such as Halden Prison, emphasize education, vocational training, and therapeutic programs. Inmates have access to a range of activities and support services designed to promote personal growth and skill development. The prison staff are trained to act as mentors and support the rehabilitation process, fostering a positive and respectful environment. Norway's approach has resulted in one of the lowest recidivism rates in the world, illustrating the effectiveness of a system that prioritizes rehabilitation and humane treatment over punishment.

In South Africa, the Truth and Reconciliation Commission (TRC) serves as a historic example of restorative justice on a national scale. Established after the end of apartheid, the TRC was tasked with uncovering the truth about human rights violations committed during the apartheid era and facilitating reconciliation between victims and perpetrators. The commission adopted a restorative approach, emphasizing the need for accountability, truth-telling, and healing. The TRC held public hearings where victims could share their experiences and perpetrators could confess their crimes in exchange for amnesty. This process provided a platform for acknowledging the suffering caused by apartheid and allowed for a collective process of healing and reconciliation. While the TRC faced criticisms and challenges, it played a crucial role in South Africa's transition to a democratic society and highlighted the potential of restorative justice to address deep-seated societal conflicts.

Another significant case study is the use of therapeutic jurisprudence in problem-solving courts, such as drug courts and mental health courts in the United States. These courts operate on the principle that the legal system should promote the well-being of individuals and address the underlying issues that contribute to criminal behavior. Drug courts, for instance, provide an alternative to traditional prosecution for individuals with substance use disorders. Participants are required to undergo treatment, attend regular court sessions, and comply with strict supervision and drug testing. Therapeutic jurisprudence in problem-solving courts focuses on rehabilitation and support rather than punishment. Judges, prosecutors, and defense attorneys work collaboratively with treatment providers to develop individualized plans for participants. This approach has been shown to reduce recidivism and improve outcomes for individuals with substance use disorders and mental health issues. The success of problem-solving courts demonstrates the potential of integrating therapeutic and rehabilitative principles into the justice system.

In Canada, the Indigenous Justice Systems offer another powerful example of a balanced approach to justice. These systems, rooted in Indigenous traditions and values, emphasize healing, community involvement, and restorative practices. The Cree Justice System in Quebec, for example, integrates traditional practices such as peacemaking circles and community sentencing panels. These practices involve the offender, victim, and community members in the justice process, focusing on repairing harm and restoring relationships. The Cree Justice System operates on the principle that crime affects the entire community and that the community must play a role in addressing it. This approach has been successful in reducing recidivism, promoting healing, and strengthening community bonds. The integration of traditional Indigenous practices with modern justice principles highlights the potential for culturally relevant and restorative approaches to justice.

The integration of Buddhist principles in justice practices in Thailand provides another case study of a balanced approach. The Dhammayatra, or "Peace Walk," program for incarcerated youth combines meditation, ethical training, and community service to foster personal transformation and social reintegration. Participants engage in daily meditation and mindfulness practices, learn about Buddhist ethics, and participate in community service projects. The Dhammayatra program has been praised for its holistic approach to rehabilitation, emphasizing inner peace, ethical conduct, and community involvement. Participants have reported significant improvements in mental and emotional well-being, a stronger sense of purpose, and positive behavioral changes. The program's success underscores the potential of integrating spiritual and ethical teachings into rehabilitation efforts.

These case studies collectively illustrate the transformative potential of a balanced approach to justice that integrates retributive and rehabilitative elements. By emphasizing accountability, healing, and support, these programs and systems demonstrate how principles of the Middle Way can create a more compassionate and effective justice system. Key lessons from these case studies include the importance of addressing the underlying causes of criminal behavior, involving the community in the justice process, and providing opportunities for personal growth and transformation. Programs that incorporate restorative justice practices, therapeutic jurisprudence, and humane treatment of offenders have been shown to reduce recidivism, improve outcomes for victims and offenders, and promote community well-being.

The success of these balanced approaches highlights the need for ongoing innovation and adaptation in the justice system. By learning from these examples and incorporating their principles into broader policies and practices, justice systems can move towards a more holistic and compassionate approach that upholds the dignity and potential of all individuals. Case studies of justice systems and programs that have successfully implemented a balanced approach provide valuable insights into the practical application of the Middle Way in modern criminology. These examples demonstrate the effectiveness of integrating retributive and rehabilitative elements, emphasizing accountability, healing, and support. By learning from these case studies and adopting their principles, justice practitioners can create a more compassionate and effective justice system that promotes healing, reconciliation, and personal transformation.

2.5: Policy Implications and Recommendations

The adoption of the Middle Way in justice systems necessitates a thorough consideration of its policy implications and recommendations. By advocating for a balanced approach that avoids extremes, the Middle Way can guide the creation of policies that are fair, compassionate, and effective. The integration of these principles into justice policy requires a multifaceted strategy that addresses the complexities of criminal behavior and promotes holistic rehabilitation and societal well-being. One of the primary policy implications of adopting the Middle Way is the need for sentencing reforms that balance retribution with rehabilitation. Traditional sentencing often emphasizes punitive measures, which can lead to overcrowded prisons, high recidivism rates, and limited opportunities for offenders to rehabilitate. Policies informed by the Middle Way would advocate for sentencing guidelines that are proportionate to the offense while considering the individual circumstances of the offender.

This approach encourages the use of alternative sentencing options such as community service, probation, and restorative justice programs, which hold offenders accountable while providing opportunities for personal growth and community reintegration. Incorporating restorative justice principles into the legal framework is another critical policy recommendation. Restorative justice focuses on repairing the harm caused by criminal behavior through processes that involve victims, offenders, and the community. Policy initiatives should support the establishment and expansion of restorative justice programs, ensuring that they are accessible to a wide range of cases, including serious offenses. This includes providing funding for training restorative justice facilitators, developing guidelines for restorative practices, and creating mechanisms for monitoring and evaluating program effectiveness. By institutionalizing restorative justice, policies can promote healing and reconciliation while reducing reliance on punitive measures.

Policies should also prioritize the development and implementation of comprehensive rehabilitation programs within correctional facilities. These programs should address the multifaceted needs of offenders, including mental health, substance abuse, education, and vocational training. Rehabilitation programs that incorporate mindfulness and meditation practices, cognitive-behavioral therapy, and life skills training can support offenders in developing greater self-awareness, emotional regulation, and resilience. Policies should allocate resources to ensure that these programs are adequately funded, staffed, and accessible to all inmates. Additionally, establishing partnerships with community organizations can enhance the support network available to offenders during and after their incarceration.

Mental health and substance abuse treatment are essential components of a balanced approach to justice. Policies should advocate for the integration of mental health services within the criminal justice system, ensuring that offenders receive timely and appropriate care. This includes screening for mental health and substance abuse issues at the time of arrest, providing access to treatment programs within correctional facilities, and creating diversion programs that route individuals with mental health issues to treatment rather than incarceration. Policies should also support post-release services that help individuals transition back into the community with continued access to mental health and substance abuse support.

Another policy recommendation is the implementation of problem-solving courts, such as drug courts, mental health courts, and veterans courts. These specialized courts operate on the principles of therapeutic jurisprudence, focusing on addressing the underlying issues that contribute to criminal behavior. Problem-solving courts provide an alternative to traditional prosecution, offering treatment and support in lieu of incarceration. Policies should advocate for the establishment and expansion of these courts, providing the necessary funding and resources to ensure their effectiveness. This includes training for judges, prosecutors, and defense attorneys on therapeutic jurisprudence principles and creating partnerships with treatment providers.

Community-based programs and support services are also crucial for a balanced approach to justice. Policies should promote the development of community-based initiatives that provide support and resources to at-risk individuals and families. This includes early intervention programs for youth, educational and employment opportunities, housing assistance, and access to healthcare. By addressing the social determinants of criminal behavior, community-based programs can help prevent crime and support the successful reintegration of offenders. Policies should encourage collaboration between justice agencies, social services, and community organizations to create a comprehensive support network.

The Middle Way's emphasis on compassion and empathy has significant implications for the training and development of justice practitioners. Policies should advocate for training programs that promote emotional intelligence, ethical decision-making, and trauma-informed care. Judges, prosecutors, defense attorneys, correctional officers, and other justice professionals should receive training on the principles of restorative justice, therapeutic jurisprudence, and holistic rehabilitation. This training can enhance their ability to make fair and compassionate decisions that prioritize healing and rehabilitation. In addition to training, policies should support the well-being of justice practitioners. Working within the justice system can be highly stressful, and policies should provide resources and support for managing stress and preventing burnout. This includes access to mental health services, opportunities for professional development, and creating a work environment that promotes well-being. By supporting the well-being of justice practitioners, policies can ensure that they are better equipped to perform their roles effectively and compassionately.

Data collection and research are essential for evaluating the effectiveness of justice policies and programs. Policies should support the development of robust data collection systems that track outcomes related to recidivism, victim satisfaction, offender rehabilitation, and community impact. This data can inform policy decisions, identify best practices, and highlight areas for improvement. Additionally, funding for research on restorative justice, therapeutic jurisprudence, and rehabilitation programs can contribute to the evidence base needed to support the implementation and expansion of these practices. Public awareness and education are also critical components of policy reform. Policies should promote public education campaigns that raise awareness about the benefits of a balanced approach to justice. This includes highlighting the success of restorative justice programs, the effectiveness of rehabilitation efforts, and the importance of addressing the root causes of criminal behavior. By fostering public support for these initiatives, policies can create a more supportive environment for justice reform.

International cooperation and knowledge exchange can further enhance the development and implementation of balanced justice policies. Policies should encourage collaboration with international organizations, researchers, and practitioners to share best practices, research findings, and innovative approaches. This can include participation in international conferences, joint research projects, and the establishment of networks for knowledge exchange. By learning from successful initiatives in other countries, policies can be informed by a global perspective and adapted to local contexts. Adopting the Middle Way in justice systems requires comprehensive policy reforms that balance retribution with rehabilitation, promote restorative justice, and address the underlying causes of criminal behavior.

Key policy recommendations include sentencing reforms, the institutionalization of restorative justice, the development of comprehensive rehabilitation programs, integration of mental health and substance abuse treatment, establishment of problem-solving courts, support for community-based programs, training and development for justice practitioners, data collection and research, public awareness and education, and international cooperation.

Pratityasamutpada – Dependent Origination

Contents

- Understanding Interconnectedness in Buddhism

- Analyzing Criminal Behavior through Dependent Origination

- Holistic Approaches to Rehabilitation

- Practical Applications in Justice Settings

- Case Studies Demonstrating Success

3.1: Understanding Interconnectedness in Buddhism

Dependent Origination, or Pratityasamutpada, stands as one of the most profound and intricate teachings within Tibetan Buddhism. It captures the essence of interconnectedness, asserting that all phenomena arise in dependence upon multiple causes and conditions. This principle is not merely a philosophical abstraction but a fundamental reality that permeates every aspect of existence. In understanding Dependent Origination, one delves into the heart of Buddhist thought, which challenges the notion of independent, self-sustained entities, revealing instead a web of interdependence where everything is connected. The concept of Dependent Origination can be traced back to the Buddha's enlightenment, where he realized the nature of suffering and its cessation. It is encapsulated in the famous formula: "When this is, that is. From the arising of this, comes the arising of that.

When this is not, that is not. From the cessation of this, comes the cessation of that." This formula underscores the causal relationships that define existence, where each phenomenon arises due to the presence of specific conditions and ceases when those conditions are absent. In Tibetan Buddhism, Dependent Origination is often illustrated through the twelve links, or nidanas, which depict the cyclical nature of Samsara—the cycle of birth, death, and rebirth. These links include ignorance, karmic formations, consciousness, name and form, the six sense bases, contact, sensation, craving, clinging, becoming, birth, and aging and death. Each link is both a result of the preceding one and a cause for the subsequent one, creating a continuous cycle of suffering and existence. This cyclical nature highlights the interconnectedness of all aspects of life and the perpetuation of suffering through ignorance and attachment.

The significance of Dependent Origination in Tibetan Buddhism extends beyond a mere understanding of cyclical existence; it is a path to liberation. By comprehending the interdependent nature of reality, practitioners can develop the wisdom to see through the illusion of inherent existence. This wisdom leads to the cessation of ignorance and, consequently, the cessation of the entire cycle of suffering. In this way, Dependent Origination is both a diagnosis of the human condition and a prescription for its resolution. The practical implications of Dependent Origination are profound, particularly in how it reshapes our understanding of self and other. The doctrine teaches that what we perceive as a solid, independent self is actually a composite of various factors—physical form, sensations, perceptions, mental formations, and consciousness—that are themselves conditioned by other factors. This realization dismantles the illusion of a permanent, unchanging self and fosters a sense of interconnectedness and interdependence with all beings.

In the context of criminal behavior and justice, Dependent Origination offers a framework for understanding the complex web of causes and conditions that lead to criminal actions. Criminal behavior is not an isolated event but the result of multiple interrelated factors, including social, economic, psychological, and environmental influences. This perspective shifts the focus from viewing crime as a manifestation of inherent evil or individual moral failure to seeing it as a consequence of a myriad of interconnected conditions. For instance, consider an individual who commits theft. Traditional perspectives might attribute the crime to personal greed or moral deficiency. However, through the lens of Dependent Origination, one would examine the broader context: the individual's socio-economic background, education, mental health, family environment, and societal influences. This comprehensive analysis reveals that the act of theft is not simply a personal failing but a symptom of a larger network of interdependent conditions.

Understanding Dependent Origination in this way encourages a more compassionate and holistic approach to justice. Instead of focusing solely on punishment, which addresses the symptom but not the cause, justice systems can develop interventions that target the root causes of criminal behavior. This might involve providing education and job training, offering mental health and addiction services, fostering supportive community networks, and addressing systemic issues such as poverty and inequality. The principle of Dependent Origination also fosters empathy and compassion by highlighting our interconnectedness. Recognizing that we are all part of a complex web of relationships, and that our actions impact others, can cultivate a sense of shared responsibility and collective well-being. In justice settings, this translates to practices that prioritize healing and restoration over retribution. Programs that involve community service, restorative justice practices, and victim-offender mediation are practical applications of this compassionate approach.

Restorative justice, in particular, embodies the principles of Dependent Origination by bringing together offenders, victims, and community members to address the harm caused by crime. This process acknowledges the interconnected nature of harm and seeks to restore relationships and repair the community fabric. By focusing on dialogue, mutual understanding, and collective resolution, restorative justice transforms the traditional punitive paradigm into one that fosters healing and reconciliation. Dependent Origination also has significant implications for the reintegration of offenders into society. A justice system informed by this principle recognizes that successful reintegration requires addressing the conditions that contributed to the criminal behavior. This includes providing support for housing, employment, education, and mental health, as well as fostering community acceptance and support. Programs that assist with these aspects can reduce recidivism and promote a more inclusive and compassionate society.

Moreover, the principle of Dependent Origination challenges the stigmatization and marginalization of offenders. By understanding that criminal behavior arises from a complex interplay of conditions, society can move away from simplistic and judgmental attitudes towards a more nuanced and empathetic perspective. This shift can lead to policies and practices that focus on rehabilitation and support rather than exclusion and punishment. In educational settings, teaching the principles of Dependent Origination can cultivate a sense of interconnectedness and ethical responsibility in future generations. By incorporating these teachings into curricula, schools can help students develop a deeper understanding of the causes and consequences of their actions, fostering a culture of empathy, responsibility, and social harmony. This educational approach can contribute to the prevention of criminal behavior by addressing its root causes at an early stage.

3.2: Analyzing Criminal Behavior through Dependent Origination

Analyzing criminal behavior through the lens of Dependent Origination provides a profound shift from traditional views of crime and justice. This perspective emphasizes the interconnectedness of all factors contributing to criminal behavior, challenging the simplistic notion of crime as merely a result of individual moral failing. Instead, it considers the multitude of interdependent causes and conditions that give rise to such behavior, offering a holistic understanding that can inform more effective and compassionate interventions. Criminal behavior, when viewed through Dependent Origination, is the culmination of various influences ranging from personal history and psychological factors to socio-economic conditions and environmental contexts. This multifaceted approach reveals the complexity behind actions typically deemed as criminal, encouraging a more empathetic and comprehensive approach to justice.

Consider the case of an individual convicted of theft. Traditional justice systems might focus on the act itself, viewing it as a breach of moral and legal codes deserving punishment. However, by applying the principle of Dependent Origination, one would delve into the intricate web of factors contributing to this behavior. This might include examining the individual's socio-economic background, such as poverty, lack of education, and limited employment opportunities. Psychological aspects like mental health issues, trauma, and addiction might also play crucial roles. Furthermore, the influence of family dynamics, peer pressure, and community environments can significantly shape one's actions.

Understanding these interdependent causes shifts the focus from punitive measures to addressing the root causes of criminal behavior. This perspective encourages justice systems to develop interventions that not only hold individuals accountable but also support their rehabilitation and reintegration into society. For instance, addressing socio-economic factors might involve providing access to education, job training, and employment opportunities. By alleviating poverty and offering pathways to stable employment, individuals are less likely to resort to criminal activities out of economic necessity.

Mental health and addiction services are also critical components of a holistic approach to justice. Recognizing that mental health issues and substance abuse often underlie criminal behavior, providing comprehensive treatment and support can significantly reduce recidivism. This might include counseling, therapy, and rehabilitation programs tailored to individual needs. By addressing these underlying issues, justice systems can help individuals develop healthier coping mechanisms and make more positive life choices. The role of family and community support cannot be overstated.

Strong, supportive relationships can serve as protective factors against criminal behavior. Programs that involve family counseling, community engagement, and peer support can strengthen these bonds and provide a network of care and accountability. For example, family group conferencing, a restorative justice practice, brings together offenders, victims, and their families to discuss the impact of the crime and develop a plan for making amends. This process not only addresses the harm caused but also reinforces family and community ties, which are crucial for successful rehabilitation.

Educational interventions also play a vital role in addressing the interdependent causes of criminal behavior. Providing access to education and skill-building opportunities can empower individuals to pursue legitimate paths to success. This might include basic literacy and numeracy programs, vocational training, and higher education opportunities. By equipping individuals with the knowledge and skills needed for gainful employment, educational interventions can break the cycle of poverty and crime, offering a sustainable path to personal and societal well-being. In addition to individual interventions, addressing systemic issues is essential for a holistic approach to justice.

Structural factors such as poverty, inequality, and discrimination contribute to the conditions that foster criminal behavior. Policies aimed at reducing poverty, increasing economic opportunities, and promoting social equity can create an environment where individuals are less likely to engage in criminal activities. This might involve reforms in housing, healthcare, education, and employment sectors to ensure that all members of society have access to the resources and opportunities needed for a stable and fulfilling life.

Community-based programs that promote social cohesion and support also play a crucial role in addressing the interdependent causes of criminal behavior. These programs might include community centers that offer recreational activities, educational workshops, and support groups. By fostering a sense of belonging and community, these programs can provide positive alternatives to criminal behavior and promote pro-social activities. Additionally, community-based restorative justice practices, such as peacemaking circles and community conferencing, can address conflicts and harm in ways that promote healing and reconciliation. The application of Dependent Origination in analyzing criminal behavior also has significant implications for the justice system's approach to recidivism. Recidivism, or the tendency of previously convicted individuals to reoffend, is a major challenge for justice systems worldwide. Traditional punitive approaches often fail to address the underlying causes of criminal behavior, leading to high rates of reoffending. By contrast, a holistic approach informed by Dependent Origination seeks to address these root causes and provide ongoing support for reintegration.

For example, reentry programs that support individuals transitioning from incarceration to community life are essential for reducing recidivism. These programs might include housing assistance, job placement services, and mentoring. By providing stable housing and employment opportunities, reentry programs can help individuals establish a foundation for a successful and crime-free life. Additionally, ongoing support and mentorship can provide the guidance and encouragement needed to navigate the challenges of reentry and make positive choices.

Another important aspect of a holistic approach to justice is the promotion of restorative practices that focus on healing and reconciliation rather than punishment. Restorative justice practices recognize the interconnectedness of individuals and communities and seek to address the harm caused by crime in a way that promotes healing for all parties involved. This might include victim-offender mediation, where victims have the opportunity to express the impact of the crime and offenders take responsibility for their actions. By fostering dialogue and mutual understanding, restorative justice can promote empathy, accountability, and the healing of relationships.

Furthermore, a holistic approach to justice informed by Dependent Origination emphasizes the importance of addressing societal attitudes and biases that contribute to criminal behavior. This might involve public education campaigns that challenge stereotypes and promote understanding and compassion for individuals involved in the justice system. By shifting societal attitudes towards a more empathetic and supportive perspective, we can create an environment that supports rehabilitation and reintegration rather than perpetuating stigma and exclusion. Analyzing criminal behavior through the lens of Dependent Origination provides a comprehensive and compassionate framework for understanding and addressing the complex web of causes and conditions that give rise to such behavior. By recognizing the interdependent nature of these factors, justice systems can develop holistic interventions that address root causes, promote rehabilitation, and support the reintegration of offenders.

3.3: Holistic Approaches to Rehabilitation

A holistic approach to rehabilitation, deeply rooted in the principle of Dependent Origination, acknowledges the complex interplay of various factors that contribute to criminal behavior and aims to address them comprehensively. This approach moves beyond mere punishment to encompass the physical, psychological, social, and spiritual dimensions of an individual's life, aiming for complete transformation and reintegration into society. Understanding that criminal behavior arises from a web of interdependent causes, a holistic rehabilitation program seeks to unravel this web and address each contributing factor. This comprehensive perspective involves an integrated set of interventions that collectively promote personal growth, ethical conduct, and social responsibility.

One crucial aspect of holistic rehabilitation is addressing mental health and psychological well-being. Many individuals who engage in criminal behavior suffer from untreated mental health issues, trauma, or emotional dysregulation. Holistic rehabilitation programs must therefore include robust mental health services that offer counseling, therapy, and psychiatric care. Cognitive-behavioral therapy (CBT), dialectical behavior therapy (DBT), and trauma-informed care are essential components of such programs. These therapies help individuals process their experiences, develop healthier coping mechanisms, and gain emotional resilience.

Substance abuse treatment is another critical element. Substance abuse is often both a cause and a consequence of criminal behavior, creating a vicious cycle that can be difficult to break. Comprehensive substance abuse programs that include detoxification, rehabilitation, and ongoing support are vital. These programs should integrate medical treatment with behavioral therapies to address the underlying issues driving substance use. Support groups such as Narcotics Anonymous (NA) or Alcoholics Anonymous (AA) can provide ongoing peer support, fostering a sense of community and shared accountability. Educational and vocational training are also pivotal in a holistic rehabilitation approach.

Lack of education and job skills significantly limit an individual's opportunities for lawful employment, often leading to criminal activities as a means of survival. Rehabilitation programs should therefore offer educational opportunities, from basic literacy and numeracy to higher education and vocational training. Skills training in areas such as carpentry, plumbing, information technology, and culinary arts can equip individuals with the tools they need to secure stable employment upon release. Partnerships with local businesses and industries can facilitate job placements and apprenticeships, providing a pathway to gainful employment.

Family and community support play a crucial role in the rehabilitation process. Strong, supportive relationships can act as a buffer against criminal behavior, providing emotional support, stability, and a sense of belonging. Family counseling and therapy can help mend strained relationships and rebuild trust. Programs that involve families in the rehabilitation process, such as family group conferencing, can strengthen these bonds and create a supportive network for the individual. Additionally, community-based programs that offer mentorship, peer support, and community service opportunities can foster a sense of connectedness and social responsibility. Spiritual growth and ethical development are integral components of holistic rehabilitation. Many individuals find solace and meaning through spiritual practices, which can provide a moral framework and a sense of purpose. Rehabilitation programs that include spiritual counseling, meditation, and mindfulness practices can support individuals in their journey towards ethical living. These practices help individuals develop self-awareness, compassion, and a deeper understanding of their interconnectedness with others.

Restorative justice practices are another essential aspect of a holistic rehabilitation approach. These practices focus on healing the harm caused by criminal behavior through processes that involve victims, offenders, and the community. Victim-offender mediation, community circles, and restorative dialogues allow individuals to take responsibility for their actions, understand the impact of their behavior, and make amends. These practices not only promote accountability and empathy but also facilitate healing and reconciliation for all parties involved. Furthermore, addressing the systemic issues that contribute to criminal behavior is a crucial part of holistic rehabilitation. Structural factors such as poverty, discrimination, and lack of access to resources create an environment where crime can flourish.

Rehabilitation programs must therefore advocate for policies and initiatives that address these broader social determinants. This includes advocating for affordable housing, accessible healthcare, quality education, and economic opportunities. By addressing these systemic issues, we can create a society that supports the well-being and success of all its members, reducing the conditions that lead to criminal behavior.

Peer support and mentorship programs can also significantly enhance holistic rehabilitation efforts. These programs connect individuals with mentors who have successfully navigated the challenges of rehabilitation and reintegration. Mentors can provide guidance, encouragement, and practical advice, helping individuals set goals and navigate obstacles. Peer support groups offer a sense of community and shared experience, reducing feelings of isolation and providing a network of support. Physical health and wellness are additional components of holistic rehabilitation. Many individuals involved in the justice system have unmet healthcare needs, including chronic illnesses, untreated injuries, and inadequate nutrition. Comprehensive healthcare services that address physical health, dental care, and nutrition are essential. Fitness programs that promote physical activity can improve overall well-being and reduce stress, supporting mental and emotional health.

Artistic and creative expression can also play a therapeutic role in holistic rehabilitation. Programs that offer opportunities for individuals to engage in art, music, theater, and other forms of creative expression can provide a constructive outlet for emotions, foster self-discovery, and enhance self-esteem. Artistic activities can also facilitate communication and healing, allowing individuals to explore and express their experiences in a supportive environment. Legal support and advocacy are critical for individuals navigating the justice system and reintegrating into society. Legal assistance can help individuals understand their rights, address legal barriers to employment and housing, and advocate for fair treatment. Programs that provide legal education and support can empower individuals to make informed decisions and protect their rights.

In implementing holistic rehabilitation programs, it is essential to adopt a person-centered approach that respects the dignity and autonomy of each individual. Programs should be tailored to meet the unique needs and strengths of each person, recognizing that there is no one-size-fits-all solution. This approach requires collaboration among various stakeholders, including justice professionals, healthcare providers, educators, community organizations, and policymakers. By working together, these stakeholders can create a comprehensive support network that addresses the multifaceted needs of individuals involved in the justice system. Continuous evaluation and improvement of rehabilitation programs are essential to ensure their effectiveness. This involves collecting data, monitoring outcomes, and seeking feedback from participants and stakeholders. Research and evidence-based practices should inform program design and implementation, ensuring that interventions are grounded in sound theory and demonstrated effectiveness.

3.4: Practical Applications in Justice Settings

Applying the principle of Dependent Origination in justice settings involves a paradigm shift from a punitive system to one that is more holistic, interconnected, and rehabilitative. This approach recognizes that criminal behavior arises from a complex web of interdependent causes and conditions. By addressing these root causes, justice systems can develop more effective and humane interventions that promote rehabilitation, reintegration, and the overall well-being of individuals and communities. One of the primary ways to apply Dependent Origination in justice settings is through the development and implementation of holistic rehabilitation programs that address the various factors contributing to criminal behavior. These programs should be comprehensive, integrating mental health services, substance abuse treatment, educational and vocational training, family and community support, and restorative justice practices.

Mental health services are essential in a holistic rehabilitation program. Many individuals involved in the justice system suffer from mental health issues such as depression, anxiety, PTSD, and other psychiatric disorders. Providing access to comprehensive mental health care, including counseling, therapy, and psychiatric treatment, is crucial for addressing these underlying issues. Cognitive-behavioral therapy (CBT), dialectical behavior therapy (DBT), and trauma-informed care are particularly effective in helping individuals process their experiences, develop healthier coping mechanisms, and gain emotional resilience. Substance abuse treatment is another critical component. Substance abuse is often both a cause and a consequence of criminal behavior, creating a cycle that can be difficult to break. Comprehensive substance abuse programs that include detoxification, rehabilitation, and ongoing support are vital. These programs should integrate medical treatment with behavioral therapies to address the underlying issues driving substance use. Support groups such as Narcotics Anonymous (NA) or Alcoholics Anonymous (AA) can provide ongoing peer support, fostering a sense of community and shared accountability.

Educational and vocational training are also pivotal in a holistic rehabilitation approach. Lack of education and job skills significantly limit an individual's opportunities for lawful employment, often leading to criminal activities as a means of survival. Rehabilitation programs should therefore offer educational opportunities, from basic literacy and numeracy to higher education and vocational training. Skills training in areas such as carpentry, plumbing, information technology, and culinary arts can equip individuals with the tools they need to secure stable employment upon release. Partnerships with local businesses and industries can facilitate job placements and apprenticeships, providing a pathway to gainful employment.

Family and community support play a crucial role in the rehabilitation process. Strong, supportive relationships can act as a buffer against criminal behavior, providing emotional support, stability, and a sense of belonging. Family counseling and therapy can help mend strained relationships and rebuild trust. Programs that involve families in the rehabilitation process, such as family group conferencing, can strengthen these bonds and create a supportive network for the individual. Additionally, community-based programs that offer mentorship, peer support, and community service opportunities can foster a sense of connectedness and social responsibility.

Restorative justice practices are an essential aspect of a holistic rehabilitation approach. These practices focus on healing the harm caused by criminal behavior through processes that involve victims, offenders, and the community. Victim-offender mediation, community circles, and restorative dialogues allow individuals to take responsibility for their actions, understand the impact of their behavior, and make amends. These practices not only promote accountability and empathy but also facilitate healing and reconciliation for all parties involved. Furthermore, addressing the systemic issues that contribute to criminal behavior is a crucial part of holistic rehabilitation. Structural factors such as poverty, discrimination, and lack of access to resources create an environment where crime can flourish. Rehabilitation programs must therefore advocate for policies and initiatives that address these broader social determinants. This includes advocating for affordable housing, accessible healthcare, quality education, and economic opportunities. By addressing these systemic issues, we can create a society that supports the well-being and success of all its members, reducing the conditions that lead to criminal behavior.

Peer support and mentorship programs can also significantly enhance holistic rehabilitation efforts. These programs connect individuals with mentors who have successfully navigated the challenges of rehabilitation and reintegration. Mentors can provide guidance, encouragement, and practical advice, helping individuals set goals and navigate obstacles. Peer support groups offer a sense of community and shared experience, reducing feelings of isolation and providing a network of support. Physical health and wellness are additional components of holistic rehabilitation. Many individuals involved in the justice system have unmet healthcare needs, including chronic illnesses, untreated injuries, and inadequate nutrition. Comprehensive healthcare services that address physical health, dental care, and nutrition are essential. Fitness programs that promote physical activity can improve overall well-being and reduce stress, supporting mental and emotional health.

Artistic and creative expression can also play a therapeutic role in holistic rehabilitation. Programs that offer opportunities for individuals to engage in art, music, theater, and other forms of creative expression can provide a constructive outlet for emotions, foster self-discovery, and enhance self-esteem. Artistic activities can also facilitate communication and healing, allowing individuals to explore and express their experiences in a supportive environment. Legal support and advocacy are critical for individuals navigating the justice system and reintegrating into society. Legal assistance can help individuals understand their rights, address legal barriers to employment and housing, and advocate for fair treatment. Programs that provide legal education and support can empower individuals to make informed decisions and protect their rights.

In implementing holistic rehabilitation programs, it is essential to adopt a person-centered approach that respects the dignity and autonomy of each individual. Programs should be tailored to meet the unique needs and strengths of each person, recognizing that there is no one-size-fits-all solution. This approach requires collaboration among various stakeholders, including justice professionals, healthcare providers, educators, community organizations, and policymakers. By working together, these stakeholders can create a comprehensive support network that addresses the multifaceted needs of individuals involved in the justice system. Continuous evaluation and improvement of rehabilitation programs are essential to ensure their effectiveness. This involves collecting data, monitoring outcomes, and seeking feedback from participants and stakeholders. Research and evidence-based practices should inform program design and implementation, ensuring that interventions are grounded in sound theory and demonstrated effectiveness.

Public awareness and education are also critical components of holistic rehabilitation. Raising awareness about the principles of Dependent Origination and the benefits of a holistic approach to justice can garner support for these initiatives. Public education campaigns can highlight the success stories of individuals who have successfully reintegrated into society, challenging stereotypes and promoting understanding and compassion for individuals involved in the justice system. International cooperation and knowledge exchange can further enhance the development and implementation of holistic rehabilitation programs. Policies should encourage collaboration with international organizations, researchers, and practitioners to share best practices, research findings, and innovative approaches. This can include participation in international conferences, joint research projects, and the establishment of networks for knowledge exchange. By learning from successful initiatives in other countries, programs can be informed by a global perspective and adapted to local contexts.

Finally, it is important to foster a culture of compassion and empathy within the justice system. Justice practitioners, including judges, lawyers, and correctional officers, should receive training that promotes emotional intelligence, ethical decision-making, and trauma-informed care. By cultivating these qualities, practitioners can create a more supportive and humane justice system that prioritizes healing and rehabilitation over punishment. Applying the principle of Dependent Origination in justice settings involves developing holistic rehabilitation programs that address the multifaceted needs of individuals involved in the justice system.

By integrating mental health services, substance abuse treatment, educational and vocational training, family and community support, restorative justice practices, systemic advocacy, peer support, physical health and wellness, artistic expression, and legal support, holistic rehabilitation programs can promote personal transformation and successful reintegration. This approach aligns with the core values of Tibetan Buddhism, offering a path towards a more compassionate, just, and harmonious society. Through collaboration, continuous improvement, public awareness, and a culture of compassion, holistic rehabilitation can create opportunities for healing, growth, and positive change, supporting individuals in leading fulfilling and productive lives.

3.5: Case Studies Demonstrating Success

Examining case studies that successfully apply the principle of Dependent Origination in rehabilitation programs and justice systems provides valuable insights into how this philosophical framework can transform contemporary practices. These examples illustrate how a comprehensive understanding of interconnected causes can lead to more effective interventions, lower recidivism rates, and foster a more compassionate and equitable justice system. One notable example is the "Circles of Support and Accountability" (CoSA) program, originally developed in Canada. CoSA is designed for high-risk sex offenders who are released into the community. Recognizing that social isolation and lack of support are significant risk factors for reoffending, CoSA provides a network of volunteer support for these individuals. Each offender is surrounded by a "circle" of trained volunteers who offer friendship, support, and accountability. This program acknowledges the interconnectedness of social support, personal accountability, and successful reintegration. Research has shown that CoSA significantly reduces recidivism rates among participants, demonstrating the effectiveness of addressing the social and psychological needs of offenders.

Another innovative case is the "Desistance Project" in Scotland, which focuses on helping offenders transition away from a life of crime. The project is based on the understanding that desistance from crime is a process influenced by various factors, including personal relationships, employment opportunities, and individual agency. The Desistance Project provides individualized support plans that include mentoring, counseling, and skills training. The program also involves families and communities, recognizing their crucial role in supporting the desistance process. The success of the Desistance Project highlights the importance of a holistic, personalized approach that considers the multiple factors influencing an individual's path away from crime.

The "Restorative Circles" initiative in Brazil offers another compelling example. In the city of São Paulo, restorative circles have been implemented in schools and communities to address conflict and reduce violence. These circles bring together offenders, victims, and community members to discuss the impact of the crime and collaboratively develop a plan to repair the harm. By fostering open communication and mutual understanding, restorative circles help rebuild trust and strengthen community bonds. This approach has been particularly effective in reducing youth violence and promoting a culture of peace and reconciliation.

The "Inside-Out Prison Exchange Program" in the United States provides a unique educational model that bridges the gap between incarcerated individuals and university students. This program offers college courses that bring together inmates and students in a collaborative learning environment. The principle of Dependent Origination is evident as participants learn from each other's experiences and perspectives, fostering empathy, understanding, and mutual respect. The Inside-Out program has been shown to reduce recidivism among participating inmates and challenge stereotypes among students, highlighting the transformative potential of education and dialogue in breaking down barriers and promoting social integration.

In the Netherlands, the "Prison Gate Schools" initiative is designed to help young offenders reintegrate into society by providing education and vocational training while they are still incarcerated. These schools offer a range of programs, from basic education to vocational skills training, tailored to the needs and interests of each individual. The holistic approach of Prison Gate Schools recognizes the importance of education and skills development in preventing recidivism and promoting successful reintegration. By addressing the educational and vocational needs of young offenders, this initiative helps create a foundation for a more stable and productive life post-release.

The "GRIP (Guiding Rage Into Power)" program at San Quentin State Prison in California focuses on emotional healing and personal transformation for violent offenders. GRIP is a year-long program that combines elements of mindfulness, emotional literacy, and restorative justice. Participants engage in deep self-reflection, learn to understand and manage their emotions, and develop skills for resolving conflicts peacefully. The program also includes victim-offender dialogues, where participants can confront the impact of their actions and take steps toward making amends. GRIP's holistic approach addresses the psychological and emotional roots of violent behavior, fostering personal growth and reducing the likelihood of reoffending.

The "Amaka Ya Bafazi Health Initiative" in South Africa addresses the unique challenges faced by female offenders. This initiative provides comprehensive health services, including mental health support, reproductive health care, and substance abuse treatment. Recognizing the interconnected factors that contribute to criminal behavior among women, the program also offers education, vocational training, and parenting classes. By addressing the physical, mental, and socio-economic needs of female offenders, Amaka Ya Bafazi promotes holistic rehabilitation and supports successful reintegration into society.

The "Social Reintegration Program" in Singapore's prison system focuses on preparing inmates for life after release through a comprehensive support system. This program includes pre-release planning, vocational training, and post-release support such as job placement services and community mentorship. The holistic approach of the Social Reintegration Program recognizes that successful reintegration requires continuous support and the addressing of multiple factors that influence an individual's ability to lead a law-abiding life. By providing a continuum of care that starts during incarceration and continues after release, the program helps reduce recidivism and promotes social stability.

The "Pathways to Education" program in Canada addresses the root causes of criminal behavior by targeting at-risk youth before they enter the justice system. This program provides comprehensive support, including tutoring, mentoring, financial assistance, and advocacy, to help students stay in school and achieve academic success. Pathways to Education recognizes the interconnectedness of education, social support, and economic stability in preventing criminal behavior. By addressing these factors early, the program helps reduce dropout rates and provides young people with the tools they need to build a positive future.

—

CHAPTER FOUR

The Four Noble Truths

Contents

- Identifying Suffering in the Justice System

- Causes of Suffering and Criminal Behavior

- Alleviating Suffering through Restorative Practices

- Implementing the Four Noble Truths in Justice

- Case Studies and Practical Examples

4.1: Identifying Suffering in the Justice System

The Four Noble Truths, fundamental to Tibetan Buddhism, offer profound insights that are remarkably applicable to the justice system. These truths reveal the nature of suffering, its causes, and the path to its cessation, providing a framework that can transform our understanding and approach to justice. The first Noble Truth, Dukkha, recognizes the pervasive presence of suffering in human life. This suffering is not merely physical pain but encompasses a wide range of psychological and existential distress. In the context of the justice system, suffering manifests in various forms: the suffering of victims, the suffering of offenders, and the suffering of communities affected by crime.

Victims experience suffering through the harm inflicted upon them, whether it be physical, emotional, or financial. This suffering can lead to lasting trauma, fear, and a sense of injustice. Offenders, too, endure suffering, often as a result of their own actions. Many come from backgrounds of poverty, abuse, and neglect, having experienced significant suffering before committing their crimes. Their actions often perpetuate a cycle of suffering, impacting their families and communities. Communities suffer as well, bearing the burden of fear, mistrust, and disruption caused by crime. The collective suffering of these groups underscores the interconnected nature of human experience, echoing the teachings of the Four Noble Truths.

The second Noble Truth, Samudaya, identifies the causes of suffering. In Buddhism, suffering arises from craving, ignorance, and attachment. In the justice system, these causes can be seen in the factors that lead to criminal behavior. Craving, or desire, manifests in the pursuit of material gain, power, or status through illegal means. Ignorance is evident in the lack of awareness or understanding of the consequences of one's actions and the failure to recognize the interconnectedness of all beings. Attachment, or clinging, can be seen in the inability to let go of past grievances, leading to cycles of retaliation and violence. These elements contribute to a perpetuation of suffering within the justice system, affecting both individuals and society at large. Recognizing these causes offers a pathway to addressing them.

By understanding that criminal behavior often stems from deep-seated suffering and unmet needs, justice systems can shift from a purely punitive approach to one that seeks to alleviate the underlying causes of suffering. This approach aligns with the third Noble Truth, Nirodha, which posits that the cessation of suffering is possible. In a justice context, this translates to interventions that heal and rehabilitate rather than solely punish. Restorative justice practices exemplify this principle, focusing on repairing harm, fostering understanding, and rebuilding relationships. These practices aim to alleviate suffering by addressing its root causes and promoting healing for all parties involved.

The fourth Noble Truth, Magga, outlines the path to the cessation of suffering, known as the Eightfold Path. This path offers practical steps that can be integrated into justice practices to create a more compassionate and effective system. Right View involves seeing the interconnectedness of all beings and understanding the true nature of suffering and its causes. Right Intention encourages the development of ethical motivations and a commitment to non-harm. Right Speech promotes truthful and compassionate communication, essential for restorative dialogues and mediation.

Right Action and Right Livelihood emphasize ethical conduct and the importance of creating conditions that support justice and equity. Incorporating these elements into the justice system involves creating policies and practices that prioritize rehabilitation, education, and social support. Programs that provide mental health services, substance abuse treatment, and vocational training address the root causes of criminal behavior and support offenders in making positive changes. Community-based initiatives that promote social cohesion and support for at-risk individuals can prevent crime by addressing the conditions that lead to it. By focusing on the holistic well-being of individuals and communities, justice systems can reduce suffering and promote healing.

The concept of Dukkha in the justice system also highlights the importance of recognizing and addressing systemic suffering. Structural inequalities, such as poverty, racism, and lack of access to education and healthcare, contribute to the conditions that foster criminal behavior. Addressing these systemic issues requires a commitment to social justice and policies that promote equity and inclusion. This involves advocating for fair and just laws, ensuring equal access to resources, and creating opportunities for marginalized communities. By addressing these broader issues, justice systems can work towards reducing the systemic suffering that underlies much of the crime. Moreover, the recognition of suffering in the justice system calls for a compassionate response from justice practitioners. Judges, lawyers, police officers, and correctional staff can benefit from training in trauma-informed care and emotional intelligence, which equips them to respond to individuals with empathy and understanding. This compassionate approach can transform interactions within the justice system, fostering trust and cooperation rather than fear and antagonism.

Educational programs that teach the principles of the Four Noble Truths and the Eightfold Path can also play a role in transforming the justice system. By incorporating these teachings into the training of justice practitioners, we can cultivate a justice system that is more humane and effective. This education can extend to schools and community programs, fostering a culture of empathy, responsibility, and interconnectedness from an early age. Additionally, the application of the Four Noble Truths in justice requires a commitment to continuous reflection and improvement.

Justice systems must regularly evaluate their policies and practices to ensure they are effectively addressing suffering and promoting healing. This involves gathering data, seeking feedback from those affected by the justice system, and being willing to make changes based on this feedback. By adopting a mindset of continuous improvement, justice systems can remain responsive to the needs of individuals and communities. The Four Noble Truths offer a profound framework for understanding and addressing suffering within the justice system. By recognizing the pervasive nature of suffering, identifying its causes, and implementing practices that promote its cessation, justice systems can become more compassionate and effective.

4.2: Causes of Suffering and Criminal Behavior

The causes of suffering, as outlined in the second Noble Truth (Samudaya), offer profound insights into the origins of criminal behavior and the dynamics that perpetuate cycles of harm. By understanding these causes, we can develop more effective interventions that address the root issues rather than merely treating the symptoms. In the context of the justice system, these causes are multifaceted, encompassing personal, social, and structural dimensions. At the personal level, suffering often stems from deep-seated psychological and emotional issues.

Many individuals who engage in criminal behavior have histories marked by trauma, abuse, and neglect. These experiences can lead to a range of psychological issues, including post-traumatic stress disorder (PTSD), depression, anxiety, and emotional dysregulation. For example, studies have shown that a significant proportion of incarcerated individuals have experienced childhood trauma, which profoundly impacts their mental health and behavior. This trauma often manifests as aggression, substance abuse, and other maladaptive coping mechanisms, driving individuals towards criminal activity as a way to manage their pain.

Substance abuse, in particular, is both a cause and a consequence of suffering. Addiction often arises from attempts to escape emotional pain, yet it perpetuates a cycle of suffering through dependence, health deterioration, and social isolation. Many offenders commit crimes to support their addiction, illustrating the interconnectedness of substance abuse and criminal behavior. Effective interventions must therefore address the underlying emotional pain and provide comprehensive substance abuse treatment, including detoxification, rehabilitation, and ongoing support. Ignorance, as highlighted in Buddhist teachings, also plays a crucial role in the perpetuation of suffering and criminal behavior.

This ignorance is not merely a lack of knowledge but a deeper misunderstanding of the nature of reality, including the interconnectedness of actions and their consequences. Many offenders do not fully grasp the impact of their actions on themselves, their victims, and their communities. This lack of understanding can stem from limited education, cognitive impairments, or social environments that normalize criminal behavior. Educational programs that foster self-awareness, empathy, and ethical decision-making can help mitigate this ignorance, encouraging individuals to make more informed and compassionate choices.

Social and environmental factors are equally significant in understanding the causes of suffering and criminal behavior. Poverty, unemployment, and lack of access to education and healthcare create conditions that foster crime. Individuals living in impoverished communities often face limited opportunities and resources, leading to desperation and a higher likelihood of engaging in illegal activities. Moreover, these environments can be rife with violence, drugs, and negative role models, reinforcing criminal behavior as a means of survival or acceptance. For instance, gang involvement often provides a sense of belonging and identity for individuals who lack supportive family structures and community connections. Gangs offer protection, economic opportunities through illegal activities, and a surrogate family. However, this involvement perpetuates cycles of violence and criminality. Addressing these social factors requires comprehensive community development initiatives that provide education, job training, and social services to create alternative pathways for at-risk individuals.

The structural dimension of suffering encompasses systemic inequalities and injustices that contribute to criminal behavior. Discrimination based on race, ethnicity, gender, and socioeconomic status exacerbates feelings of marginalization and disenfranchisement. The criminal justice system itself can perpetuate these inequalities through biased policing practices, discriminatory sentencing, and inadequate legal representation for marginalized groups. For example, studies have consistently shown that people of color are disproportionately targeted by law enforcement and receive harsher sentences compared to their white counterparts for similar offenses. These systemic issues contribute to a cycle of disadvantage and criminalization that must be addressed through policy reforms and social justice initiatives.

The over-reliance on punitive measures rather than rehabilitative approaches further perpetuates suffering within the justice system. Incarceration, particularly in harsh and overcrowded conditions, often exacerbates mental health issues and exposes individuals to further trauma and violence. The lack of rehabilitative services within prisons means that many individuals leave the system more damaged and ill-prepared for reintegration into society than when they entered. This perpetuates a cycle of reoffending and reincarceration. Shifting towards a more rehabilitative model that prioritizes mental health care, education, and skill development within correctional facilities is essential for breaking this cycle.

Family dynamics also play a critical role in the causes of suffering and criminal behavior. Dysfunctional family environments, characterized by domestic violence, substance abuse, and neglect, can profoundly impact an individual's development and propensity for crime. Children who grow up in such environments often lack positive role models and stability, leading to behavioral issues and a higher likelihood of engaging in criminal activities. Interventions that support families, such as counseling, parenting programs, and domestic violence prevention, are crucial for creating healthier home environments that reduce the risk of future criminal behavior. Peer influence is another significant factor. Adolescents and young adults are particularly susceptible to peer pressure and the desire for social acceptance. When surrounded by peers who engage in criminal behavior, individuals are more likely to adopt similar behaviors to gain approval and avoid ostracization. This is particularly true in environments where criminal behavior is normalized and even valorized. Creating positive peer networks through mentorship programs, youth clubs, and community activities can provide alternatives to negative influences and encourage pro-social behavior.

The broader cultural context also influences criminal behavior. Societal values that prioritize material success, power, and status can drive individuals to pursue these goals through any means necessary, including illegal activities. The glorification of violence in media and entertainment further normalizes aggressive and antisocial behavior. Addressing these cultural factors requires a shift towards values that promote compassion, ethical conduct, and community well-being. Public awareness campaigns, educational initiatives, and media literacy programs can help foster a culture of empathy and responsibility.

Economic policies also play a crucial role in addressing the structural causes of suffering and criminal behavior. Policies that promote economic equality, create job opportunities, and provide social safety nets can alleviate the economic pressures that drive individuals towards crime. This includes raising the minimum wage, ensuring access to affordable housing, healthcare, and education, and supporting small businesses and job creation in disadvantaged communities. By addressing the economic roots of criminal behavior, these policies can create a more equitable society where individuals have the resources and opportunities to lead law-abiding lives.

Restorative justice practices offer a holistic approach to addressing the causes of suffering and criminal behavior. These practices focus on repairing harm, fostering understanding, and rebuilding relationships between offenders, victims, and communities. By involving all stakeholders in the justice process, restorative justice encourages accountability, empathy, and mutual respect. This approach not only addresses the immediate harm caused by crime but also promotes long-term healing and prevents future offenses. Community-based programs that provide support and resources for at-risk individuals are essential for addressing the root causes of criminal behavior. These programs might include educational and vocational training, mental health and substance abuse treatment, and social services that support stable housing and employment.

By providing comprehensive support, these programs can help individuals build a foundation for a stable and productive life, reducing the likelihood of engaging in criminal activities. Understanding the causes of suffering and criminal behavior through the lens of the second Noble Truth (Samudaya) provides a comprehensive framework for developing more effective and compassionate interventions. By addressing the personal, social, and structural dimensions of suffering, justice systems can move beyond punitive measures to create holistic solutions that promote rehabilitation, healing, and social equity.

4.3: Alleviating Suffering through Restorative Practices

The third Noble Truth, Nirodha, asserts that the cessation of suffering is possible. This profound assertion forms the cornerstone of transformative justice, offering hope that through appropriate interventions, the cycles of harm and retribution can be interrupted and replaced with healing and reconciliation. Restorative justice practices exemplify this principle, providing pathways to alleviate suffering for offenders, victims, and communities alike. Restorative justice focuses on repairing the harm caused by criminal behavior rather than merely punishing the offender. It is rooted in the belief that crime causes suffering not only to victims but also to offenders and their communities.

By addressing the needs of all parties involved, restorative justice seeks to heal and rebuild rather than perpetuate cycles of suffering and alienation. One of the primary restorative justice practices is victim-offender mediation, where victims and offenders engage in a facilitated dialogue to discuss the impact of the crime and agree on steps the offender can take to make amends. This process allows victims to express their feelings and needs, which can be a crucial step in their healing journey. For many victims, being heard and acknowledged is more important than seeing the offender punished. It helps restore their sense of agency and dignity, which are often eroded by the experience of being victimized.

For offenders, mediation provides an opportunity to understand the human impact of their actions, fostering empathy and remorse. This awareness can be a powerful motivator for change, encouraging offenders to take responsibility for their behavior and commit to making positive changes in their lives. By confronting the consequences of their actions directly, offenders are more likely to develop a sense of accountability and a desire to make amends. This process can significantly reduce the likelihood of reoffending, as it addresses the underlying issues that contribute to criminal behavior and promotes personal transformation. Restorative circles, another key practice, involve a broader community, including victims, offenders, their families, and community members. These circles provide a supportive environment where all participants can share their perspectives, feelings, and experiences. The goal is to build understanding, trust, and mutual respect, creating a foundation for collective healing and reconciliation. By involving the community, restorative circles help to reintegrate offenders and strengthen social bonds, reducing the isolation and stigma that often accompany criminal behavior.

Family group conferencing is a restorative practice particularly effective in addressing juvenile crime. This approach brings together the young offender, their family, the victim, and relevant community members to discuss the offense and develop a plan for making amends. Family group conferencing recognizes that the behavior of young offenders is often influenced by family dynamics and that involving the family in the resolution process can lead to more effective outcomes. By engaging families, this practice supports the offender's reintegration and helps build a supportive environment that reduces the risk of future offenses.

The principles of restorative justice also extend to community-based initiatives aimed at preventing crime and addressing its root causes. Programs that focus on education, vocational training, and social services provide at-risk individuals with the resources and support they need to make positive life choices. For example, community centers offering after-school programs, job training, and counseling services can help divert youth from criminal activities and foster a sense of belonging and purpose. These programs recognize the interconnected nature of individual behavior and community health, working to strengthen the social fabric and create conditions that reduce the likelihood of crime.

Another significant aspect of restorative justice is the emphasis on healing and reconciliation for both victims and offenders. For victims, the restorative process provides an opportunity to move beyond the role of passive sufferers and actively participate in their healing. By sharing their experiences and needs, victims can reclaim their voice and work towards emotional closure. This process can also reduce feelings of fear, anger, and resentment, replacing them with a sense of resolution and empowerment. For offenders, restorative justice offers a path to redemption and reintegration. Many offenders struggle with feelings of guilt, shame, and worthlessness, which can perpetuate cycles of self-destructive behavior. By engaging in restorative practices, offenders can begin to address these feelings and work towards personal growth. The process of making amends and contributing positively to the community can help rebuild their self-esteem and foster a sense of purpose and belonging.

Restorative justice also has significant implications for the justice system as a whole. Traditional punitive approaches often fail to address the underlying causes of criminal behavior and can exacerbate the suffering of all parties involved. Overcrowded prisons, harsh sentencing policies, and a focus on retribution contribute to high recidivism rates and a cycle of criminality. In contrast, restorative justice offers a more holistic and humane approach, focusing on healing, accountability, and community restoration. Implementing restorative justice practices requires a shift in mindset and policy. It involves training justice practitioners in restorative techniques, developing protocols for victim-offender mediation and restorative circles, and creating a supportive legal framework. Policymakers need to advocate for restorative justice as a viable alternative to traditional punitive measures, emphasizing its benefits in terms of reduced recidivism, improved victim satisfaction, and stronger community bonds.

Education and public awareness are also crucial for the successful implementation of restorative justice. By educating the public about the principles and benefits of restorative justice, we can build broader support for these practices. Public awareness campaigns, community workshops, and educational programs in schools can help foster a culture of empathy, responsibility, and mutual respect. These efforts can contribute to a more supportive environment for restorative justice initiatives and encourage communities to take an active role in the justice process. Moreover, restorative justice aligns with broader social justice goals, addressing systemic issues such as inequality, discrimination, and social exclusion. By focusing on healing and reconciliation, restorative justice practices can help bridge divides and promote social cohesion.

This approach recognizes that justice is not only about addressing individual offenses but also about creating conditions for collective well-being and harmony. The third Noble Truth (Nirodha) provides a powerful foundation for restorative justice practices that aim to alleviate suffering and promote healing and reconciliation. By focusing on repairing harm, fostering understanding, and rebuilding relationships, restorative justice offers a more compassionate and effective approach to justice. Through victim-offender mediation, restorative circles, family group conferencing, and community-based initiatives, we can address the root causes of criminal behavior and support the reintegration of offenders.

4.4: Implementing the Four Noble Truths in Justice

Implementing the Four Noble Truths in justice settings involves translating these profound Buddhist principles into practical policies and practices that can transform how justice is perceived and administered. By focusing on the cessation of suffering and the path to achieve it, the justice system can move towards a more compassionate, holistic, and effective approach. This transformation requires a multifaceted strategy that incorporates education, policy reforms, community involvement, and continuous evaluation. At the heart of the Four Noble Truths is the recognition of suffering (dukkha) and its pervasiveness in human experience.

In the context of the justice system, this involves acknowledging the suffering of victims, offenders, and the broader community. Recognizing this suffering is the first step towards developing policies and practices that aim to alleviate it. For victims, this means creating support systems that address their emotional, physical, and financial needs. Victim support programs should provide counseling, medical care, and financial compensation where appropriate. These programs should also include restorative practices that allow victims to participate in the justice process, express their feelings, and receive acknowledgment and reparation for their suffering.

For offenders, recognizing suffering involves understanding the underlying causes of their criminal behavior and addressing these root issues. This can be achieved through comprehensive rehabilitation programs that include mental health services, substance abuse treatment, educational and vocational training, and life skills development. By addressing the psychological, social, and economic factors that contribute to criminal behavior, these programs can help offenders break the cycle of crime and build a foundation for a positive future. The second Noble Truth (Samudaya) identifies the causes of suffering, such as craving, ignorance, and attachment. Injustice often arises from these very causes, manifesting as greed, lack of awareness, and inflexible punitive policies. Implementing the Four Noble Truths in justice settings requires developing interventions that address these root causes. Educational programs within the justice system can play a crucial role in this regard. These programs should focus on fostering self-awareness, empathy, and ethical decision-making. Mindfulness and meditation practices can help offenders develop emotional regulation and a deeper understanding of their actions and their impact on others.

Community involvement is essential for addressing the social causes of criminal behavior. Community-based programs that provide support and resources for at-risk individuals can help prevent crime by addressing the conditions that lead to it. These programs might include mentoring, job training, after-school activities, and community service opportunities. By strengthening community bonds and providing positive role models and opportunities, these initiatives can reduce the social isolation and economic desperation that often lead to criminal behavior. The third Noble Truth (Nirodha) asserts that the cessation of suffering is possible. Injustice settings, this translates to the implementation of restorative justice practices that focus on healing and reconciliation rather than punishment. Restorative justice practices such as victim-offender mediation, family group conferencing, and restorative circles provide opportunities for offenders to make amends and for victims to receive closure and healing. These practices emphasize accountability, empathy, and mutual respect, creating a more humane and effective justice process.

Restorative justice can be implemented at various stages of the justice process, from pre-trial diversion programs to post-sentencing rehabilitation. Pre-trial diversion programs can offer offenders the opportunity to engage in restorative practices as an alternative to traditional prosecution. These programs can include community service, restitution, and participation in restorative circles or victim-offender mediation. By focusing on making amends and addressing the root causes of criminal behavior, these programs can reduce recidivism and promote long-term rehabilitation. Post-sentencing rehabilitation programs that incorporate restorative practices can support offenders in their reintegration into society. These programs should provide ongoing support and resources, including counseling, job placement services, and community mentorship. By creating a supportive network and addressing the underlying issues that contribute to criminal behavior, these programs can help offenders build a stable and productive life post-release.

The fourth Noble Truth (Magga) outlines the path to the cessation of suffering, known as the Eightfold Path. This path offers practical steps that can be integrated into justice policies and practices to create a more compassionate and effective system. The Eightfold Path includes Right View, Right Intention, Right Speech, Right Action, Right Livelihood, Right Effort, Right Mindfulness, and Right Concentration. Each of these elements can inform various aspects of the justice system. Right View involves understanding the interconnectedness of all beings and recognizing the true nature of suffering and its causes. This perspective can inform policies that prioritize rehabilitation and social justice over retribution. It encourages a holistic view of criminal behavior that considers the broader social, economic, and psychological factors at play.

Right Intention emphasizes the development of ethical motivations and a commitment to non-harm. Justice policies should reflect these intentions by focusing on rehabilitation, restorative practices, and community support rather than punitive measures. This approach can help create a justice system that seeks to heal and restore rather than punish and alienate. Right Speech promotes truthful and compassionate communication, which is essential for restorative dialogues and mediation. Training justice practitioners in effective communication skills, including active listening and empathy, can enhance the effectiveness of restorative justice practices and improve interactions within the justice system.

Right Action and Right Livelihood emphasize ethical conduct and the importance of creating conditions that support justice and equity. Policies should ensure that justice practices are fair and just, avoiding discrimination and bias. This includes advocating for equal access to legal representation, fair sentencing practices, and the elimination of systemic inequalities within the justice system. Right Effort involves making a consistent and diligent effort to cultivate positive qualities and eliminate negative ones. Injustice settings, this means continuously working to improve policies and practices to better address the causes of criminal behavior and promote rehabilitation. This requires a commitment to ongoing training, research, and evaluation to ensure that interventions are effective and based on the best available evidence.

Right Mindfulness and Right Concentration involve cultivating awareness and focus, which are essential for effective decision-making and emotional regulation. Mindfulness and meditation practices can be integrated into rehabilitation programs to help offenders develop these skills. Additionally, training justice practitioners in mindfulness can enhance their ability to make fair and compassionate decisions. Implementing the Four Noble Truths in justice settings also involves creating a supportive legal framework that encourages restorative practices and rehabilitation. Policymakers should advocate for legislation that supports these approaches, including funding for restorative justice programs, mental health services, and community-based initiatives. Legal reforms should also address systemic issues such as sentencing disparities, discriminatory policing practices, and the overuse of incarceration.

Education and public awareness are crucial for fostering support for these transformative approaches. By educating the public about the principles and benefits of restorative justice and rehabilitation, we can build broader support for these initiatives. Public awareness campaigns, community workshops, and educational programs in schools can help foster a culture of empathy, responsibility, and mutual respect. International cooperation and knowledge exchange can further enhance the implementation of the Four Noble Truths in justice settings. Collaborating with international organizations, researchers, and practitioners to share best practices, research findings, and innovative approaches can inform and improve justice practices. This can include participation in international conferences, joint research projects, and the establishment of networks for knowledge exchange.

Continuous reflection and improvement are essential for the successful implementation of the Four Noble Truths in justice settings. Justice systems must regularly evaluate their policies and practices to ensure they are effectively addressing suffering and promoting healing. This involves gathering data, seeking feedback from those affected by the justice system, and being willing to make changes based on this feedback. By adopting a mindset of continuous improvement, justice systems can remain responsive to the needs of individuals and communities. Implementing the Four Noble Truths in justice settings involves developing policies and practices that recognize and address the root causes of suffering, promote healing and reconciliation, and create conditions that support justice and equity. This approach aligns with the principles of Tibetan Buddhism, emphasizing interconnectedness, empathy, and holistic well-being.

4.5: Case Studies and Practical Examples

Exploring case studies that successfully apply the Four Noble Truths in justice settings offers a wealth of insights into how these principles can transform justice practices. By examining new examples, we can further understand how recognizing suffering, addressing its causes, promoting its cessation, and following a path that alleviates it can lead to effective and compassionate justice. One impactful case study is the "Transforming Justice Initiative" in Oakland, California. This initiative focuses on addressing the systemic causes of criminal behavior through community-based restorative justice programs.

The initiative involves community circles where residents, including victims and offenders, come together to discuss conflicts and find collaborative solutions. By fostering open dialogue and mutual understanding, these circles help to repair relationships and address the root causes of criminal behavior. The program also includes mentoring and support for at-risk youth, providing them with positive role models and alternative pathways to success. The success of this initiative highlights the power of community involvement in addressing suffering and promoting healing.

The "Common Justice" program in New York City provides another compelling example. This program offers an alternative to incarceration for young adults charged with violent felonies. Instead of traditional court proceedings, offenders participate in restorative justice circles where they meet with victims and community members to discuss the impact of their actions and develop plans for making amends. Common Justice emphasizes accountability, empathy, and personal growth, helping participants understand the harm they have caused and take responsibility for their actions. By focusing on rehabilitation rather than punishment, the program has achieved significant reductions in recidivism and high levels of victim satisfaction.

The "LEAD (Law Enforcement Assisted Diversion)" program in Seattle, Washington, exemplifies the implementation of the Four Noble Truths by addressing the root causes of criminal behavior through a harm reduction approach. LEAD allows police officers to redirect individuals engaged in low-level drug and prostitution offenses to community-based services instead of arresting them. These services include housing assistance, substance abuse treatment, mental health care, and vocational training. By addressing the underlying issues that lead to criminal behavior, LEAD helps participants stabilize their lives and reduce recidivism. The program's success demonstrates the importance of compassionate, community-based interventions in alleviating suffering.

The "Restorative Opportunities" program in Ontario, Canada, offers restorative justice interventions for federally incarcerated individuals. The program facilitates victim-offender dialogues, allowing offenders to understand the impact of their crimes directly from those affected. These dialogues provide a platform for victims to express their feelings and needs, while offenders have the opportunity to take responsibility and make amends. The program also includes community service and educational components to support offenders' rehabilitation and reintegration. Restorative Opportunities highlights the effectiveness of restorative justice in fostering empathy, accountability, and healing for both victims and offenders.

The "Project Return" program in Nashville, Tennessee, focuses on supporting formerly incarcerated individuals in their reentry into society. The program provides a comprehensive range of services, including job training, employment placement, housing assistance, and mental health support. By addressing the multiple challenges faced by returning citizens, Project Return helps them build stable, productive lives and reduces the likelihood of reoffending. The program's holistic approach underscores the importance of continuous support in the successful reintegration of formerly incarcerated individuals.

In Germany, the "Social Therapeutic Institutions" (Sozialtherapeutische Anstalten) offer a unique approach to addressing the psychological and social causes of criminal behavior. These institutions provide intensive therapeutic programs for inmates with severe psychological issues and high recidivism risk. The programs include individual and group therapy, educational and vocational training, and social skills development. By focusing on the underlying psychological factors that contribute to criminal behavior, these institutions help inmates achieve personal growth and reduce the likelihood of reoffending. The success of Social Therapeutic Institutions demonstrates the importance of addressing mental health in rehabilitation efforts.

The "Community Conferencing Center" in Baltimore, Maryland, utilizes restorative justice principles to address conflicts and reduce youth involvement in the criminal justice system. The center facilitates community conferences where offenders, victims, and community members come together to discuss the impact of the crime and develop a plan to repair the harm. These conferences emphasize accountability, empathy, and community support, helping to resolve conflicts and prevent future offenses. By involving the community in the justice process, the Community Conferencing Center promotes social cohesion and mutual respect.

The "PEACE (Project for Empowerment and Community Enhancement)" program in South Africa focuses on supporting young people in impoverished communities to prevent their involvement in crime. The program provides educational support, vocational training, and mentorship, helping participants develop the skills and confidence needed to pursue positive life paths. PEACE also includes community-building activities that foster a sense of belonging and purpose. The program's success highlights the importance of addressing the socio-economic factors that contribute to criminal behavior and supporting at-risk youth. The "Hollow Water Community Holistic Healing Circle" in Manitoba, Canada, provides a culturally grounded approach to justice for Indigenous communities. The program integrates traditional Indigenous healing practices with restorative justice principles to address the impacts of sexual abuse and violence. The Healing Circle involves victims, offenders, their families, and community members in a collective process of healing and reconciliation. By addressing the deep-rooted trauma and fostering a sense of communal responsibility, the program promotes healing and reduces recidivism. The Hollow Water Healing Circle illustrates the importance of culturally relevant approaches in justice practices.

The "Justice Reinvestment Initiative" in Australia seeks to reduce incarceration rates by redirecting funds from the criminal justice system to community-based programs that address the root causes of crime. The initiative involves local communities in developing and implementing strategies to reduce crime and support at-risk individuals. These strategies include education and employment programs, mental health services, and substance abuse treatment. By investing in community-based solutions, the Justice Reinvestment Initiative aims to create safer and more resilient communities.

The initiative's success demonstrates the potential of reallocating resources to address the social determinants of criminal behavior. These case studies illustrate the transformative potential of applying the Four Noble Truths in justice settings. By recognizing and addressing the root causes of suffering, promoting healing and reconciliation, and providing comprehensive support, these programs demonstrate the effectiveness of a holistic approach to justice. These examples highlight the importance of community involvement, education, restorative practices, and continuous support in creating a justice system that fosters personal growth, healing, and social harmony.

References

- Abrahamsen, D. (1950). Psychiatric Aspects of Delinquency. The Journal of Educational Sociology, 24(1), 40–44. https://doi.org/10.2307/2263986
- Alarid, L. F., & Wang, H.-M. (2001). Mercy and Punishment: Buddhism and the Death Penalty. Social Justice, 28(1 (83)), 231–247. http://www.jstor.org/stable/29768067
- Alschuler, A. W. (2003). The Changing Purposes of Criminal Punishment: A Retrospective on the past Century and Some Thoughts about the Next. The University of Chicago Law Review, 70(1), 1–22. https://doi.org/10.2307/1600541
- ANDERSEN, S. N., & HYATT, J. M. (2018). Building a Policy "Sandbox": An Opportunity for Comparative Sentencing and Corrections. Federal Sentencing Reporter, 31(1), 14–20. https://www.jstor.org/stable/26586181
- Brudholm, T. (2003). The Justice of Truth and Reconciliation. Hypatia, 18(2), 189–196. http://www.jstor.org/stable/3811020

- Chinchore, M. (1987). SOME THOUGHTS ON SIGNIFICANT CONTRIBUTIONS OF BUDDHIST LOGICIANS. Journal of Indian Philosophy, 15(2), 155–171. http://www.jstor.org/stable/23445442
- Eltschinger, V. (2014). The Four Nobles' Truths and Their 16 Aspects. Journal of Indian Philosophy, 42(2/3), 249–273. http://www.jstor.org/stable/43497602
- France, A., Freiberg, K., & Homel, R. (2010). Beyond Risk Factors: Towards a Holistic Prevention Paradigm for Children and Young People. The British Journal of Social Work, 40(4), 1192–1210. http://www.jstor.org/stable/43687515
- Garfield, J. L. (2001). Nāgārjuna's Theory of Causality. Philosophy East and West, 51(4), 507–524. http://www.jstor.org/stable/1400165
- Gómez, L. O. (1975). Some Aspects of the Free-Will Question in the Nikāyas. Philosophy East and West, 25(1), 81–90. https://doi.org/10.2307/1398436
- Gross, R. M. (1987). The Three-Yāna Journey in Tibetan Vajrayāna Buddhism. Buddhist-Christian Studies, 7, 87–104. https://doi.org/10.2307/1390236
- Herbert, S., Beckett, K., & Stuart, F. (2018). Policing Social Marginality: Contrasting Approaches. Law & Social Inquiry, 43(4), 1491–1513. http://www.jstor.org/stable/26630969
- Jeffery, C. R. (1965). Criminal Behavior and Learning Theory. The Journal of Criminal Law, Criminology, and Police Science, 56(3), 294–300. https://doi.org/10.2307/1141238
- Jennifer Graber. (2012). Engaging the Trope of Redemptive Suffering. Pennsylvania History: A Journal of Mid-Atlantic Studies, 79(2), 209–233. https://doi.org/10.5325/pennhistory.79.2.0209
- Junqing, W. (2019). Sex in the Cloister: Behind the Image of the "Criminal Monk" in Ming Courtroom Tales. T'oung Pao, 105(5/6), 545–586. https://www.jstor.org/stable/27067802
- Kang, C. (2011). SARKAR ON THE BUDDHA'S FOUR NOBLE TRUTHS. Philosophy East and West, 61(2), 303–323. http://www.jstor.org/stable/23015315
- Kenny, A. (1960). THE BALANCE OF JUSTICE. Blackfriars, 41(485), 356–363. http://www.jstor.org/stable/43816038
- Kværne, P. (1972). Aspects of the Origin of the Buddhist Tradition in Tibet. Numen, 19(1), 22–40. https://doi.org/10.2307/3269585

- Laub, J. H., & Sampson, R. J. (2001). Understanding Desistance from Crime. Crime and Justice, 28, 1–69. http://www.jstor.org/stable/1147672
- Luke, A. (1996). Tackling Crime by Other Means. Journal of Applied Philosophy, 13(2), 179–188. http://www.jstor.org/stable/24354301
- Loy, D. (1983). The Difference between Saṁsāra and Nirvāṇa. Philosophy East and West, 33(4), 355–365. https://doi.org/10.2307/1398594
- Loy, D. R. (2014). Why Buddhism and the Modern World Need Each Other. Buddhist-Christian Studies, 34, 39–50. http://www.jstor.org/stable/24801350
- Macy, J. R. (1979). Dependent Co-arising. The Journal of Religious Ethics, 7(1), 38–52. http://www.jstor.org/stable/40018242
- Murakami, S. (2002). Vedāntic Interpretation and Criticism of the Buddhist Dependent Origination. Zeitschrift Der Deutschen Morgenländischen Gesellschaft, 152(2), 269–294. http://www.jstor.org/stable/43381085
- Nathan, M. A. (2009). THE ENCOUNTER OF BUDDHISM AND LAW IN EARLY TWENTIETH-CENTURY KOREA. Journal of Law and Religion, 25(1), 1–32. http://www.jstor.org/stable/25654351
- Omvedt, G. (2001). The Buddha as a Political Philosopher. Economic and Political Weekly, 36(21), 1801–1804. http://www.jstor.org/stable/4410659
- Reichenbach, B. R. (1988). The Law of Karma and the Principle of Causation. Philosophy East and West, 38(4), 399–410. https://doi.org/10.2307/1399118
- Rusk, H. A., & Wilson, D. V. (1960). New Resources for Rehabilitation and Health. The Annals of the American Academy of Political and Social Science, 329, 97–106. http://www.jstor.org/stable/1034410
- Ryōjin, S., & Van Bragt, J. (2000). A Savior on Earth. The Eastern Buddhist, 32(2), 157–169. http://www.jstor.org/stable/44362261
- Schuster, N. (1979). [Review of God as Mother, a Feminine Theology in India, by C. M. Brown]. Philosophy East and West, 29(1), 112–114. https://doi.org/10.2307/1398908
- Sered, D. (2011). A New Approach to Victim Services. Federal Sentencing Reporter, 24(1), 50–53. https://doi.org/10.1525/fsr.2011.24.1.50

- Shulman, E. (2008). Early Meanings of Dependent-Origination. Journal of Indian Philosophy, 36(2), 297–317. http://www.jstor.org/stable/23497292
- Simmer-Brown, J. (1996). Suffering and Social Justice. Buddhist-Christian Studies, 16, 99–112. https://doi.org/10.2307/1390159
- Thorpe, G. L., & Marett, S. (1981). [Review of Controlling Stress and Tension: A Holistic Approach, by D. Girdano & G. Everly]. The Journal of Mind and Behavior, 2(1), 113–116. http://www.jstor.org/stable/43852847
- Toshio, K., & Stone, J. I. (1996). The Imperial Law and the Buddhist Law. Japanese Journal of Religious Studies, 23(3/4), 271–285. http://www.jstor.org/stable/30233575
- Tuckness, A. (2010). Retribution and Restitution in Locke's Theory of Punishment. The Journal of Politics, 72(3), 720–732. https://doi.org/10.1017/s0022381610000125
- Welch, H. (1961). Buddhism under the Communists. The China Quarterly, 6, 1–14. http://www.jstor.org/stable/651751
- Wayman, A. (1971). Buddhist Dependent Origination. History of Religions, 10(3), 185–203. http://www.jstor.org/stable/1062009
- Vaughan, B. (2007). THE INTERNAL NARRATIVE OF DESISTANCE. The British Journal of Criminology, 47(3), 390–404. http://www.jstor.org/stable/23639547

Part II: The Eightfold Path in Rehabilitation

—

CHAPTER FIVE

Right View and Right Intention

Contents

- Developing Ethical Perspectives in Offenders

- Fostering Positive Intentions for Change

- Practical Applications in Rehabilitation Programs

- Case Studies of Ethical Transformation

- Long-Term Benefits for Offenders and Society

5.1: Developing Ethical Perspectives in Offenders

The concept of Right View in Buddhism is foundational for cultivating ethical perspectives, especially in the context of rehabilitation. Right View involves seeing the world as it truly is, understanding the nature of reality, and recognizing the interconnectedness of all things. For offenders, developing an ethical perspective through the lens of Right View means transforming their understanding of themselves, their actions, and their relationships with others. In rehabilitation, fostering an ethical perspective begins with education and counseling that focus on the fundamental principles of Right View. Offenders are encouraged to explore the causes and conditions that led to their criminal behavior, recognizing that their actions are often the result of complex interactions between personal choices, social influences, and environmental factors. This understanding helps them to see that they are not inherently bad but have made harmful decisions influenced by various conditions.

Education programs play a crucial role in this transformative process. Through structured courses, offenders learn about ethical principles, the impact of their actions, and the broader implications of their behavior on society. These programs often include discussions on moral philosophy, the nature of justice, and the importance of ethical conduct. By engaging with these concepts, offenders begin to develop a more nuanced understanding of right and wrong, moving beyond simplistic notions of good and evil. Counseling sessions complement educational efforts by providing a safe space for offenders to reflect on their experiences and explore their motivations. Skilled counselors guide them through a process of self-examination, helping them to identify the underlying beliefs and attitudes that have shaped their behavior. This introspective work is essential for fostering self-awareness and encouraging personal growth. Offenders learn to take responsibility for their actions and to understand the impact of their behavior on others.

One effective technique for fostering ethical perspectives is the use of reflective exercises and journaling. Offenders are encouraged to keep journals where they document their thoughts, feelings, and reflections on their past actions. These journals serve as tools for self-discovery, allowing offenders to track their progress and gain insights into their behavior. Reflective exercises, such as writing letters of apology to their victims (whether sent or unsent), help offenders to articulate their remorse and to begin the process of making amends. Group discussions and peer support groups also play a vital role in developing ethical perspectives. In these settings, offenders share their experiences and listen to the stories of others, fostering a sense of empathy and mutual understanding. These interactions challenge offenders to see beyond their own perspectives and to appreciate the diverse experiences of their peers. Through group activities and facilitated discussions, offenders learn to recognize the common humanity they share with others, which is a key component of ethical thinking.

Role-playing scenarios are another powerful tool for cultivating ethical perspectives. Offenders participate in simulated situations that mirror real-life ethical dilemmas, allowing them to practice decision-making in a controlled environment. These exercises help offenders to develop critical thinking skills and to explore the consequences of different actions. By stepping into the shoes of others, offenders gain a deeper understanding of the impact of their behavior and learn to consider the well-being of others in their decisions. In addition to these techniques, mindfulness practices are integrated into rehabilitation programs to support the development of ethical perspectives. Mindfulness encourages offenders to be present in the moment and to observe their thoughts and feelings without judgment. This practice cultivates a sense of inner calm and self-awareness, which are essential for ethical decision-making. Through mindfulness, offenders learn to pause and reflect before acting, reducing impulsivity and fostering thoughtful consideration of their actions.

Mentorship programs also contribute significantly to fostering ethical perspectives. Offenders are paired with mentors who provide guidance, support, and positive role models. Mentors share their own experiences and offer insights into how to navigate ethical challenges. This relationship helps offenders to build trust and to develop a sense of accountability. Mentorship provides a continuous source of encouragement and reinforcement of ethical principles, aiding offenders in their journey towards rehabilitation. Successful case studies highlight the transformative power of cultivating ethical perspectives through Right View.

For instance, in one program, offenders who participated in an intensive ethics course showed significant improvements in their attitudes towards crime and justice. They reported increased empathy for their victims, a stronger sense of personal responsibility, and a commitment to making positive changes in their lives. Follow-up studies indicated lower recidivism rates among these participants compared to those who did not receive the same ethical training.

Another example comes from a restorative justice initiative where offenders engaged in dialogue with their victims. These interactions provided offenders with firsthand accounts of the pain and suffering caused by their actions, profoundly impacting their understanding of the consequences of their behavior. Offenders who participated in these dialogues demonstrated a greater willingness to accept responsibility and to work towards repairing the harm they had caused. The integration of Buddhist principles into rehabilitation programs has also proven effective in fostering ethical perspectives. Programs that incorporate teachings on compassion, interdependence, and non-harm resonate deeply with offenders, offering them a new framework for understanding their actions. By aligning their behavior with these principles, offenders find a sense of purpose and direction, which supports their rehabilitation and reintegration into society.

5.2: Fostering Positive Intentions for Change

Teaching offenders about the impact of their actions on victims, families, and communities is crucial for fostering an understanding of the far-reaching consequences of criminal behavior. This process involves comprehensive education programs, workshops, and real-life case studies designed to illustrate the ripple effects of crime. By gaining insights into these consequences, offenders can develop empathy and a sense of responsibility, which are essential for their rehabilitation and reintegration into society. Educational programs that focus on the consequences of criminal actions typically begin with a thorough exploration of the concept of harm. Offenders learn about the different forms of harm that their actions can cause, including physical, emotional, psychological, and financial harm. They are introduced to the idea that crime affects not only the direct victims but also their families, friends, and the broader community. This understanding lays the foundation for deeper reflection on the personal impact of their behavior.

Workshops and interactive sessions play a crucial role in this educational process. These sessions often involve role-playing and simulated scenarios where offenders must confront the effects of their actions. For example, offenders might role-play as victims, experiencing firsthand the fear, pain, and anxiety that their actions can cause. This experiential learning helps to break down the psychological barriers that often prevent offenders from empathizing with their victims. By stepping into the shoes of others, they gain a more visceral understanding of the suffering they have caused.

Victim impact panels are another powerful tool used to illustrate the consequences of crime. In these panels, victims of crime share their personal stories and describe how the crime has affected their lives. Listening to these testimonies can be a profound and transformative experience for offenders. Victims recount the physical injuries, emotional trauma, and long-term psychological effects they have endured. They also discuss the broader impact on their families, such as strained relationships, financial hardships, and a pervasive sense of fear and insecurity.

For many offenders, hearing directly from victims is a pivotal moment that triggers a deeper awareness of the human cost of their actions. It challenges them to confront the reality of the harm they have caused, moving beyond abstract notions of crime to the concrete and often devastating effects on real people. These interactions often evoke strong emotional responses, including guilt, shame, and remorse, which are critical for the process of moral reckoning and personal transformation. In addition to victim impact panels, restorative justice practices such as victim-offender mediation provide opportunities for direct dialogue between offenders and victims.

In these mediated sessions, offenders hear firsthand accounts of how their actions have affected the victims and their families. This direct interaction fosters a deeper level of empathy and understanding. Offenders are encouraged to take responsibility for their actions, express their remorse, and work towards making amends. Victims, in turn, have the opportunity to express their feelings and needs, which can be an important step in their healing process.

Case studies of offenders who have successfully transformed their perspectives provide valuable insights and inspiration for current participants. These case studies often highlight individuals who have gone through similar educational programs and have come to understand the impact of their actions on others. They serve as role models, demonstrating that personal change and redemption are possible. By sharing their journeys of transformation, these individuals offer hope and practical guidance to others on the path to rehabilitation. Programs and workshops also use multimedia resources, such as documentaries and films, to illustrate the consequences of crime.

These visual and auditory materials can be powerful tools for conveying the emotional and psychological impact of criminal behavior. For example, documentaries that follow the lives of victims and their families over time can show the long-term effects of crime, including ongoing trauma, struggles with trust and security, and efforts to rebuild their lives. These stories humanize the abstract concepts of harm and suffering, making them more relatable and impactful for offenders.

One effective program is the "Impact of Crime on Victims" (ICV) workshop, which is part of many correctional education curricula. In ICV workshops, offenders participate in structured sessions where they learn about the physical, emotional, and financial impacts of crime. The program often includes guest speakers, victim impact statements, and interactive activities designed to foster empathy and understanding. Offenders are encouraged to reflect on their own experiences and consider how their actions have affected others. This reflection process is facilitated by trained counselors who guide discussions and help offenders process their emotions. Another example is the "Restorative Dialogue Program" used in some juvenile justice systems.

This program brings together young offenders, their families, victims, and community members in a series of facilitated dialogues. These dialogues focus on the harm caused by the offense, the needs of the victims, and the responsibilities of the offenders. The program emphasizes accountability and the importance of making amends. Young offenders who participate in restorative dialogues often report a greater understanding of the consequences of their actions and a stronger commitment to changing their behavior.

Educational initiatives also extend to family members of offenders, helping them understand the broader impact of crime and their role in the rehabilitation process. Family therapy sessions and support groups provide a platform for family members to express their feelings and concerns, discuss the effects of the crime on their lives, and develop strategies for supporting their loved one's rehabilitation. These sessions highlight the interconnectedness of family dynamics and criminal behavior, emphasizing the importance of a supportive and understanding family environment in the offender's journey towards rehabilitation. The integration of technology in education programs has also proven effective in illustrating the consequences of criminal actions.

Virtual reality (VR) simulations, for example, are being used to create immersive experiences that allow offenders to see the world from the perspective of their victims. These VR experiences can be powerful tools for fostering empathy and understanding. By virtually stepping into the shoes of victims, offenders can gain a deeper appreciation of the fear, pain, and trauma their actions have caused. This innovative approach leverages technology to create impactful learning experiences that resonate deeply with participants.

Furthermore, community involvement is essential for reinforcing the lessons learned in educational programs. Community service projects that require offenders to engage with the people and neighborhoods affected by their actions provide practical opportunities for making amends. These projects might include cleaning up vandalized areas, participating in community-building activities, or working with local organizations that support victims of crime. By contributing positively to the community, offenders can begin to rebuild trust and demonstrate their commitment to change.

Evaluating the effectiveness of these educational programs and workshops is crucial for continuous improvement. Longitudinal studies that track the progress of participants over time provide valuable data on recidivism rates, changes in attitudes and behaviors, and the overall impact of the programs. Feedback from offenders, victims, and facilitators helps to refine and enhance the curriculum, ensuring that it remains relevant and effective. Continuous evaluation and adaptation are key to maintaining the success of these initiatives.

5.3: Practical Applications in Rehabilitation Programs

Developing empathy and compassion in offenders is a crucial element of rehabilitation, transforming individuals' attitudes and behaviors by fostering an understanding of others' feelings and experiences. Empathy, the ability to perceive and share another's emotions, and compassion, the desire to alleviate others' suffering, are fundamental for ethical conduct and social harmony. Programs and exercises designed to cultivate these qualities can lead to reduced recidivism and more successful reintegration into society.

One of the primary methods for fostering empathy and compassion in offenders is through structured exercises and programs that encourage self-reflection and understanding of others. These exercises often begin with activities that help offenders recognize and articulate their own emotions. By developing emotional literacy, offenders become more aware of their feelings and the impact of those feelings on their behavior. This self-awareness is the first step towards understanding the emotions of others.

Mindfulness meditation is a powerful tool for developing this emotional awareness. Regular mindfulness practice helps individuals become more attuned to their thoughts and feelings, fostering a sense of presence and non-judgmental awareness. Offenders who engage in mindfulness meditation learn to observe their emotions without being overwhelmed by them. This practice enhances their ability to stay calm and reflective, even in stressful situations, which is essential for developing empathy.

Another effective exercise is guided imagery, where offenders are led through scenarios that encourage them to imagine themselves in the shoes of others. These scenarios might involve visualizing a day in the life of a victim, considering the challenges and emotions the victim faces. By mentally placing themselves in these situations, offenders can gain insights into the feelings and experiences of those they have harmed. This imaginative exercise can be a powerful catalyst for empathy, helping offenders see beyond their own perspectives.

Role-playing exercises are also instrumental in fostering empathy. In these exercises, offenders take on the roles of victims, witnesses, or community members affected by their actions. By acting out these roles, they experience firsthand the fear, pain, and confusion that crime can cause. Role-playing helps offenders develop a deeper understanding of the emotional and psychological impact of their behavior. These exercises are often followed by group discussions where participants share their experiences and reflections, further reinforcing empathetic understanding.

Victim impact statements are another crucial component of empathy-building programs. These statements, written or spoken by victims or their families, describe the emotional, physical, and financial impact of the crime. Listening to these statements can be a profound experience for offenders, as they confront the real-life consequences of their actions. Victim impact statements provide a direct and personal account of suffering, which can evoke strong emotional responses and foster a sense of responsibility and remorse in offenders.

Restorative justice practices, such as victim-offender mediation and restorative circles, offer opportunities for direct dialogue between offenders and victims. In these settings, offenders hear directly from victims about how the crime has affected their lives. Victims share their stories, express their emotions, and ask questions, while offenders listen and respond. This direct interaction helps offenders understand the human impact of their actions and fosters a sense of accountability. The process is often transformative, leading to genuine remorse and a desire to make amends.

Empathy and compassion can also be cultivated through storytelling and literature. Programs that include reading and discussing literature, especially narratives that highlight human suffering and resilience, can open offenders' eyes to different perspectives. Stories of struggle, redemption, and forgiveness can resonate deeply, helping offenders relate to characters' experiences and emotions. Literature can serve as a bridge to understanding complex human emotions and ethical dilemmas, fostering a sense of empathy and compassion.

Educational programs that incorporate teachings from psychology and neuroscience also contribute to empathy development. Understanding how the brain processes emotions and the psychological mechanisms behind empathy can demystify these concepts for offenders. Knowledge of mirror neurons, for example, which are believed to play a role in empathy, can provide a scientific basis for understanding how and why we feel empathy for others. This scientific perspective can make the concept of empathy more tangible and relatable for offenders. Group therapy sessions provide a supportive environment for offenders to explore and develop their empathetic abilities. In these sessions, participants share their experiences, listen to others, and offer support and feedback. Group therapy encourages offenders to practice active listening and to respond with understanding and compassion. The group dynamic helps build a sense of community and mutual support, reinforcing the importance of empathy in social interactions.

Mentorship programs connect offenders with mentors who serve as positive role models and guides. Mentors share their own experiences, offer advice, and provide emotional support. This relationship helps offenders develop trust and learn from someone who has successfully navigated similar challenges. Mentors demonstrate empathy and compassion in their interactions, providing offenders with a practical example of these qualities in action. Community service projects offer practical opportunities for offenders to develop and express empathy and compassion. By engaging in activities that benefit others, such as helping at a homeless shelter, participating in community clean-up efforts, or working with disadvantaged youth, offenders experience the positive impact of their actions on others. Community service fosters a sense of connection and purpose, helping offenders see the value of contributing to the well-being of others.

Evaluating the effectiveness of empathy and compassion-building programs is crucial for continuous improvement. Longitudinal studies that track changes in offenders' attitudes, behaviors, and recidivism rates provide valuable data on the impact of these programs. Feedback from participants, victims, and facilitators helps to refine and enhance the curriculum, ensuring that it remains effective and relevant. Continuous evaluation and adaptation are key to maintaining the success of these initiatives. Cultural and spiritual practices also play a role in developing empathy and compassion. Programs that incorporate elements of spirituality, such as meditation, prayer, or ethical teachings from various religious traditions, can resonate deeply with offenders. These practices often emphasize interconnectedness, compassion, and ethical behavior, aligning closely with the goals of empathy-building programs. Integrating cultural and spiritual elements can provide offenders with a broader framework for understanding and practicing empathy and compassion.

5.4: Case Studies of Ethical Transformation

Fostering positive intentions in offenders is a fundamental aspect of rehabilitation, as it encourages individuals to shift their focus from harmful behaviors to constructive goals. Positive intentions, rooted in the Buddhist concept of Right Intention, involve cultivating thoughts and motivations that align with ethical and compassionate living. Developing these intentions in offenders requires a multifaceted approach, incorporating educational programs, therapeutic interventions, and practical exercises designed to inspire and reinforce positive change. One effective method for fostering positive intentions is through structured goal-setting programs. These programs guide offenders in identifying their personal aspirations and developing actionable plans to achieve them. Goal-setting workshops often begin with exercises that help individuals reflect on their values, strengths, and interests. Offenders are encouraged to envision a future where they contribute positively to society, setting specific, measurable, achievable, relevant, and time-bound (SMART) goals. This process helps offenders to focus their energy on constructive activities and provides a sense of direction and purpose.

Cognitive-behavioral therapy (CBT) is another critical tool in fostering positive intentions. CBT helps offenders recognize and change negative thought patterns that lead to destructive behaviors. Through individual and group therapy sessions, offenders learn to identify cognitive distortions, such as all-or-nothing thinking, overgeneralization, and catastrophizing, that contribute to negative intentions. Therapists work with offenders to challenge these distortions and replace them with more realistic and positive thoughts. This cognitive restructuring supports the development of healthier intentions and behaviors. Positive psychology interventions, which focus on building strengths and fostering well-being, are also valuable in promoting positive intentions. These interventions include activities that enhance gratitude, optimism, and resilience. For example, gratitude journaling exercises encourage offenders to regularly write about things they are thankful for, shifting their focus from negative experiences to positive aspects of their lives. Similarly, exercises that promote optimism, such as visualizing successful outcomes and reflecting on past successes, help offenders develop a more positive outlook and set intentions aligned with their goals.

Mentorship programs play a crucial role in fostering positive intentions. Offenders are paired with mentors who provide guidance, support, and positive role models. Mentors share their own experiences of overcoming challenges and achieving personal growth, offering practical advice and encouragement. This relationship helps offenders to develop trust and gain insights into how to navigate obstacles and pursue positive goals. Mentors also hold offenders accountable, encouraging them to stay committed to their intentions and providing feedback on their progress. The "Phoenix Prison Trust" in the United Kingdom is an excellent example of a program that integrates yoga and meditation to foster positive intentions. The trust offers yoga and meditation classes to inmates, helping them to develop mindfulness, self-discipline, and inner peace. These practices encourage offenders to reflect on their behavior, cultivate self-awareness, and set intentions for personal growth and positive change. Participants in the Phoenix Prison Trust program have reported significant improvements in their emotional well-being and a stronger commitment to leading ethical lives post-release.

The "Insight Garden Program" (IGP) in California prisons is another innovative initiative that fosters positive intentions through horticulture therapy. IGP combines gardening with mindfulness practices, helping inmates connect with nature, develop patience, and cultivate a sense of responsibility. Working in the garden provides offenders with a tangible sense of accomplishment and an opportunity to nurture life. The program also includes environmental education and vocational training, equipping participants with skills that can be applied to positive endeavors after release. Through gardening, inmates learn to set and achieve goals, fostering positive intentions and a sense of purpose. Art therapy programs provide a creative outlet for offenders to explore their emotions and set positive intentions. Through various forms of artistic expression, such as painting, drawing, music, and writing, offenders can process their experiences and envision a better future. Art therapy encourages self-expression and introspection, helping offenders to articulate their hopes and aspirations. It also provides a non-verbal means of communication, which can be particularly valuable for individuals who struggle with traditional forms of therapy. By creating art, offenders can develop a deeper understanding of themselves and their goals, fostering positive intentions and a commitment to change.

The "Prison Entrepreneurship Program" (PEP) in Texas offers a unique approach to fostering positive intentions by combining business education with character development. PEP provides inmates with intensive training in business skills, including marketing, finance, and management, while also emphasizing the importance of ethical behavior and personal responsibility. Participants develop business plans, receive mentorship from successful entrepreneurs, and participate in character-building activities. This holistic approach helps offenders to set ambitious but achievable goals, develop a sense of purpose, and build a foundation for a successful and ethical life post-release. PEP graduates have demonstrated significantly lower recidivism rates and higher employment rates, highlighting the program's effectiveness in fostering positive intentions. Incorporating restorative justice principles into rehabilitation programs also supports the development of positive intentions. Restorative justice focuses on repairing harm and restoring relationships, encouraging offenders to take responsibility for their actions and make amends. Programs such as victim-offender dialogue and community circles provide opportunities for offenders to express remorse, seek forgiveness, and commit to positive change. These interactions help offenders to develop empathy, accountability, and a sense of purpose, aligning their intentions with the well-being of others.

Peer support groups offer a supportive environment where offenders can share their experiences, set goals, and encourage each other in their journey towards positive change. These groups provide a sense of community and mutual support, reinforcing the importance of positive intentions. Facilitators guide discussions on topics such as goal-setting, overcoming obstacles, and celebrating successes. By participating in peer support groups, offenders learn from each other's experiences, gain motivation, and hold each other accountable to their intentions. Life skills training programs equip offenders with the practical skills needed to pursue positive goals and intentions. These programs cover a wide range of topics, including financial literacy, communication skills, conflict resolution, and time management. By developing these essential skills, offenders are better prepared to achieve their goals and navigate challenges. Life skills training empowers offenders to take control of their lives, set realistic goals, and develop a plan for achieving them.

The "TROSA (Triangle Residential Options for Substance Abusers)" program in North Carolina provides comprehensive support for individuals recovering from substance abuse. TROSA combines residential treatment with vocational training, education, and life skills development. Participants set personal and professional goals, receive counseling and mentorship, and engage in community service. This holistic approach helps individuals to rebuild their lives, develop positive intentions, and achieve long-term recovery and success. TROSA's emphasis on goal-setting and personal development fosters a sense of purpose and direction, supporting positive change. Community engagement initiatives provide offenders with opportunities to contribute positively to society and develop a sense of purpose.

These initiatives might include volunteering with local organizations, participating in community service projects, or mentoring at-risk youth. By giving back to the community, offenders can build positive relationships, gain a sense of accomplishment, and reinforce their commitment to ethical behavior. Community engagement helps offenders to see themselves as valuable members of society, capable of making positive contributions. Evaluating the effectiveness of programs that foster positive intentions is crucial for continuous improvement. Longitudinal studies that track changes in offenders' attitudes, behaviors, and recidivism rates provide valuable data on the impact of these programs. Feedback from participants, facilitators, and community members helps to refine and enhance the curriculum, ensuring that it remains relevant and effective. Continuous evaluation and adaptation are key to maintaining the success of these initiatives.

5.5: Long-Term Benefits for Offenders and Society

Integrating ethical perspectives into daily life is essential for offenders as they transition from correctional facilities to their communities. This process involves practical strategies, role-playing scenarios, mindfulness practices, support systems, and mentorship programs designed to reinforce ethical behavior and promote successful reintegration. By embedding ethical principles into everyday actions, offenders can develop habits that foster personal growth and contribute positively to society. Practical strategies for applying ethical perspectives in everyday situations begin with establishing routines that prioritize ethical decision-making. Offenders are encouraged to start their day with reflective practices such as journaling or meditation, which help them set positive intentions and align their actions with their values. Writing down their goals and reflecting on their progress helps offenders stay focused and committed to their ethical principles. This practice not only fosters self-discipline but also provides a daily reminder of their commitment to positive change.

Role-playing scenarios are an effective tool for helping offenders practice ethical behavior in a controlled environment. These scenarios simulate real-life situations where ethical dilemmas may arise, allowing offenders to explore different responses and their consequences. For example, a role-playing exercise might involve a scenario where an offender is tempted to engage in illegal activity to solve a financial problem. Through guided discussions and feedback, offenders can analyze the situation, consider ethical alternatives, and practice making decisions that align with their values. These exercises help offenders develop critical thinking skills and prepare them for real-world challenges. Mindfulness practices play a crucial role in integrating ethical perspectives into daily life. Mindfulness involves paying attention to the present moment with a non-judgmental attitude, which helps offenders become more aware of their thoughts, feelings, and actions. By practicing mindfulness, offenders learn to pause before reacting, allowing them to consider the ethical implications of their choices. Mindfulness meditation, body scans, and mindful breathing exercises are simple yet powerful techniques that can be incorporated into daily routines. These practices help offenders develop self-awareness, emotional regulation, and a greater sense of control over their actions.

Support systems are vital for reinforcing ethical behavior. Offenders need a network of supportive individuals who can provide encouragement, guidance, and accountability. Family members, friends, mentors, and community organizations play a key role in this support system. Regular check-ins, support group meetings, and community activities help offenders stay connected and committed to their ethical goals. These support systems provide a sense of belonging and remind offenders that they are not alone in their journey towards positive change. Mentorship programs are particularly effective in supporting the integration of ethical perspectives into daily life. Mentors serve as role models, offering practical advice, emotional support, and encouragement. They help offenders navigate challenges, set realistic goals, and stay focused on their ethical commitments. Mentors also provide a source of accountability, encouraging offenders to stay true to their values and make responsible choices. The relationship between mentor and mentee fosters trust and mutual respect, which are essential for personal growth and ethical development.

Community engagement is another important aspect of integrating ethical perspectives into daily life. Offenders are encouraged to participate in community service projects, volunteer work, and local organizations that align with their values. These activities provide opportunities to apply ethical principles in real-world settings, build positive relationships, and contribute to the well-being of the community. By giving back, offenders reinforce their commitment to ethical living and gain a sense of purpose and fulfillment. Educational programs that focus on ethical principles and decision-making skills are also crucial. These programs provide offenders with the knowledge and tools they need to navigate ethical dilemmas and make responsible choices. Courses on moral philosophy, ethics, and social responsibility help offenders understand the theoretical foundations of ethical behavior and how to apply them in everyday situations. By engaging with these concepts, offenders develop a deeper understanding of the importance of ethical conduct and are better prepared to integrate these principles into their lives.

Peer support groups offer a collaborative environment where offenders can share their experiences, challenges, and successes in applying ethical perspectives. These groups provide a platform for mutual learning and support, reinforcing the importance of ethical behavior. Group discussions, workshops, and activities help offenders practice ethical decision-making and build confidence in their ability to make positive choices. Peer support groups also foster a sense of community and accountability, which are crucial for maintaining ethical behavior. Technology can also play a role in supporting the integration of ethical perspectives into daily life. Mobile apps and online platforms that offer resources, reminders, and support for ethical living can be valuable tools for offenders. These technologies provide easy access to mindfulness exercises, goal-setting tools, and educational materials. They can also facilitate communication with mentors and support groups, helping offenders stay connected and motivated. By leveraging technology, offenders can integrate ethical practices into their daily routines and receive continuous support and guidance.

Continuous self-reflection is essential for maintaining ethical behavior. Offenders are encouraged to regularly evaluate their actions, reflect on their choices, and consider the impact of their behavior on others. Journaling, mindfulness meditation, and discussions with mentors or support groups can facilitate this reflective process. By regularly examining their behavior and its alignment with their values, offenders can identify areas for improvement and reinforce their commitment to ethical living. Case studies of individuals who have successfully integrated ethical perspectives into their daily lives provide valuable insights and inspiration. These stories highlight the challenges and triumphs of applying ethical principles in real-world situations. By learning from the experiences of others, offenders can gain practical strategies and motivation to stay committed to their ethical goals. Case studies also demonstrate the positive impact of ethical behavior on personal well-being and community relationships, reinforcing the importance of ethical living.

Restorative justice practices, such as restorative circles and victim-offender dialogues, offer opportunities for offenders to apply ethical principles in their interactions with others. These practices emphasize accountability, empathy, and mutual respect, helping offenders develop a deeper understanding of the impact of their actions and the importance of making amends. By participating in restorative justice activities, offenders practice ethical behavior and build stronger relationships with their victims and communities. Life skills training programs equip offenders with the practical skills needed to navigate daily challenges and make ethical choices. These programs cover topics such as financial literacy, communication skills, conflict resolution, and time management. By developing these essential skills, offenders are better prepared to handle real-world situations and make decisions that align with their values. Life skills training empowers offenders to take control of their lives and build a foundation for ethical and responsible living.

Community-based initiatives that promote ethical behavior and social responsibility can also support offenders in integrating ethical perspectives into their daily lives. Programs that encourage civic engagement, environmental stewardship, and social justice provide opportunities for offenders to apply ethical principles in meaningful ways. By participating in these initiatives, offenders contribute to the common good and reinforce their commitment to ethical living. Evaluating the effectiveness of programs that support the integration of ethical perspectives is crucial for continuous improvement. Longitudinal studies that track changes in offenders' behavior, attitudes, and recidivism rates provide valuable data on the impact of these programs. Feedback from participants, mentors, and community members helps to refine and enhance the curriculum, ensuring that it remains effective and relevant. Continuous evaluation and adaptation are key to maintaining the success of these initiatives.

CHAPTER SIX

Right Speech and Right Action

Contents

- Promoting Honest Communication in Justice

- Encouraging Compassionate Behavior

- Practical Techniques for Implementing Right Speech

- Case Studies of Behavioral Change

- Integrating Right Action in Rehabilitation Programs

6.1: Promoting Honest Communication in Justice

The power of words in shaping relationships and society is immense. Speech can build bridges or erect barriers, heal wounds or inflict pain. In the context of rehabilitation, understanding the impact of words is crucial for fostering healthy interactions and promoting personal growth. Offenders often come from backgrounds where communication patterns have been destructive, contributing to cycles of conflict and misunderstanding. Programs that teach effective communication and conflict resolution can transform these patterns, enabling offenders to engage in more constructive and empathetic dialogues. Effective communication begins with the awareness that words carry weight. Every spoken word has the potential to influence thoughts, emotions, and actions. For offenders, recognizing this power is the first step towards using speech responsibly. This awareness is cultivated through educational programs that explore the psychology of communication. Offenders learn about the impact of their words on others, understanding that speech can either uplift or degrade, foster trust or sow discord. These insights help offenders appreciate the importance of thoughtful and considerate communication.

Restorative justice circles offer a practical setting for offenders to experience the transformative power of words. In these circles, participants engage in open dialogue, sharing their experiences and listening to others. The process emphasizes respectful and non-judgmental communication, allowing offenders to express themselves honestly while considering the perspectives of others. This practice not only fosters empathy but also helps offenders understand the repercussions of harmful speech. Through restorative justice circles, offenders learn that words can be tools for healing and reconciliation, rather than weapons of harm. Conflict resolution workshops further enhance offenders' communication skills. These workshops teach techniques for managing and resolving disputes peacefully. Offenders learn to identify the underlying issues in conflicts, rather than reacting impulsively. Techniques such as active listening, which involves fully concentrating on the speaker and reflecting back what is heard, help offenders understand the emotions and needs behind the words. This understanding can de-escalate tensions and lead to more productive resolutions. Role-playing exercises in these workshops allow offenders to practice these skills in a safe and supportive environment, building their confidence in handling real-life conflicts.

Active listening is a cornerstone of effective communication and is emphasized in many rehabilitation programs. Offenders are taught to listen with the intent to understand, rather than to respond. This involves paying attention to the speaker's words, tone, and body language, and reflecting back their message to ensure accurate understanding. Active listening fosters empathy, as it requires offenders to step outside their own perspectives and consider those of others. By practicing active listening, offenders can build stronger, more respectful relationships and reduce misunderstandings and conflicts. Communication workshops also address the importance of non-verbal communication. Offenders learn that body language, facial expressions, and tone of voice significantly impact how messages are received. Misaligned non-verbal cues can undermine spoken words, leading to confusion and mistrust. Through exercises that focus on congruent communication, offenders become more aware of their non-verbal signals and learn to align them with their verbal messages. This holistic approach to communication enhances clarity and trust in interactions.

Another vital aspect of communication training is teaching offenders the value of assertive communication. Assertiveness involves expressing one's thoughts and feelings honestly and respectfully, without aggression or passivity. Offenders often struggle with either aggressive or passive communication styles, which can lead to conflicts or unmet needs. Assertiveness training helps offenders find a balance, enabling them to stand up for themselves while respecting the rights of others. This skill is particularly important in high-stress environments like correctional facilities, where clear and respectful communication can prevent misunderstandings and altercations. Mindfulness practices are integrated into communication training to help offenders remain present and attentive during interactions. Mindfulness enhances self-awareness and emotional regulation, enabling offenders to respond thoughtfully rather than react impulsively. Techniques such as mindful breathing and meditation are taught to help offenders manage stress and maintain focus during conversations. By cultivating a mindful approach to communication, offenders can engage more fully with others and handle challenging interactions with greater calm and clarity.

Educational programs also emphasize the ethical dimensions of communication. Offenders are encouraged to reflect on the moral implications of their words, considering how their speech aligns with their values and principles. Discussions on topics such as honesty, respect, and integrity help offenders understand the broader social impact of ethical communication. These discussions are often framed within the context of the Buddhist principle of Right Speech, which advocates for truthful, beneficial, and harmonious communication. By aligning their speech with these ethical standards, offenders can contribute to a more just and compassionate society. Case studies and real-life examples are used to illustrate the consequences of harmful and beneficial speech. Offenders examine scenarios where words have led to either positive outcomes or negative repercussions. These case studies provide concrete examples of how communication can build or destroy relationships, influence social dynamics, and impact individual well-being. Analyzing these examples helps offenders understand the practical application of communication principles and the importance of choosing words wisely.

Support networks within correctional facilities play a crucial role in reinforcing effective communication skills. Peer support groups, mentorship programs, and counseling sessions provide ongoing opportunities for offenders to practice and refine their communication abilities. In these supportive environments, offenders receive feedback, encouragement, and guidance, helping them to navigate the challenges of interpersonal interactions. The continuous practice and reinforcement of effective communication skills in these settings help offenders internalize these behaviors, making them more likely to carry these skills into their lives post-release. Training staff and volunteers in communication principles is essential for creating a supportive environment within correctional facilities. Staff members who model effective communication behaviors set a positive example for offenders and contribute to a culture of respect and understanding. Training programs for staff and volunteers focus on skills such as active listening, assertiveness, conflict resolution, and empathy. By fostering a consistent and supportive communication environment, staff and volunteers can enhance the rehabilitation process and help offenders develop the skills needed for successful reintegration.

Community involvement is also important in promoting healthy dialogue and effective communication. Programs that connect offenders with community members through restorative justice initiatives, community service projects, and volunteer opportunities provide practical settings for applying communication skills. These interactions help offenders build positive relationships, gain confidence in their communication abilities, and contribute to the well-being of their communities. Community involvement reinforces the importance of effective communication in building trust and fostering social cohesion.

Evaluating the effectiveness of communication programs is crucial for continuous improvement. Longitudinal studies that track changes in offenders' communication skills, relationships, and conflict resolution abilities provide valuable data on the impact of these programs. Feedback from offenders, staff, and community members helps to refine and enhance the curriculum, ensuring that it remains relevant and effective. Continuous evaluation and adaptation are key to maintaining the success of communication initiatives.

6.2: Encouraging Compassionate Behavior

Honest and compassionate communication forms the bedrock of healthy relationships and effective rehabilitation. For offenders, developing these communication skills is crucial for rebuilding trust, resolving conflicts, and fostering meaningful connections. Techniques for fostering honesty and compassion in communication are diverse, encompassing workshops, exercises, and therapeutic practices designed to encourage self-awareness, empathy, and responsible expression. One of the foundational techniques for fostering honesty in communication is the practice of self-reflection. Offenders are encouraged to engage in regular self-reflection to examine their thoughts, feelings, and motivations. This process helps individuals become more aware of their inner states and the ways in which these states influence their communication. Through journaling, offenders can track their emotional responses, identify patterns, and recognize areas where honesty may be lacking. Self-reflection promotes a deeper understanding of oneself, which is essential for cultivating authenticity in interactions with others.

Workshops focused on active listening and empathy are central to developing compassionate communication. Active listening involves fully concentrating on the speaker, understanding their message, and responding thoughtfully. Exercises in active listening teach offenders to pay attention not only to the words being spoken but also to the emotions and intentions behind them. By practicing active listening, offenders learn to create a safe space for others to express themselves, fostering mutual respect and understanding. These workshops often include role-playing scenarios where offenders practice listening without interrupting, reflecting back what they have heard, and validating the speaker's feelings. Empathy exercises are designed to help offenders connect with the emotions and experiences of others. These exercises might include sharing personal stories in group settings, where each participant has the opportunity to speak and be heard. Group members practice responding with empathy, acknowledging the speaker's feelings, and offering support. Such exercises highlight the importance of emotional resonance in communication, teaching offenders to move beyond their own perspectives and consider the experiences of others. By fostering empathy, these activities help offenders build deeper, more compassionate relationships.

The development of honest communication is also supported by techniques that encourage transparency and accountability. Offenders are taught to express their thoughts and feelings openly, without fear of judgment or retribution. This involves learning to articulate one's needs and boundaries clearly and respectfully. Workshops on assertive communication are particularly effective in this regard. Assertiveness training helps offenders find a balance between passive and aggressive communication styles, enabling them to express themselves honestly while respecting the rights of others. Through role-playing and feedback, offenders practice using "I" statements, which focus on their own experiences and feelings rather than blaming or criticizing others. This approach promotes honesty and reduces defensiveness in conversations. Building trust is a key component of fostering honest and compassionate communication. Trust-building exercises help offenders develop the confidence to be vulnerable and authentic in their interactions. Activities such as trust falls, guided discussions, and collaborative problem-solving tasks create opportunities for offenders to rely on and support one another. These exercises emphasize the importance of reliability, consistency, and mutual respect in building trust. As offenders learn to trust themselves and others, they become more comfortable with honest communication, knowing that their words will be received with understanding and respect.

Therapeutic practices, such as cognitive-behavioral therapy (CBT), play a significant role in developing honest and compassionate communication. CBT helps offenders identify and challenge cognitive distortions that hinder honest expression and empathy. Therapists guide offenders through the process of recognizing automatic negative thoughts, examining the evidence for and against these thoughts, and developing more balanced and realistic perspectives. By addressing these cognitive distortions, CBT helps offenders develop a more honest and compassionate outlook, which is reflected in their communication. Mindfulness practices are integrated into communication training to enhance self-awareness and emotional regulation. Mindfulness involves paying attention to the present moment with a non-judgmental attitude, which helps offenders become more aware of their thoughts, feelings, and bodily sensations. By practicing mindfulness, offenders learn to observe their internal states without reacting impulsively, allowing them to respond more thoughtfully in conversations. Techniques such as mindful breathing, body scans, and meditation are taught to help offenders manage stress and maintain focus during interactions. Mindfulness fosters a calm and centered presence, which is essential for honest and compassionate communication.

Workshops on nonviolent communication (NVC) provide offenders with a structured approach to expressing their needs and feelings without aggression or judgment. NVC emphasizes the importance of empathy, honesty, and mutual respect in communication. Offenders learn to identify their underlying needs, express them clearly, and listen to the needs of others with empathy. This approach helps de-escalate conflicts and fosters a collaborative spirit in resolving disagreements. Through role-playing and feedback, offenders practice using NVC techniques in various scenarios, building their confidence and skill in compassionate communication. Restorative justice practices, such as victim-offender dialogues and restorative circles, offer powerful opportunities for offenders to practice honest and compassionate communication. In these settings, offenders engage in direct dialogue with victims, listening to their experiences and expressing their remorse. The process emphasizes accountability, empathy, and mutual respect, helping offenders understand the impact of their actions and commit to making amends. By participating in restorative justice activities, offenders practice honest and compassionate communication in a structured and supportive environment, reinforcing these skills for future interactions.

Mentorship programs provide ongoing support for offenders as they develop their communication skills. Mentors serve as role models and guides, offering practical advice, emotional support, and feedback. Regular check-ins with mentors help offenders stay accountable to their communication goals and address challenges as they arise. The mentor-mentee relationship fosters trust and mutual respect, providing offenders with a safe space to practice honest and compassionate communication. Community engagement initiatives offer practical opportunities for offenders to apply their communication skills in real-world settings. Volunteering with local organizations, participating in community service projects, and engaging in civic activities provide offenders with contexts to practice honest and compassionate communication.

These interactions help offenders build positive relationships, gain confidence in their abilities, and contribute to the well-being of their communities. Community engagement reinforces the importance of honest and compassionate communication in building trust and fostering social cohesion. Evaluating the effectiveness of communication programs is crucial for continuous improvement. Longitudinal studies that track changes in offenders' communication skills, relationships, and conflict resolution abilities provide valuable data on the impact of these programs. Feedback from offenders, mentors, and community members helps to refine and enhance the curriculum, ensuring that it remains effective and relevant. Continuous evaluation and adaptation are key to maintaining the success of communication initiatives.

6.3: Practical Techniques for Implementing Right Speech

Understanding Right Action and its importance in rehabilitation involves delving into the principles of ethical behavior and personal accountability. For offenders, adopting ethical behaviors and taking responsibility for their actions are crucial steps towards rehabilitation and reintegration into society. This process requires comprehensive programs that emphasize personal responsibility, ethical decision-making, and the development of moral reasoning. By exploring the principles of Right

Action and providing practical tools for implementing these principles, offenders can transform their behavior and contribute positively to their communities. One of the foundational aspects of understanding Right Action is recognizing the moral implications of one's behavior. Educational programs that focus on moral philosophy and ethical reasoning help offenders explore the concepts of right and wrong, justice and injustice, and the impact of their actions on others. These programs often include discussions on the nature of ethical behavior, the role of intention in moral decision-making, and the consequences of unethical actions. By engaging with these concepts, offenders develop a deeper understanding of the importance of ethical conduct and are better prepared to make responsible choices.

Ethics workshops and courses provide a structured environment for offenders to examine their values and beliefs. These workshops often involve guided discussions, case studies, and reflective exercises that encourage offenders to think critically about their actions and the principles that guide them. Offenders are encouraged to reflect on past behaviors, identify areas where they have acted unethically, and consider how they can align their future actions with their values. This process of self-examination and reflection is essential for fostering a sense of personal responsibility and commitment to ethical behavior. Role-playing scenarios are an effective tool for teaching ethical decision-making. In these scenarios, offenders are presented with ethical dilemmas that require them to make choices based on their values and principles. By exploring different responses and their consequences, offenders learn to navigate complex moral situations and develop strategies for making ethical decisions. Role-playing helps offenders practice applying ethical principles in real-life contexts, building their confidence and competence in making responsible choices.

Cognitive-behavioral therapy (CBT) is another crucial component of programs that emphasize personal responsibility and ethical decision-making. CBT helps offenders identify and challenge cognitive distortions that contribute to unethical behavior, such as rationalization, minimization, and externalization of blame. Therapists guide offenders through the process of recognizing these distortions, examining the evidence for and against them, and developing more balanced and realistic perspectives. By addressing these cognitive distortions, CBT helps offenders develop a greater sense of personal accountability and a commitment to ethical behavior. Mindfulness practices are integrated into programs to support the development of ethical behavior and personal responsibility. Mindfulness involves paying attention to the present moment with a non-judgmental attitude, which helps offenders become more aware of their thoughts, feelings, and actions. By practicing mindfulness, offenders learn to observe their internal states without reacting impulsively, allowing them to respond more thoughtfully in challenging situations. Techniques such as mindful breathing, body scans, and meditation are taught to help offenders manage stress and maintain focus during ethical decision-making. Mindfulness fosters a calm and centered presence, which is essential for acting ethically and responsibly.

Mentorship programs provide ongoing support for offenders as they develop their understanding of Right Action and personal responsibility. Mentors serve as role models and guides, offering practical advice, emotional support, and feedback. Regular check-ins with mentors help offenders stay accountable to their ethical goals and address challenges as they arise. The mentor-mentee relationship fosters trust and mutual respect, providing offenders with a safe space to explore their values and develop strategies for acting ethically. Mentorship programs also offer opportunities for offenders to learn from the experiences of others who have successfully navigated similar challenges, providing inspiration and motivation for their own journeys. Restorative justice practices, such as victim-offender mediation and restorative circles, offer powerful opportunities for offenders to practice ethical behavior and personal responsibility. In these settings, offenders engage in direct dialogue with victims, listening to their experiences and expressing their remorse. The process emphasizes accountability, empathy, and mutual respect, helping offenders understand the impact of their actions and commit to making amends. By participating in restorative justice activities, offenders practice taking responsibility for their actions and develop a deeper understanding of the principles of Right Action.

Community service projects provide practical opportunities for offenders to apply their understanding of Right Action in real-world settings. These projects might include volunteering with local organizations, participating in community clean-up efforts, or working with disadvantaged youth. By engaging in activities that benefit others, offenders experience the positive impact of their actions and reinforce their commitment to ethical behavior. Community service helps offenders build positive relationships, gain a sense of accomplishment, and contribute to the well-being of their communities. Support networks within correctional facilities play a crucial role in reinforcing ethical behavior and personal responsibility. Peer support groups, counseling sessions, and educational programs provide ongoing opportunities for offenders to practice and refine their understanding of Right Action.

In these supportive environments, offenders receive feedback, encouragement, and guidance, helping them to navigate the challenges of ethical decision-making. The continuous practice and reinforcement of ethical behavior in these settings help offenders internalize these principles, making them more likely to carry these skills into their lives post-release. Evaluating the effectiveness of programs that emphasize personal responsibility and ethical decision-making is crucial for continuous improvement. Longitudinal studies that track changes in offenders' behavior, attitudes, and recidivism rates provide valuable data on the impact of these programs. Feedback from offenders, mentors, and community members helps to refine and enhance the curriculum, ensuring that it remains effective and relevant. Continuous evaluation and adaptation are key to maintaining the success of these initiatives.

6.4: Case Studies of Behavioral Change

Practical applications of Right Speech and Right Action require concrete strategies and tools to help offenders practice ethical communication and behavior in real-life situations. Incorporating mindfulness and reflection into daily routines, creating role-playing scenarios, and engaging support networks and community involvement are essential components. By integrating these practices, offenders can develop habits that promote positive interactions, ethical decision-making, and successful reintegration into society. Role-playing scenarios are one of the most effective ways to practice Right Speech and Right Action.

In controlled environments, offenders are presented with common social and ethical dilemmas that they may encounter upon reintegration into society. These scenarios might include dealing with conflict at work, responding to a provocation without resorting to violence, or making ethical decisions under pressure. Through guided role-play, offenders can explore various responses, receive feedback, and refine their approach to ensure that their speech and actions align with ethical principles.

Mindfulness practices are crucial in helping offenders maintain awareness and control over their thoughts, emotions, and behaviors. Daily mindfulness routines, such as meditation, mindful breathing, and body scans, enhance self-awareness and emotional regulation. By practicing mindfulness, offenders can cultivate a state of calm and focus, which is essential for making thoughtful and ethical decisions. For example, a mindfulness exercise might involve offenders taking a few moments each day to reflect on their interactions and consider how their words and actions impacted others. This practice fosters a habit of introspection and continuous improvement in communication and behavior. Incorporating ethical reflection into daily routines helps offenders stay aligned with their values and principles. Reflective journaling is an effective tool for this purpose. Offenders are encouraged to keep a daily journal where they document their thoughts, feelings, and experiences. They can reflect on situations where they faced ethical dilemmas, consider the choices they made, and evaluate the outcomes. This practice helps offenders identify areas for improvement and reinforces their commitment to ethical behavior. Regular journaling also provides a written record of their progress, which can be motivating and empowering.

Mentorship programs play a significant role in reinforcing the practical application of Right Speech and Right Action. Mentors provide guidance, support, and accountability, helping offenders navigate the challenges of ethical living. Regular meetings with mentors allow offenders to discuss their experiences, seek advice, and receive constructive feedback. Mentors can share their own experiences and insights, offering practical strategies for dealing with difficult situations. This ongoing support helps offenders stay focused on their goals and maintain their commitment to ethical behavior. The "Second Chance Pell Pilot Program" in the United States provides an example of how educational opportunities can support the practical application of ethical principles. This program allows incarcerated individuals to receive Pell Grants to pursue higher education. Educational courses often include components that focus on ethical reasoning, communication skills, and personal development. By engaging in higher education, offenders not only gain valuable knowledge and skills but also learn to apply ethical principles in their academic and personal lives. The structure and discipline required for academic success further reinforce positive habits and behaviors.

The "Forgiveness Project" is another initiative that provides practical tools for offenders to practice Right Speech and Right Action. This project uses storytelling to promote forgiveness and reconciliation. Offenders are encouraged to share their stories, reflect on their actions, and consider the perspectives of those they have harmed. By engaging in this process, offenders learn to express remorse, seek forgiveness, and commit to making amends. The storytelling approach helps offenders understand the impact of their words and actions, fostering empathy and accountability. Community service projects offer practical opportunities for offenders to apply ethical principles in real-world settings. Participating in community service not only benefits the community but also provides offenders with a sense of purpose and accomplishment. Through activities such as cleaning up public spaces, helping at food banks, or mentoring at-risk youth, offenders can demonstrate their commitment to positive change and build relationships based on mutual respect and trust. Community service reinforces the importance of ethical behavior and helps offenders develop a reputation for integrity and responsibility.

Support networks within correctional facilities and in the community are essential for reinforcing ethical communication and behavior. Peer support groups, therapy sessions, and educational programs provide ongoing opportunities for offenders to practice and refine their skills. These support networks offer a safe space for offenders to share their challenges, celebrate their successes, and receive encouragement. The sense of community and mutual support helps offenders stay motivated and committed to their goals. The "Sycamore Tree Project" is an example of a restorative justice initiative that provides practical applications of Right Speech and Right Action. This project brings together offenders and victims in facilitated dialogue sessions. Offenders listen to the experiences of victims, reflect on the impact of their actions, and engage in discussions about accountability and restitution. Through this process, offenders practice empathetic listening, honest communication, and ethical decision-making. The Sycamore Tree Project emphasizes the importance of making amends and rebuilding trust, helping offenders develop a deeper understanding of their responsibilities and the principles of Right Speech and Right Action.

The "Reducing Reoffending Through Family Engagement" (RRFE) program in the United Kingdom focuses on strengthening family relationships as a means of supporting rehabilitation. This program involves family therapy sessions, communication workshops, and parenting classes. Offenders learn to communicate more effectively with their family members, resolve conflicts peacefully, and build stronger, more supportive relationships. By practicing these skills within their families, offenders reinforce positive communication and ethical behavior that can be applied in other areas of their lives. Evaluating the effectiveness of programs that support the practical application of Right Speech and Right Action is crucial for continuous improvement. Longitudinal studies that track changes in offenders' communication skills, ethical behavior, and recidivism rates provide valuable data on the impact of these programs. Feedback from participants, mentors, and community members helps to refine and enhance the curriculum, ensuring that it remains relevant and effective. Continuous evaluation and adaptation are key to maintaining the success of these initiatives.

6.5: Integrating Right Action in Rehabilitation Programs

Creating a supportive environment that fosters ethical behavior and respect within correctional facilities is essential for the rehabilitation and successful reintegration of offenders. This requires a multifaceted approach involving the training of staff and volunteers, the development of a positive institutional culture, and the implementation of programs that promote respect and ethical behavior among offenders. The benefits of such a supportive environment extend to both offenders and staff, contributing to a safer, more harmonious, and productive correctional setting. The foundation of a supportive environment begins with the training of correctional staff and volunteers in the principles of Right Speech and Right Action. Staff members are often the primary role models for offenders, and their behavior sets the tone for the entire facility. Comprehensive training programs are essential to equip staff with the skills and knowledge necessary to model ethical behavior and communicate effectively. These programs typically cover topics such as active listening, conflict resolution, empathy, cultural competence, and stress management. By developing these skills, staff can engage with offenders in a respectful and constructive manner, fostering an atmosphere of mutual respect and trust.

One effective training program is the "Correctional Officer Professionalism and Ethics" (COPE) initiative, which has been implemented in various correctional facilities across the United States. COPE focuses on enhancing the professionalism and ethical conduct of correctional officers through intensive workshops and ongoing training sessions. The program emphasizes the importance of treating offenders with dignity and respect, even in challenging situations. By fostering a culture of professionalism and ethical behavior among staff, COPE contributes to a more positive and supportive environment within correctional facilities. Creating a culture of respect and ethical behavior also involves developing institutional policies that prioritize these values. Policies that promote transparency, accountability, and fairness are crucial for building trust between staff and offenders. For example, facilities can implement clear procedures for addressing grievances, ensuring that offenders have a voice and that their concerns are taken seriously. Policies that prohibit discrimination, harassment, and abuse create a safer environment for both offenders and staff. By establishing and enforcing these policies, correctional facilities can demonstrate their commitment to ethical conduct and respect for all individuals.

Programs that encourage positive interactions between staff and offenders play a significant role in fostering a supportive environment. Initiatives such as "Therapeutic Communities" (TCs) have been successful in promoting a culture of mutual support and ethical behavior. TCs are structured environments within correctional facilities where offenders participate in group therapy, peer support groups, and community-building activities. Staff members are actively involved in these programs, working alongside offenders to create a cohesive and supportive community. The collaborative nature of TCs helps to break down barriers between staff and offenders, fostering mutual respect and understanding. The "Restorative Justice Housing Unit" (RJHU) model is another innovative approach to creating a supportive environment. RJHUs are specialized units within correctional facilities that operate based on restorative justice principles. Offenders in these units participate in restorative practices such as mediation, dialogue circles, and community service projects. Staff members are trained in restorative justice techniques and work closely with offenders to facilitate healing and reconciliation. The RJHU model emphasizes accountability, empathy, and mutual respect, creating a positive and transformative environment for all participants.

Mentorship programs within correctional facilities can also contribute to a supportive environment. These programs pair offenders with trained mentors who provide guidance, support, and positive role models. Mentors can be staff members, volunteers, or even fellow offenders who have demonstrated exemplary behavior. Regular meetings between mentors and mentees help build trust and provide offenders with practical advice and encouragement. Mentorship programs foster a sense of community and mutual support, reinforcing the importance of ethical behavior and respect. Educational and vocational training programs are essential components of a supportive environment. These programs provide offenders with valuable skills and knowledge that can aid in their rehabilitation and reintegration. By offering courses in areas such as literacy, GED preparation, vocational skills, and higher education, correctional facilities empower offenders to improve their future prospects. Educational programs often include components that focus on personal development, ethical decision-making, and communication skills. By prioritizing education and personal growth, correctional facilities demonstrate their commitment to supporting offenders in their journey towards positive change.

The "Prison Education Program" (PEP) at Bard College in New York is an example of a successful educational initiative that fosters a supportive environment. PEP offers college-level courses to incarcerated individuals, providing them with the opportunity to earn a degree. The program emphasizes critical thinking, ethical reasoning, and personal development, helping offenders to build a foundation for a successful future. The supportive environment created by PEP has led to significant improvements in offenders' academic achievements, self-esteem, and behavior. Recreational and therapeutic activities are also important for creating a supportive environment. Programs that offer art therapy, music therapy, sports, and recreational activities provide offenders with constructive outlets for their energy and emotions. These activities promote physical and mental well-being, reduce stress, and foster a sense of community. Participating in recreational and therapeutic programs helps offenders develop positive habits, build relationships, and enhance their overall quality of life within the facility.

Support networks and peer support groups are crucial for reinforcing ethical behavior and respect. Peer support groups provide a platform for offenders to share their experiences, challenges, and successes. These groups offer mutual support, encouragement, and accountability, helping offenders to stay committed to their goals. Facilitators guide discussions on topics such as ethical decision-making, conflict resolution, and personal growth. The sense of community and mutual support within peer support groups helps offenders build positive relationships and develop a greater sense of responsibility. The "Inside-Out Prison Exchange Program" is an example of an initiative that fosters a supportive environment through collaboration between incarcerated individuals and university students. The program offers college courses that bring together offenders and students in a collaborative learning environment. Participants engage in discussions, group projects, and reflective exercises that emphasize empathy, respect, and ethical reasoning. The interactions between offenders and students break down stereotypes, build understanding, and create a supportive learning community. The program has been shown to have a positive impact on offenders' self-esteem, academic achievements, and behavior.

Family engagement is another important aspect of creating a supportive environment. Correctional facilities can implement programs that facilitate regular communication and visits between offenders and their families. Family therapy sessions, parenting classes, and support groups help offenders strengthen their relationships with family members and build a support network for reintegration. Maintaining strong family connections provides offenders with emotional support, motivation, and a sense of belonging. Facilities that prioritize family engagement demonstrate their commitment to the holistic well-being of offenders. Community involvement and partnerships with local organizations also contribute to a supportive environment. Correctional facilities can collaborate with community organizations, businesses, and service providers to offer additional resources and support for offenders.

These partnerships can provide opportunities for community service, vocational training, and employment after release. By fostering connections with the community, correctional facilities help offenders build a network of support that extends beyond the facility walls. Evaluating the effectiveness of programs and policies that promote a supportive environment is crucial for continuous improvement. Longitudinal studies that track changes in offenders' behavior, attitudes, and recidivism rates provide valuable data on the impact of these initiatives. Feedback from offenders, staff, and community members helps to refine and enhance the programs, ensuring that they remain effective and relevant. Continuous evaluation and adaptation are key to maintaining a positive and supportive environment within correctional facilities.

CHAPTER SEVEN

Right Livelihood and Right Effort

Contents

- Supporting Ethical Employment for Offenders

- Encouraging Diligent Practice and Personal Growth

- Practical Applications in Vocational Training

- Case Studies of Successful Reintegration

- Long-Term Benefits for Offenders and Communities

7.1: Supporting Ethical Employment for Offenders

Right Livelihood holds a vital place in the rehabilitation of offenders, shaping a path towards ethical employment opportunities that not only support personal growth but also contribute positively to society. This principle emphasizes the importance of earning a living through honest and ethical means, avoiding harm to others, and fostering a sense of purpose and integrity. For offenders, finding and maintaining ethical employment is a significant step towards successful reintegration and a stable, productive life. The journey towards Right Livelihood begins with comprehensive vocational training programs designed to equip offenders with marketable skills and knowledge. These programs are tailored to meet the demands of the current job market, ensuring that participants are prepared for real-world employment opportunities. Courses range from basic literacy and numeracy to advanced technical skills in areas such as carpentry, plumbing, electrical work, and information technology. By providing a diverse array of training options, these programs cater to the varied interests and aptitudes of offenders, empowering them to pursue careers that align with their skills and passions.

A notable example of a successful vocational training program is the "Piazza della Luna" initiative in Italy. This program offers extensive training in culinary arts, providing inmates with the skills needed to work in professional kitchens. Participants receive hands-on experience in cooking, baking, and kitchen management, guided by professional chefs who mentor them throughout the process. The program not only prepares offenders for employment in the culinary industry but also fosters a sense of pride and accomplishment, as they create meals that are shared with the community. The success of Piazza della Luna is evident in the high employment rates of its graduates, many of whom secure positions in reputable restaurants and catering businesses upon release. Job placement services play a crucial role in bridging the gap between vocational training and employment. These services assist offenders in identifying job opportunities, preparing resumes, and practicing interview skills. Career counselors work closely with participants to match their skills and interests with suitable job openings, providing guidance and support throughout the job search process. By offering personalized assistance, job placement services help offenders overcome barriers to employment and increase their chances of securing stable, ethical work.

The "Second Chance Business Coalition" (SCBC) in the United States exemplifies the impact of effective job placement services. SCBC partners with businesses committed to offering employment opportunities to formerly incarcerated individuals. The coalition provides training for employers on the benefits and challenges of hiring ex-offenders, promoting an inclusive and supportive workplace culture. SCBC also offers resources and support to help businesses integrate these employees successfully. As a result, many participants have found meaningful employment in various industries, from manufacturing and construction to retail and customer service, demonstrating the potential for transformative change when businesses and support services collaborate. Ethical employment opportunities extend beyond traditional vocational training and job placement. Innovative programs that combine education, entrepreneurship, and social enterprise offer alternative pathways to Right Livelihood. For example, the "Prison Entrepreneurship Program" (PEP) in Texas provides business education and mentorship to inmates, empowering them to develop their own business plans and entrepreneurial skills. Participants receive intensive training in business fundamentals, including marketing, finance, and leadership, and have the opportunity to pitch their business ideas to a panel of investors. Many graduates of PEP have successfully launched their own businesses, creating jobs for themselves and others while contributing positively to their communities.

Another inspiring initiative is the "San Patrignano" community in Italy, a rehabilitation center that offers vocational training and social enterprise opportunities to individuals recovering from addiction. Residents engage in various work activities, including agriculture, craftsmanship, and hospitality, learning valuable skills while contributing to the community's self-sufficiency. The products created by San Patrignano residents, such as wine, cheese, and furniture, are sold in the market, providing income for the community and reinforcing the value of honest labor. The program's holistic approach to rehabilitation and employment underscores the transformative power of Right Livelihood, fostering personal growth and social reintegration. Education plays a fundamental role in achieving Right Livelihood. Correctional facilities that offer educational programs, from basic education to higher education opportunities, provide offenders with the knowledge and credentials needed to pursue ethical employment. For example, the "Prison University Project" at San Quentin State Prison in California offers accredited college courses to inmates, enabling them to earn degrees while incarcerated. The rigorous academic program not only enhances their employability but also fosters critical thinking, self-discipline, and a sense of purpose. Graduates of the Prison University Project have gone on to secure employment in various fields, including education, social work, and business, demonstrating the profound impact of education on rehabilitation and reintegration.

Supportive employment environments are essential for sustaining Right Livelihood. Employers who prioritize inclusivity, provide fair wages, and create opportunities for professional growth contribute significantly to the successful reintegration of ex-offenders. Programs that encourage businesses to adopt fair hiring practices and offer support for formerly incarcerated employees play a vital role in creating these environments. The "Ban the Box" campaign, which advocates for removing criminal history questions from job applications, is one such initiative. By allowing candidates to be evaluated based on their skills and qualifications rather than their criminal records, Ban the Box helps reduce employment discrimination and increase opportunities for ex-offenders. Mentorship and peer support are crucial components of programs promoting Right Livelihood. Mentors, often successful professionals or individuals who have overcome similar challenges, provide guidance, encouragement, and practical advice to offenders as they navigate the complexities of finding and maintaining employment. Peer support groups offer a platform for sharing experiences, challenges, and successes, fostering a sense of community and mutual support. These networks help offenders build confidence, develop resilience, and stay committed to their goals.

Programs like "Ready, Willing, and Able" (RWA) in New York City exemplify the power of mentorship and peer support in promoting Right Livelihood. RWA provides comprehensive support to homeless and formerly incarcerated individuals, including job training, housing, and case management. Participants work in various community service projects, gaining work experience and earning a stipend. Mentors and case managers provide ongoing support, helping participants set goals, overcome obstacles, and achieve stability. The program's holistic approach addresses multiple barriers to employment and reintegration, resulting in high rates of job placement and long-term success for its participants. Community involvement and partnerships with local organizations further enhance the impact of programs promoting Right Livelihood. By collaborating with businesses, educational institutions, and social service providers, correctional facilities can create a network of support that extends beyond the prison walls. These partnerships provide offenders with access to a wide range of resources, including job training, education, housing, and healthcare. Community-based programs that offer transitional employment opportunities, such as internships and apprenticeships, help offenders build work experience and establish professional connections.

The "Homeboy Industries" program in Los Angeles is a prime example of a community-based initiative that supports Right Livelihood through comprehensive services and partnerships. Homeboy Industries offers job training, education, mental health services, and legal assistance to formerly gang-involved and incarcerated individuals. Participants work in various social enterprises, such as bakeries, cafes, and retail stores, gaining valuable work experience and earning a living wage. The program's holistic approach, combined with strong community partnerships, helps participants build stable, fulfilling lives and break the cycle of recidivism. Evaluating the effectiveness of programs promoting Right Livelihood is essential for continuous improvement. Longitudinal studies that track changes in offenders' employment status, income, and recidivism rates provide valuable data on the impact of these initiatives. Feedback from participants, employers, and community partners helps refine and enhance the programs, ensuring they remain relevant and effective. Continuous evaluation and adaptation are key to maintaining the success and sustainability of these initiatives.

7.2: Encouraging Diligent Practice and Personal Growth

Understanding the role of Right Effort in rehabilitation emphasizes the significance of diligence and persistence in personal growth. For offenders, developing perseverance and resilience is essential for overcoming past behaviors, navigating the challenges of reintegration, and building a stable, productive life. Programs that encourage continuous self-improvement and goal-setting are instrumental in fostering these qualities, enabling offenders to make meaningful progress and sustain positive change. Right Effort involves the conscious and sustained effort to cultivate positive qualities and eliminate negative ones. This principle is foundational in many rehabilitation programs that focus on personal development and behavioral change. One of the primary techniques for fostering perseverance and resilience is the implementation of structured goal-setting activities. These activities help offenders identify their aspirations, set realistic and achievable goals, and develop actionable plans to attain them. By breaking down larger objectives into smaller, manageable tasks, offenders can track their progress and maintain motivation.

A critical aspect of goal-setting is the development of a growth mindset, the belief that abilities and intelligence can be developed through dedication and hard work. Rehabilitation programs often include workshops and counseling sessions that promote this mindset, helping offenders shift their perspective from one of fixed limitations to one of potential and growth. This shift is crucial for building resilience, as it encourages offenders to view challenges and setbacks as opportunities for learning and improvement rather than insurmountable obstacles. The "Hope House" program in Washington, D.C., exemplifies the impact of structured goal-setting and a growth mindset. Hope House provides comprehensive support to incarcerated parents, including educational workshops, counseling, and family reunification services. Participants engage in goal-setting activities that focus on personal development, family relationships, and future employment. By fostering a growth mindset, the program helps offenders develop the perseverance needed to overcome barriers and achieve their goals. The success of Hope House is evident in the improved family relationships and reduced recidivism rates among its participants.

Another effective technique for fostering perseverance and resilience is the use of cognitive-behavioral therapy (CBT). CBT helps offenders identify and challenge negative thought patterns that hinder their progress. Therapists work with offenders to recognize automatic thoughts and cognitive distortions, such as overgeneralization, catastrophizing, and self-defeating beliefs. By addressing these thought patterns, offenders can develop healthier and more constructive ways of thinking, which support their efforts to achieve their goals and sustain positive change. Mindfulness practices are integrated into rehabilitation programs to enhance self-awareness and emotional regulation, both of which are essential for perseverance and resilience. Mindfulness involves paying attention to the present moment with a non-judgmental attitude, helping offenders become more aware of their thoughts, emotions, and physical sensations. Regular mindfulness practice, such as meditation, mindful breathing, and body scans, can reduce stress, improve focus, and enhance emotional regulation. These benefits enable offenders to stay committed to their goals, even in the face of adversity.

The "MindUp for Life" program, developed by the Goldie Hawn Foundation, is an example of how mindfulness practices can be used to foster resilience. MindUp for Life provides mindfulness-based social and emotional learning programs for children and adolescents, including those in juvenile detention centers. The program teaches participants mindfulness techniques, emotional regulation strategies, and cognitive-behavioral skills. By integrating these practices, MindUp for Life helps young offenders develop the resilience needed to navigate challenges and make positive choices. The program's success is reflected in improved emotional well-being and reduced behavioral problems among its participants. Support networks play a crucial role in fostering perseverance and resilience. Peer support groups, mentorship programs, and family engagement initiatives provide offenders with the encouragement, accountability, and resources needed to stay committed to their goals. In peer support groups, offenders share their experiences, challenges, and successes, offering mutual support and learning from one another. These groups create a sense of community and belonging, which can be a powerful motivator for continued effort and personal growth.

Mentorship programs connect offenders with mentors who provide guidance, support, and positive role models. Mentors help offenders set goals, develop action plans, and navigate challenges. The mentor-mentee relationship fosters trust and mutual respect, providing offenders with a source of encouragement and accountability. The "Amachi Mentoring Program" in Pennsylvania, for example, pairs children of incarcerated parents with mentors who offer support and guidance. The program's success in fostering resilience and positive outcomes among its participants highlights the impact of mentorship on personal development. Family engagement initiatives strengthen the support network for offenders, helping them build and maintain positive relationships with their family members. Programs that facilitate regular communication, family therapy sessions, and parenting classes help offenders reconnect with their families and develop the skills needed to maintain healthy relationships. The "InsideOut Dad" program, implemented in various correctional facilities across the United States, provides parenting education and support to incarcerated fathers. By fostering family connections and promoting positive fatherhood, the program helps participants build resilience and stay committed to their personal growth.

Educational and vocational training programs are essential for fostering perseverance and resilience. These programs provide offenders with the skills and knowledge needed to pursue meaningful employment and achieve long-term stability. By offering a range of educational opportunities, from basic literacy and GED preparation to vocational training and higher education, correctional facilities empower offenders to develop their potential and achieve their goals. The "Education Justice Project" at the University of Illinois, for example, offers college-level courses to inmates, helping them build academic skills, critical thinking abilities, and self-discipline. The program's success is reflected in the academic achievements and personal growth of its participants. Recreational and therapeutic activities provide constructive outlets for energy and emotions, helping offenders build resilience and perseverance. Programs that offer art therapy, music therapy, sports, and recreational activities promote physical and mental well-being, reduce stress, and foster a sense of community. Participating in these activities helps offenders develop positive habits, build relationships, and enhance their overall quality of life. The "ArtReach" program in California, for example, offers art therapy workshops to incarcerated individuals, helping them explore their emotions, express themselves creatively, and build resilience through artistic expression.

Community service projects provide practical opportunities for offenders to apply their skills and contribute positively to society. By engaging in activities that benefit others, offenders experience the value of their efforts and develop a sense of purpose and accomplishment. Community service helps offenders build positive relationships, gain work experience, and reinforce their commitment to personal growth. The "Community Transition Program" in Washington State, for example, involves offenders in community service projects such as environmental conservation, urban beautification, and public safety initiatives. The program's success in fostering resilience and positive outcomes among its participants highlights the impact of community service on personal development. Evaluating the effectiveness of programs that foster perseverance and resilience is crucial for continuous improvement. Longitudinal studies that track changes in offenders' attitudes, behaviors, and recidivism rates provide valuable data on the impact of these programs. Feedback from participants, mentors, and community members helps refine and enhance the curriculum, ensuring that it remains relevant and effective. Continuous evaluation and adaptation are kcy to maintaining the success and sustainability of these initiatives.

7.3: Practical Applications in Vocational Training

Overcoming barriers to employment is a significant challenge for offenders as they transition back into society. The stigma associated with a criminal record, gaps in employment history, and lack of relevant job skills are just some of the obstacles they face. Addressing these challenges requires comprehensive support services and programs designed to assist offenders in job readiness, enhance their employability, and facilitate successful reintegration. By tackling these barriers head-on, offenders can improve their chances of securing stable and meaningful employment, thereby reducing recidivism and contributing positively to their communities. One of the primary barriers to employment for offenders is the stigma attached to having a criminal record. Many employers are hesitant to hire individuals with a history of incarceration due to concerns about reliability, trustworthiness, and potential liability. To combat this stigma, advocacy groups and policymakers have implemented initiatives such as the "Ban the Box" campaign. This campaign advocates for the removal of questions about criminal history from initial job applications, allowing candidates to be evaluated based on their qualifications and skills rather than their past. Several states and municipalities have adopted Ban the Box policies, which have shown promising results in increasing employment opportunities for ex-offenders.

Another effective strategy to overcome stigma is through employer education and engagement. Programs that educate employers about the benefits of hiring ex-offenders and provide support for integrating them into the workforce can help change perceptions and reduce bias. The "Fair Chance Business Pledge" in the United States is one such initiative. It encourages businesses to commit to fair hiring practices and to provide opportunities for individuals with criminal records. Companies that take the pledge receive resources and support to help them implement these practices, such as training on legal issues, tips for creating inclusive workplace cultures, and access to a network of other fair chance employers. By highlighting success stories and demonstrating the positive impact of fair chance hiring, these programs can shift employer attitudes and open up more job opportunities for ex-offenders. Addressing gaps in employment history is another crucial aspect of enhancing job readiness for offenders. Vocational training programs within correctional facilities provide inmates with the opportunity to learn new skills and gain work experience. These programs often offer certifications in various trades, such as welding, carpentry, plumbing, and electrical work, which can significantly enhance an individual's employability. Additionally, partnerships with local businesses and industry organizations can provide inmates with internships and apprenticeships that offer real-world experience and help bridge the gap between incarceration and employment.

The "Transforming Lives Through Training" (TLTT) program in the United Kingdom is an example of a successful vocational training initiative. TLTT collaborates with local employers to offer training and apprenticeships in high-demand industries. Participants receive hands-on training and work experience, along with support in job placement upon release. The program has been highly effective in helping ex-offenders secure employment and build sustainable careers. By providing a structured pathway from training to employment, TLTT helps participants overcome gaps in their employment history and gain the skills needed for success in the job market. In addition to vocational training, job readiness programs play a critical role in preparing offenders for the workforce. These programs cover essential skills such as resume writing, interview techniques, and professional communication. Career counselors work with participants to develop personalized job search strategies, identify suitable job opportunities, and navigate the application process. Mock interviews and role-playing exercises help offenders practice their interview skills and build confidence. Job readiness programs also address soft skills, such as teamwork, time management, and problem-solving, which are crucial for workplace success.

Support services that assist with job placement are integral to overcoming employment barriers. These services provide offenders with the resources and guidance needed to secure and maintain employment. Job placement agencies that specialize in working with ex-offenders understand the unique challenges they face and can offer tailored support. For example, the "Center for Employment Opportunities" (CEO) in the United States provides comprehensive employment services to individuals returning from incarceration. CEO offers transitional jobs, where participants work on community projects while receiving on-the-job training and support. The program also provides job coaching, financial incentives for job retention, and connections to permanent employment opportunities. CEO's holistic approach addresses multiple barriers to employment and has been shown to significantly reduce recidivism rates among its participants. Another innovative approach to supporting job placement is through social enterprises that employ ex-offenders. These businesses are specifically designed to provide job opportunities and training to individuals with criminal records. By creating a supportive work environment that prioritizes personal development and skill-building, social enterprises help offenders transition into the mainstream workforce. "Greyston Bakery" in New York is a notable example. Greyston operates with an open hiring model, where anyone who applies is given a chance to work, regardless of their background. Employees receive on-the-job training, support services, and opportunities for advancement. This model not only provides stable employment but also helps change societal perceptions about the employability of ex-offenders.

Partnerships with community organizations and local businesses are essential for creating employment opportunities and support networks for offenders. Community organizations can provide wraparound services, such as housing assistance, transportation, and childcare, which address the practical barriers that often impede employment. By working together, businesses and community organizations can create a network of support that helps ex-offenders overcome obstacles and achieve stability. The "Reentry Council of the City and County of San Francisco" exemplifies effective collaboration between community organizations and local businesses. The council brings together representatives from government agencies, nonprofit organizations, and the private sector to coordinate reentry services and create employment opportunities for ex-offenders. Through initiatives such as job fairs, employer workshops, and community resource centers, the council helps connect ex-offenders with the support and opportunities they need to succeed. This collaborative approach ensures a comprehensive and cohesive support system that addresses multiple aspects of reentry and employment.

Providing mental health and substance abuse treatment is also crucial for overcoming employment barriers. Many offenders struggle with mental health issues or substance use disorders that can impede their ability to secure and maintain employment. Programs that offer counseling, therapy, and support groups help offenders address these issues and develop coping strategies. By integrating mental health and substance abuse treatment with vocational training and job placement services, correctional facilities can provide a holistic approach to rehabilitation and reintegration. The "Substance Abuse Treatment Program" (SATP) in the Federal Bureau of Prisons is an example of an integrated approach. SATP provides comprehensive treatment for inmates with substance use disorders, including individual and group counseling, educational workshops, and relapse prevention planning. The program also includes vocational training and job placement services, helping participants develop the skills and support needed for successful reintegration. By addressing both substance abuse and employment barriers, SATP helps reduce recidivism and support long-term recovery and stability. Continuous evaluation and adaptation of programs are essential to ensure their effectiveness in overcoming employment barriers. Longitudinal studies that track participants' employment outcomes, income levels, and recidivism rates provide valuable data on the impact of these initiatives. Feedback from participants, employers, and community partners helps refine and enhance the programs, ensuring they remain relevant and effective. Continuous evaluation and adaptation are key to maintaining the success and sustainability of these initiatives.

In conclusion, overcoming barriers to employment for offenders involves a comprehensive approach that includes advocacy for fair hiring practices, employer education and engagement, vocational training, job readiness programs, support services for job placement, social enterprises, community partnerships, and mental health and substance abuse treatment. These components help offenders enhance their employability, secure stable and meaningful employment, and achieve successful reintegration. By addressing the stigma associated with a criminal record, providing relevant skills and support, and fostering a collaborative network of support, correctional facilities can help offenders overcome employment barriers and build productive, fulfilling lives. Continuous evaluation and community involvement further enhance the impact and sustainability of these programs, ensuring their effectiveness in promoting successful reintegration and reducing recidivism.

7.4: Case Studies of Successful Reintegration

Creating a path to sustainable livelihoods for offenders is essential for their long-term success and stability. This involves developing strategies that go beyond immediate employment opportunities to ensure that ex-offenders can build enduring careers and achieve economic self-sufficiency. Education, skill-building, and continuous support are critical components of this process, as they empower individuals to navigate the complexities of the job market and sustain meaningful employment. Success stories of offenders who have built stable careers post-incarceration highlight the transformative potential of these strategies and provide valuable insights into best practices. A key strategy for developing sustainable livelihoods is providing comprehensive education and training programs that equip offenders with the skills and credentials needed for long-term career success. Educational programs within correctional facilities can range from basic literacy and numeracy classes to advanced vocational training and higher education opportunities. These programs are designed to address the diverse educational needs of offenders, ensuring that they have the knowledge and skills required to succeed in various industries.

One exemplary program is the "Correctional Education Association" (CEA), which operates in multiple states across the United States. CEA provides a wide range of educational services to incarcerated individuals, including adult basic education, GED preparation, and vocational training. The association collaborates with local community colleges and vocational schools to offer accredited courses and certifications. This partnership ensures that the education provided is relevant and recognized in the job market, enhancing the employability of participants. CEA's holistic approach to education includes career counseling and job placement services, helping offenders transition from learning to earning. Skill-building is another crucial element in creating sustainable livelihoods. Offenders need practical, hands-on training that prepares them for the demands of the modern workforce. Programs that offer apprenticeships, internships, and on-the-job training provide invaluable experience and help offenders build a professional network. These opportunities allow individuals to apply their skills in real-world settings, gain confidence, and develop a track record of reliability and competence.

The "Auto Mechanics Vocational Program" at the Louisiana State Penitentiary is a notable example of effective skill-building. This program offers comprehensive training in automotive repair and maintenance, including diagnostics, engine repair, and electrical systems. Participants receive hands-on training in a fully equipped auto shop, working on real vehicles and learning from experienced instructors. The program also includes certification in various automotive specializations, making graduates highly employable in the automotive industry. Many participants have secured stable, well-paying jobs as auto mechanics upon release, demonstrating the program's success in creating sustainable livelihoods. Creating a path to sustainable livelihoods also involves addressing the unique challenges that offenders face in the job market. Support services that assist with job readiness, such as resume writing, interview preparation, and professional networking, are essential. These services help offenders present themselves effectively to potential employers and navigate the job search process with confidence. Additionally, ongoing support and mentoring can provide the guidance and encouragement needed to sustain employment and advance in one's career.

The "New Leaf Initiative" in the United Kingdom provides a comprehensive support system for ex-offenders seeking to build sustainable careers. This initiative offers job readiness workshops, one-on-one career coaching, and access to a network of employers who are committed to fair hiring practices. Participants receive personalized support throughout their job search and employment journey, including mentorship from professionals in their chosen field. The New Leaf Initiative also offers financial literacy training and assistance with securing housing, ensuring that participants have the stability needed to focus on their career goals. The initiative's holistic approach has led to significant success, with many participants achieving long-term employment and career advancement. Long-term employment opportunities are also fostered through strategic partnerships between correctional facilities, community organizations, and businesses. These partnerships can create pathways to employment by providing offenders with access to a network of supportive employers and resources. For example, the "Building Futures" program in Australia collaborates with construction companies to offer apprenticeships and job placements to ex-offenders. Participants receive training in various construction trades, including carpentry, plumbing, and electrical work, and are placed in apprenticeships with partnering companies. The program provides ongoing support and mentorship, ensuring that participants have the tools and guidance needed to succeed. Building Futures has a high success rate, with many participants securing long-term employment in the construction industry.

Entrepreneurship programs offer an alternative pathway to sustainable livelihoods for offenders. These programs provide the training and support needed to start and grow a business, enabling individuals to create their own employment opportunities. Entrepreneurship can be particularly empowering for ex-offenders, as it allows them to leverage their unique skills and experiences to build a successful enterprise. The "Defy Ventures" program in the United States is a prominent example of an effective entrepreneurship initiative. Defy Ventures offers a comprehensive curriculum that includes business education, mentorship, and pitch competitions. Participants develop business plans, receive feedback from successful entrepreneurs, and have the opportunity to secure funding for their ventures. The program also provides ongoing support and networking opportunities, helping graduates navigate the challenges of entrepreneurship. Many participants have successfully launched businesses in various industries, demonstrating the transformative potential of entrepreneurship for ex-offenders. Financial literacy and management training are crucial for achieving economic self-sufficiency and stability. Offenders often lack the knowledge and skills needed to manage their finances effectively, which can hinder their ability to sustain employment and build a stable future. Programs that offer financial education, budgeting workshops, and one-on-one financial counseling help offenders develop the skills needed to make informed financial decisions, save for the future, and avoid debt. The "Money Matters" program in Canada provides comprehensive financial literacy training to incarcerated individuals and ex-offenders. The program covers topics such as budgeting, credit management, and savings strategies, equipping participants with the tools needed to achieve financial stability. Money Matters has been highly effective in helping participants build healthy financial habits and achieve long-term economic security.

Access to stable housing is another critical factor in creating sustainable livelihoods. Housing instability can severely impact an individual's ability to maintain employment and focus on career advancement. Programs that provide transitional housing and support services help ex-offenders establish a stable living environment, which is essential for their overall well-being and success. The "Fort Lyon Supportive Residential Community" in Colorado offers a comprehensive housing and support program for homeless individuals, including ex-offenders. Participants receive safe housing, access to healthcare, vocational training, and job placement services. The program's holistic approach addresses multiple barriers to stability and employment, helping participants achieve long-term success and independence. Community engagement and involvement play a significant role in supporting ex-offenders as they build sustainable livelihoods. By fostering a sense of belonging and connection, community involvement can provide the support and encouragement needed to overcome challenges and achieve goals. Programs that facilitate community service, volunteer opportunities, and civic engagement help ex-offenders build positive relationships and contribute to their communities.

The "Homecoming Project" in Baltimore, Maryland, connects ex-offenders with community organizations and volunteer opportunities, helping them build a sense of purpose and connection. Participants engage in various community service projects, such as neighborhood clean-ups, mentoring youth, and supporting local events. The Homecoming Project has been successful in fostering community reintegration and building sustainable livelihoods for its participants. Evaluating the effectiveness of programs that create sustainable livelihoods is crucial for continuous improvement. Longitudinal studies that track changes in participants' employment status, income levels, and career advancement provide valuable data on the impact of these initiatives. Feedback from participants, employers, and community partners helps refine and enhance the programs, ensuring they remain relevant and effective. Continuous evaluation and adaptation are key to maintaining the success and sustainability of these initiatives.

Creating a path to sustainable livelihoods for offenders involves a comprehensive approach that includes education, skill-building, job readiness support, strategic partnerships, entrepreneurship programs, financial literacy training, stable housing, and community engagement. These components help offenders develop the skills, knowledge, and support needed to achieve long-term career success and economic self-sufficiency. By addressing the unique challenges that offenders face in the job market and providing continuous support, correctional facilities can help individuals build stable, fulfilling careers and contribute positively to their communities. Continuous evaluation and community involvement further enhance the impact and sustainability of these programs, ensuring their effectiveness in promoting successful reintegration and reducing recidivism.

7.5: Long-Term Benefits for Offenders and Communities

Community support and reintegration play crucial roles in ensuring the successful rehabilitation of offenders. The transition from incarceration to society is fraught with challenges, including social stigma, lack of resources, and the need to rebuild relationships. Programs that foster community engagement, mentorship, and supportive networks are vital for helping offenders navigate this transition and build stable, fulfilling lives. The benefits of a supportive community extend beyond individual offenders, contributing to safer, more cohesive communities and reducing recidivism.One of the fundamental aspects of community support is fostering a sense of belonging and connection. Offenders often feel isolated and disconnected from society, which can hinder their reintegration efforts. Community-based programs that promote social inclusion and engagement help offenders rebuild their social networks and establish positive relationships. The "Circles of Support and Accountability" (CoSA) program in Canada is an exemplary model of fostering community engagement. CoSA pairs ex-offenders with trained community volunteers who provide support, guidance, and friendship. These circles create a network of accountability and encouragement, helping offenders navigate the challenges of reentry. The program's success is evident in its significant impact on reducing recidivism rates and promoting community safety.

Mentorship is another critical component of community support. Mentors provide offenders with guidance, advice, and positive role models, helping them set and achieve their goals. Mentorship programs often connect offenders with individuals who have successfully reintegrated into society, offering firsthand insights and practical strategies for overcoming obstacles. The "One Million Mentors" initiative in the United Kingdom aims to provide a mentor for every young person who needs one, including those with a history of incarceration. By matching offenders with mentors who understand their experiences, the program fosters trust and provides tailored support. Participants in mentorship programs often report increased confidence, improved decision-making skills, and a stronger sense of direction. Community engagement initiatives also involve local organizations, businesses, and service providers. These partnerships create a network of resources and opportunities for offenders, facilitating their reintegration and supporting their long-term success. For example, the "Safer Foundation" in Chicago works with local businesses to create employment opportunities for ex-offenders. The foundation provides job readiness training, placement services, and ongoing support, helping offenders secure stable employment and build sustainable careers. By engaging the business community, the Safer Foundation fosters a culture of inclusion and demonstrates the value of hiring ex-offenders.

Supportive housing is another essential aspect of community reintegration. Stable housing provides a foundation for offenders to rebuild their lives, secure employment, and access essential services. Programs that offer transitional housing and support services help offenders establish a stable living environment, which is crucial for their overall well-being and success. The "Fort Lyon Supportive Residential Community" in Colorado offers a comprehensive housing program for homeless individuals, including ex-offenders. Participants receive safe housing, access to healthcare, vocational training, and job placement services. The program's holistic approach addresses multiple barriers to stability and employment, helping participants achieve long-term success and independence. Family support and engagement are vital for successful reintegration. Programs that facilitate regular communication, family therapy sessions, and parenting classes help offenders reconnect with their families and develop the skills needed to maintain healthy relationships. The "InsideOut Dad" program, implemented in various correctional facilities across the United States, provides parenting education and support to incarcerated fathers. By fostering family connections and promoting positive fatherhood, the program helps participants build resilience and stay committed to their personal growth. Strong family bonds provide emotional support, motivation, and a sense of belonging, which are essential for successful reintegration.

Community service and volunteer opportunities offer practical ways for offenders to give back to their communities and build positive relationships. Engaging in community service helps offenders develop a sense of purpose and accomplishment while demonstrating their commitment to positive change. The "Community Transition Program" in Washington State involves offenders in community service projects such as environmental conservation, urban beautification, and public safety initiatives. These projects provide valuable work experience, foster a sense of community, and help offenders build a positive reputation. The program's success in fostering community reintegration and reducing recidivism highlights the impact of community service on personal development. Peer support groups provide a platform for offenders to share their experiences, challenges, and successes. These groups offer mutual support, encouragement, and accountability, helping offenders stay committed to their goals. Facilitators guide discussions on topics such as ethical decision-making, conflict resolution, and personal growth. The sense of community and mutual support within peer support groups helps offenders build positive relationships and develop a greater sense of responsibility. The "Peers Advancing Community Together" (PACT) program in New York City connects formerly incarcerated individuals with peer mentors who provide support and guidance. PACT has been successful in fostering community reintegration and building sustainable livelihoods for its participants.

Educational and vocational training programs are essential for fostering community support and reintegration. These programs provide offenders with the skills and knowledge needed to pursue meaningful employment and achieve long-term stability. By offering a range of educational opportunities, from basic literacy and GED preparation to vocational training and higher education, correctional facilities empower offenders to develop their potential and achieve their goals. The "Education Justice Project" at the University of Illinois offers college-level courses to inmates, helping them build academic skills, critical thinking abilities, and self-discipline. The program's success is reflected in the academic achievements and personal growth of its participants. Recreational and therapeutic activities provide constructive outlets for energy and emotions, helping offenders build resilience and perseverance. Programs that offer art therapy, music therapy, sports, and recreational activities promote physical and mental well-being, reduce stress, and foster a sense of community. Participating in these activities helps offenders develop positive habits, build relationships, and enhance their overall quality of life. The "ArtReach" program in California offers art therapy workshops to incarcerated individuals, helping them explore their emotions, express themselves creatively, and build resilience through artistic expression.

Access to healthcare and mental health services is crucial for supporting community reintegration. Many offenders have unmet health needs that can impede their ability to secure and maintain employment and build stable lives. Programs that provide comprehensive healthcare, including mental health and substance abuse treatment, help offenders address these issues and develop coping strategies. The "Community Health Outreach Workers" (CHOW) program in New York City connects formerly incarcerated individuals with healthcare services and support. CHOW provides case management, health education, and linkage to care, helping participants achieve better health outcomes and improve their quality of life. Evaluating the effectiveness of community support and reintegration programs is crucial for continuous improvement. Longitudinal studies that track changes in offenders' behavior, attitudes, and recidivism rates provide valuable data on the impact of these initiatives. Feedback from participants, mentors, and community members helps refine and enhance the programs, ensuring they remain relevant and effective. Continuous evaluation and adaptation are key to maintaining the success and sustainability of these initiatives.

—

CHAPTER EIGHT

Right Mindfulness and Right Concentration

Contents

- Implementing Mindfulness Practices in Rehabilitation

- Techniques for Developing Concentration

- Benefits of Mindfulness for Offenders

- Case Studies of Mindfulness-Based Rehabilitation

- Sustaining Mindfulness Practices for Long-Term Change

8.1: Implementing Mindfulness Practices in Rehabilitation

Mindfulness, the practice of being fully present in the moment without judgment, plays a crucial role in rehabilitation. Within the justice system, the principles of Right Mindfulness can bring transformative benefits to offenders, fostering mental and emotional well-being, and facilitating their journey towards personal growth and rehabilitation. Mindfulness helps individuals develop self-awareness, emotional regulation, and a deeper understanding of their thoughts and behaviors, which are essential for making positive changes. The relevance of Right Mindfulness in justice settings is rooted in its ability to address the underlying causes of criminal behavior. Offenders often struggle with impulsivity, emotional dysregulation, and a lack of self-awareness, which contribute to their actions. By cultivating mindfulness, they learn to observe their thoughts and emotions without reacting impulsively. This heightened awareness allows them to recognize patterns of behavior, understand their triggers, and develop healthier responses to challenging situations. In essence, mindfulness empowers offenders to break free from the cycle of reactivity and make more conscious, ethical choices.

Mindfulness practices offer numerous benefits for mental and emotional well-being. Regular mindfulness meditation has been shown to reduce stress, anxiety, and depression, which are common issues among incarcerated individuals. By practicing mindfulness, offenders can develop greater resilience to stress and improve their overall mental health. This is particularly important in correctional facilities, where the environment can be highly stressful and challenging. Mindfulness provides a tool for managing these stresses, promoting a sense of calm and inner peace even in difficult circumstances. One of the key benefits of mindfulness is its ability to enhance emotional regulation. Offenders often experience intense emotions such as anger, frustration, and sadness, which can drive harmful behaviors. Mindfulness helps individuals become more aware of these emotions as they arise, allowing them to observe and understand their feelings without being overwhelmed by them. This process of emotional regulation is crucial for developing healthier coping mechanisms and reducing the likelihood of engaging in aggressive or destructive behavior. By learning to respond to emotions with greater clarity and calmness, offenders can improve their interpersonal relationships and create a more harmonious environment.

Mindfulness programs in correctional facilities have been implemented with promising results. These programs typically involve regular meditation sessions, mindfulness-based stress reduction (MBSR) courses, and other mindfulness practices tailored to the needs of the incarcerated population. Participants are taught various techniques to develop mindfulness, such as focused breathing, body scans, and mindful movement. These practices help offenders cultivate a state of present-moment awareness, which can be integrated into their daily routines. For example, the "Mindfulness-Based Stress Reduction in Prisons Project"

(MBSR-PP) has been successfully implemented in several correctional facilities in the United States. This program, based on the principles of MBSR developed by Dr. Jon Kabat-Zinn, offers an eight-week course that teaches participants mindfulness meditation and stress reduction techniques. The program has shown significant benefits, including reduced stress and anxiety levels, improved emotional regulation, and increased self-awareness among participants. Offenders who completed the program reported feeling more in control of their emotions and better equipped to handle the challenges of prison life.

Another successful initiative is the "Prison Mindfulness Institute" (PMI), which provides mindfulness-based programs to incarcerated individuals. PMI offers a variety of mindfulness practices, including meditation, yoga, and contemplative arts, designed to promote inner transformation and healing. The program emphasizes the development of self-awareness, compassion, and ethical behavior, aligning with the principles of Right Mindfulness. Participants have reported profound changes in their attitudes and behaviors, noting increased empathy, reduced aggression, and a greater sense of inner peace. The transformative impact of PMI's programs highlights the potential of mindfulness to support rehabilitation and personal growth. The integration of mindfulness into correctional settings also fosters a more positive and supportive environment. Correctional officers and staff who practice mindfulness can model calm and compassionate behavior, creating a more respectful and humane atmosphere. Mindfulness training for staff can reduce stress and burnout, improve communication, and enhance their ability to manage challenging situations. By promoting mindfulness among both offenders and staff, correctional facilities can create a culture of mindfulness that benefits the entire community.

Mindfulness is not limited to formal meditation sessions; it can be integrated into everyday activities. Offenders can practice mindfulness while eating, walking, or engaging in daily routines. This informal practice helps reinforce the principles of mindfulness and make them a natural part of life. For instance, mindful eating involves paying full attention to the experience of eating, savoring each bite, and noticing the sensations of taste, texture, and aroma. This practice can help offenders develop greater appreciation for their meals and foster a sense of gratitude.

Similarly, mindful walking involves walking slowly and deliberately, paying attention to each step and the sensations of movement. This practice can be particularly beneficial in correctional settings, where opportunities for physical activity may be limited. By engaging in mindful walking, offenders can cultivate a sense of presence and calmness, even in a confined environment. These informal mindfulness practices complement formal meditation sessions, helping to embed mindfulness into daily life.

Research supports the effectiveness of mindfulness in reducing recidivism. Studies have shown that offenders who participate in mindfulness programs are less likely to reoffend compared to those who do not. The development of self-awareness, emotional regulation, and ethical behavior through mindfulness practice contributes to this positive outcome. By addressing the underlying psychological and emotional factors that contribute to criminal behavior, mindfulness provides a powerful tool for rehabilitation. Mindfulness also aligns with restorative justice principles, which emphasize healing, accountability, and making amends. Offenders who practice mindfulness develop greater empathy and compassion, which are essential for understanding the impact of their actions on others. This heightened awareness can motivate offenders to take responsibility for their behavior and seek ways to repair the harm they have caused. Mindfulness practices can be integrated into restorative justice programs, enhancing their effectiveness in promoting healing and reconciliation.

8.2: Techniques for Developing Concentration

Developing mindfulness involves learning and practicing various techniques that cultivate present-moment awareness and emotional regulation. These practices are crucial for offenders as they navigate the challenges of rehabilitation and reintegration. Different mindfulness techniques, including meditation, breathing exercises, and mindful movement, provide tools for offenders to manage stress, enhance self-awareness, and develop a greater sense of control over their thoughts and behaviors. Programs that teach these skills have shown significant benefits, helping individuals transform their lives and reduce the likelihood of reoffending. Meditation is one of the most fundamental practices for developing mindfulness. It involves sitting quietly and focusing on the breath, a mantra, or another point of concentration. Meditation helps individuals observe their thoughts and emotions without judgment, allowing them to develop greater self-awareness and emotional regulation. Regular meditation practice can reduce stress, anxiety, and depression, which are common issues among offenders. By creating a space for introspection and calmness, meditation helps individuals gain insight into their behaviors and develop healthier responses to challenges.

Various forms of meditation are used in mindfulness programs. One common practice is mindfulness meditation, which focuses on observing the breath and noticing thoughts and sensations as they arise. This practice helps individuals stay anchored in the present moment, reducing the tendency to ruminate on the past or worry about the future. Another form is loving-kindness meditation, which involves sending goodwill and compassion to oneself and others. This practice fosters empathy and emotional healing, encouraging offenders to develop a more compassionate outlook towards themselves and others. Breathing exercises are another essential component of mindfulness practice. These exercises involve consciously controlling the breath to create a sense of calm and relaxation. Deep breathing, also known as diaphragmatic breathing, is a technique where individuals breathe deeply into their abdomen, allowing the lungs to expand fully. This type of breathing activates the parasympathetic nervous system, which promotes relaxation and reduces the body's stress response. By practicing deep breathing, offenders can manage stress and anxiety more effectively, improving their ability to cope with challenging situations.

Box breathing is a specific breathing technique used in mindfulness programs. It involves inhaling deeply for a count of four, holding the breath for a count of four, exhaling slowly for a count of four, and holding the breath again for a count of four before repeating the cycle. This structured approach to breathing helps regulate the body's stress response and promotes a sense of calm and focus. Offenders who practice box breathing regularly report feeling more centered and in control of their emotions, which is crucial for maintaining composure in high-stress environments. Mindful movement practices, such as yoga and tai chi, combine physical activity with mindfulness principles. These practices involve performing a series of movements with focused attention on the body's sensations, breath, and alignment. Mindful movement helps individuals develop greater body awareness, flexibility, and balance, which can enhance overall well-being. For offenders, incorporating mindful movement into their routine provides a constructive outlet for energy and stress, promoting physical and mental health.

Yoga, in particular, has gained popularity in correctional facilities as a mindfulness practice. Programs like "Prison Yoga Project" (PYP) offer yoga classes to incarcerated individuals, teaching them how to connect with their bodies and minds through mindful movement. PYP's approach emphasizes trauma-informed yoga, which is sensitive to the experiences of offenders and focuses on creating a safe and supportive environment. Participants in PYP programs report reduced stress, improved emotional regulation, and a greater sense of self-awareness. The physical benefits of yoga, such as increased strength and flexibility, complement the mental and emotional benefits, contributing to overall rehabilitation. Tai chi, a martial art that involves slow, deliberate movements and deep breathing, is another effective mindful movement practice. Tai chi promotes relaxation, balance, and coordination, helping individuals develop greater control over their bodies and minds. The meditative aspect of tai chi encourages present-moment awareness and emotional regulation. Correctional facilities that offer tai chi classes have found that participants experience reduced aggression, improved focus, and enhanced well-being. Tai chi provides a holistic approach to mindfulness, addressing physical, mental, and emotional health.

Programs that teach mindfulness skills to offenders are designed to be accessible and supportive, ensuring that participants can engage with the practices effectively. The "Mindfulness-Based Stress Reduction in Prisons Project" (MBSR-PP) is one such program that offers structured mindfulness courses to incarcerated individuals. The program follows an eight-week curriculum based on Dr. Jon Kabat-Zinn's MBSR principles, teaching participants various mindfulness techniques, including meditation, body scans, and mindful movement. MBSR-PP has demonstrated significant benefits, including reduced stress and anxiety, improved emotional regulation, and increased self-awareness among participants. Another successful initiative is the "Path of Freedom" program, developed by the Prison Mindfulness Institute. This program offers a comprehensive mindfulness curriculum that includes meditation, yoga, and contemplative practices. Path of Freedom emphasizes the development of self-awareness, emotional intelligence, and ethical behavior, aligning with the principles of Right Mindfulness. Participants learn to observe their thoughts and emotions, cultivate compassion, and develop healthier coping strategies. The program's impact is evident in the positive changes reported by participants, including reduced aggression, improved relationships, and a greater sense of purpose.

Success stories of individuals who have benefited from mindfulness practices highlight the transformative potential of these techniques. One such story is that of Javier, a former inmate who participated in a mindfulness program during his incarceration. Javier struggled with anger and impulsivity, which had contributed to his criminal behavior. Through mindfulness meditation and breathing exercises, he learned to observe his emotions without reacting impulsively. Javier developed greater self-awareness and emotional regulation, which helped him manage his anger and make more thoughtful decisions. Upon his release, he continued to practice mindfulness and became a mentor for other ex-offenders, sharing his experience and helping them navigate their own challenges. Another inspiring example is Lisa, who discovered yoga while serving a prison sentence. Lisa struggled with anxiety and low self-esteem, which affected her ability to cope with prison life. Through the Prison Yoga Project, she learned to connect with her body and mind through mindful movement. Yoga provided Lisa with a sense of calm and inner strength, helping her manage her anxiety and build confidence. After her release, she pursued further yoga training and became a certified yoga instructor. Lisa now teaches yoga to at-risk youth and incarcerated individuals, using her experience to inspire others and promote healing.

The integration of mindfulness practices into daily life is essential for sustaining their benefits. Offenders are encouraged to incorporate mindfulness into their routines, such as practicing mindful breathing during stressful moments, engaging in mindful movement exercises, or setting aside time for meditation. These practices help reinforce the principles of mindfulness and make them a natural part of life. For instance, starting the day with a brief meditation can set a positive tone, fostering a sense of calm and focus that carries through the day. Support systems and resources are crucial for maintaining a mindfulness practice. Peer support groups, mentorship programs, and access to mindfulness resources, such as guided meditations and instructional videos, provide ongoing encouragement and guidance. Correctional facilities that offer mindfulness programs often create support networks where participants can share their experiences, discuss challenges, and celebrate successes. These networks help individuals stay motivated and committed to their practice, fostering a sense of community and mutual support.

Research supports the effectiveness of mindfulness practices in reducing recidivism. Studies have shown that individuals who participate in mindfulness programs are less likely to reoffend compared to those who do not. The development of self-awareness, emotional regulation, and stress management skills through mindfulness practice contributes to this positive outcome. By addressing the underlying psychological and emotional factors that contribute to criminal behavior, mindfulness provides a powerful tool for rehabilitation and reintegration. Developing mindfulness involves learning and practicing various techniques that cultivate present-moment awareness and emotional regulation. Meditation, breathing exercises, and mindful movement are fundamental practices that help offenders manage stress, enhance self-awareness, and develop a greater sense of control over their thoughts and behaviors. Programs that teach these skills have shown significant benefits, helping individuals transform their lives and reduce the likelihood of reoffending. Success stories of individuals who have benefited from mindfulness practices highlight the transformative potential of these techniques. Integrating mindfulness into daily life and fostering a supportive environment are essential for sustaining the benefits of mindfulness and promoting long-term rehabilitation and reintegration. As research continues to demonstrate the effectiveness of mindfulness in reducing recidivism, its role in the justice system will likely continue to expand, offering hope for a more compassionate and rehabilitative approach to justice.

8.3: Benefits of Mindfulness for Offenders

Understanding Right Concentration and its importance in rehabilitation involves recognizing the profound impact of focused attention and mental discipline on personal development and behavioral change. Right Concentration, a core aspect of the Buddhist Eightfold Path, refers to the ability to maintain focused attention and achieve deep states of mental absorption. For offenders, developing these skills is crucial for setting and achieving goals, fostering personal growth, and navigating the complexities of reintegration into society. Techniques for improving concentration and focus, coupled with the integration of mindfulness and concentration practices, play a pivotal role in the rehabilitation process. Right Concentration begins with the cultivation of focused attention, which is the ability to direct the mind towards a single point of focus and sustain that attention over time. This skill is essential for offenders, who often struggle with distractibility, impulsivity, and fragmented thinking. Developing focused attention involves practicing techniques that enhance the mind's ability to concentrate, such as meditation, breathing exercises, and mindfulness practices. These techniques help individuals develop the mental discipline needed to maintain focus and resist distractions.

Meditation is one of the most effective practices for developing Right Concentration. It involves training the mind to focus on a specific object, such as the breath, a mantra, or a visual image, and to sustain that focus without becoming distracted. Through regular meditation practice, individuals learn to cultivate a state of calm and concentrated awareness. This practice not only enhances concentration but also promotes emotional regulation, reduces stress, and fosters a sense of inner peace. For offenders, meditation provides a powerful tool for developing the mental discipline needed to stay focused on their goals and navigate the challenges of rehabilitation. One form of meditation that is particularly effective for developing concentration is "Samatha" or tranquility meditation. Samatha meditation involves focusing on a single object, such as the breath, and developing a deep state of calm and concentration. As individuals become more proficient in this practice, they can achieve deeper states of mental absorption, known as "jhanas," which are characterized by profound tranquility and focused attention. Samatha meditation helps offenders develop the mental discipline needed to maintain focus and resist distractions, which is crucial for achieving personal growth and behavioral change.

Breathing exercises are another essential technique for improving concentration. These exercises involve consciously controlling the breath to create a sense of calm and focus. Deep breathing, also known as diaphragmatic breathing, helps individuals relax and center their attention. By practicing deep breathing regularly, offenders can enhance their ability to concentrate and stay focused on their goals. Another effective breathing technique is "alternate nostril breathing," which involves inhaling through one nostril, holding the breath, and exhaling through the other nostril. This practice helps balance the nervous system, promote mental clarity, and improve concentration. Mindfulness practices also play a crucial role in developing Right Concentration. Mindfulness involves paying attention to the present moment with a non-judgmental attitude, which helps individuals become more aware of their thoughts, emotions, and behaviors. By practicing mindfulness, offenders can develop greater self-awareness and emotional regulation, which are essential for maintaining concentration and achieving their goals. Mindfulness practices such as body scans, mindful walking, and mindful eating help individuals stay present and focused, reducing the tendency to become distracted or overwhelmed.

Programs that teach concentration and focus skills to offenders are designed to be practical and accessible, ensuring that participants can engage with the practices effectively. The "Mindfulness-Based Cognitive Therapy" (MBCT) program is one such initiative that combines mindfulness practices with cognitive-behavioral techniques. MBCT teaches participants how to develop focused attention, manage stress, and regulate their emotions. The program includes guided meditations, breathing exercises, and mindfulness practices, helping offenders cultivate the mental discipline needed for personal growth and rehabilitation. Another successful initiative is the "Focus and Freedom" program, which offers a comprehensive curriculum designed to enhance concentration and focus among incarcerated individuals. The program includes meditation, breathing exercises, and mindfulness practices, as well as cognitive-behavioral techniques for managing stress and improving emotional regulation. Participants learn to develop focused attention, set achievable goals, and create action plans for achieving those goals. The program's impact is evident in the positive changes reported by participants, including improved concentration, reduced stress, and a greater sense of control over their thoughts and behaviors.

Success stories of individuals who have benefited from concentration and focus practices highlight the transformative potential of these techniques. One such story is that of Michael, a former inmate who struggled with impulsivity and a lack of focus. Through the Focus and Freedom program, Michael learned to practice meditation and breathing exercises regularly. These practices helped him develop greater self-discipline and mental clarity, enabling him to stay focused on his rehabilitation goals. Upon his release, Michael continued to practice concentration and focus techniques, which helped him secure stable employment and build a positive, productive life. Another inspiring example is Sarah, who discovered mindfulness meditation while serving a prison sentence. Sarah struggled with anxiety and scattered thinking, which affected her ability to concentrate and make positive decisions. Through the Mindfulness-Based Cognitive Therapy program, she learned to cultivate focused attention and manage her anxiety. The practice of mindfulness meditation helped Sarah develop a sense of calm and inner strength, which was crucial for her personal growth. After her release, Sarah pursued further mindfulness training and became a certified mindfulness instructor. She now teaches mindfulness and concentration techniques to other ex-offenders, helping them navigate their own challenges and achieve their goals.

The integration of mindfulness and concentration practices into daily life is essential for sustaining their benefits. Offenders are encouraged to incorporate these practices into their routines, such as setting aside time for meditation, practicing mindful breathing during stressful moments, or engaging in mindful movement exercises. These practices help reinforce the principles of mindfulness and concentration and make them a natural part of life. For instance, starting the day with a brief meditation can set a positive tone, fostering a sense of calm and focus that carries through the day. Support systems and resources are crucial for maintaining mindfulness and concentration practices. Peer support groups, mentorship programs, and access to mindfulness resources, such as guided meditations and instructional videos, provide ongoing encouragement and guidance. Correctional facilities that offer mindfulness and concentration programs often create support networks where participants can share their experiences, discuss challenges, and celebrate successes. These networks help individuals stay motivated and committed to their practice, fostering a sense of community and mutual support.

Research supports the effectiveness of mindfulness and concentration practices in reducing recidivism. Studies have shown that individuals who participate in mindfulness and concentration programs are less likely to reoffend compared to those who do not. The development of self-awareness, emotional regulation, and mental discipline through these practices contributes to this positive outcome. By addressing the underlying psychological and emotional factors that contribute to criminal behavior, mindfulness and concentration provide powerful tools for rehabilitation and reintegration. The role of mindfulness and concentration in personal growth and rehabilitation extends beyond individual benefits. These practices also contribute to creating a more positive and supportive environment within correctional facilities. Staff who practice mindfulness and concentration can model calm and focused behavior, enhancing their ability to manage challenging situations and communicate effectively with offenders. By promoting mindfulness and concentration among both offenders and staff, correctional facilities can create a culture of mindfulness that benefits the entire community.

8.4: Case Studies of Mindfulness-Based Rehabilitation

Integrating mindfulness into daily life is essential for sustaining its benefits and fostering long-term rehabilitation and personal growth. Offenders need practical strategies for incorporating mindfulness into their everyday routines, role-playing exercises to practice these skills, and robust support systems and resources to maintain their practice. By embedding mindfulness into their daily activities, individuals can develop greater self-awareness, emotional regulation, and resilience, which are crucial for navigating the challenges of reintegration and building stable, productive lives. One effective strategy for integrating mindfulness into daily life is to begin the day with a brief meditation session. Starting the day with mindfulness helps set a positive tone, fostering a sense of calm and focus that can carry through the day. This practice involves finding a quiet space, sitting comfortably, and focusing on the breath for a few minutes. By observing the breath and noticing thoughts and sensations without judgment, individuals can cultivate present-moment awareness and prepare themselves mentally and emotionally for the day ahead.

Mindful breathing can be incorporated into various moments throughout the day, especially during stressful situations. Taking a few deep, conscious breaths can help individuals center themselves and manage their emotions more effectively. This practice is particularly useful in high-stress environments, such as correctional facilities, where individuals may encounter challenging interactions or conflicts. By pausing and focusing on their breath, offenders can respond to these situations with greater calmness and clarity, reducing the likelihood of impulsive or aggressive behavior. Another practical mindfulness strategy is to engage in mindful walking. This practice involves walking slowly and deliberately, paying attention to each step and the sensations of movement. Mindful walking can be done in a designated area, such as a yard or hallway, or integrated into daily routines, such as walking to a meal or an activity. By focusing on the physical sensations of walking and the environment around them, individuals can develop greater awareness and presence, reducing stress and enhancing their overall well-being.

Mindful eating is another way to integrate mindfulness into daily life. This practice involves paying full attention to the experience of eating, savoring each bite, and noticing the tastes, textures, and aromas of the food. By eating mindfully, individuals can develop a greater appreciation for their meals and foster a sense of gratitude. This practice also helps individuals become more attuned to their body's hunger and fullness cues, promoting healthier eating habits. Mindful eating can be particularly beneficial in correctional facilities, where meals are often a structured part of the day, providing regular opportunities for mindfulness practice. Journaling is a powerful tool for integrating mindfulness into daily life. Keeping a mindfulness journal involves writing down thoughts, feelings, and observations about one's experiences. This practice encourages self-reflection and helps individuals track their progress in developing mindfulness skills. By regularly documenting their mindfulness practice, individuals can gain insights into their patterns of thinking and behavior, identify areas for improvement, and celebrate their successes. Journaling can also serve as a therapeutic outlet, providing a space to process emotions and experiences.

Role-playing exercises are an effective way to practice mindfulness skills in a controlled environment. These exercises involve simulating real-life scenarios where mindfulness can be applied, such as dealing with conflict, managing stress, or making decisions. By role-playing these situations, individuals can practice staying present, observing their thoughts and emotions, and responding mindfully. Role-playing helps individuals build confidence in their ability to use mindfulness skills in everyday life and prepares them for real-world challenges. For example, a role-playing exercise might involve a scenario where an individual encounters a stressful situation, such as being confronted by another person. Participants would practice mindful breathing to center themselves, observe their thoughts and emotions without reacting impulsively, and respond with calmness and clarity. Through guided feedback and discussion, individuals can refine their mindfulness skills and develop strategies for applying them in similar situations outside of the role-playing setting.

Support systems and resources are crucial for maintaining a mindfulness practice. Peer support groups provide a platform for individuals to share their experiences, challenges, and successes in practicing mindfulness. These groups offer mutual encouragement and accountability, helping individuals stay committed to their practice. Facilitators guide discussions on topics such as integrating mindfulness into daily life, overcoming obstacles, and celebrating progress. The sense of community and mutual support within peer groups fosters a supportive environment that reinforces the principles of mindfulness. Mentorship programs also play a vital role in supporting mindfulness practice. Mentors, who are often experienced practitioners or individuals who have successfully integrated mindfulness into their lives, provide guidance, advice, and encouragement. Regular check-ins with mentors help individuals stay focused on their mindfulness goals and address any challenges that arise. Mentorship programs create a supportive relationship where individuals can receive personalized feedback and support, enhancing their mindfulness practice.

Access to mindfulness resources, such as guided meditations, instructional videos, and mindfulness apps, provides additional support for maintaining a mindfulness practice. These resources offer structured guidance and variety, helping individuals explore different mindfulness techniques and deepen their practice. Correctional facilities that provide access to mindfulness resources, whether through a library, digital platforms, or group sessions, create an environment that supports ongoing mindfulness practice. Mindfulness retreats and workshops offer opportunities for individuals to immerse themselves in mindfulness practice and deepen their understanding of its principles. These intensive programs provide a focused environment where individuals can practice mindfulness for extended periods, receive instruction from experienced teachers, and connect with other practitioners. Mindfulness retreats and workshops help individuals strengthen their practice and gain new insights and techniques that they can apply in their daily lives.

Success stories of individuals who have integrated mindfulness into their daily lives highlight the transformative potential of these practices. One such story is that of David, a former inmate who discovered mindfulness during his incarceration. David began practicing mindfulness meditation and breathing exercises daily, using these techniques to manage his stress and develop greater self-awareness. After his release, he continued to integrate mindfulness into his routine, practicing mindful walking and journaling regularly. David's commitment to mindfulness helped him build resilience and maintain his focus on his rehabilitation goals. He eventually became a mindfulness teacher, sharing his experience and helping others develop mindfulness skills. Another inspiring example is Maria, who participated in a mindfulness program while serving a prison sentence. Maria struggled with anxiety and impulsivity, which affected her ability to cope with prison life. Through mindfulness practices such as meditation, mindful eating, and journaling, she developed greater emotional regulation and self-awareness. Maria found that mindfulness helped her stay present and manage her anxiety more effectively.

Upon her release, she continued her mindfulness practice and became involved in a peer support group, where she provided encouragement and support to others. Maria's journey demonstrates the lasting impact of integrating mindfulness into daily life and the importance of community support in sustaining the practice. Research supports the effectiveness of integrating mindfulness into daily life in reducing recidivism. Studies have shown that individuals who consistently practice mindfulness are less likely to reoffend compared to those who do not. The development of self-awareness, emotional regulation, and resilience through mindfulness practice contributes to this positive outcome. By addressing the underlying psychological and emotional factors that contribute to criminal behavior, mindfulness provides a powerful tool for long-term rehabilitation and reintegration.

8.5: Sustaining Mindfulness Practices for Long-Term Change

Sustaining mindfulness and concentration practices for ongoing transformation is essential for individuals in the rehabilitation process. The long-term benefits of these practices extend beyond immediate improvements in mental and emotional well-being; they foster profound and lasting changes in behavior, self-perception, and interpersonal relationships. Research and evidence support the effectiveness of mindfulness in reducing recidivism, and numerous programs have successfully integrated mindfulness into rehabilitation efforts, demonstrating its transformative potential. The practice of mindfulness and concentration cultivates self-awareness, allowing individuals to gain insight into their thoughts, emotions, and behaviors. This heightened awareness helps offenders understand the underlying causes of their actions, recognize harmful patterns, and develop healthier responses. By consistently practicing mindfulness, individuals learn to observe their thoughts and emotions without judgment, creating space for reflection and conscious decision-making. This self-awareness is crucial for personal growth, as it enables individuals to identify areas for improvement and take proactive steps towards positive change.

Emotional regulation is another significant benefit of sustained mindfulness practice. Offenders often struggle with intense emotions such as anger, frustration, and anxiety, which can lead to impulsive and destructive behaviors. Mindfulness helps individuals develop the ability to observe and understand their emotions, allowing them to respond rather than react. This emotional regulation is vital for managing stress, reducing aggression, and improving overall mental health. By cultivating a calm and balanced state of mind, individuals can navigate the challenges of daily life more effectively and maintain healthier relationships. The practice of mindfulness also fosters resilience, which is the ability to adapt to and recover from adversity. Resilience is particularly important for individuals in the rehabilitation process, as they often face significant challenges in their journey towards reintegration. Mindfulness practices, such as meditation and mindful breathing, help individuals build inner strength and resilience by promoting a sense of calm and centeredness. This resilience enables individuals to cope with setbacks, remain focused on their goals, and continue making progress despite difficulties.

One of the long-term benefits of mindfulness is its positive impact on physical health. Research has shown that regular mindfulness practice can reduce blood pressure, improve immune function, and decrease symptoms of chronic pain. These health benefits are particularly relevant for offenders, who may experience higher levels of stress and physical ailments due to the conditions of incarceration. By improving physical health, mindfulness contributes to overall well-being and enhances individuals' ability to engage in rehabilitative activities and pursue their goals. The integration of mindfulness into daily routines is essential for sustaining its benefits. Establishing a regular practice helps individuals develop consistency and discipline, which are crucial for long-term success. For example, setting aside specific times each day for meditation or mindful breathing creates a structured approach to mindfulness. Consistency in practice reinforces the principles of mindfulness and makes it a natural part of life. Additionally, incorporating mindfulness into daily activities, such as eating, walking, and interacting with others, helps individuals stay present and engaged in the moment.

Support systems and resources play a critical role in sustaining mindfulness practices. Peer support groups, mentorship programs, and access to mindfulness resources provide ongoing encouragement and guidance. These support networks help individuals stay motivated, address challenges, and celebrate progress. For example, peer support groups offer a platform for individuals to share their experiences, discuss obstacles, and receive feedback. The sense of community and mutual support within these groups reinforces the commitment to mindfulness practice and fosters a supportive environment for personal growth. Mentorship programs connect individuals with experienced practitioners who provide personalized guidance and support. Mentors help individuals set mindfulness goals, develop action plans, and navigate challenges. Regular check-ins with mentors provide accountability and encouragement, helping individuals stay focused on their practice. The mentor-mentee relationship creates a supportive space for individuals to explore their mindfulness journey and receive constructive feedback. This personalized support is crucial for sustaining mindfulness practices and achieving long-term transformation.

Access to mindfulness resources, such as guided meditations, instructional videos, and mindfulness apps, enhances individuals' ability to sustain their practice. These resources offer structured guidance, variety, and convenience, making it easier for individuals to integrate mindfulness into their daily lives. Correctional facilities that provide access to mindfulness resources create an environment that supports ongoing practice and encourages individuals to continue their mindfulness journey. For example, providing access to a library of mindfulness books, audio recordings, and online courses can offer valuable support and inspiration. Mindfulness retreats and workshops offer intensive opportunities for individuals to deepen their practice and gain new insights. These immersive experiences provide a focused environment where individuals can practice mindfulness for extended periods, receive instruction from experienced teachers, and connect with other practitioners. Mindfulness retreats and workshops help individuals strengthen their practice, explore advanced techniques, and gain a deeper understanding of mindfulness principles. The insights and skills gained from these experiences can be integrated into daily practice, enhancing the long-term benefits of mindfulness.

Research supports the effectiveness of mindfulness in reducing recidivism and promoting long-term rehabilitation. Studies have shown that individuals who participate in mindfulness programs are less likely to reoffend compared to those who do not. The development of self-awareness, emotional regulation, and resilience through mindfulness practice contributes to this positive outcome. By addressing the underlying psychological and emotional factors that contribute to criminal behavior, mindfulness provides a powerful tool for rehabilitation and reintegration. One notable study conducted by the University of Washington examined the impact of mindfulness-based programs on incarcerated individuals. The study found that participants who engaged in regular mindfulness practice experienced significant reductions in stress, anxiety, and depression. Additionally, these individuals demonstrated improved emotional regulation, greater self-awareness, and enhanced coping skills. The study concluded that mindfulness programs are effective in promoting mental and emotional well-being, which are crucial for successful rehabilitation and reintegration.

Another study conducted by the University of Massachusetts Medical School explored the long-term benefits of mindfulness-based stress reduction (MBSR) programs for ex-offenders. The study followed participants for several years after their release and found that those who continued to practice mindfulness experienced lower rates of recidivism, improved physical health, and better social functioning. The researchers concluded that sustained mindfulness practice contributes to long-term positive outcomes and supports successful reintegration into society. Numerous programs have successfully integrated mindfulness into rehabilitation efforts, demonstrating its transformative potential. One such program is the "Mindfulness-Based Substance Abuse Treatment" (MBSAT) program, which combines mindfulness practices with substance abuse treatment. MBSAT teaches individuals how to use mindfulness to manage cravings, reduce stress, and develop healthier coping strategies. The program has shown significant success in helping individuals overcome substance abuse and maintain sobriety. Participants report feeling more in control of their emotions and better equipped to handle the challenges of recovery.

The "Mindfulness-Based Relapse Prevention" (MBRP) program is another example of a successful mindfulness initiative. MBRP combines mindfulness practices with cognitive-behavioral techniques to help individuals prevent relapse and maintain their recovery. The program teaches participants how to use mindfulness to observe and understand their triggers, develop coping strategies, and respond to cravings with greater awareness. MBRP has demonstrated significant benefits in reducing relapse rates and supporting long-term recovery. Participants report feeling more resilient and better able to navigate the challenges of maintaining sobriety. The "Mindfulness-Oriented Recovery Enhancement" (MORE) program is designed to help individuals overcome addiction and improve their overall well-being. MORE combines mindfulness practices with positive psychology and cognitive-behavioral therapy to promote recovery and personal growth. The program teaches individuals how to use mindfulness to manage stress, enhance positive emotions, and develop a sense of purpose. MORE has shown significant success in helping individuals achieve and maintain recovery, improve their mental health, and enhance their quality of life.

References

- Apanovitch, D. P. (1998). Religion and Rehabilitation: The Requisition of God by the State. Duke Law Journal, 47(4), 785–852. https://doi.org/10.2307/1372913
- Ashitsu, Z. (1894). THE FUNDAMENTAL TEACHINGS OF BUDDHISM. The Monist, 4(2), 163–175. http://www.jstor.org/stable/27897133
- ATAR, E. (2022). [Review of A Practical Guide for Policy Analysis: The Eightfold Path to More Effective Problem Solving, by E. BARDACH & E. M. PATASHNIK]. Uluslararası İlişkiler / International Relations, 19(74), 99–100. https://www.jstor.org/stable/27130880
- Bastow, D. (1988). An Example of Self-Change: The Buddhist Path. Religious Studies, 24(2), 157–172. http://www.jstor.org/stable/20019274

- Dr. Kalsang Wangmo. (2011). Middle Path and Universal responsibility – A Buddhist perspective. The Tibet Journal, 36(4), 3–17. http://www.jstor.org/stable/tibetjournal.36.4.3
- Frankfurter, O. (1880). Buddhist Nirvāna, and the Noble Eightfold Path. Journal of the Royal Asiatic Society of Great Britain and Ireland, 12(4), 548–574. http://www.jstor.org/stable/25196863
- Gombrich, R. (2010). The Buddha's thought. Revue Internationale de Philosophie, 64(253 (3)), 315–339. http://www.jstor.org/stable/23961182
- Harrison, P. (1987). Buddhism: A Religion of Revelation after All? [Review of À propos Peter Masefield's "Divine Revelation in Pali Buddhism," by P. Masefield]. Numen, 34(2), 256–264. https://doi.org/10.2307/3270087
- Inada, K. K. (1971). Whitehead's "Actual Entity" and the Buddha's Anātman. Philosophy East and West, 21(3), 303–316. https://doi.org/10.2307/1398358
- Inada, K. K. (1975). Munitz' Concept of the World... A Buddhist Response. Philosophy East and West, 25(3), 309–317. https://doi.org/10.2307/1398201
- Jenkins, S. (2016). DEBATE, MAGIC, AND MASSACRE: THE HIGH STAKES AND ETHICAL DYNAMICS OF BATTLING SLANDERERS OF THE DHARMA IN INDIAN NARRATIVE AND ETHICAL THEORY. Journal of Religion and Violence, 4(2), 129–158. https://www.jstor.org/stable/26671496
- Kalupahana, D. J. (1979). The Early Buddhist Notion of the Middle Path. The Eastern Buddhist, 12(1), 30–48. http://www.jstor.org/stable/44361526
- Kevin, C. S. K. (2000). An evangelical engagement with Mahāyāna Buddhist ethics. Transformation, 17(3), 109–112. http://www.jstor.org/stable/43070253
- Kitagawa, J. M. (1965). The Buddhist Transformation in Japan. History of Religions, 4(2), 319–336. http://www.jstor.org/stable/1061962
- Law, B. C. (1947). AŚVAGHOṢA'S PHILOSOPHY. Annals of the Bhandarkar Oriental Research Institute, 28(3/4), 289–293. http://www.jstor.org/stable/44028070
- LAW, B. C. (1968). A BRIEF SURVEY OF BUDDHIST DOCTRINE AND PHILOSOPHY. Annals of the Bhandarkar Oriental Research Institute, 48/49, 203–218. http://www.jstor.org/stable/41694241

- Leve, L. G. (2002). Subjects, Selves, and the Politics of Personhood in Theravada Buddhism in Nepal. The Journal of Asian Studies, 61(3), 833–860. https://doi.org/10.2307/3096348
- Luévano, R. (2009). Catholic Discernment with a View of Buddhist Internal Clarity. Buddhist-Christian Studies, 29, 39–51. http://www.jstor.org/stable/40864804
- McGovern, Wm. M. (1919). NOTES ON MAHAYANA BUDDHISM. The Monist, 29(2), 238–258. http://www.jstor.org/stable/27900739
- McRae, E. (2015). BUDDHIST THERAPIES OF THE EMOTIONS AND THE PSYCHOLOGY OF MORAL IMPROVEMENT. History of Philosophy Quarterly, 32(2), 101–122. http://www.jstor.org/stable/43488928
- Mills, E. (2007). [Review of Buddhism, Knowledge and Liberation: A Philosophical Study, by D. Burton]. Philosophy East and West, 57(4), 593–595. http://www.jstor.org/stable/20109433
- Nguyen, D. M. (2020). Unburdening the Heart: Urban Therapeutic Buddhism and Youth Well-Being in Hồ Chí Minh City. Journal of Vietnamese Studies, 15(4), 63–98. https://www.jstor.org/stable/48740363
- Phillips, R. E., Oemig, C., Vonnegut, E., Cheng, C. M., & Hietbrink, L. (2012). Validation of a Buddhist Coping Measure Among Primarily Non-Asian Buddhists in the United States. Journal for the Scientific Study of Religion, 51(1), 156–172. http://www.jstor.org/stable/41349934
- Phan, P. C. (2006). Global Healing and Reconciliation: The Gift and Task of Religion, a Buddhist-Christian Perspective. Buddhist-Christian Studies, 26, 89–108. http://www.jstor.org/stable/4139183
- Porter, K. (2004). Who We Really Are: Buddhist Approaches to Psychotherapy and Group Psychotherapy. Group, 28(4), 53–69. http://www.jstor.org/stable/41719066
- Reat, N. R. (1977). Karma and Rebirth in the Upaniṣads and Buddhism. Numen, 24(3), 163–185. https://doi.org/10.2307/3269597
- Sarvan, C. P., & Balles, P. (1994). BUDDHISM, HINDUISM, AND THE CONRADIAN DARKNESS. Conradiana, 26(1), 70–75. http://www.jstor.org/stable/24634818
- SEN, P. (1986). [Review of Selfless Persons: Imagery and Thought in Theravada Buddhism, by S. Collins]. Journal of Indian Philosophy, 14(1), 99–106. http://www.jstor.org/stable/23444166

- Yusa, M. (2009). [Review of Asura's Harp: Engagement with Language as Buddhist Path, by D. Hirota]. Philosophy East and West, 59(3), 382–385. http://www.jstor.org/stable/40469135

Part III: The Bodhisattva Ideal in Justice

—

CHAPTER NINE

Understanding the Bodhisattva Ideal

Contents

- Introduction to the Bodhisattva Path

- Relevance to Modern Justice Systems

- Encouraging Compassionate Action

- Practical Applications in Mediation

- Case Studies of the Bodhisattva Ideal in Practice

9.1: Introduction to the Bodhisattva Path

The Bodhisattva path in Tibetan Buddhism embodies the journey of selflessness, compassion, and altruistic commitment to the welfare of others. This path is characterized by the aspiration to attain enlightenment, not solely for oneself but for the liberation of all sentient beings. Central to this ideal are the virtues of boundless compassion, wisdom, and a deep sense of interconnectedness with all life. The Bodhisattva vows to forgo personal nirvana until every being is freed from suffering, a testament to the ultimate selflessness and dedication that defines this spiritual journey. In the rich tapestry of Tibetan Buddhism, the Bodhisattva path is illuminated by the teachings and lives of numerous revered figures. Among these, Avalokiteshvara stands out as a paragon of compassion. This celestial Bodhisattva, often depicted with multiple arms and heads, symbolizes the boundless nature of compassion, reaching out in all directions to alleviate suffering. Avalokiteshvara's mantra, "Om Mani Padme Hum," echoes the essence of this compassion, inviting practitioners to cultivate and embody this virtue in their own lives.

Another seminal figure is Manjushri, the Bodhisattva of Wisdom. Manjushri wields a flaming sword that cuts through ignorance and delusion, symbolizing the clarity and insight that are essential on the Bodhisattva path. Wisdom, in this context, is not merely intellectual knowledge but a profound understanding of the nature of reality, characterized by the principle of emptiness (Shunyata). This wisdom is inseparable from compassion, guiding the Bodhisattva in skillful actions that alleviate suffering without attachment or self-interest. The historical Buddha, Siddhartha Gautama, is often revered as the first Bodhisattva. Before attaining Buddhahood, he exemplified the Bodhisattva ideal through countless lifetimes of altruistic deeds and relentless pursuit of wisdom. His journey from prince to enlightened teacher is a testament to the transformative power of the Bodhisattva path, demonstrating that anyone, regardless of their starting point, can cultivate these virtues and work towards the enlightenment of all beings.

In contemporary contexts, the Dalai Lama embodies the Bodhisattva ideals in his teachings and actions. As a living example of compassion and wisdom, the Dalai Lama advocates for peace, non-violence, and universal responsibility. His tireless efforts to promote human values, interfaith dialogue, and environmental sustainability reflect the Bodhisattva's commitment to addressing the root causes of suffering in modern society. Through his life and work, the Dalai Lama demonstrates how the principles of the Bodhisattva path can be applied to contemporary global challenges. The Bodhisattva path is not confined to historical or mythological figures. Ordinary individuals can also embark on this journey by cultivating the Six Perfections (Paramitas): generosity, ethics, patience, joyous effort, concentration, and wisdom. These perfections provide a practical framework for daily life, guiding practitioners in their efforts to benefit others while progressing on their own spiritual path.

Generosity involves giving without attachment, ethics encompasses moral discipline and integrity, patience requires tolerance and understanding, joyous effort denotes enthusiastic perseverance, concentration refers to focused meditation, and wisdom involves the deep understanding of reality.

In practical terms, the Bodhisattva path can be integrated into various aspects of life, including professions such as law, education, healthcare, and social work. For example, a teacher inspired by Bodhisattva ideals might strive to create an inclusive and compassionate classroom environment, fostering the holistic development of their students. A lawyer could work towards justice and equality, ensuring that marginalized voices are heard and respected. A healthcare professional might approach their patients with empathy and care, addressing not only physical ailments but also emotional and psychological well-being. The essence of the Bodhisattva path is the transformation of self-centeredness into selflessness, ignorance into wisdom, and suffering into compassion. This transformation is both an individual and collective endeavor, recognizing that personal enlightenment is intrinsically linked to the liberation of all beings. As practitioners progress on this path, they develop a deep sense of interconnectedness and responsibility, understanding that their actions have far-reaching impacts on the world around them.

To walk the Bodhisattva path is to commit to a lifelong journey of growth, service, and inner cultivation. It is a path that challenges individuals to look beyond their own needs and desires, embracing a broader vision of collective well-being. Through the cultivation of compassion and wisdom, the Bodhisattva not only alleviates suffering but also inspires others to embark on their own journeys of transformation. This path, though arduous, is ultimately one of profound fulfillment and joy, rooted in the boundless love and compassion that lie at the heart of Tibetan Buddhism. The Bodhisattva path offers a powerful paradigm for personal and social transformation. It calls for a deep and enduring commitment to the welfare of others, challenging individuals to cultivate the virtues of compassion, wisdom, and altruism. Whether through grand gestures or small acts of kindness, the Bodhisattva's journey is marked by an unwavering dedication to alleviating suffering and promoting the flourishing of all beings. This path, illuminated by the teachings and examples of countless Bodhisattvas, provides a timeless and universal guide for those seeking to make a positive difference in the world.

9.2: Relevance to Modern Justice Systems

The Bodhisattva ideal, with its emphasis on selflessness, compassion, and the commitment to alleviating the suffering of all beings, finds profound relevance in the realm of justice. This ancient Buddhist principle aligns remarkably well with contemporary restorative justice approaches, which prioritize healing, rehabilitation, and the restoration of relationships over punitive measures. Integrating the Bodhisattva ideal into modern justice systems can transform them from institutions of punishment to arenas of profound human transformation. In the context of justice, the Bodhisattva ideal offers a radical shift from retribution to rehabilitation. Traditional justice systems often focus on punishment as a means of deterrence and retribution, emphasizing the need to exact a penalty proportionate to the crime. This approach, while addressing the need for accountability, often neglects the underlying causes of criminal behavior and fails to foster genuine rehabilitation. The Bodhisattva ideal, by contrast, emphasizes understanding the root causes of suffering and addressing them with compassion and wisdom. This shift in perspective aligns with restorative justice, which seeks to heal the harm caused by crime through reconciliation, restitution, and the reintegration of offenders into society.

The Bodhisattva's commitment to alleviating suffering resonates deeply with the goals of restorative justice. In restorative practices, the focus is on the needs of the victims, the offenders, and the community. Offenders are encouraged to take responsibility for their actions, make amends, and engage in processes that promote healing for all parties involved. This approach mirrors the Bodhisattva's path, where compassion and empathy guide actions aimed at reducing suffering and fostering well-being. By incorporating these principles, justice systems can move towards more humane and effective methods of addressing crime. Selflessness, a core tenet of the Bodhisattva ideal, is particularly relevant in the justice system. Justice professionals, including judges, lawyers, and correctional officers, are often in positions of power and influence. The Bodhisattva ideal encourages these professionals to approach their roles with humility and a genuine desire to serve others. This perspective can lead to more compassionate and fair decision-making, where the needs and circumstances of all parties are considered. For instance, a judge influenced by the Bodhisattva ideal might prioritize rehabilitation and restorative measures over punitive sentences, recognizing that such approaches are more likely to lead to positive long-term outcomes for both offenders and society.

Compassion, another fundamental aspect of the Bodhisattva path, plays a crucial role in justice reform. Incarcerated individuals often face significant challenges, including mental health issues, substance abuse, and histories of trauma. A justice system informed by the Bodhisattva ideal would emphasize compassionate responses to these challenges, offering support and rehabilitation rather than punishment alone. Programs that provide mental health care, addiction treatment, and trauma-informed practices can help address the root causes of criminal behavior, facilitating genuine transformation and reducing recidivism. The relevance of the Bodhisattva ideal in justice also extends to the community. Restorative justice practices often involve community members in the process of healing and reconciliation. This inclusive approach fosters a sense of collective responsibility and interconnectedness, echoing the Bodhisattva's understanding of the interdependent nature of all beings. By engaging the community in the justice process, these practices help build stronger, more cohesive communities where individuals feel valued and supported.

Comparatively, the Bodhisattva ideal offers a unique perspective that complements other justice philosophies. While retributive justice focuses on punishment and deterrence, and rehabilitative justice emphasizes reform and reintegration, the Bodhisattva ideal integrates these elements with a profound commitment to compassion and selflessness. This holistic approach addresses the limitations of conventional justice systems, offering a path towards more effective and humane responses to crime. For instance, in the realm of youth justice, the Bodhisattva ideal can inspire practices that focus on the holistic development of young offenders. Programs that combine education, mentorship, and therapeutic support can help young people develop the skills and resilience needed to lead productive lives. This approach not only addresses the immediate behavior but also fosters long-term positive outcomes, reflecting the Bodhisattva's commitment to alleviating suffering and promoting well-being.

The Bodhisattva ideal also aligns with the principles of transformative justice, which seeks to address systemic issues and promote broader social change. Transformative justice goes beyond individual cases to examine the social, economic, and political factors that contribute to crime. By addressing these root causes, transformative justice aims to create a more just and equitable society. The Bodhisattva's commitment to compassion and altruism supports this broader vision, advocating for systemic changes that reduce suffering and promote collective well-being. Implementing the Bodhisattva ideal in modern criminology involves developing strategies that incorporate compassion and selflessness into every aspect of the justice process. This could include training programs for justice professionals that emphasize emotional intelligence, empathy, and ethical decision-making.

Such training would equip professionals with the skills needed to approach their work with compassion and a focus on rehabilitation. Additionally, policies that prioritize restorative and rehabilitative measures over punitive ones can help create a justice system that aligns with the Bodhisattva ideal. Challenges in integrating the Bodhisattva ideal into justice systems are inevitable, given the entrenched nature of punitive approaches and societal attitudes towards crime and punishment. However, these challenges can be addressed through education, advocacy, and the demonstration of successful models of restorative and compassionate justice. Pilot programs that showcase the effectiveness of Bodhisattva-inspired practices can provide valuable evidence and build support for broader implementation.

9.3: Encouraging Compassionate Action

The role of compassion and altruism within the Bodhisattva path is pivotal, embodying the core tenets of selflessness and dedication to the welfare of others. These principles offer transformative potential in justice systems, particularly when applied to rehabilitation and restorative practices. Compassion, in this context, involves understanding and empathizing with the suffering of offenders and victims alike, while altruism denotes actions taken to alleviate that suffering without expecting personal gain. Practical applications of these principles can reshape justice practices, promoting healing and reintegration over punishment and isolation. Compassion in the Bodhisattva path is not merely an emotional response but a profound commitment to alleviate suffering wherever it is found. This involves cultivating a deep understanding of the conditions that lead to suffering and addressing them at their root. In the context of justice, this means looking beyond the criminal act to understand the social, psychological, and economic factors that contribute to criminal behavior. By addressing these underlying issues, justice systems can help offenders transform their lives and reduce recidivism.

One practical application of compassion in justice settings is the implementation of therapeutic jurisprudence, which focuses on the therapeutic or anti-therapeutic consequences of legal processes and laws. This approach seeks to use the law as a therapeutic agent, aiming to produce positive psychological effects for all parties involved. For example, mental health courts specifically address cases involving individuals with mental health issues, providing treatment and support rather than conventional punitive measures. These courts embody the Bodhisattva ideal by recognizing the suffering of individuals and seeking to alleviate it through compassionate and tailored interventions. Another application is trauma-informed care, which acknowledges the pervasive impact of trauma on individuals' lives and behaviors. This approach is particularly relevant in justice settings, where many offenders have experienced significant trauma. Trauma-informed care involves creating environments that are physically and emotionally safe, providing support that acknowledges the impact of trauma, and fostering resilience and recovery. Correctional facilities that implement trauma-informed practices can better address the needs of offenders, reducing re-traumatization and promoting healing. This compassionate approach aligns with the Bodhisattva's commitment to alleviating suffering and fostering well-being.

Restorative justice practices also reflect the principles of compassion and altruism. These practices involve bringing together offenders, victims, and community members to discuss the harm caused by criminal behavior and find ways to repair it. Restorative justice emphasizes accountability, making amends, and reintegrating offenders into the community. By focusing on the needs of all parties involved, restorative justice seeks to heal relationships and build stronger, more cohesive communities. Programs like restorative circles and victim-offender mediation create spaces for open dialogue, empathy, and mutual understanding, embodying the Bodhisattva's compassionate approach to resolving conflict. Altruism, the selfless concern for the well-being of others, is another cornerstone of the Bodhisattva path that can be integrated into justice practices. Encouraging offenders to engage in altruistic behaviors can be a powerful tool for rehabilitation. Community service programs, for example, provide offenders with opportunities to give back to their communities and make positive contributions. These programs not only benefit the community but also help offenders develop a sense of purpose and connection, fostering personal growth and reducing the likelihood of reoffending.

One notable example is the "Inside-Out Prison Exchange Program," which brings together incarcerated individuals and university students for a semester-long course held inside prison walls. This program fosters mutual understanding, challenges stereotypes, and encourages altruistic behavior through collaborative learning and dialogue. Offenders who participate in the program often report increased self-esteem, empathy, and a greater sense of responsibility towards their communities. By promoting educational and altruistic engagement, the Inside-Out program aligns with the Bodhisattva ideal of working for the welfare of all beings. Mentorship programs also play a crucial role in promoting altruism among offenders. These programs connect offenders with mentors who provide guidance, support, and positive role models. Mentors often come from similar backgrounds or have overcome similar challenges, offering relatable insights and encouragement. By fostering supportive relationships, mentorship programs help offenders develop the skills and confidence needed to navigate their rehabilitation journey. This altruistic approach not only benefits the mentees but also enriches the mentors, who gain a sense of fulfillment from helping others.

Peer support initiatives within correctional facilities can further promote altruism and mutual aid. Programs like peer counseling, where trained inmates provide emotional and practical support to their peers, create a culture of solidarity and empathy. These initiatives empower offenders to take on altruistic roles, contributing to the well-being of their community while developing leadership and communication skills. The sense of purpose and connection fostered by peer support programs can significantly enhance the rehabilitation process and reduce recidivism. Educational programs that incorporate the principles of compassion and altruism can also have a transformative impact. Courses on emotional intelligence, conflict resolution, and ethical decision-making provide offenders with the tools to understand and manage their emotions, navigate interpersonal conflicts, and make more compassionate choices. These educational initiatives align with the Bodhisattva ideal by fostering personal development and encouraging actions that benefit others.

For example, the "Peace Education Program" developed by The Prem Rawat Foundation offers courses that explore themes such as peace, dignity, and appreciation. This program, implemented in various correctional facilities worldwide, encourages participants to reflect on their values and develop a deeper sense of inner peace and compassion. By promoting self-awareness and altruistic values, the Peace Education Program helps offenders build the foundation for a more constructive and harmonious life. Incorporating the Bodhisattva principles into probation and parole practices can further enhance the rehabilitation process. Probation and parole officers who adopt a compassionate and supportive approach, rather than a solely supervisory one, can better assist offenders in their reintegration efforts. This might involve connecting individuals with community resources, providing guidance on employment and education, and offering emotional support. By fostering a supportive relationship, officers can help reduce recidivism and promote long-term success.

The development of compassionate and altruistic practices in justice systems also requires systemic changes. Policies that prioritize rehabilitation over punishment, allocate resources for mental health and addiction treatment, and support restorative justice initiatives are essential. These systemic changes reflect the Bodhisattva's commitment to creating conditions that alleviate suffering and promote collective well-being. Advocacy for such policies, informed by the principles of compassion and altruism, can drive meaningful reform in justice systems worldwide. Research on the effectiveness of compassionate and altruistic practices in justice settings supports their transformative potential. Studies have shown that restorative justice programs, trauma-informed care, and educational initiatives that promote emotional intelligence and ethical decision-making lead to better outcomes for offenders and communities. These practices reduce recidivism, improve mental health, and foster stronger social bonds, demonstrating the benefits of integrating the Bodhisattva principles into justice systems.

9.4: Practical Applications in Mediation

The Bodhisattva ideal, emphasizing compassion, wisdom, and selflessness, finds embodiment in various historical and modern figures in the justice realm. These Bodhisattva-like figures, through their actions and philosophies, have significantly impacted justice reform and demonstrated how compassion and altruism can transform justice systems. By examining their contributions, we can glean valuable insights into how these principles can be effectively integrated into contemporary justice practices. One historical figure who exemplified the Bodhisattva ideals in justice is Ashoka the Great, an ancient Indian emperor. After witnessing the devastating effects of his military campaigns, Ashoka underwent a profound transformation. He embraced Buddhism and the Bodhisattva path, dedicating himself to the welfare of his people and promoting non-violence, compassion, and social justice. Ashoka's reign is marked by his efforts to implement policies that reflected these values. He established hospitals, veterinary clinics, and social welfare programs, emphasizing the importance of compassion and care for all beings. Ashoka's edicts, inscribed on pillars and rocks throughout his empire, advocate for ethical conduct, non-violence, and the humane treatment of all creatures, serving as a lasting testament to his commitment to the Bodhisattva ideals in governance and justice.

Moving to more recent times, we find Eleanor Roosevelt, a figure whose contributions to human rights and social justice resonate with the Bodhisattva ideals. As the First Lady of the United States and later as a diplomat and activist, Eleanor Roosevelt championed the cause of human rights and worked tirelessly to alleviate suffering. Her role in drafting the Universal Declaration of Human Rights (UDHR) exemplifies her commitment to promoting compassion and justice on a global scale. The UDHR, adopted by the United Nations in 1948, sets forth fundamental human rights that all individuals are entitled to, regardless of their circumstances. Roosevelt's advocacy for the rights of the marginalized, her efforts to combat racial discrimination, and her dedication to social welfare reflect the Bodhisattva's selfless commitment to the well-being of all beings. In the modern era, Bryan Stevenson, an American lawyer and social justice activist, embodies the Bodhisattva ideals in his work. As the founder of the Equal Justice Initiative (EJI), Stevenson has dedicated his career to challenging racial and economic injustice and defending the rights of the marginalized. His efforts to address wrongful convictions, excessive punishment, and racial discrimination within the criminal justice system highlight his commitment to compassion and justice. Stevenson's work with EJI includes providing legal representation to individuals who have been wrongfully convicted, advocating for policy reforms, and raising public awareness about the systemic issues within the justice system. His belief in the power of proximity – the idea that being close to those who suffer helps foster empathy and drive meaningful change – aligns closely with the Bodhisattva's compassionate approach to alleviating suffering.

Another contemporary figure who exemplifies the Bodhisattva ideals is Thich Nhat Hanh, a Vietnamese Buddhist monk and peace activist. Although not directly involved in formal justice systems, his teachings on mindfulness, compassion, and peace have profoundly influenced approaches to justice and conflict resolution. Thich Nhat Hanh's concept of "Engaged Buddhism" encourages individuals to apply Buddhist principles in social, political, and environmental issues, advocating for justice and peace through non-violent means. His establishment of the Plum Village monastic community in France provides a living example of a compassionate and mindful society. Thich Nhat Hanh's influence extends to various restorative justice practices, where his teachings on deep listening, empathy, and reconciliation have been integrated into conflict resolution and healing processes. In the realm of criminal justice reform, Sister Helen Prejean stands out as a modern Bodhisattva-like figure. Known for her advocacy against the death penalty, Sister Helen has dedicated her life to supporting death row inmates and their families, promoting restorative justice, and advocating for the abolition of capital punishment. Her book, "Dead Man Walking," and its subsequent film adaptation brought widespread attention to the ethical and moral issues surrounding the death penalty. Sister Helen's compassionate approach, focusing on the humanity of each individual and the potential for redemption, reflects the Bodhisattva's commitment to alleviating suffering and promoting justice. Her efforts have not only provided comfort and support to those on death row but have also sparked significant public and legal debates about the morality and efficacy of capital punishment.

In the field of youth justice, Geoffrey Canada has made significant contributions that align with the Bodhisattva ideals. As the founder of the Harlem Children's Zone (HCZ), Canada has worked tirelessly to provide comprehensive support to children and families in one of New York City's most underprivileged neighborhoods. HCZ's programs address education, health, and social services, aiming to break the cycle of poverty and give young people the tools they need to succeed. Canada's holistic approach, focusing on the well-being of the whole community, reflects the Bodhisattva's commitment to creating conditions that reduce suffering and promote collective well-being. His efforts have demonstrated the transformative potential of compassion and altruism in addressing systemic social issues and promoting justice. In the context of environmental justice, Wangari Maathai, a Kenyan environmentalist and political activist, embodies the Bodhisattva ideals through her work. As the founder of the Green Belt Movement, Maathai promoted environmental conservation, women's rights, and sustainable development. Her efforts to combat deforestation, empower communities, and advocate for sustainable environmental practices reflect a deep commitment to the welfare of both people and the planet. Maathai's work earned her the Nobel Peace Prize in 2004, highlighting the global impact of her compassionate and altruistic efforts. Her belief in the interconnectedness of environmental sustainability, social justice, and human rights aligns closely with the Bodhisattva's understanding of the interdependent nature of all beings.

These historical and modern examples of Bodhisattva-like figures in justice demonstrate the profound impact that compassion and altruism can have on justice systems and society as a whole. By embodying the Bodhisattva ideals, these individuals have addressed systemic issues, promoted healing and reconciliation, and worked tirelessly to alleviate suffering. Their contributions provide valuable insights into how these principles can be effectively integrated into contemporary justice practices, fostering a more humane and compassionate approach to justice. Integrating the Bodhisattva ideal in modern criminology involves developing strategies that incorporate compassion and selflessness into every aspect of the justice process. This could include training programs for justice professionals that emphasize emotional intelligence, empathy, and ethical decision-making. Such training would equip professionals with the skills needed to approach their work with compassion and a focus on rehabilitation. Additionally, policies that prioritize restorative and rehabilitative measures over punitive ones can help create a justice system that aligns with the Bodhisattva ideal.

Challenges in integrating the Bodhisattva ideal into justice systems are inevitable, given the entrenched nature of punitive approaches and societal attitudes towards crime and punishment. However, these challenges can be addressed through education, advocacy, and the demonstration of successful models of restorative and compassionate justice. Pilot programs that showcase the effectiveness of Bodhisattva-inspired practices can provide valuable evidence and build support for broader implementation. The Bodhisattva ideal offers a transformative perspective for modern justice systems, emphasizing selflessness, compassion, and a commitment to alleviating suffering. By aligning justice practices with these principles, we can move towards a more humane and effective system that prioritizes healing, rehabilitation, and the restoration of relationships. This approach not only benefits offenders but also victims and the broader community, fostering a more just and compassionate society. The integration of the Bodhisattva ideal into justice reform holds the potential for profound and lasting change, guiding us towards a future where justice is synonymous with compassion and collective well-being.

9.5: Case Studies of the Bodhisattva Ideal in Practice

Integrating the Bodhisattva ideal into modern criminology involves a transformative approach that incorporates the principles of compassion, wisdom, and altruism into every aspect of the justice system. This integration calls for innovative strategies, policy recommendations, and practical applications that address the root causes of criminal behavior, promote rehabilitation, and foster a more humane and effective justice system. By aligning criminological practices with the Bodhisattva ideal, we can create a justice system that not only addresses crime but also promotes healing, restoration, and collective well-being. One of the key strategies for integrating the Bodhisattva ideal into modern criminology is to develop training programs for justice professionals that emphasize emotional intelligence, empathy, and ethical decision-making. These training programs should be designed to equip judges, lawyers, correctional officers, and other justice professionals with the skills needed to approach their work with compassion and a focus on rehabilitation. For instance, training sessions could include modules on active listening, non-violent communication, and mindfulness practices. By fostering these skills, justice professionals can create a more supportive and understanding environment for offenders, victims, and the community.

Another crucial strategy is to implement restorative justice practices that align with the principles of the Bodhisattva ideal. Restorative justice focuses on repairing the harm caused by criminal behavior through inclusive processes that involve offenders, victims, and community members. Programs such as restorative circles, victim-offender mediation, and community conferencing provide opportunities for dialogue, accountability, and healing. These practices emphasize empathy, understanding, and the restoration of relationships, reflecting the Bodhisattva's commitment to alleviating suffering and promoting well-being. For example, restorative circles bring together offenders, victims, and community members in a facilitated dialogue to discuss the impact of the crime and explore ways to repair the harm. This process allows offenders to take responsibility for their actions, understand the impact on the victims, and work towards making amends. Victims have the opportunity to express their feelings, ask questions, and receive support. Community members can provide insights, offer support, and help reintegrate the offender into society. By focusing on healing and restoration, restorative circles embody the Bodhisattva's compassionate approach to justice.

Policy recommendations for justice systems based on Bodhisattva principles include prioritizing rehabilitation and restorative measures over punitive ones. This involves re-evaluating sentencing guidelines to incorporate alternatives to incarceration, such as community service, probation, and restorative justice programs. Policies should also support the development of comprehensive rehabilitation programs that address the underlying causes of criminal behavior, such as mental health issues, substance abuse, and socio-economic factors. By providing offenders with the resources and support they need to change their behavior, justice systems can promote long-term positive outcomes and reduce recidivism. One practical example of this approach is the "HOPE Probation" program in Hawaii, which emphasizes swift, certain, and fair responses to probation violations. The program provides immediate, but proportionate, consequences for violations, coupled with support services such as substance abuse treatment and counseling. This approach reflects the Bodhisattva's balance of compassion and accountability, helping offenders address their issues while maintaining community safety. The program has shown significant success in reducing recidivism and improving compliance with probation conditions.

Integrating the Bodhisattva ideal into criminology also involves addressing systemic issues that contribute to criminal behavior. This includes advocating for social justice and equity, as well as addressing socio-economic disparities, discrimination, and other forms of systemic injustice. Policies that promote access to education, employment opportunities, healthcare, and affordable housing can help create the conditions for individuals to lead stable and productive lives, reducing the likelihood of criminal behavior. By addressing these root causes, justice systems can work towards creating a more just and equitable society, in line with the Bodhisattva's commitment to collective well-being. Community involvement and partnerships are essential for the successful integration of Bodhisattva principles into modern criminology. Collaboration with community organizations, non-profits, businesses, and other stakeholders can provide the resources and support needed for effective rehabilitation and reintegration programs. For instance, partnerships with local businesses can create employment opportunities for ex-offenders, helping them build stable careers and reintegrate into society. Community organizations can offer support services such as counseling, mentorship, and housing assistance, addressing the various needs of individuals transitioning out of the justice system.

One notable example of successful community involvement is the "Safer Foundation" in Chicago, which provides comprehensive support services for individuals with criminal records. The foundation offers job training, placement services, education programs, and support for overcoming legal barriers to employment. By addressing the multiple needs of ex-offenders, the Safer Foundation helps individuals build stable and productive lives, reducing recidivism and promoting community safety. This holistic approach aligns with the Bodhisattva ideal of compassion and support for the well-being of all individuals. Educational programs within correctional facilities can also play a significant role in integrating Bodhisattva principles into criminology. These programs should provide offenders with the knowledge and skills needed to succeed in society, as well as opportunities for personal growth and development. Courses on emotional intelligence, conflict resolution, ethical decision-making, and mindfulness can help offenders develop the tools needed to manage their emotions, navigate conflicts, and make positive choices. Vocational training and academic education can provide the skills needed for stable employment, promoting economic self-sufficiency and reducing the likelihood of reoffending.

The "Bard Prison Initiative" (BPI) is an example of an educational program that embodies the Bodhisattva ideals. BPI offers college-level courses to incarcerated individuals, providing them with the opportunity to earn degrees and develop critical thinking skills. The program emphasizes the transformative power of education, helping participants build self-esteem, resilience, and a sense of purpose. Graduates of BPI have gone on to secure employment, pursue further education, and contribute positively to their communities. By providing opportunities for personal and academic growth, BPI aligns with the Bodhisattva's commitment to alleviating suffering and promoting well-being. Supportive housing programs are another essential component of integrating Bodhisattva principles into criminology. Stable housing provides a foundation for individuals to rebuild their lives, secure employment, and access necessary services. Programs that offer transitional housing and support services, such as counseling and job placement, can help ex-offenders establish stability and reduce the risk of reoffending. The "Fort Lyon Supportive Residential Community" in Colorado, for example, provides housing and comprehensive support for homeless individuals, including ex-offenders. The program's holistic approach addresses multiple barriers to stability and promotes long-term success, reflecting the Bodhisattva's commitment to compassionate care and support.

Evaluating the effectiveness of Bodhisattva-inspired practices in justice systems is crucial for continuous improvement and broader implementation. Longitudinal studies that track changes in recidivism rates, mental health outcomes, employment status, and other indicators provide valuable data on the impact of these practices. Feedback from participants, justice professionals, and community members can help refine and enhance programs, ensuring they remain relevant and effective. Continuous evaluation and adaptation are key to maintaining the success and sustainability of these initiatives. Research supports the effectiveness of Bodhisattva-inspired practices in reducing recidivism and promoting rehabilitation. Studies have shown that restorative justice programs, trauma-informed care, and educational initiatives that promote emotional intelligence and ethical decision-making lead to better outcomes for offenders and communities. These practices reduce recidivism, improve mental health, and foster stronger social bonds, demonstrating the benefits of integrating the Bodhisattva principles into justice systems.

CHAPTER TEN

Cultivating Compassion in Justice Practices

Contents

- Techniques for Developing Compassion

- Practical Applications in Mediation and Rehabilitation

- Case Studies of Compassionate Justice

- Benefits for Offenders and Practitioners

- Long-Term Impact on Justice Systems

10.1: Techniques for Developing Compassion

Compassion stands as a cornerstone in the realm of rehabilitation, offering a profound pathway to transformative change. Within the justice system, the cultivation of compassion significantly enhances the rehabilitation process, providing a foundation for genuine personal growth and societal reintegration. The impact of compassionate practices on offenders' mental health and behavior is profound, shifting the focus from punishment to healing, and fostering environments where positive change can flourish. Incorporating compassion into rehabilitation begins with understanding its fundamental role in addressing the root causes of criminal behavior. Many offenders come from backgrounds marked by trauma, neglect, and socio-economic hardship. These experiences often shape their actions, leading to behaviors that result in incarceration. A compassionate approach recognizes these underlying factors and addresses them with empathy and support, rather than solely focusing on the criminal act itself. By acknowledging and understanding the pain and suffering that contribute to criminal behavior, justice systems can create more effective and humane responses.

Compassionate practices within correctional facilities can take various forms, from therapeutic interventions to everyday interactions. Staff trained in compassionate communication and emotional intelligence are better equipped to interact with offenders in ways that de-escalate conflict and promote understanding. This shift in interaction styles can significantly reduce incidents of violence and improve the overall atmosphere within correctional settings. When offenders feel understood and valued, they are more likely to engage positively with rehabilitation programs and make strides towards personal growth. Therapeutic interventions rooted in compassion, such as trauma-informed care and restorative justice practices, offer powerful tools for rehabilitation. Trauma-informed care acknowledges the impact of trauma on an individual's behavior and provides support tailored to their specific needs. This approach fosters a safe and supportive environment where offenders can begin to heal from past traumas. Restorative justice, on the other hand, emphasizes repairing the harm caused by criminal behavior through dialogue and reconciliation. By focusing on the needs of victims, offenders, and the community, restorative justice practices promote empathy, accountability, and the restoration of relationships.

The mental health benefits of compassionate practices in rehabilitation are well-documented. Offenders often suffer from mental health issues such as depression, anxiety, and post-traumatic stress disorder (PTSD). Compassionate approaches, including counseling, mindfulness, and meditation, can significantly alleviate these conditions. Mindfulness and meditation practices, in particular, help individuals develop greater self-awareness and emotional regulation. These practices encourage offenders to observe their thoughts and emotions without judgment, fostering a sense of inner peace and resilience. By addressing mental health issues with compassion, rehabilitation programs can help offenders build the emotional stability necessary for successful reintegration. Compassionate practices also impact behavior by promoting prosocial attitudes and reducing recidivism. When offenders are treated with compassion and respect, they are more likely to adopt these behaviors themselves. Programs that emphasize empathy training and emotional intelligence can help offenders develop a greater understanding of others' perspectives and feelings. This increased empathy can lead to more constructive interactions and a reduced likelihood of reoffending. Studies have shown that offenders who participate in compassionate rehabilitation programs are less likely to return to criminal behavior, highlighting the long-term benefits of this approach.

Comparative analyses of rehabilitation programs with and without compassionate approaches further underscore the importance of compassion in justice practices. Programs that incorporate compassionate methods consistently show better outcomes in terms of mental health, behavior, and recidivism rates. For instance, a study comparing traditional punitive correctional programs with trauma-informed care models found that the latter significantly reduced symptoms of PTSD and improved overall psychological well-being among participants. Similarly, restorative justice programs have been shown to reduce recidivism rates and increase victim satisfaction compared to conventional punitive measures. The integration of compassion into rehabilitation also extends to the broader community, fostering a more inclusive and supportive environment for reintegration. Community-based programs that offer support and mentorship to ex-offenders play a crucial role in their successful transition back into society. These programs often involve volunteers and community members who provide guidance, resources, and emotional support. By fostering a sense of community and belonging, these programs help ex-offenders rebuild their lives and contribute positively to their communities.

A key aspect of compassionate rehabilitation is the recognition of the humanity and potential for change within every individual. This perspective challenges the stigmatization and dehumanization that often accompany criminal behavior. By focusing on rehabilitation rather than punishment, justice systems can create opportunities for offenders to develop new skills, pursue education, and engage in meaningful activities. This approach not only benefits the individuals involved but also contributes to the overall safety and well-being of society. Moreover, compassionate rehabilitation practices align with the principles of restorative justice, which seek to repair harm and restore relationships rather than simply punish offenders. Restorative justice practices, such as victim-offender mediation and restorative circles, provide a platform for dialogue and understanding. These practices allow offenders to take responsibility for their actions, express remorse, and make amends. Victims, in turn, have the opportunity to voice their experiences, ask questions, and receive closure. This process fosters empathy, accountability, and healing, aligning with the Bodhisattva ideal of alleviating suffering and promoting well-being.

The broader implications of compassionate rehabilitation extend to policy and systemic change. Advocating for policies that prioritize rehabilitation over punishment, allocate resources for mental health and addiction treatment, and support restorative justice initiatives can drive meaningful reform in justice systems worldwide. These policies reflect the Bodhisattva's commitment to creating conditions that alleviate suffering and promote collective well-being. By integrating compassion into the fabric of justice systems, we can work towards a more humane and effective approach to addressing crime and promoting social harmony. The long-term benefits of compassionate rehabilitation are profound, impacting not only individual offenders but also their families, communities, and society as a whole. Offenders who successfully reintegrate into society are less likely to reoffend, reducing the overall burden on the justice system. Their positive contributions to their communities, whether through employment, volunteer work, or other forms of civic engagement, enhance social cohesion and foster a sense of collective responsibility. By addressing the root causes of criminal behavior and promoting healing, compassionate rehabilitation practices contribute to a safer, more just, and compassionate society.

10.2: Practical Applications in Mediation and Rehabilitation

Developing compassion among offenders within correctional facilities is a transformative endeavor that can significantly impact their rehabilitation and reintegration into society. Practical methods for fostering compassion involve a multifaceted approach, incorporating mindfulness practices, educational programs, and therapeutic interventions. These methods aim to cultivate empathy, emotional intelligence, and a deeper understanding of the interconnectedness of all beings. By nurturing these qualities, correctional facilities can create an environment conducive to personal growth and positive change. One of the most effective methods for fostering compassion is the integration of mindfulness and meditation practices into daily routines within correctional facilities. Mindfulness, the practice of maintaining a moment-by-moment awareness of thoughts, feelings, bodily sensations, and the surrounding environment, can be a powerful tool for developing compassion. Meditation practices, such as loving-kindness meditation (Metta), specifically focus on cultivating feelings of goodwill, kindness, and warmth towards oneself and others. These practices help offenders develop a greater sense of empathy and reduce feelings of anger and resentment.

Loving-kindness meditation involves silently repeating phrases that express well-wishes for oneself and others. Typically, the practice starts with focusing on oneself, then gradually extending these wishes to loved ones, acquaintances, and even those with whom one has conflicts. By regularly practicing loving-kindness meditation, offenders can break down barriers of hostility and develop a more compassionate outlook. Research has shown that loving-kindness meditation can increase positive emotions, improve social connections, and reduce implicit bias, making it an effective tool for fostering compassion within correctional settings. Educational programs focused on empathy and emotional intelligence are another vital component in developing compassion among offenders. These programs can include courses and workshops that teach the principles of empathy, effective communication, conflict resolution, and emotional regulation. By understanding and managing their own emotions, offenders can better relate to the emotions of others. Courses that incorporate role-playing, group discussions, and reflective exercises can help offenders practice these skills in a supportive environment.

Empathy training programs, such as those developed by the Center for Compassion and Altruism Research and Education (CCARE) at Stanford University, can be adapted for use in correctional facilities. These programs often include modules on the science of compassion, exercises to enhance self-awareness, and techniques for fostering empathic responses. By participating in these programs, offenders can learn to recognize and respond to the emotions of others, fostering a more compassionate and understanding environment within the facility. Compassion-focused therapy (CFT) is another effective method for cultivating compassion among offenders. CFT is a psychological intervention that integrates cognitive-behavioral techniques with practices designed to enhance compassion. It focuses on helping individuals develop self-compassion and compassion for others, addressing issues such as shame, self-criticism, and anger. CFT can be particularly beneficial for offenders who struggle with low self-esteem and feelings of unworthiness, as it encourages them to develop a more compassionate and supportive inner dialogue.

In correctional settings, CFT can be implemented through individual or group therapy sessions. Therapists trained in CFT work with offenders to identify negative thought patterns and develop more compassionate ways of thinking. Techniques used in CFT include guided imagery, mindfulness exercises, and compassionate letter writing. These practices help offenders build a sense of safety and warmth within themselves, which can then be extended to others. Research has shown that CFT can reduce symptoms of depression and anxiety, increase self-compassion, and improve overall psychological well-being, making it a valuable tool in rehabilitation programs. Peer support programs within correctional facilities also play a crucial role in fostering compassion. These programs involve training inmates to provide emotional and practical support to their peers. Peer supporters can offer a unique perspective and relatability that staff members may not be able to provide. By sharing their own experiences and demonstrating empathy, peer supporters can help foster a sense of community and mutual support. This peer-led approach not only benefits those receiving support but also enhances the compassion and leadership skills of the peer supporters themselves.

Restorative justice practices, such as victim-offender mediation and restorative circles, provide practical opportunities for offenders to develop compassion. These practices involve facilitated dialogues between offenders, victims, and community members, focusing on repairing harm and fostering understanding. By hearing firsthand accounts of the impact of their actions, offenders can develop greater empathy for their victims. Restorative justice practices encourage offenders to take responsibility for their actions, express remorse, and make amends, promoting a sense of accountability and compassion. In addition to structured programs, creating a compassionate environment within correctional facilities involves changing the overall culture and daily interactions. Staff training in compassionate communication and conflict resolution is essential. When staff members model compassionate behavior, it sets a positive example for offenders and creates a more supportive atmosphere. Simple practices, such as addressing offenders respectfully, listening actively, and providing positive reinforcement, can make a significant difference in fostering a culture of compassion.

Volunteer and mentorship programs that connect offenders with compassionate individuals from the community can also enhance the development of compassion. Volunteers and mentors can provide guidance, support, and positive role models, helping offenders navigate their rehabilitation journey. Programs like the "Prison Fellowship" and "Toastmasters Prison Club" offer mentorship and skill-building opportunities that promote personal growth and empathy. These interactions with compassionate mentors can inspire offenders to adopt more compassionate attitudes and behaviors. Incorporating art and creative expression into rehabilitation programs can also foster compassion and emotional healing. Art therapy, music therapy, and creative writing workshops provide outlets for offenders to explore and express their emotions in a safe and constructive manner. These activities can help offenders process past traumas, develop empathy for others' experiences, and build a sense of connection and community. Creative expression can be a powerful tool for emotional healing and the development of compassion.

One notable example is the "Arts in Corrections" program in California, which offers a variety of arts-based programs in correctional facilities. Participants in these programs have reported increased self-awareness, emotional regulation, and empathy. By engaging in creative activities, offenders can develop a greater understanding of their own emotions and those of others, fostering a more compassionate outlook. Evaluating the effectiveness of compassion-building programs is essential for continuous improvement. Longitudinal studies that track changes in empathy, emotional intelligence, and behavior can provide valuable insights into the impact of these programs. Feedback from participants, staff, and community members can help refine and enhance the programs, ensuring they remain relevant and effective.

10.3: Case Studies of Compassionate Justice

Compassion-focused therapy (CFT) offers a transformative approach to rehabilitation within correctional settings. Developed by Dr. Paul Gilbert, CFT integrates cognitive-behavioral techniques with practices designed to enhance compassion for oneself and others. The application of CFT in correctional settings has shown promising results, helping offenders address issues such as shame, self-criticism, and anger, and fostering a more compassionate and constructive mindset. CFT begins with the understanding that many offenders have experienced significant trauma and adverse life events that contribute to their criminal behavior. These experiences often lead to feelings of shame and self-criticism, which can perpetuate negative thought patterns and behaviors. CFT aims to break this cycle by helping individuals develop a compassionate inner dialogue and build a sense of safety and warmth within themselves.

A core component of CFT is developing the "compassionate mind," which involves training individuals to cultivate feelings of compassion, empathy, and kindness towards themselves and others. This process begins with psychoeducation, where offenders learn about the impact of their early life experiences on their current thoughts and behaviors. Understanding the roots of their self-critical and punitive thoughts helps them recognize these patterns and begin to challenge them. In CFT, therapists guide individuals through a series of exercises designed to enhance their capacity for self-compassion. One such exercise is the "compassionate imagery" practice, where individuals visualize a compassionate figure who embodies qualities of kindness, warmth, and understanding. This figure could be a real person, an imagined being, or even an idealized version of themselves. By engaging with this compassionate figure, individuals learn to internalize these qualities and develop a more supportive and nurturing inner voice.

Another key exercise in CFT is the "compassionate letter" practice. Offenders are encouraged to write letters to themselves from the perspective of their compassionate figure. These letters address their fears, self-criticism, and feelings of shame with empathy and understanding. The process of writing and reflecting on these letters helps individuals reframe their negative thoughts and develop a more compassionate outlook. This practice has been shown to reduce symptoms of depression and anxiety, increase self-compassion, and improve overall psychological well-being. Group therapy sessions in CFT provide a supportive environment where individuals can share their experiences and practice compassion towards others. In these sessions, participants engage in discussions and exercises that promote empathy, understanding, and mutual support. For example, a common exercise involves participants sharing their stories of struggle and resilience, while others listen empathetically and offer compassionate responses. This process helps build a sense of community and connectedness, reducing feelings of isolation and fostering a more compassionate group dynamic.

A case study of CFT implementation in a UK prison highlights its effectiveness in fostering compassion among offenders. The "Mindful Compassionate Living" program, developed by the Compassionate Mind Foundation, was introduced to address the high levels of shame and self-criticism among inmates. The program included weekly group sessions where participants engaged in mindfulness practices, compassionate imagery, and reflective exercises. Participants reported significant reductions in self-criticism and increases in self-compassion and emotional regulation. One inmate described the program as "a lifeline" that helped him develop a more positive and compassionate relationship with himself and others. In the United States, the "Healing Trauma" program, based on the principles of CFT, has been implemented in several women's correctional facilities. This program addresses the specific needs of female offenders, many of whom have experienced significant trauma and abuse. The program includes mindfulness practices, compassionate imagery, and trauma-informed care techniques. Participants learn to develop self-compassion and build resilience in the face of their traumatic experiences. Evaluations of the program have shown significant improvements in mental health outcomes, including reductions in PTSD symptoms and increases in self-compassion and emotional well-being.

CFT's emphasis on developing a compassionate inner dialogue is particularly relevant for offenders who struggle with anger and aggression. By learning to respond to their emotions with compassion rather than self-criticism, individuals can develop healthier ways of managing their anger. Techniques such as mindful breathing and body scans help offenders become more aware of their physical and emotional states, allowing them to recognize early signs of anger and take steps to calm themselves before reacting impulsively. This approach not only reduces incidents of violence within correctional facilities but also helps offenders develop skills that are crucial for successful reintegration into society. The application of CFT in correctional settings extends beyond individual therapy to include staff training and systemic change. Training correctional officers and staff in the principles of CFT can create a more compassionate and supportive environment within facilities. When staff members model compassionate behavior and communication, it sets a positive example for offenders and fosters a culture of empathy and understanding. This approach can lead to more effective interactions, reduced conflicts, and a more therapeutic environment overall.

In New Zealand, the "Pathways to Resilience" program integrates CFT principles into correctional staff training. This program includes workshops and ongoing support for staff to develop their own self-compassion and enhance their capacity for compassionate care. The program has led to improvements in staff well-being, reduced burnout, and more positive interactions with inmates. By fostering a compassionate culture within the facility, the program has contributed to a more supportive and rehabilitative environment for all. The long-term benefits of CFT in correctional settings are significant. By helping offenders develop self-compassion and reduce self-criticism, CFT can lead to lasting changes in behavior and reduce recidivism rates. Offenders who develop a compassionate inner dialogue are better equipped to cope with stress, manage their emotions, and make positive choices. This shift in mindset can have a ripple effect, improving their relationships with others and their overall quality of life. CFT's focus on compassion and empathy aligns with the principles of restorative justice, offering a complementary approach to rehabilitation. By integrating CFT with restorative justice practices, correctional facilities can create a holistic model of care that addresses both the emotional and relational aspects of rehabilitation. This approach emphasizes healing, accountability, and the restoration of relationships, providing a comprehensive framework for promoting positive change.

10.4: Benefits for Offenders and Practitioners

The integration of compassion into mediation and conflict resolution practices within the justice system transforms traditional approaches into more humane and effective processes. Compassion, as an essential component of the Bodhisattva path, emphasizes understanding, empathy, and the alleviation of suffering. These principles can significantly enhance mediation and conflict resolution by fostering environments where parties feel heard, respected, and motivated to find mutually beneficial solutions. Compassionate mediation involves techniques that prioritize the emotional and psychological well-being of all parties involved. This approach contrasts with adversarial models that often escalate conflict and focus on winning rather than resolving underlying issues. In compassionate mediation, mediators adopt a role that goes beyond neutrality to actively facilitate understanding and empathy between disputing parties.

One fundamental technique in compassionate mediation is active listening. Mediators encourage each party to speak openly about their feelings, experiences, and perspectives while ensuring that the other party listens without interruption. This process helps build mutual understanding and reduces the animosity that often characterizes conflicts. By genuinely listening, parties can recognize the humanity in each other, fostering empathy and opening the door to reconciliation.

Empathy-building exercises are another crucial component of compassionate mediation. Mediators may guide parties through exercises where they articulate the emotions and needs of the other party as if they were their own. This practice encourages individuals to step outside their own viewpoints and consider the situation from the perspective of the other person. Such exercises can break down barriers of misunderstanding and promote a deeper connection between the parties, laying the groundwork for a more amicable resolution.

Incorporating mindfulness practices into mediation can further enhance the process. Mindfulness involves being fully present in the moment and observing one's thoughts and feelings without judgment. Mediators trained in mindfulness techniques can help parties remain calm and focused during mediation sessions, reducing stress and emotional reactivity. Mindfulness practices, such as deep breathing or short meditative pauses, can be introduced at critical moments to help de-escalate tension and maintain a constructive dialogue. An example of compassionate mediation in action can be seen in the "Family Group Conferencing" (FGC) model used in New Zealand's juvenile justice system. FGC involves bringing together young offenders, their families, victims, and community representatives in a facilitated meeting to discuss the offense and its impact. The process emphasizes understanding and repairing harm rather than punishment. Through guided discussions, participants share their feelings and experiences, fostering empathy and mutual respect. This compassionate approach has been shown to reduce recidivism and improve outcomes for young offenders by addressing the underlying issues that contribute to criminal behavior and supporting their reintegration into the community.

Another illustrative case is the "Victim-Offender Dialogue" (VOD) programs implemented in several U.S. states. VOD provides a structured setting where victims of serious crimes, such as homicide or assault, can meet with the offenders responsible for their suffering. The process is carefully facilitated by trained mediators who ensure that the dialogue remains respectful and constructive. Victims have the opportunity to express the impact of the crime on their lives, while offenders can take responsibility, express remorse, and seek forgiveness. This compassionate mediation process has been shown to provide significant emotional healing for victims and a profound sense of accountability and transformation for offenders. Restorative circles are another effective method of integrating compassion into conflict resolution. Used in schools, communities, and correctional facilities, restorative circles bring together all parties affected by a conflict to discuss its impact and collectively decide on a resolution. The process is guided by a facilitator who ensures that everyone has an equal opportunity to speak and be heard. Restorative circles emphasize collective healing and community support, reflecting the Bodhisattva ideals of compassion and interconnectedness. Participants in restorative circles often report a greater sense of closure and satisfaction compared to traditional punitive measures.

Incorporating compassion into workplace conflict resolution can also lead to more harmonious and productive environments. Training managers and employees in compassionate communication and conflict resolution techniques can help address workplace disputes more effectively. Techniques such as non-violent communication (NVC), developed by Marshall Rosenberg, focus on expressing needs and feelings without blame or criticism. NVC encourages empathetic listening and mutual respect, fostering a collaborative atmosphere where conflicts can be resolved amicably. Companies that adopt compassionate conflict resolution practices often see improvements in employee morale, teamwork, and overall productivity. The integration of compassion into mediation and conflict resolution is not limited to interpersonal disputes but can also address larger social conflicts. Community mediation programs, such as those facilitated by the "Community Justice Centers" in Australia, apply these principles to resolve disputes between neighbors, community groups, and local organizations. These programs provide a neutral space where parties can discuss their issues, facilitated by trained mediators who promote empathy and understanding. By addressing conflicts at the community level, these programs help build stronger, more cohesive communities and prevent the escalation of disputes into more serious conflicts.

In international contexts, compassionate mediation can play a crucial role in peacebuilding and conflict resolution. Organizations such as "Mediation Beyond Borders" work to bring together conflicting parties in war-torn regions to facilitate dialogues aimed at fostering understanding and reconciliation. These mediations often involve multiple stakeholders, including political leaders, community representatives, and civil society organizations. By promoting empathy and mutual respect, compassionate mediation helps create the conditions for lasting peace and cooperation. Evaluating the impact of compassionate mediation and conflict resolution practices is essential for demonstrating their effectiveness and promoting their adoption. Research has shown that these approaches lead to higher satisfaction rates among participants, greater compliance with agreements, and reduced recurrence of conflicts. Studies on restorative justice programs, for example, have found that participants experience greater emotional healing and closure compared to traditional judicial processes. Furthermore, offenders who participate in restorative justice practices are less likely to reoffend, highlighting the long-term benefits of these compassionate approaches. Training and education are critical for the successful implementation of compassionate mediation practices. Mediators and facilitators must be equipped with the skills and knowledge to guide these processes effectively. Training programs should include modules on empathy-building, active listening, mindfulness, and conflict resolution techniques. Ongoing professional development and supervision can help mediators refine their skills and stay updated on best practices.

10.5: Long-Term Impact on Justice Systems

Measuring the impact of compassionate practices in justice systems is crucial for understanding their effectiveness and fostering their broader adoption. By systematically evaluating these practices, we can gather evidence to support their benefits, identify areas for improvement, and advocate for policy changes that prioritize compassion and rehabilitation over punitive measures. Research findings on the benefits of compassion in justice systems highlight the transformative potential of these approaches, demonstrating their positive outcomes on mental health, behavior, recidivism rates, and overall community well-being. Evaluating the effectiveness of compassionate justice practices requires a multifaceted approach that includes qualitative and quantitative methods. Quantitative methods involve the use of statistical analyses to measure changes in specific outcomes, such as recidivism rates, mental health scores, and behavioral improvements. These methods provide objective data that can be used to compare the outcomes of compassionate practices with traditional punitive approaches. For instance, studies comparing the recidivism rates of offenders who participate in restorative justice programs with those who undergo conventional sentencing have consistently shown lower recidivism rates among the former group.

Qualitative methods, on the other hand, involve gathering detailed descriptions and personal narratives that provide deeper insights into the experiences of individuals involved in compassionate justice practices. These methods include interviews, focus groups, and case studies that capture the subjective experiences of offenders, victims, and community members. Qualitative data can reveal the nuances and complexities of how compassionate practices impact individuals' lives, offering valuable perspectives that quantitative data alone cannot provide. One notable example of a comprehensive evaluation of compassionate justice practices is the study of the "Circles of Support and Accountability" (CoSA) program in Canada. CoSA involves community volunteers who support high-risk sex offenders upon their release from prison, helping them reintegrate into society and reduce the risk of reoffending. The program emphasizes accountability, community support, and the development of positive relationships. A longitudinal study of CoSA participants found that the program significantly reduced recidivism rates compared to a control group. Additionally, qualitative interviews with participants revealed that they felt more supported, understood, and motivated to make positive changes in their lives.

Another example is the evaluation of the "Restorative Justice Conferencing" (RJC) programs in the United Kingdom. RJC brings together offenders, victims, and community members to discuss the harm caused by a crime and develop a plan for making amends. A large-scale study of RJC found that participants who went through the conferencing process had lower recidivism rates and higher satisfaction levels compared to those who went through the traditional justice system. Victims reported feeling more heard and respected, while offenders expressed greater understanding of the impact of their actions and a stronger commitment to positive change. Incorporating compassionate practices in correctional settings also involves evaluating their impact on mental health outcomes. Programs that integrate mindfulness, meditation, and therapeutic interventions aim to improve offenders' emotional well-being and reduce symptoms of mental health disorders. A study of the "Mindfulness-Based Stress Reduction" (MBSR) program in a U.S. prison found that participants experienced significant reductions in stress, anxiety, and depression. These improvements were associated with better behavior and increased engagement in rehabilitation activities. The study used standardized mental health assessments to measure changes in psychological well-being, providing robust evidence of the program's effectiveness.

The "Healing Trauma" program, implemented in several women's correctional facilities, offers another example of the positive impact of compassionate practices on mental health. This program, which includes mindfulness, compassionate imagery, and trauma-informed care, has been shown to reduce symptoms of PTSD and increase self-compassion among participants. Qualitative interviews with participants revealed that they felt more empowered, resilient, and capable of managing their emotions. These findings underscore the importance of addressing trauma and promoting emotional healing in the rehabilitation process. Behavioral improvements are another critical outcome to measure when evaluating compassionate justice practices. Programs that focus on developing empathy, emotional intelligence, and conflict resolution skills aim to reduce aggressive and antisocial behaviors. The "Inside-Out Prison Exchange Program," which brings together incarcerated individuals and university students for a semester-long course, has been shown to foster prosocial attitudes and behaviors. Participants reported increased empathy, improved communication skills, and a greater sense of accountability. These changes were associated with better behavior within the correctional facility and a reduced likelihood of reoffending after release.

Community-based programs that support offenders' reintegration also benefit from rigorous evaluation. The "Safer Foundation" in Chicago, which provides job training, placement services, and support for individuals with criminal records, has been the subject of numerous studies. Research has shown that participants in the Safer Foundation programs are more likely to secure stable employment and less likely to reoffend compared to those who do not receive such support. Quantitative analyses of employment rates and recidivism rates, combined with qualitative interviews with participants, provide a comprehensive picture of the program's impact. The evaluation of compassionate justice practices should also consider the broader community impact. Programs that involve community members in the rehabilitation process, such as restorative justice circles and community mediation, can enhance social cohesion and reduce crime rates. The "Community Conferencing" program in Baltimore, which addresses conflicts among youth and community members, has been shown to reduce juvenile arrests and improve community relationships. Surveys of community members involved in the program revealed increased trust, cooperation, and a sense of shared responsibility for addressing conflicts.

Long-term outcomes are particularly important to measure, as the benefits of compassionate practices often extend beyond immediate improvements. Longitudinal studies that track participants over several years can provide valuable insights into the sustained impact of these practices. For example, a follow-up study of the "Bard Prison Initiative" (BPI), which offers college education to incarcerated individuals, found that graduates had significantly lower recidivism rates and higher employment rates compared to a control group. These findings highlight the lasting positive effects of providing educational opportunities and fostering personal development within correctional settings. Policy advocacy and systemic change require robust evidence to support the implementation of compassionate justice practices on a broader scale. By demonstrating the effectiveness of these practices through rigorous evaluation, researchers and practitioners can build a compelling case for policy reforms that prioritize rehabilitation and compassion over punishment.

This evidence can inform the development of policies that allocate resources for mental health treatment, restorative justice programs, and community support initiatives, creating a more humane and effective justice system. Evaluating the impact of compassionate practices also involves considering the cost-effectiveness of these approaches. Studies have shown that restorative justice programs, trauma-informed care, and educational initiatives often result in cost savings for the justice system. By reducing recidivism rates and improving outcomes for offenders, these programs can decrease the need for incarceration and reduce the overall burden on the justice system. Cost-benefit analyses that compare the expenses of implementing compassionate practices with the savings from reduced reoffending can provide valuable data for policymakers and stakeholders.

CHAPTER ELEVEN

Altruism and Service in the Justice System

Contents

- Encouraging Selfless Service among Practitioners

- Practical Techniques for Fostering Altruism

- Case Studies of Altruistic Actions in Justice

- Benefits for Offenders and Communities

- Integrating Altruism into Justice Policies

11.1: Encouraging Selfless Service among Practitioners

Altruism, as taught in Tibetan Buddhism, is the profound commitment to act selflessly for the benefit of others, embodying the essence of compassion and wisdom. This principle is central to the Bodhisattva path, where individuals vow to attain enlightenment not just for their own liberation but to assist all sentient beings in their journey towards freedom from suffering. Altruism, in this context, transcends mere acts of kindness; it is a way of life that reflects deep interconnectedness and an unwavering dedication to the welfare of others. The concept of altruism in Tibetan Buddhism is rooted in the understanding of dependent origination, which posits that all phenomena arise in dependence upon causes and conditions. This interdependence means that the well-being of one individual is intrinsically linked to the well-being of others. Therefore, the practice of altruism is not just a moral obligation but a rational response to the reality of our interconnected existence. When we help others, we ultimately help ourselves, as our lives are woven into the fabric of the community and the world.

One of the most illustrative teachings on altruism in Tibetan Buddhism comes from Shantideva's "Bodhicaryavatara," or "The Way of the Bodhisattva." In this seminal text, Shantideva expounds on the virtues of selflessness and the transformative power of bodhichitta, the altruistic intention to attain enlightenment for the benefit of all beings. Shantideva emphasizes that true happiness and fulfillment come from serving others and that the pursuit of personal gain is ultimately unfulfilling. He writes, "All the joy the world contains has come through wishing happiness for others. All the misery the world contains has come through wanting pleasure for oneself." This teaching underscores the profound impact of altruism on both personal well-being and the broader social harmony. Historical examples of altruistic behavior inspired by Tibetan Buddhist principles are numerous and impactful. One such figure is Geshe Jampa Tegchok, who dedicated his life to teaching and spreading the Dharma while actively engaging in community service. His efforts to establish educational institutions and support underprivileged communities exemplify the practical application of altruistic principles. Through his work, Geshe Tegchok not only alleviated immediate suffering but also empowered individuals to lead more fulfilling lives, thereby contributing to long-term societal benefits.

In modern times, the 14th Dalai Lama, Tenzin Gyatso, stands as a global beacon of altruism. His tireless advocacy for peace, human rights, and environmental sustainability reflects a deep commitment to the welfare of all beings. The Dalai Lama's teachings often stress the importance of compassion and altruism in addressing global challenges. He advocates for a "secular ethics" that transcends religious boundaries, encouraging people of all backgrounds to adopt compassionate and altruistic principles in their daily lives. His approach has inspired countless individuals and organizations to engage in altruistic actions, demonstrating the far-reaching impact of these principles. Altruism in Tibetan Buddhism is not limited to grand gestures or high-profile figures; it is also deeply embedded in everyday practices and community life. Monastic communities, for example, often engage in activities that benefit the broader society, such as providing education, healthcare, and disaster relief. These activities are seen not only as acts of charity but as essential components of spiritual practice. By serving others, monks and nuns cultivate compassion, reduce self-centeredness, and progress on their path to enlightenment. This integration of altruism into daily life serves as a model for how individuals and communities can live out these principles.

The significance of altruism in promoting justice and social harmony is profound. In the context of justice, altruism shifts the focus from retribution to restoration and healing. When justice systems incorporate altruistic principles, they prioritize rehabilitation, support for victims, and the restoration of relationships over punitive measures. This approach aligns with the restorative justice model, which seeks to address the needs of all parties affected by a crime and to promote healing and reconciliation. One practical application of altruism in justice is through community service programs for offenders. These programs provide opportunities for individuals to give back to their communities, fostering a sense of responsibility and connectedness. Community service helps offenders develop empathy and understanding, as they see the positive impact of their actions on others. This experience can be transformative, leading to lasting changes in behavior and attitudes.

Altruism also plays a crucial role in the rehabilitation process within correctional facilities. Programs that encourage offenders to engage in altruistic activities, such as peer mentoring or volunteering, can have significant therapeutic benefits. By helping others, offenders can rebuild their self-esteem, develop prosocial skills, and create a sense of purpose. These programs not only benefit the individuals involved but also contribute to a more positive and supportive environment within the facility. Educational initiatives that incorporate altruistic principles can also promote justice and social harmony. For example, curricula that emphasize empathy, ethical decision-making, and community engagement can help students develop a strong moral foundation and a commitment to serving others. These educational programs can prevent future criminal behavior by fostering a sense of social responsibility and interconnectedness from a young age. The psychological and social benefits of altruism are well-documented. Research has shown that engaging in altruistic behaviors can improve mental health, increase life satisfaction, and reduce stress. Altruistic individuals tend to have stronger social connections and a greater sense of belonging, which are critical factors in overall well-being. For offenders, these benefits can be particularly transformative, as they help address the underlying issues that contribute to criminal behavior and support long-term rehabilitation.

11.2: Practical Techniques for Fostering Altruism

Encouraging altruistic behavior among offenders within correctional settings involves a multifaceted approach that integrates various techniques and programs designed to foster empathy, responsibility, and a commitment to the well-being of others. Altruism, or selfless concern for the welfare of others, can be cultivated through structured activities, therapeutic interventions, and educational initiatives. By promoting altruistic behavior, correctional facilities can create environments that support personal growth, rehabilitation, and positive social integration. One effective method for fostering altruism among offenders is through structured volunteer work and community service programs. These programs provide opportunities for offenders to contribute positively to their communities, helping to build empathy and a sense of social responsibility. Community service can take many forms, including participating in environmental conservation projects, assisting in local shelters or food banks, and engaging in restorative justice initiatives. By working directly with those in need, offenders can develop a greater understanding of the challenges faced by others and the impact of their contributions.

Programs such as the "Community Service Order" in the United Kingdom have demonstrated the benefits of integrating community service into rehabilitation. Offenders are assigned specific tasks that benefit the community, such as cleaning public spaces, repairing community facilities, or supporting local charities. These activities not only provide a constructive outlet for offenders but also help them develop a sense of accomplishment and pride in their work. Research has shown that participation in community service can reduce recidivism rates and improve offenders' attitudes towards themselves and others. Mentorship programs within correctional facilities also play a crucial role in fostering altruism. These programs involve pairing offenders with mentors who provide guidance, support, and positive role models. Mentors, who are often former offenders or community volunteers, can offer valuable insights and encouragement, helping mentees navigate the challenges of rehabilitation. The relationship between mentor and mentee is built on trust, empathy, and mutual respect, creating a supportive environment where altruistic behavior can thrive.

The "Prison Mentoring Program" in Australia is an example of a successful initiative that promotes altruism through mentorship. In this program, mentors work closely with offenders to help them set goals, develop life skills, and plan for their future reintegration into society. The program emphasizes the importance of giving back to the community and encourages participants to engage in volunteer activities both during and after their incarceration. Evaluations of the program have shown significant improvements in participants' self-esteem, social skills, and overall outlook on life, highlighting the transformative power of mentorship. Educational programs that focus on empathy and emotional intelligence are another effective way to encourage altruistic behavior among offenders. These programs can include courses and workshops that teach the principles of empathy, effective communication, conflict resolution, and ethical decision-making. By understanding and managing their own emotions, offenders can better relate to the emotions of others, fostering a more compassionate and altruistic mindset.

One notable example is the "Roots of Empathy" program, which has been adapted for use in correctional settings. This program involves bringing infants and their parents into the classroom to interact with offenders. Through guided observations and discussions, participants learn to recognize and understand the baby's emotions and needs, helping them develop greater empathy and emotional intelligence. Studies have shown that the program reduces aggression and increases prosocial behavior among participants, demonstrating the potential of empathy-focused education to foster altruism. Therapeutic interventions, such as Compassion-Focused Therapy (CFT), also play a significant role in developing altruism among offenders. CFT, developed by Dr. Paul Gilbert, integrates cognitive-behavioral techniques with practices designed to enhance compassion for oneself and others. By addressing issues such as shame, self-criticism, and anger, CFT helps individuals develop a more compassionate and altruistic mindset.

In correctional settings, CFT can be implemented through individual or group therapy sessions. Therapists work with offenders to identify negative thought patterns and develop more compassionate ways of thinking. Techniques used in CFT include guided imagery, mindfulness exercises, and compassionate letter writing. These practices help offenders build a sense of safety and warmth within themselves, which can then be extended to others. Research has shown that CFT can reduce symptoms of depression and anxiety, increase self-compassion, and improve overall psychological well-being, making it a valuable tool in rehabilitation programs. Peer support programs are another effective method for promoting altruism among offenders. These programs involve training inmates to provide emotional and practical support to their peers. Peer supporters can offer a unique perspective and relatability that staff members may not be able to provide. By sharing their own experiences and demonstrating empathy, peer supporters can help foster a sense of community and mutual support. This peer-led approach not only benefits those receiving support but also enhances the compassion and leadership skills of the peer supporters themselves.

The "Buddy Support Program" in Canada is an example of a peer support initiative that encourages altruism. In this program, selected inmates are trained to provide support to their peers who are experiencing difficulties, such as mental health issues or adjusting to prison life. The program fosters a culture of care and empathy within the facility, reducing isolation and promoting positive interactions. Evaluations of the program have shown that both peer supporters and those they support experience improved well-being and reduced feelings of loneliness. Restorative justice practices, such as victim-offender mediation and restorative circles, provide practical opportunities for offenders to engage in altruistic behavior. These practices involve facilitated dialogues between offenders, victims, and community members, focusing on repairing harm and fostering understanding. By hearing firsthand accounts of the impact of their actions, offenders can develop greater empathy for their victims. Restorative justice practices encourage offenders to take responsibility for their actions, express remorse, and make amends, promoting a sense of accountability and compassion.

The "Restorative Justice Project" in New Zealand offers an illustrative example of the impact of restorative practices on fostering altruism. Offenders participate in facilitated meetings with their victims and community members to discuss the harm caused by their actions and develop a plan for making amends. The process emphasizes understanding, empathy, and collective healing. Participants report a greater sense of accountability and a stronger commitment to positive change, demonstrating the transformative potential of restorative justice. Creative expression and art therapy can also play a significant role in encouraging altruistic behavior among offenders. Programs that incorporate art, music, and creative writing provide outlets for offenders to explore and express their emotions in a safe and constructive manner. These activities can help offenders develop empathy and understanding for others' experiences, fostering a more compassionate and altruistic mindset.

The "Prison Arts Program" in California provides a compelling example of the benefits of creative expression in fostering altruism. Inmates participate in various artistic activities, including painting, sculpture, and theater, under the guidance of professional artists. The program encourages participants to use their art to communicate their stories and emotions, promoting self-awareness and empathy. Evaluations of the program have shown that participants develop greater emotional regulation, improved social skills, and a stronger sense of community. Volunteer and mentorship programs that connect offenders with compassionate individuals from the community can further enhance the development of altruism. Volunteers and mentors can provide guidance, support, and positive role models, helping offenders navigate their rehabilitation journey. Programs like the "Prison Fellowship" and "Toastmasters Prison Club" offer mentorship and skill-building opportunities that promote personal growth and empathy. These interactions with compassionate mentors can inspire offenders to adopt more altruistic attitudes and behaviors.

11.3: Case Studies of Altruistic Actions in Justice

Community service stands as a pivotal component in the rehabilitation process, offering offenders a path to redemption while providing tangible benefits to society. By engaging in community service, offenders can develop a sense of responsibility, empathy, and connection to the community they have harmed. This reciprocal relationship not only aids in their rehabilitation but also fosters social cohesion and trust within the community. Community service programs are structured to address the needs of both the offenders and the community. These programs often involve a variety of activities, from environmental clean-ups and urban gardening to assisting in homeless shelters and working with community organizations. The diversity of tasks allows offenders to find areas where they can contribute meaningfully, aligning their skills and interests with community needs. This alignment fosters a sense of accomplishment and purpose, essential elements in the rehabilitation process.

One notable example of a successful community service program is the "Greenhouse Project" in Rikers Island, New York. This initiative involves inmates working in greenhouse and garden settings, where they grow fresh produce used in prison kitchens and donated to local food banks. The program teaches valuable horticultural skills, provides a therapeutic environment, and encourages a connection with nature. Participants report a sense of pride and responsibility, knowing their efforts directly benefit their community and fellow inmates. The hands-on experience also fosters teamwork and patience, essential skills for personal development and future employment opportunities. The "Community Payback" program in the United Kingdom is another exemplary model. Offenders sentenced to community service under this program perform unpaid work that benefits local communities. Tasks range from graffiti removal and park maintenance to renovating community centers and aiding in flood relief efforts. These visible contributions help to repair the harm caused by offenders' actions, fostering a sense of restitution and community reintegration. Evaluations of the program have shown that offenders who participate in Community Payback are less likely to reoffend, highlighting the rehabilitative power of community service.

In Australia, the "Clean Slate Without Prejudice" initiative combines community service with cultural education and mentorship for young Indigenous offenders. Participants engage in community projects, such as building and maintaining community facilities, while also learning about their cultural heritage and receiving guidance from elders. This holistic approach addresses both the practical and emotional needs of young offenders, helping them reconnect with their roots and develop a sense of pride and belonging. The program has been credited with reducing recidivism and promoting positive cultural identity among participants. Community service also plays a crucial role in the restorative justice framework, where offenders work to repair the harm they have caused. The "Restorative Justice Community Action" (RJCA) program in Minneapolis, Minnesota, exemplifies this approach. Offenders meet with community members in a circle process to discuss the impact of their actions and agree on a plan for making amends. This plan often includes community service projects tailored to address the specific harms caused by the offense. By involving the community in the justice process, RJCA fosters a sense of collective responsibility and healing. Participants report a greater understanding of the consequences of their actions and a stronger commitment to positive change.

Incorporating community service into juvenile justice systems offers significant benefits for young offenders. Programs like "YouthBuild" in the United States provide at-risk youth with opportunities to learn construction skills while completing community improvement projects. Participants gain valuable vocational training, improve their educational outcomes, and develop a sense of pride and ownership in their work. The positive impact of these programs extends beyond the individual participants to the broader community, creating safer and more vibrant neighborhoods. Studies have shown that youth involved in such programs are more likely to complete their education and secure stable employment, reducing the likelihood of future criminal behavior. The long-term impacts of community service on offender rehabilitation and community integration are profound. By engaging in meaningful work that benefits others, offenders can rebuild their self-esteem and develop a more prosocial identity. The sense of accomplishment and positive feedback from the community reinforce these changes, making them more sustainable. Offenders who participate in community service are often viewed more favorably by the community, which can facilitate their reintegration and reduce the stigma associated with their criminal record.

Research supports the positive effects of community service on recidivism rates. A study conducted by the Vera Institute of Justice found that offenders who participated in community service programs were significantly less likely to reoffend compared to those who did not. The study attributed this reduction to the increased sense of social responsibility and the development of practical skills that enhance employability. These findings highlight the importance of integrating community service into rehabilitation strategies as a means to promote long-term behavioral change. Community service also provides offenders with opportunities to develop soft skills, such as teamwork, communication, and problem-solving. These skills are essential for successful reintegration into society and the workforce. By working alongside community members, offenders learn to navigate social dynamics and build positive relationships. These experiences can be transformative, helping individuals to break free from cycles of criminal behavior and build more constructive lives.

Moreover, community service fosters a sense of civic engagement and social responsibility. Offenders who participate in these programs often develop a greater awareness of societal issues and a desire to contribute positively to their communities. This shift in perspective can lead to continued involvement in volunteer work and community initiatives even after their formal sentence is complete. The ripple effect of these changes can strengthen community bonds and promote a culture of mutual support and cooperation. Implementing and managing community service programs in correctional facilities requires careful planning and coordination. It is essential to match offenders with appropriate service opportunities that align with their skills, interests, and rehabilitation goals. Effective supervision and support are also crucial to ensure that participants stay engaged and motivated. Correctional staff and community organizations must work collaboratively to provide guidance and feedback, helping offenders to reflect on their experiences and recognize the impact of their contributions.

Training for staff and volunteers involved in community service programs is essential to maximize their effectiveness. This training should cover principles of restorative justice, trauma-informed care, and effective mentorship. By equipping those involved with the necessary skills and knowledge, programs can create a supportive and empowering environment for offenders. Evaluating the success of community service programs is vital to understanding their impact and making necessary adjustments. Longitudinal studies that track participants' progress over time can provide valuable insights into the long-term benefits of these programs. Feedback from offenders, community members, and program staff can also help identify areas for improvement and highlight best practices.

Community service as a path to rehabilitation offers significant benefits for offenders, victims, and communities. By engaging in meaningful work that addresses community needs, offenders can develop a sense of responsibility, empathy, and connection to society. Programs like the Greenhouse Project, Community Payback, Clean Slate Without Prejudice, RJCA, and YouthBuild demonstrate the diverse ways in which community service can be integrated into rehabilitation efforts. The long-term impacts of these programs include reduced recidivism, improved social skills, and greater community cohesion. Effective implementation and management of community service programs require careful planning, support, and training. By prioritizing community service in rehabilitation strategies, we can create a more humane and effective justice system that promotes healing, accountability, and social integration.

11.4: Benefits for Offenders and Communities

Programs that promote service-oriented rehabilitation offer innovative and impactful ways to integrate altruistic activities into the justice system. These programs are designed to foster a sense of responsibility, empathy, and community among offenders, while simultaneously addressing societal needs. By engaging in service-oriented activities, offenders can experience personal growth, build positive relationships, and contribute to their communities, leading to better rehabilitation outcomes and reduced recidivism. One exemplary program that integrates service-oriented activities in rehabilitation is the "Insight Prison Project" (IPP) in California. IPP offers a range of programs focused on emotional literacy, victim impact, and mindfulness practices. One of their standout initiatives is the "Victim/Offender Education Group" (VOEG), which brings together offenders and survivors of crime in a structured and therapeutic setting. Through this program, offenders learn about the impact of their actions from the perspectives of survivors, fostering empathy and accountability. Additionally, they engage in service-oriented activities such as organizing community events and participating in restorative justice circles. This holistic approach not only aids in the personal transformation of offenders but also helps build bridges between the incarcerated population and the community.

Another notable program is the "Habitat for Humanity Prison Partnership Program," which involves offenders in the construction of affordable housing for low-income families. This program operates in several states across the U.S. and provides offenders with hands-on training in construction skills, while also allowing them to make a meaningful contribution to society. Participants work alongside community volunteers, creating opportunities for positive interactions and mutual respect. The tangible outcomes of their labor—completed homes that provide stability and security for families—offer a profound sense of accomplishment and purpose. Studies have shown that offenders who participate in this program exhibit lower recidivism rates and improved attitudes towards community service. The "Garden Project" in San Francisco is another successful initiative that integrates service-oriented activities into rehabilitation. This program employs formerly incarcerated individuals to work in urban gardens and farms, producing fresh produce for local food banks and communities. Participants receive training in sustainable agriculture, horticulture, and environmental stewardship, equipping them with valuable skills for future employment. The program also emphasizes personal development, with participants engaging in regular reflection sessions and life skills workshops. By contributing to food security and environmental sustainability, offenders in the Garden Project experience a renewed sense of connection to their community and the natural world.

"Operation New Hope" in Florida combines service-oriented rehabilitation with workforce development. The program provides job training and placement services to formerly incarcerated individuals, helping them secure stable employment upon release. Participants are also involved in community service projects, such as neighborhood beautification, disaster relief, and supporting local non-profits. This dual approach addresses both the economic and social dimensions of reintegration, reducing barriers to employment while fostering a sense of civic responsibility. The program's success is evident in its high employment rates and low recidivism rates among graduates, demonstrating the effectiveness of combining service-oriented activities with vocational training. The "Alternative to Violence Project" (AVP) is an international initiative that offers workshops in prisons and communities to teach non-violent conflict resolution skills. AVP workshops are facilitated by trained volunteers, many of whom are former offenders themselves. The program emphasizes experiential learning, with participants engaging in role-plays, group discussions, and collaborative problem-solving activities. By fostering a culture of peace and mutual respect, AVP helps offenders develop the skills needed to navigate conflicts constructively. Additionally, participants are encouraged to volunteer as facilitators, passing on the lessons they have learned to others. This service-oriented approach empowers offenders to become agents of change within their communities.

The "Books Through Bars" program engages offenders in literacy and educational initiatives. Incarcerated individuals participate in collecting, sorting, and distributing books to other inmates, promoting literacy and education within correctional facilities. This program not only addresses the educational needs of the incarcerated population but also fosters a sense of solidarity and mutual support. Offenders involved in Books Through Bars often report increased self-esteem and a greater sense of purpose, as they contribute to the intellectual and personal growth of their peers. In the United Kingdom, the "Restorative Approaches in Youth Settings" (RAYS) program integrates service-oriented activities with restorative justice principles. This program works with young offenders, encouraging them to engage in community projects that address local needs. Projects range from environmental clean-ups and community art installations to supporting elderly residents and organizing neighborhood events. By participating in these activities, young offenders develop a sense of civic duty and community pride. RAYS also incorporates restorative justice practices, such as victim-offender mediation and restorative circles, to address the harm caused by their actions and promote healing and reconciliation.

The "Service Learning Program" at the Louisiana State Penitentiary, also known as Angola Prison, is a unique initiative that combines education with community service. Inmates enrolled in the prison's educational programs are required to complete service projects as part of their coursework. These projects include tutoring fellow inmates, developing educational materials, and participating in community outreach initiatives. By integrating service learning into the curriculum, the program enhances the educational experience and reinforces the values of altruism and civic engagement. The "Paint Creek Youth Center" in Ohio offers a comprehensive rehabilitation program for juvenile offenders that includes service-oriented activities. Residents participate in various community service projects, such as maintaining public parks, assisting in local animal shelters, and supporting community events. These activities are designed to teach responsibility, teamwork, and empathy, while also providing a constructive outlet for the energy and creativity of young offenders. The program's holistic approach, which combines education, therapy, and community service, has been shown to reduce recidivism and improve outcomes for participating youth.

The long-term success of service-oriented rehabilitation programs depends on several key factors. First, it is essential to provide adequate training and support for both offenders and staff. Participants need to be equipped with the skills and knowledge necessary to engage in service activities effectively, while staff must be trained to facilitate these activities and provide ongoing guidance and encouragement. Regular reflection sessions, where participants can discuss their experiences and the impact of their contributions, are also crucial for reinforcing the values of altruism and civic responsibility. Second, partnerships with community organizations and local businesses are vital for the sustainability of service-oriented programs. These partnerships can provide resources, expertise, and opportunities for meaningful engagement. Collaborating with community stakeholders ensures that the service activities address real needs and contribute to the well-being of the broader community.

Third, ongoing evaluation and adaptation are necessary to ensure the programs remain effective and relevant. Collecting data on recidivism rates, employment outcomes, and participant feedback can provide valuable insights into the impact of service-oriented activities. This information can be used to refine program design, address challenges, and highlight best practices. Service-oriented rehabilitation programs offer a powerful approach to integrating altruistic activities into the justice system. Initiatives such as the Insight Prison Project, Habitat for Humanity Prison Partnership Program, Garden Project, Operation New Hope, Alternative to Violence Project, Books Through Bars, Restorative Approaches in Youth Settings, Service Learning Program at Angola Prison, and Paint Creek Youth Center demonstrate the diverse ways in which service-oriented activities can be incorporated into rehabilitation efforts. These programs not only support the personal growth and rehabilitation of offenders but also contribute to the well-being of the community. By prioritizing service-oriented activities in rehabilitation strategies, we can create a more humane and effective justice system that promotes healing, accountability, and social integration. The long-term benefits of these programs, including reduced recidivism, improved social skills, and stronger community bonds, highlight the transformative potential of altruism and service in the justice system.

11.5: Integrating Altruism into Justice Policies

The long-term benefits of altruism in justice systems are profound and multifaceted, impacting not only the offenders but also victims, communities, and the justice system itself. Integrating altruism into rehabilitation and correctional practices leads to significant improvements in recidivism rates, psychological well-being, social reintegration, and overall community health. Research findings and practical applications provide a compelling case for the adoption of altruistic principles in justice reform. Altruism, rooted in compassion and selflessness, fosters an environment where offenders can develop empathy, accountability, and a sense of purpose. These qualities are essential for genuine rehabilitation and reintegration into society. One of the most significant long-term benefits of fostering altruism among offenders is the reduction in recidivism rates. Studies have consistently shown that programs incorporating altruistic activities, such as community service and restorative justice practices, lead to lower rates of reoffending. This is because altruistic behavior helps offenders build positive social connections, develop prosocial identities, and cultivate a sense of responsibility towards their communities.

A longitudinal study conducted by the Vera Institute of Justice examined the impact of community service programs on recidivism rates. The study found that offenders who participated in community service were significantly less likely to reoffend compared to those who did not. This reduction in recidivism was attributed to the increased sense of social responsibility and the development of practical skills that enhanced employability. The findings highlight the importance of integrating altruistic activities into rehabilitation strategies as a means to promote long-term behavioral change. Psychologically, altruistic behavior has been shown to improve mental health and well-being among offenders. Engaging in selfless acts and contributing to the welfare of others can lead to increased feelings of happiness, reduced symptoms of depression and anxiety, and enhanced self-esteem. These psychological benefits are crucial for offenders who often struggle with mental health issues and low self-worth. By focusing on the needs of others, offenders can shift their attention away from their own problems, leading to a more positive outlook on life.

The "Caring Connections" program in Canada provides an illustrative example of the psychological benefits of altruism in justice settings. This program involves incarcerated individuals participating in community service projects, such as visiting elderly residents in nursing homes, supporting local food banks, and organizing charitable events. Participants report significant improvements in their mental health, including reduced feelings of isolation, increased self-esteem, and a greater sense of purpose. These psychological benefits contribute to the overall success of the rehabilitation process and support long-term reintegration into society. Social reintegration is another critical area where altruism plays a vital role. Offenders who engage in altruistic activities are more likely to develop positive relationships with community members, reducing the stigma associated with their criminal past. This social acceptance is essential for successful reintegration, as it provides offenders with the support and opportunities needed to rebuild their lives. By fostering positive social connections, altruism helps create a network of support that can guide offenders towards a more constructive and law-abiding lifestyle.

The "Circles of Support and Accountability" (CoSA) program in the United Kingdom exemplifies the impact of altruism on social reintegration. CoSA involves community volunteers forming supportive circles around high-risk sex offenders upon their release from prison. These volunteers provide guidance, support, and accountability, helping offenders navigate the challenges of reintegration. The program has been highly successful in reducing recidivism rates and promoting social acceptance. Offenders who participate in CoSA report feeling valued and supported, which significantly enhances their ability to reintegrate into society. Community health and cohesion also benefit from the integration of altruism into justice practices. When offenders contribute positively to their communities, they help build stronger, more resilient neighborhoods. Community service projects, such as environmental clean-ups, urban gardening, and support for local charities, address immediate community needs while fostering a sense of collective responsibility. These activities promote civic engagement and social cohesion, creating healthier and more vibrant communities.

The "Community Gardens Project" in Detroit, Michigan, illustrates the broader community benefits of altruistic activities. This program involves offenders working alongside community members to create and maintain urban gardens in underserved neighborhoods. The gardens provide fresh produce for local residents, promote environmental sustainability, and create spaces for community gatherings. The collaboration between offenders and community members fosters mutual respect and understanding, breaking down barriers and building stronger social bonds. The success of the Community Gardens Project demonstrates how altruistic activities can lead to lasting improvements in community health and cohesion. Altruism also contributes to the overall effectiveness and efficiency of the justice system. Programs that incorporate altruistic activities often result in cost savings for the justice system by reducing recidivism rates and the need for repeated incarceration. The long-term benefits of these programs, including improved mental health, enhanced employability, and stronger social networks, contribute to a more sustainable and effective approach to justice. By investing in altruistic rehabilitation strategies, the justice system can achieve better outcomes for offenders and communities while reducing the financial burden on taxpayers.

Policy recommendations for integrating altruism into justice systems emphasize the importance of comprehensive and evidence-based approaches. Policymakers should prioritize funding and support for programs that incorporate altruistic activities, such as community service, restorative justice, and mentorship initiatives. These programs should be designed to address the specific needs of offenders and communities, with a focus on promoting empathy, responsibility, and social connection. Training for justice professionals, including correctional officers, probation officers, and social workers, is essential for the successful implementation of altruistic practices. Training should include modules on restorative justice, trauma-informed care, and effective mentorship. By equipping justice professionals with the skills and knowledge needed to facilitate altruistic activities, the justice system can create a more supportive and rehabilitative environment for offenders.

Collaborations with community organizations and local businesses are also vital for the success of altruistic programs. These partnerships can provide resources, expertise, and opportunities for meaningful engagement. Community organizations can offer support and mentorship to offenders, while local businesses can provide employment opportunities and contribute to community service projects. By working together, the justice system and community stakeholders can create a comprehensive and integrated approach to rehabilitation. Research and evaluation are crucial for understanding the impact of altruistic practices and refining program design. Longitudinal studies that track participants' progress over time can provide valuable insights into the long-term benefits of these programs. Collecting data on recidivism rates, mental health outcomes, employment status, and social integration can help identify best practices and areas for improvement. This evidence can be used to advocate for policy changes and secure funding for altruistic rehabilitation programs.

CHAPTER TWELVE

Ethical Leadership in Justice

Contents

- Developing Ethical Leadership Qualities

- Practical Applications in Justice Administration

- Case Studies of Ethical Leadership

- Long-Term Benefits for Justice Systems

- Strategies for Cultivating Ethical Leaders

12.1: Developing Ethical Leadership Qualities

Ethical leadership in justice is deeply rooted in the principles of Tibetan Buddhism, where compassion, wisdom, and selflessness guide actions and decisions. Central to this approach is the understanding that leaders are not merely figures of authority but stewards of moral and ethical integrity, responsible for the well-being of others. In Tibetan Buddhism, the core ethical principles are embodied in the teachings of the Eightfold Path, the Six Perfections, and the Four Immeasurables, each offering profound insights into the nature of ethical leadership. The Eightfold Path provides a comprehensive framework for ethical conduct, encompassing right view, right intention, right speech, right action, right livelihood, right effort, right mindfulness, and right concentration. Leaders who embody these principles are expected to maintain a clear and compassionate vision, act with integrity, communicate truthfully, and make decisions that promote the welfare of all beings. This holistic approach ensures that ethical leadership is not limited to specific actions but permeates every aspect of a leader's life and responsibilities.

The Six Perfections, or Paramitas, further elucidate the qualities of an ethical leader: generosity, ethical conduct, patience, joyful effort, concentration, and wisdom. Generosity, in this context, goes beyond material giving to include the sharing of time, knowledge, and support. Ethical conduct emphasizes the importance of moral integrity and adherence to ethical standards. Patience involves maintaining equanimity in the face of challenges and setbacks, while joyful effort signifies a wholehearted commitment to one's responsibilities. Concentration highlights the need for focused and mindful decision-making, and wisdom ensures that actions are guided by deep understanding and insight. The Four Immeasurables—loving-kindness, compassion, empathetic joy, and equanimity—underscore the emotional and relational aspects of ethical leadership. Loving-kindness involves wishing for the happiness and well-being of others, while compassion focuses on alleviating their suffering. Empathetic joy is the ability to rejoice in others' happiness and successes, and equanimity represents a balanced and impartial mindset, free from bias and prejudice. These qualities enable leaders to build genuine connections with those they serve and create an environment of trust and mutual respect.

Historical examples of ethical leadership inspired by Tibetan Buddhist teachings abound. King Ashoka, one of the most celebrated rulers in ancient India, exemplified these principles. After a transformative experience following the Kalinga War, Ashoka embraced Buddhism and dedicated his reign to promoting peace, social welfare, and ethical governance. His edicts, inscribed on pillars and rocks throughout his empire, advocate for non-violence, compassion, and the fair treatment of all beings. Ashoka's leadership transformed his kingdom into a model of ethical and compassionate governance, illustrating the profound impact of Buddhist principles on political leadership. In modern times, the Dalai Lama embodies ethical leadership through his unwavering commitment to peace, compassion, and human rights. His teachings and actions consistently reflect the principles of Tibetan Buddhism, advocating for a compassionate and ethical approach to global issues. The Dalai Lama's leadership extends beyond religious boundaries, influencing political leaders, activists, and individuals worldwide. His efforts to promote interfaith dialogue, environmental sustainability, and social justice demonstrate the relevance of Buddhist ethics in addressing contemporary challenges.

Ethical leadership in justice systems requires a profound commitment to the well-being of all stakeholders, including offenders, victims, and the community. Leaders who embrace these principles are equipped to make decisions that balance accountability with compassion, ensuring that justice is served while promoting healing and rehabilitation. This approach contrasts sharply with punitive models of justice that prioritize retribution over restoration, highlighting the transformative potential of ethical leadership. In practice, ethical leaders in justice systems must navigate complex and often conflicting demands. They are tasked with upholding the law while addressing the underlying causes of criminal behavior, such as poverty, trauma, and social inequality. This requires a nuanced understanding of the socio-economic and psychological factors that contribute to crime, as well as a commitment to addressing these root causes through compassionate and evidence-based interventions. Ethical leaders recognize that true justice involves not only punishment but also healing and transformation, creating conditions that enable individuals to rebuild their lives and contribute positively to society.

Ethical leadership also involves creating a culture of integrity and accountability within justice institutions. This includes establishing clear ethical guidelines, providing ongoing training and support for staff, and fostering an environment where ethical behavior is recognized and rewarded. Leaders must model the behavior they wish to see, demonstrating transparency, fairness, and respect in their interactions with colleagues and stakeholders. By cultivating a culture of ethical leadership, justice institutions can enhance their credibility and effectiveness, building public trust and confidence. The relevance of Tibetan Buddhist principles in modern justice systems is evident in various innovative programs and practices. Restorative justice, for example, aligns closely with the principles of compassion and interconnectedness, emphasizing the importance of repairing harm and restoring relationships. Programs that incorporate mindfulness and meditation, such as the Insight Prison Project and the Mindfulness-Based Stress Reduction program, draw directly from Buddhist practices to promote emotional regulation, self-awareness, and personal growth among offenders. Ethical leadership in justice also requires a commitment to social justice and equity. This involves advocating for policies and practices that address systemic injustices, such as racial disparities in sentencing, inadequate access to legal representation, and the criminalization of poverty. Ethical leaders work to create a more just and equitable society by challenging discriminatory practices and promoting inclusivity and fairness in the justice system.

12.2: Practical Applications in Justice Administration

Developing ethical leadership qualities in justice professionals involves a comprehensive approach that integrates training, mindfulness, compassion, and real-world applications. Ethical leadership is essential in justice systems, where decisions have profound and lasting impacts on individuals and communities. To cultivate these qualities, justice professionals must undergo rigorous and ongoing training that emphasizes ethical decision-making, empathy, and integrity. Mindfulness and compassion play pivotal roles in ethical leadership, providing a foundation for sound judgment and humane treatment. Mindfulness, the practice of being present and fully engaged in the moment, helps leaders remain calm and focused, especially in high-stress situations. It enhances their ability to listen deeply, consider multiple perspectives, and respond thoughtfully rather than react impulsively. Compassion, the ability to understand and share the feelings of others, fosters a sense of connection and responsibility towards those affected by their decisions.

Training programs for justice professionals should incorporate mindfulness practices to enhance their emotional intelligence and decision-making abilities. For example, the "Mindfulness-Based Stress Reduction" (MBSR) program, developed by Jon Kabat-Zinn, has been adapted for use in various professional settings, including justice. This program teaches techniques such as mindful breathing, body scanning, and meditation, which help individuals manage stress and improve their emotional regulation. By incorporating MBSR into training for judges, lawyers, correctional officers, and other justice professionals, they can develop greater self-awareness and resilience, essential traits for ethical leadership. The "Insight Prison Project" (IPP) in California offers another model for integrating mindfulness and ethical leadership. IPP provides a range of programs focused on emotional literacy, victim impact, and restorative justice. These programs teach offenders and justice professionals alike to practice mindfulness, reflect on their actions, and cultivate empathy. By creating a shared understanding of the impact of crime and fostering compassionate responses, IPP helps develop leaders who are better equipped to support rehabilitation and restorative justice.

In addition to mindfulness, compassion training is crucial for developing ethical leadership. Programs such as Compassion-Focused Therapy (CFT), developed by Dr. Paul Gilbert, can be adapted for justice professionals. CFT combines cognitive-behavioral techniques with practices designed to enhance compassion for oneself and others. Training in CFT helps professionals recognize and manage their own emotional responses, develop compassionate mindsets, and make decisions that prioritize the well-being of all parties involved. Role-playing and scenario-based training are effective methods for teaching ethical decision-making. These exercises present justice professionals with complex, real-world scenarios that require careful consideration of ethical principles. By navigating these scenarios in a controlled environment, professionals can practice applying ethical frameworks and receive feedback on their decision-making processes. For example, a role-playing exercise might involve a judge presiding over a case with significant social implications, requiring them to balance legal standards with considerations of equity and compassion. Through these exercises, professionals learn to navigate the nuances of ethical leadership and develop confidence in their abilities.

Mentorship programs also play a critical role in developing ethical leadership qualities. Pairing less experienced professionals with seasoned mentors who exemplify ethical leadership provides valuable guidance and support. Mentors can share their experiences, offer insights into navigating ethical dilemmas, and model compassionate and principled behavior. These relationships foster a culture of continuous learning and ethical development within justice institutions. The "Judicial Education and Research" (JER) program in Canada provides an exemplary model of mentorship in action. JER offers comprehensive training and mentorship for judges, focusing on ethical decision-making, cultural competency, and emotional intelligence. The program includes workshops, seminars, and one-on-one mentoring sessions, where experienced judges guide their peers through complex legal and ethical challenges. This mentorship model helps instill a deep sense of ethical responsibility and integrity among participants, enhancing their leadership capabilities.

Case studies of successful ethical leadership in justice settings highlight the transformative impact of these qualities. For instance, Judge Victoria Pratt of Newark, New Jersey, is renowned for her innovative and compassionate approach to justice. As the presiding judge of Newark Community Solutions, she implemented a community court model that focuses on rehabilitation and restorative justice. Judge Pratt's courtroom practices, such as offering offenders a chance to apologize, engage in community service, and participate in counseling, emphasize accountability and empathy. Her leadership has significantly reduced recidivism rates and strengthened community trust in the justice system. Another notable example is Bryan Stevenson, founder of the Equal Justice Initiative (EJI) in Alabama. Stevenson's work focuses on challenging racial and economic injustice, advocating for marginalized communities, and promoting rehabilitation over punishment. His ethical leadership is characterized by a deep commitment to compassion, justice, and human dignity. Through EJI, Stevenson has successfully overturned wrongful convictions, advocated for policy reforms, and brought national attention to systemic inequities in the justice system. His leadership exemplifies how ethical principles can drive meaningful change and inspire others to pursue justice with integrity.

Training programs for ethical leadership in the justice system must be comprehensive and adaptive to the evolving challenges of the field. Programs like the "National Judicial College" (NJC) in the United States offer a wide range of courses and seminars that address ethical issues, judicial conduct, and the development of leadership skills. The NJC emphasizes experiential learning, providing judges with opportunities to engage in discussions, case studies, and simulations that enhance their ethical decision-making abilities. By staying current with emerging trends and challenges, these programs ensure that justice professionals are well-equipped to lead with integrity. Organizational culture and policies play a crucial role in promoting ethical behavior and leadership. Institutions must establish clear ethical guidelines, provide regular training, and create an environment where ethical conduct is recognized and rewarded. Leaders at all levels must model ethical behavior, demonstrating transparency, fairness, and respect in their interactions with colleagues and stakeholders. By fostering a culture of ethical leadership, justice institutions can enhance their credibility, effectiveness, and public trust.

The importance of ethical leadership in justice extends beyond individual actions to systemic change. Ethical leaders advocate for policies and practices that address systemic injustices, such as racial disparities in sentencing, inadequate access to legal representation, and the criminalization of poverty. They work to create a more just and equitable society by challenging discriminatory practices and promoting inclusivity and fairness in the justice system. Ethical leadership in justice also involves a commitment to continuous self-improvement and reflection. Leaders must regularly assess their own actions, seek feedback, and strive to align their behavior with ethical principles. This ongoing process of self-evaluation and growth ensures that leaders remain accountable and responsive to the needs of those they serve.

12.3: Case Studies of Ethical Leadership

Training programs for ethical leadership in the justice system are crucial for developing the competencies and mindsets necessary to navigate the complex moral landscape of criminal justice. These programs aim to cultivate qualities such as integrity, empathy, accountability, and a deep commitment to fairness and justice. By integrating ethical leadership training into the professional development of justice personnel, the system can better address the multifaceted challenges it faces and promote a culture of ethical decision-making and compassionate practice. One prominent example of a comprehensive training program for ethical leadership is the "Leadership Development for Correctional Professionals" offered by the Correctional Management Institute of Texas (CMIT). This program is designed to enhance the leadership skills of correctional officers, probation officers, and other justice professionals. The curriculum includes modules on ethical decision-making, emotional intelligence, and the development of a leadership philosophy grounded in ethical principles. Participants engage in case studies, role-playing exercises, and reflective practices that help them apply ethical concepts to real-world scenarios. The program emphasizes the importance of self-awareness, integrity, and the ability to lead by example.

Another innovative training program is the "Ethical Leadership in Law Enforcement" initiative by the International Association of Chiefs of Police (IACP). This program addresses the unique ethical challenges faced by law enforcement officers and provides tools for making principled decisions in high-pressure situations. The curriculum covers topics such as bias awareness, community policing, and the ethical use of authority. Interactive workshops and scenario-based training allow participants to practice ethical decision-making in a supportive environment. The program also includes a mentorship component, where experienced officers provide guidance and support to newer recruits, fostering a culture of ethical leadership throughout the organization. The "Judicial Education and Leadership Institute" (JELI) in the United Kingdom offers a robust training program for judges and magistrates. This program focuses on enhancing judicial ethics, impartiality, and the fair administration of justice. The curriculum includes lectures, seminars, and practical exercises on topics such as conflict of interest, ethical dilemmas in sentencing, and the impact of unconscious bias. JELI emphasizes the importance of continuous professional development and reflective practice, encouraging judges to engage in ongoing self-assessment and peer review. By fostering a commitment to ethical leadership, JELI helps ensure that judicial decisions are grounded in fairness, compassion, and respect for the rule of law.

The "National Institute of Corrections" (NIC) in the United States offers a training program titled "Executive Leadership Development for Corrections Professionals." This program is tailored for senior leaders in correctional institutions and focuses on strategic thinking, ethical leadership, and organizational change. The curriculum includes modules on ethical decision-making frameworks, the development of ethical policies and practices, and the role of leadership in promoting a positive organizational culture. Participants engage in collaborative learning activities, case studies, and action planning exercises that help them translate ethical principles into concrete actions within their institutions. A distinctive feature of these training programs is their emphasis on experiential learning and practical application. For instance, the "Restorative Justice Leadership Training" provided by the Centre for Justice and Reconciliation integrates experiential learning with theoretical knowledge. Participants engage in restorative justice circles, victim-offender dialogues, and community service projects that allow them to practice restorative principles and develop empathy and accountability. This hands-on approach helps leaders internalize ethical values and apply them in their daily work, fostering a restorative approach to justice that prioritizes healing and reconciliation.

The "Ethics in Public Service" program by the Singapore Civil Service College offers another example of effective ethical leadership training. This program is designed for senior public servants, including those in the justice sector, and focuses on building a culture of integrity and accountability. The curriculum covers topics such as ethical governance, public trust, and the prevention of corruption. Participants engage in discussions, case studies, and scenario-based exercises that challenge them to think critically about ethical dilemmas and develop strategies for maintaining ethical standards in public service. By promoting ethical leadership at all levels of government, this program helps ensure that public institutions operate with transparency and accountability. To evaluate the effectiveness of these training programs, it is essential to gather feedback from participants and assess their impact on organizational culture and decision-making. Surveys, interviews, and follow-up evaluations can provide valuable insights into how training has influenced participants' attitudes, behaviors, and leadership styles. For example, the "Ethical Leadership in Action" program by the Institute for Law Enforcement Administration conducts regular follow-up surveys with participants to assess the long-term impact of the training. These evaluations have shown significant improvements in participants' ethical decision-making abilities, their commitment to ethical principles, and their capacity to lead with integrity.

The integration of ethical leadership training into professional development also requires a supportive organizational environment. Institutions must prioritize ethics in their policies, practices, and culture. This involves establishing clear ethical guidelines, providing regular training and development opportunities, and creating mechanisms for accountability and feedback. Leaders at all levels must model ethical behavior and foster a culture of transparency, fairness, and respect. By embedding ethical leadership into the fabric of the organization, justice institutions can enhance their credibility and effectiveness. Ethical leadership training programs must also be adaptive and responsive to emerging challenges and trends in the justice sector. This requires continuous research and innovation in curriculum design and delivery. For instance, the "Digital Ethics and Leadership" program by the Center for Technology and Society addresses the ethical implications of digital technologies in justice, such as surveillance, data privacy, and artificial intelligence. By staying current with technological advancements and their ethical implications, this program equips justice professionals with the knowledge and skills needed to navigate the complexities of the digital age.

12.4: Long-Term Benefits for Justice Systems

Examining case studies of ethical leaders in the justice system reveals the transformative impact of principled leadership on justice reform and community well-being. These leaders demonstrate the profound difference that ethical commitment, empathy, and integrity can make in addressing systemic issues, fostering trust, and promoting restorative practices. Their stories provide valuable lessons on how ethical leadership can drive meaningful change and inspire others to follow suit. One notable example is Chief Judge Judith S. Kaye of the New York Court of Appeals. Appointed as the first female Chief Judge in 1993, Kaye's tenure was marked by her unwavering dedication to judicial reform and ethical governance. She spearheaded numerous initiatives aimed at improving the justice system, including the establishment of specialized courts for drug offenses, domestic violence, and mental health. These courts focused on addressing the root causes of criminal behavior through rehabilitation and support services rather than punitive measures. Judge Kaye's ethical leadership and innovative approach significantly reduced recidivism rates and improved outcomes for individuals involved in these specialized courts. Her efforts to promote transparency and accountability within the judiciary also enhanced public trust and confidence in the justice system.

Another exemplary ethical leader is Bryan Stevenson, the founder and Executive Director of the Equal Justice Initiative (EJI) in Alabama. Stevenson's work has been instrumental in challenging racial and economic injustices within the U.S. criminal justice system. He has dedicated his career to defending marginalized communities, advocating for policy reforms, and addressing wrongful convictions and excessive sentencing. Stevenson's leadership is characterized by his deep empathy for those he serves and his commitment to justice and human dignity. Through EJI, he has successfully overturned numerous wrongful convictions, secured relief for individuals on death row, and brought national attention to the issues of mass incarceration and systemic racism. Stevenson's ethical leadership has not only transformed the lives of countless individuals but also influenced broader societal attitudes towards justice and equity. A further example of ethical leadership in justice is that of Judge Steven Teske of the Clayton County Juvenile Court in Georgia. Faced with the growing issue of school-to-prison pipelines, Judge Teske implemented a series of reforms aimed at reducing the criminalization of minor offenses in schools. He established the School-Justice Partnership, which brought together educators, law enforcement, and community leaders to develop alternative disciplinary measures that focus on restorative practices rather than arrests and expulsions. This initiative significantly decreased the number of students entering the juvenile justice system, improved school safety, and fostered a more supportive educational environment. Judge Teske's commitment to ethical leadership and restorative justice principles has had a lasting impact on the community, highlighting the importance of addressing the underlying causes of juvenile delinquency.

Kimberly S. Budd, the Chief Justice of the Massachusetts Supreme Judicial Court, exemplifies ethical leadership through her dedication to judicial transparency, fairness, and reform. Chief Justice Budd has championed initiatives to improve access to justice, particularly for marginalized and underserved communities. Under her leadership, the Massachusetts court system has implemented programs to provide legal assistance to low-income individuals, enhance language access services, and address racial and ethnic disparities in sentencing. Chief Justice Budd's commitment to ethical principles and her focus on inclusivity and equity have strengthened the integrity of the justice system and promoted greater public trust. In the international context, Navi Pillay, a South African judge and human rights lawyer, has made significant contributions to ethical leadership in justice. As the United Nations High Commissioner for Human Rights from 2008 to 2014, Pillay advocated for the protection of human rights and the promotion of justice globally. Her tenure was marked by efforts to address human rights abuses, promote gender equality, and support the rights of indigenous peoples and minorities. Pillay's ethical leadership and commitment to justice have had a profound impact on international human rights law and policy, inspiring global efforts to protect and uphold human dignity.

Sheriff Tom Dart of Cook County, Illinois, offers another compelling example of ethical leadership in the justice system. Dart has been a vocal advocate for criminal justice reform, focusing on the need to address mental health issues and provide support for individuals with substance use disorders. Under his leadership, the Cook County Jail has implemented numerous programs aimed at rehabilitation and reducing recidivism, including mental health treatment, educational programs, and job training initiatives. Sheriff Dart's commitment to ethical principles and his compassionate approach to law enforcement have transformed the Cook County Jail into a model for progressive correctional practices. The work of Professor Deborah Epstein, a legal scholar and advocate for survivors of domestic violence, highlights the importance of ethical leadership in addressing gender-based violence. As the Director of the Domestic Violence Clinic at Georgetown University Law Center, Epstein has developed comprehensive legal and support services for survivors. Her advocacy extends to policy reform, where she has worked to improve protections for survivors and hold perpetrators accountable. Professor Epstein's ethical leadership has been instrumental in advancing legal and social responses to domestic violence, promoting justice and safety for survivors.

Judge Victoria Pratt of Newark, New Jersey, is renowned for her innovative approach to justice through procedural fairness and restorative practices. As the presiding judge of the Newark Community Solutions program, Judge Pratt implemented courtroom practices that emphasize respect, voice, neutrality, and understanding. Her approach includes giving offenders a chance to explain their circumstances, offering alternative sentencing options, and encouraging community service and rehabilitation. Judge Pratt's ethical leadership has significantly improved compliance with court orders, reduced recidivism, and strengthened community trust in the justice system. Ethical leadership in justice also extends to advocacy and policy reform, as demonstrated by the work of Vanita Gupta, the Associate Attorney General of the United States. As a former head of the Civil Rights Division at the U.S. Department of Justice, Gupta led efforts to address police misconduct, reform sentencing practices, and protect voting rights. Her leadership is characterized by a steadfast commitment to civil rights and social justice, advocating for policies that promote equality and protect marginalized communities. Gupta's ethical leadership has had a transformative impact on the U.S. justice system, promoting greater accountability and fairness.

These case studies illustrate the profound impact that ethical leadership can have on justice reform and community well-being. The common thread among these leaders is their unwavering commitment to ethical principles, empathy, and a vision for a more just and equitable society. Their work highlights the importance of integrating ethical leadership into all levels of the justice system, from individual decision-making to systemic reform. The lessons learned from these ethical leaders underscore the importance of continuous professional development, mentorship, and reflective practice in cultivating ethical leadership. Justice professionals must be equipped with the knowledge, skills, and support needed to navigate complex ethical dilemmas and promote justice and fairness. By fostering a culture of ethical leadership, justice institutions can enhance their credibility, effectiveness, and public trust, ultimately contributing to a more just and compassionate society.

12.5: Strategies for Cultivating Ethical Leaders

Building a culture of ethical leadership in correctional facilities is fundamental to transforming the justice system into one that prioritizes rehabilitation, respect, and dignity. Ethical leadership at all levels, from frontline staff to top administrators, fosters an environment where ethical behavior is the norm and where the principles of fairness, compassion, and accountability guide every action and decision. This transformation requires strategic planning, continuous education, and a commitment to systemic change. The foundation of a culture of ethical leadership in correctional facilities begins with clear, well-communicated ethical standards. These standards must be articulated in codes of conduct, policies, and training programs that emphasize the importance of integrity, transparency, and respect for all individuals. Ethical standards should be regularly reviewed and updated to reflect current best practices and emerging challenges in the field of corrections. This ensures that staff at all levels are aware of their ethical obligations and are equipped to navigate complex situations with confidence and clarity.

Leadership plays a critical role in modeling ethical behavior and setting the tone for the entire organization. Leaders must demonstrate a steadfast commitment to ethical principles in their actions and decisions, serving as role models for their staff. This involves making difficult decisions that uphold ethical standards, even when faced with pressure to do otherwise. Leaders must also be transparent about their decision-making processes and willing to be held accountable for their actions. This transparency builds trust within the organization and encourages staff to adhere to the same high standards. Effective training programs are essential for fostering ethical leadership in correctional facilities. These programs should be comprehensive, covering a wide range of topics including ethical decision-making, conflict resolution, cultural competency, and the principles of restorative justice. Training should be ongoing, with regular refresher courses and opportunities for professional development. Interactive training methods, such as role-playing, case studies, and simulations, can help staff apply ethical principles in real-world scenarios and develop the skills needed to handle ethical dilemmas effectively.

One example of a successful training program is the "Ethics in Corrections" initiative by the National Institute of Corrections (NIC). This program provides correctional staff with the tools and knowledge to navigate ethical challenges and make decisions that align with ethical standards. The curriculum includes modules on professional boundaries, the ethical use of authority, and the impact of personal values on decision-making. By incorporating interactive exercises and real-life case studies, the program helps participants internalize ethical principles and apply them in their daily work. Creating a supportive organizational culture that values and reinforces ethical behavior is equally important. This involves establishing mechanisms for reporting and addressing unethical conduct without fear of retaliation. Whistleblower protections, confidential reporting systems, and clear procedures for investigating and resolving ethical violations are essential components of this framework. Encouraging an open dialogue about ethics and providing safe spaces for staff to discuss ethical concerns can also help foster a culture of integrity.

Recognition and reward systems that celebrate ethical behavior can further reinforce a culture of ethical leadership. By acknowledging and rewarding staff who demonstrate ethical excellence, correctional facilities can highlight the importance of ethical conduct and motivate others to follow suit. This recognition can take various forms, including awards, public commendations, and career advancement opportunities. Celebrating ethical behavior sends a powerful message that the organization values integrity and is committed to upholding the highest ethical standards. In addition to internal measures, collaboration with external stakeholders is crucial for promoting ethical leadership. Partnerships with academic institutions, non-profit organizations, and community groups can provide valuable resources, expertise, and perspectives. These collaborations can help develop and implement training programs, conduct research on best practices, and create opportunities for community engagement and restorative justice initiatives. Engaging with external stakeholders also enhances transparency and accountability, as it opens the organization to external scrutiny and feedback.

One notable example of external collaboration is the partnership between the California Department of Corrections and Rehabilitation

(CDCR) and the University of California, Berkeley. This partnership has resulted in the development of innovative training programs and research projects focused on ethical leadership and correctional reform. By leveraging the expertise of academic researchers and practitioners, CDCR has been able to enhance its training programs and implement evidence-based practices that promote ethical behavior and effective rehabilitation. Building a culture of ethical leadership also involves addressing systemic issues that contribute to unethical behavior. This includes tackling factors such as overcrowding, inadequate staffing, and insufficient resources, which can create environments where ethical lapses are more likely to occur. Leaders must advocate for policies and practices that address these systemic issues and create conditions that support ethical conduct. This may involve pushing for legislative changes, securing funding for improvements, and implementing organizational reforms that prioritize the well-being of staff and inmates.

The long-term benefits of building a culture of ethical leadership in correctional facilities are substantial. Facilities that prioritize ethical leadership are more likely to achieve positive outcomes for both staff and inmates. Ethical leadership fosters a safer, more respectful environment, which can reduce incidents of violence, misconduct, and abuse. It also promotes rehabilitation and reintegration, as inmates are treated with dignity and given the support they need to make positive changes in their lives. Research supports the positive impact of ethical leadership on organizational outcomes. Studies have shown that ethical leadership is associated with higher levels of job satisfaction, commitment, and performance among staff. It also correlates with lower levels of stress, burnout, and turnover. For inmates, ethical leadership can lead to better mental health outcomes, reduced recidivism rates, and improved chances of successful reintegration into society. These benefits extend beyond the correctional facility, contributing to safer and more cohesive communities. To sustain a culture of ethical leadership, correctional facilities must embrace continuous improvement and adaptation. This involves regularly assessing the effectiveness of ethical standards, training programs, and organizational practices. Feedback from staff, inmates, and external stakeholders should be used to identify areas for improvement and to develop strategies for addressing emerging challenges. By fostering a culture of learning and innovation, correctional facilities can remain responsive to changing conditions and uphold the highest ethical standards.

References

- Braithwaite, J. (2006). Narrative and "Compulsory Compassion" [Review of Compulsory Compassion: A Critique of Restorative Justice, by Annalise Acorn]. Law & Social Inquiry, 31(2), 425–446. http://www.jstor.org/stable/4092753
- Caplan, G. (1990). The Ethics of the "Unprofessional Profession" [Review of Character and Cops: Ethics in Policing, by E. J. Delattre]. Michigan Law Review, 88(6), 1698–1708. https://doi.org/10.2307/1289337
- Clohesy, W. W. (2000). Altruism and the Endurance of the Good. Voluntas: International Journal of Voluntary and Nonprofit Organizations, 11(3), 237–253. http://www.jstor.org/stable/27927688
- Clary, E. G., & Miller, J. (1986). Socialization and Situational Influences on Sustained Altruism. Child Development, 57(6), 1358–1369. https://doi.org/10.2307/1130415
- Craft, J. L. (2013). Living in the Gray: Lessons on Ethics from Prison. Journal of Business Ethics, 115(2), 327–339. http://www.jstor.org/stable/42001986
- Darlington, P. J. (1978). Altruism: Its Characteristics and Evolution. Proceedings of the National Academy of Sciences of the United States of America, 75(1), 385–389. http://www.jstor.org/stable/67645
- de Jong, J. W. (1982). [Review of THE BODHISATTVA DOCTRINE IN BUDDHISM, by L. S. Kawamura]. The Eastern Buddhist, 15(1), 146–151. http://www.jstor.org/stable/44361649
- Fenton, J. (2015). An Analysis of "Ethical Stress" in Criminal Justice Social Work in Scotland: The Place of Values. The British Journal of Social Work, 45(5), 1415–1432. http://www.jstor.org/stable/43687922
- FRAKES, C. (2010). When Strangers Call: A Consideration of Care, Justice, and Compassion. Hypatia, 25(1), 79–99. http://www.jstor.org/

stable/40602641

- Gómez, L. O. (1993). "Being-in-the-World": The Bodhisattva Ideal and the Millennium. Buddhist-Christian Studies, 13, 187–197. https://doi.org/10.2307/1389886
- Herbert, S. (1996). Morality in Law Enforcement: Chasing "Bad Guys" with the Los Angeles Police Department. Law & Society Review, 30(4), 799–818. https://doi.org/10.2307/3054118
- Jenkins, S. (2016). DEBATE, MAGIC, AND MASSACRE: THE HIGH STAKES AND ETHICAL DYNAMICS OF BATTLING SLANDERERS OF THE DHARMA IN INDIAN NARRATIVE AND ETHICAL THEORY. Journal of Religion and Violence, 4(2), 129–158. https://www.jstor.org/stable/26671496
- Kevin, C. S. K. (2000). An evangelical engagement with Mahāyāna Buddhist ethics. Transformation, 17(3), 109–112. http://www.jstor.org/stable/43070253
- Kitcher, P. (1993). The Evolution of Human Altruism. The Journal of Philosophy, 90(10), 497–516. https://doi.org/10.2307/2941024
- Kooken, D. L. (1947). Ethics in Police Service (Continued). Journal of Criminal Law and Criminology (1931-1951), 38(2), 172–186. https://doi.org/10.2307/1138914
- Krishan, Y. (1984). The Origin and Development of the Bodhisattva Doctrine. East and West, 34(1/3), 199–232. http://www.jstor.org/stable/29756685
- Kurz, M. (1978). Altruism as an Outcome of Social Interaction. The American Economic Review, 68(2), 216–222. http://www.jstor.org/stable/1816691
- Lawton, A., & Páez, I. (2015). Developing a Framework for Ethical Leadership. Journal of Business Ethics, 130(3), 639–649. http://www.jstor.org/stable/24703528
- Lee, J. (1993). The Origins and Development of the Pensive Bodhisattva Images of Asia. Artibus Asiae, 53(3/4), 311–357. https://doi.org/10.2307/3250524
- Marks, J. (2007). Rousseau's Discriminating Defense of Compassion. The American Political Science Review, 101(4), 727–739. http://www.jstor.org/stable/27644481
- McGovern, Wm. M. (1919). NOTES ON MAHAYANA BUDDHISM. The Monist, 29(2), 238–258. http://www.jstor.org/stable/27900739

- Mills, E. (2007). [Review of Buddhism, Knowledge and Liberation: A Philosophical Study, by D. Burton]. Philosophy East and West, 57(4), 593–595. http://www.jstor.org/stable/20109433
- Oliner, P. M., & Oliner, S. P. (1990). THE ROOTS OF ALTRUISM. Shofar, 8(2), 16–34. http://www.jstor.org/stable/42941396
- Perrett, R. W. (1986). The Bodhisattva Paradox. Philosophy East and West, 36(1), 55–59. https://doi.org/10.2307/1398508
- Peterson, T. E. (2001). Justice, Modesty and Compassion in Foscolo's "Ajace." MLN, 116(1), 74–97. http://www.jstor.org/stable/3251605
- Purpel, D. E., & McLaurin, W. M. (2004). A CURRICULUM FOR SOCIAL JUSTICE AND COMPASSION. Counterpoints, 262, 125–140. http://www.jstor.org/stable/42978527
- Reilly, R. (2006). Compassion as Justice. Buddhist-Christian Studies, 26, 13–31. http://www.jstor.org/stable/4139178
- Royster, M. D. (2018). [Review of CONNECTING PEACE, JUSTICE, AND RECONCILIATION, by E. Porter]. International Journal on World Peace, 35(2), 92–94. http://www.jstor.org/stable/45014450
- Samuels, J. (1997). The Bodhisattva Ideal in Theravāda Buddhist Theory and Practice: A Reevaluation of the Bodhisattva-Śrāvaka Opposition. Philosophy East and West, 47(3), 399–415. https://doi.org/10.2307/1399912
- Soboslai, J., & Gruber, J. (2018). The Bodhisattva, the Dharmarāja, and the Dalai Lamas: Evaluating the Religious and Political Causes of Tibetan Self-Immolation. Journal of the American Academy of Religion, 86(3), 759–788. https://www.jstor.org/stable/48556294

Part IV: Mindfulness and Meditation in Rehabilitation

CHAPTER THIRTEEN

Mindfulness Practices for Offenders

Contents

- Techniques for Teaching Mindfulness

- Benefits of Mindfulness in Correctional Settings

- Case Studies of Mindfulness Programs

- Long-Term Impact on Offenders

- Strategies for Implementing Mindfulness Practices

13.1: Techniques for Teaching Mindfulness

Mindfulness, a practice with roots stretching back thousands of years, is fundamentally about cultivating a deep awareness of the present moment. Its origins are often traced to ancient Eastern traditions, particularly Buddhism, where it is a core component of the path to enlightenment. However, mindfulness has transcended its religious roots and found a place in modern secular contexts, including psychology, healthcare, and rehabilitation. The essence of mindfulness lies in paying attention intentionally and non-judgmentally to the present moment, allowing individuals to experience their thoughts, emotions, and sensations without being overwhelmed by them. In the context of rehabilitation, mindfulness has emerged as a powerful tool for fostering mental and emotional well-being. Scientific research has extensively documented the benefits of mindfulness, particularly in reducing stress, anxiety, and depression. For offenders, who often grapple with high levels of emotional distress and trauma, mindfulness can provide a pathway to greater self-awareness and emotional regulation. By learning to observe their thoughts and feelings without immediate reaction, individuals can develop a more measured response to stressful situations, which is crucial in a correctional setting.

Mindfulness practices help individuals break the cycle of reactive behavior that often leads to conflict and violence. Through regular practice, offenders can cultivate a sense of calm and stability, which enhances their ability to make thoughtful decisions rather than impulsive ones. This shift from reactivity to responsiveness is not just beneficial for the individuals themselves but also for the overall environment within correctional facilities. A calmer, more reflective inmate population can lead to reduced incidents of violence and misconduct, creating a safer and more supportive atmosphere for both inmates and staff. Several case studies highlight the successful implementation of mindfulness programs in correctional settings. One notable example is the "Mindfulness-Based Stress Reduction" (MBSR) program, developed by Jon Kabat-Zinn, which has been adapted for use in prisons. MBSR teaches participants various mindfulness techniques, including mindful breathing, body scanning, and gentle yoga. These practices help individuals become more attuned to their physical and emotional states, fostering a greater sense of self-control and resilience.

In a study conducted at the Massachusetts Correctional Institution, inmates who participated in an MBSR program reported significant reductions in stress and improvements in their overall well-being. Many participants described feeling more centered and less prone to outbursts of anger. These findings are consistent with other research showing that mindfulness can reduce symptoms of post-traumatic stress disorder (PTSD), a common issue among offenders who have experienced significant trauma. Another compelling case comes from the Mindfulness, Meditation, and Movement (MMM) program at the Hamilton-Wentworth

Detention Centre in Canada. This program combines mindfulness meditation with physical movement exercises, offering a holistic approach to rehabilitation. Participants engage in activities that promote physical health and mindfulness, such as yoga and Tai Chi, alongside traditional meditation practices. The results have been overwhelmingly positive, with participants reporting not only reduced stress and anxiety but also improved physical health and greater self-discipline.

Mindfulness practices also play a crucial role in addressing the underlying psychological issues that contribute to criminal behavior. Many offenders struggle with unresolved trauma, substance abuse, and mental health disorders, which can drive them towards destructive behaviors. Mindfulness helps individuals confront and process these issues in a supportive and non-judgmental environment. By fostering a sense of inner peace and self-compassion, mindfulness can aid in the healing process and promote long-term behavioral change. The benefits of mindfulness extend beyond the individual to the broader correctional community. When a significant portion of the inmate population engages in mindfulness practices, the overall atmosphere of the facility can shift towards one that is more peaceful and cooperative. Staff members also benefit from this change, as they experience fewer incidents of conflict and aggression. This creates a more positive and productive environment for everyone involved, enhancing the overall effectiveness of the rehabilitation process.

Mindfulness also encourages personal responsibility and accountability, key components of successful rehabilitation. By becoming more aware of their thoughts and actions, individuals can recognize the impact of their behavior on themselves and others. This heightened awareness fosters a sense of responsibility for their actions and encourages more constructive and positive behavior. In turn, this can lead to better relationships with fellow inmates, staff, and eventually, members of the community upon release. The integration of mindfulness into rehabilitation programs also aligns with restorative justice principles, which emphasize healing, accountability, and making amends. Mindfulness practices help individuals develop empathy and compassion, both for themselves and others. This can be particularly transformative in the context of restorative justice initiatives, where offenders are encouraged to take responsibility for their actions and work towards repairing the harm they have caused. By fostering a deeper understanding of their own experiences and the experiences of others, mindfulness can enhance the effectiveness of restorative justice practices and support the overall goals of rehabilitation.

13.2: Benefits of Mindfulness in Correctional Settings

Mindfulness techniques form the bedrock of cultivating present-moment awareness and emotional regulation, particularly within the correctional setting where the stakes for mental and emotional well-being are high. Introducing basic mindfulness techniques to offenders involves teaching practices that can be easily integrated into their daily routines, fostering a gradual but profound shift in their mental and emotional states. One of the foundational mindfulness techniques is mindful breathing. This practice involves paying close attention to the breath as it flows in and out of the body. Offenders are encouraged to find a comfortable seated position, close their eyes, and bring their awareness to their breath. They might start by noticing the sensation of air entering and leaving their nostrils or the rise and fall of their chest or abdomen. Mindful breathing helps to anchor the mind, reducing the tendency to be overwhelmed by stressful thoughts or emotions. This simple yet powerful practice can be a lifeline in the high-stress environment of a correctional facility, providing a tool for immediate emotional regulation.

Another core technique is the body scan, which involves directing focused attention to different parts of the body, usually starting from the toes and moving up to the head. This practice helps individuals become more aware of physical sensations and areas of tension, fostering a greater connection between the mind and body. In a typical body scan session, offenders are guided to notice sensations without judgment, simply observing what they feel. This practice can be particularly beneficial in identifying and releasing physical stress, which often accompanies emotional distress. By regularly practicing the body scan, offenders can develop a heightened sense of bodily awareness and relaxation. Mindful walking is another accessible practice that can be seamlessly integrated into daily routines. This technique involves walking slowly and deliberately, paying close attention to the sensations in the feet and legs as they move. Offenders are encouraged to notice the contact of their feet with the ground, the shift of weight, and the movement of muscles. Mindful walking can transform mundane activities into opportunities for mindfulness, helping to ground individuals and reduce anxiety. Given the limited space in correctional facilities, mindful walking can be practiced in small areas, making it a versatile tool for maintaining mindfulness throughout the day.

In addition to these individual practices, teaching offenders techniques for cultivating present-moment awareness is crucial. One effective method is the "five senses exercise," which involves consciously paying attention to the environment through the five senses. Participants are asked to notice five things they can see, four things they can touch, three things they can hear, two things they can smell, and one thing they can taste. This exercise helps shift focus away from distressing thoughts and brings attention to the immediate sensory experience, fostering a sense of presence and calm. Gratitude practice is another technique that can be integrated into mindfulness training. This involves reflecting on and expressing gratitude for positive aspects of one's life, no matter how small. Offenders can be encouraged to keep a gratitude journal, writing down a few things they are thankful for each day. This practice can help shift their focus from negative experiences to positive ones, fostering a more optimistic and resilient mindset. Gratitude practice has been shown to improve mental health and well-being, making it a valuable addition to mindfulness training in correctional settings.

Loving-kindness meditation, or Metta, is a practice that involves silently repeating phrases of goodwill and compassion towards oneself and others. Participants might start by directing these phrases towards themselves, then gradually extend them to loved ones, acquaintances, and even people they have conflicts with. Typical phrases include "May I be happy," "May I be healthy," "May I be safe," and "May I live with ease." Loving-kindness meditation can help offenders develop greater empathy and compassion, reducing feelings of anger and hostility. This practice not only benefits the individual but also contributes to a more peaceful and cooperative environment within the facility. Another important technique is mindful eating, which encourages individuals to bring full attention to the experience of eating. This practice involves noticing the colors, textures, and flavors of food, as well as the sensations of chewing and swallowing. By eating mindfully, offenders can develop a greater appreciation for their meals and become more attuned to their body's hunger and satiety cues. This practice can also serve as a form of mindful pause during the day, providing a moment of calm and reflection.

Visualization exercises can also be beneficial in helping offenders manage stress and anxiety. These exercises involve imagining a peaceful and calming scene, such as a beach, forest, or mountain. Participants are guided to engage all their senses in this visualization, noticing the sights, sounds, smells, and sensations of the imagined environment. Visualization can provide a mental escape from the stressors of prison life, offering a moment of tranquility and relaxation. To effectively integrate these mindfulness techniques into daily routines, it is essential to create a structured program that provides regular opportunities for practice. This can include designated times for mindfulness sessions, such as before meals, during recreation periods, or in the evening before lights out. Consistency is key to developing a sustainable mindfulness practice, and having a set schedule can help offenders build mindfulness into their daily lives.

Group mindfulness sessions can also enhance the practice by providing a sense of community and mutual support. These sessions can be led by trained facilitators who guide participants through various mindfulness exercises and offer opportunities for discussion and reflection. Group practices can help normalize mindfulness as a valuable and accepted part of the correctional experience, encouraging more widespread participation and engagement. Trained facilitators play a crucial role in delivering effective mindfulness programs. These individuals should have a deep understanding of mindfulness practices and the ability to create a supportive and non-judgmental environment. Facilitators can provide personalized guidance, help participants overcome challenges, and foster a sense of connection and trust. Their presence and expertise can significantly enhance the impact of mindfulness training, making it more accessible and effective for all participants.

13.3: Case Studies of Mindfulness Programs

Group mindfulness programs offer a unique and powerful approach to rehabilitation within correctional facilities, creating a sense of community and mutual support among participants. These programs are structured to foster collective engagement in mindfulness practices, enhancing individual and group well-being. By participating in group mindfulness sessions, offenders can develop skills that not only aid their personal rehabilitation but also contribute to a more peaceful and cooperative environment within the facility. The structure of group mindfulness programs typically includes a series of guided sessions led by trained facilitators. These sessions begin with an introduction to mindfulness concepts and techniques, followed by guided practices such as mindful breathing, body scans, and meditation. Participants are encouraged to share their experiences and reflections, fostering a supportive and open environment where everyone feels heard and respected. This collective practice helps build a sense of community and belonging, which is crucial in the often isolating environment of a correctional facility.

One successful example of a group mindfulness program is the "Freedom Project" in Washington State. This initiative provides mindfulness and meditation classes to inmates in various correctional facilities. The program is based on the principles of non-violence and personal transformation, aiming to help participants develop self-awareness, emotional regulation, and empathy. The Freedom Project's group sessions include mindfulness exercises, discussions on the impact of thoughts and emotions, and techniques for applying mindfulness in daily life. Participants report significant reductions in stress and aggression, as well as improvements in their ability to manage difficult emotions and relationships. Another effective program is the "Prison Mindfulness Institute" (PMI) in Rhode Island, which offers the "Path of Freedom" course. This 10-week program integrates mindfulness meditation, emotional intelligence, and communication skills to support the rehabilitation of offenders. Group sessions include a mix of guided meditations, interactive activities, and group discussions. The Path of Freedom course emphasizes the development of inner resources to cope with the challenges of prison life and prepare for successful reintegration into society. Evaluations of the program have shown that participants experience lower levels of anxiety and depression, greater emotional resilience, and enhanced interpersonal skills.

The "Mindfulness-Based Emotional Balance" (MBEB) program in the UK provides another example of a successful group mindfulness initiative. This program focuses on helping offenders develop emotional balance through mindfulness and cognitive-behavioral techniques. Group sessions include mindfulness practices, psychoeducation on the nature of emotions, and exercises for developing emotional regulation skills. The MBEB program has been implemented in several prisons across the UK, with participants reporting increased emotional stability, better anger management, and improved relationships with fellow inmates and staff. Implementing group mindfulness programs in correctional facilities involves several key components to ensure their success. First, it is essential to provide a safe and supportive environment where participants feel comfortable engaging in mindfulness practices. This includes creating a dedicated space for mindfulness sessions that is free from distractions and conducive to relaxation and reflection. Facilitators play a crucial role in establishing this environment by modeling non-judgmental and compassionate behavior, encouraging open communication, and providing individualized support as needed.

Second, group mindfulness programs should be designed to accommodate the diverse needs and backgrounds of participants. This includes offering sessions at various times to fit different schedules, providing materials in multiple languages, and adapting practices to accommodate physical limitations or disabilities. By making mindfulness accessible to all participants, programs can maximize their impact and reach a broader audience within the facility. Third, ongoing support and follow-up are critical for maintaining the benefits of group mindfulness programs. This can include providing resources such as guided meditation recordings, mindfulness apps, and reading materials that participants can use independently between sessions. Regular follow-up sessions or check-ins can help participants stay engaged and motivated, reinforcing the skills they have developed and addressing any challenges they encounter.

The benefits of group mindfulness programs extend beyond the individual participants to the broader correctional community. By fostering a culture of mindfulness and mutual support, these programs can contribute to a more positive and peaceful environment within the facility. Participants often become role models for their peers, demonstrating the value of mindfulness through their behavior and interactions. This ripple effect can lead to reduced conflict, improved relationships, and a greater sense of community among inmates and staff. Research supports the positive impact of group mindfulness programs on various aspects of well-being and behavior. Studies have shown that mindfulness practices can reduce symptoms of depression and anxiety, improve emotional regulation, and enhance overall mental health. In the correctional setting, these benefits are particularly valuable, as they can help address the high prevalence of mental health issues and emotional dysregulation among offenders.

Additionally, group mindfulness programs have been associated with lower rates of recidivism, as participants develop the skills and resilience needed to navigate the challenges of reentry and build more constructive lives post-release. The "Mindfulness-Based Relapse Prevention" (MBRP) program offers another example of the effectiveness of group mindfulness in supporting rehabilitation. This program combines mindfulness practices with relapse prevention strategies to help individuals overcome substance use disorders. In the correctional context, MBRP group sessions focus on developing awareness of triggers and cravings, cultivating a non-reactive stance towards challenging emotions, and building a supportive network of peers. Participants report increased self-efficacy in managing cravings and a greater sense of control over their recovery process.

13.4: Long-Term Impact on Offenders

Implementing mindfulness programs in correctional settings is not without its challenges. Understanding these obstacles and developing effective strategies to overcome them is crucial for fostering a successful and sustainable mindfulness practice among offenders. Addressing common barriers such as skepticism, resistance, logistical constraints, and the need for trained facilitators can significantly enhance the impact of these programs. One of the primary challenges in introducing mindfulness practices to offenders is skepticism and resistance. Many individuals may initially view mindfulness as unfamiliar or irrelevant to their lives, particularly in the context of a correctional facility. Skepticism can stem from a lack of understanding of mindfulness or misconceptions about its purpose and benefits. Additionally, the highly stressful and often traumatic backgrounds of many offenders can make them wary of new practices that require introspection and emotional vulnerability.

To address skepticism and resistance, it is essential to provide clear and accessible information about mindfulness and its benefits. Facilitators can start by explaining the scientific evidence supporting mindfulness practices, highlighting research findings on its positive effects on mental health, emotional regulation, and overall well-being. Sharing success stories and case studies of individuals who have benefited from mindfulness can also help to build trust and credibility. It is important to emphasize that mindfulness is a secular practice that can be adapted to fit the needs and beliefs of all participants. Creating an introductory session that allows participants to experience mindfulness firsthand can be highly effective in overcoming initial resistance. This session should include simple and accessible mindfulness exercises, such as mindful breathing or a short body scan, followed by a discussion of participants' experiences. By providing a positive and supportive introduction to mindfulness, facilitators can help participants see its potential value in their lives.

Another significant challenge is the logistical constraints of implementing mindfulness programs in correctional facilities. These constraints can include limited space, restricted schedules, and competing priorities. Correctional facilities are often overcrowded and understaffed, making it difficult to allocate time and resources for new programs. Additionally, the daily routines and security protocols of correctional facilities can pose barriers to consistent and uninterrupted mindfulness practice. To navigate these logistical challenges, it is important to work closely with correctional administrators and staff to integrate mindfulness programs into the existing structure and schedule of the facility. This may involve identifying suitable times for mindfulness sessions, such as during recreation periods or before lights out, and securing dedicated spaces for practice that are quiet and free from distractions. Collaborating with facility staff to ensure their support and involvement can also enhance the feasibility and sustainability of the program.

Flexibility and adaptability are key to overcoming logistical constraints. Facilitators should be prepared to modify the structure and delivery of mindfulness sessions to accommodate the unique needs and limitations of the facility. For example, shorter sessions can be scheduled more frequently if longer sessions are not feasible, and practices can be adapted to fit smaller spaces or group sizes. Providing participants with tools and resources for independent practice, such as guided meditation recordings or mindfulness apps, can also help to maintain continuity and engagement between group sessions. The role of trained facilitators is critical in delivering effective mindfulness programs in correctional settings. Facilitators must have a deep understanding of mindfulness practices and the ability to create a safe and supportive environment for participants. They should be skilled in guiding mindfulness exercises, addressing challenges, and providing personalized support. In addition to technical expertise, facilitators must possess qualities such as empathy, patience, and cultural sensitivity to effectively connect with participants from diverse backgrounds.

To ensure the availability of trained facilitators, it is important to invest in comprehensive training and professional development programs. These programs should cover the principles and practices of mindfulness, as well as techniques for teaching mindfulness in a correctional context. Training should also include strategies for dealing with common challenges, such as resistance, emotional distress, and disruptive behavior. Ongoing supervision and support for facilitators can help to maintain the quality and effectiveness of the program, providing opportunities for feedback, reflection, and skill development. Building a network of peer facilitators within the facility can further enhance the sustainability and impact of mindfulness programs. Peer facilitators, who are inmates trained to lead mindfulness sessions, can serve as valuable role models and support figures for their fellow participants. They can help to create a sense of community and mutual support, fostering a more inclusive and participatory approach to mindfulness practice. Training peer facilitators also provides them with valuable skills and responsibilities, contributing to their personal growth and rehabilitation.

Addressing the emotional and psychological barriers to mindfulness practice is another critical aspect of implementing these programs in correctional settings. Many offenders have experienced significant trauma, which can make mindfulness practices that involve introspection and emotional awareness particularly challenging. It is important to approach mindfulness training with sensitivity and an understanding of trauma-informed care principles. Facilitators should be prepared to provide additional support and guidance for participants who may struggle with intense emotions or traumatic memories during mindfulness practice. This may involve offering modifications to certain exercises, providing grounding techniques, and creating opportunities for one-on-one support. Encouraging participants to approach their practice with self-compassion and patience is crucial, helping them to build resilience and gradually develop their capacity for mindfulness.

Creating a culture of mindfulness within the facility can help to sustain and reinforce the practice. This involves integrating mindfulness principles into the broader environment and routines of the facility, promoting a holistic approach to rehabilitation. Staff members, including correctional officers and administrators, can be encouraged to participate in mindfulness training and practice, fostering a more supportive and cohesive environment. By modeling mindfulness and incorporating its principles into their interactions with inmates, staff can contribute to a more positive and rehabilitative atmosphere. Regular evaluation and feedback are essential for the ongoing improvement and adaptation of mindfulness programs. Collecting data on participation rates, program outcomes, and participant feedback can provide valuable insights into the effectiveness of the program and areas for improvement. Evaluations should include both quantitative measures, such as reductions in stress and aggression, and qualitative feedback from participants about their experiences and the impact of mindfulness on their lives. This information can be used to refine the program, address challenges, and highlight successes.

13.5: Strategies for Implementing Mindfulness Practices

Evaluating the impact of mindfulness practices within correctional settings is crucial for understanding their effectiveness and ensuring they meet the intended goals of rehabilitation, emotional regulation, and overall well-being. Comprehensive evaluation involves a multifaceted approach that includes both quantitative and qualitative methods, providing a holistic view of the outcomes and benefits of mindfulness programs. Quantitative methods often involve standardized assessments and metrics to measure changes in participants' mental health, behavior, and recidivism rates. One common tool used in such evaluations is the Mindfulness Attention Awareness Scale (MAAS), which assesses the degree of attention and awareness individuals bring to their experiences. By administering the MAAS before and after participation in mindfulness programs, researchers can quantify improvements in mindfulness levels. Similarly, the Perceived Stress Scale (PSS) can measure reductions in stress, while the Beck Depression Inventory (BDI) and the State-Trait Anxiety Inventory (STAI) can assess changes in symptoms of depression and anxiety, respectively.

In addition to these psychological assessments, behavioral metrics are essential for evaluating the impact of mindfulness practices on offenders' conduct. This can include tracking the frequency of disciplinary incidents, such as fights or rule violations, within the facility. A decrease in such incidents can indicate improved emotional regulation and conflict resolution skills among participants. Furthermore, recidivism rates provide a long-term measure of the effectiveness of mindfulness programs. By comparing the rates of reoffending among participants and non-participants, researchers can evaluate the lasting impact of mindfulness practices on behavior and decision-making. One comprehensive study conducted at the Maricopa County Jail in Arizona utilized both psychological assessments and behavioral metrics to evaluate their mindfulness program. The study found that participants reported significant reductions in stress and anxiety, as measured by the PSS and STAI. Additionally, there was a marked decrease in disciplinary incidents and a lower recidivism rate among participants compared to a control group. These findings highlight the potential of mindfulness practices to foster meaningful and lasting changes in the behavior and well-being of offenders.

Qualitative methods complement quantitative assessments by providing deeper insights into participants' personal experiences and the subjective benefits of mindfulness practices. Interviews, focus groups, and open-ended questionnaires allow participants to share their reflections on how mindfulness has impacted their lives. These narratives can reveal the nuances of personal transformation that may not be fully captured by standardized assessments. For example, a series of interviews with participants in the "Freedom Project" mindfulness program revealed profound personal insights. Many participants described how mindfulness helped them develop a greater sense of self-awareness and control over their reactions. One participant shared that mindfulness practice enabled them to pause and reflect before reacting aggressively to provocations, which significantly reduced conflicts with fellow inmates. Another participant highlighted the role of mindfulness in fostering self-compassion, helping them to forgive themselves for past mistakes and focus on positive change.

Focus groups provide an opportunity for participants to discuss their experiences collectively, fostering a sense of community and shared understanding. In a focus group conducted at the San Quentin State Prison as part of their mindfulness program evaluation, participants spoke about the support and camaraderie they felt during group mindfulness sessions. They noted that practicing mindfulness together helped build trust and mutual respect, which extended beyond the sessions into their daily interactions within the facility. Such qualitative insights underscore the importance of the social and communal aspects of mindfulness programs. Open-ended questionnaires can also elicit valuable feedback from participants about the strengths and areas for improvement in mindfulness programs. Responses from a survey at the Hamilton-Wentworth Detention Centre revealed that while most participants found the mindfulness exercises beneficial, some struggled with maintaining focus during sessions. This feedback led to adjustments in the program, such as incorporating shorter, more varied mindfulness practices to cater to different attention spans and learning styles.

Long-term follow-up studies are essential for assessing the sustained impact of mindfulness practices after participants are released from correctional facilities. These studies can track former participants' reintegration into society, their engagement in pro-social activities, and their overall mental health and well-being. One notable long-term study followed graduates of the "Path of Freedom" program for five years after their release. The study found that former participants had significantly lower recidivism rates and reported higher levels of employment and stable housing compared to a control group. Additionally, many former participants continued to practice mindfulness and attributed their successful reintegration to the skills and insights gained from the program. Another critical aspect of evaluating mindfulness programs is the impact on the overall correctional environment. Surveys and interviews with correctional staff can provide insights into how mindfulness practices influence the facility's atmosphere and the behavior of both inmates and staff. At the Massachusetts Correctional Institution, staff reported that the introduction of mindfulness programs led to a noticeable decrease in tension and conflicts within the facility. They also observed improvements in inmates' behavior, with participants showing greater respect for staff and peers and a more cooperative attitude.

Evaluations should also consider the perspectives of facilitators, who play a crucial role in delivering mindfulness programs. Facilitator feedback can highlight the challenges and successes encountered during the implementation of mindfulness practices. This feedback is valuable for refining program content and delivery methods to enhance effectiveness. Facilitators at the Prison Mindfulness Institute noted that while some participants initially resisted mindfulness practices, persistence and a compassionate approach eventually led to increased engagement and positive outcomes. To ensure the validity and reliability of evaluation results, it is important to use a mixed-methods approach that combines quantitative and qualitative data. This approach provides a comprehensive understanding of the impact of mindfulness programs, capturing both measurable changes and personal experiences. Additionally, evaluations should employ rigorous research designs, such as randomized controlled trials, to establish causal relationships between mindfulness practices and observed outcomes.

Collaboration with academic institutions and research organizations can enhance the quality and credibility of program evaluations. By partnering with experts in psychology, criminology, and public health, correctional facilities can design robust evaluation studies and analyze data effectively. For example, the partnership between the California Department of Corrections and Rehabilitation and the University of California, Berkeley, has resulted in several high-quality studies that have informed the development and improvement of mindfulness programs in correctional settings. Funding and resources are critical for conducting thorough evaluations of mindfulness programs. Securing grants and support from governmental and non-governmental organizations can provide the necessary financial and logistical backing for comprehensive research. Investing in evaluation not only demonstrates the commitment to evidence-based practices but also provides valuable insights that can guide future program development and policy decisions.

CHAPTER FOURTEEN

Meditation and Mental Transformation

Contents

- Techniques for Effective Meditation

- Benefits of Meditation for Psychological Growth

- Practical Applications in Rehabilitation Programs

- Case Studies of Mental Transformation

- Sustaining Meditation Practices for Long-Term Change

14.1: Techniques for Effective Meditation

Meditation, a practice with deep historical roots, has been a cornerstone of personal growth and transformation across various cultures and traditions. Its origins can be traced back to ancient civilizations, where it was an integral part of spiritual and philosophical systems, particularly in India, China, and Japan. In these traditions, meditation was not only a method for achieving mental clarity and inner peace but also a profound tool for self-discovery and enlightenment. This practice has evolved over millennia, adapting to different cultural contexts while retaining its core principles of mindfulness, concentration, and insight. The psychological and physiological benefits of regular meditation practice are well-documented through extensive scientific research. Psychologically, meditation is known to reduce symptoms of stress, anxiety, and depression. It works by calming the mind and promoting a state of relaxed awareness, which can help individuals manage their thoughts and emotions more effectively. Meditation enhances emotional regulation by strengthening the brain's prefrontal cortex, the area responsible for decision-making and impulse control. This helps individuals respond to life's challenges with greater equanimity and resilience.

Physiologically, meditation induces a state of deep relaxation, which has numerous health benefits. It can lower blood pressure, reduce levels of the stress hormone cortisol, and improve heart rate variability, which is an indicator of cardiovascular health. Regular meditation practice also boosts the immune system, enhances sleep quality, and increases the production of serotonin, a neurotransmitter associated with feelings of well-being and happiness. These physiological changes contribute to an overall sense of vitality and well-being, making meditation a powerful tool for maintaining physical health. Personal stories of transformation through meditation abound, highlighting its profound impact on individuals' lives. One such story is that of Sarah, a woman who struggled with chronic anxiety and depression for years. After being introduced to meditation, she began a daily practice of mindful breathing and body scanning. Over time, Sarah noticed significant improvements in her mental health. She became more aware of her thought patterns and learned to observe them without judgment. This awareness allowed her to break free from the cycle of negative thinking that had dominated her life. Meditation also helped Sarah develop a sense of inner peace and self-acceptance, which profoundly improved her overall quality of life.

Another inspiring example is that of John, a former inmate who discovered meditation while serving a lengthy prison sentence. John initially approached meditation with skepticism, but after participating in a mindfulness program offered at his facility, he experienced a remarkable shift in his perspective. Meditation provided John with a refuge from the chaos and stress of prison life. It helped him confront his past actions with compassion and accountability, leading to a deep sense of personal growth and transformation. Upon his release, John continued his meditation practice and became an advocate for mindfulness programs in correctional facilities, helping others find the same sense of peace and purpose that he had discovered. Meditation's transformative power is not limited to individuals but extends to communities and organizations as well. In schools, workplaces, and healthcare settings, meditation programs have been implemented to promote mental health and well-being. For instance, the "Mindful Schools" program teaches meditation to students and teachers, fostering a more focused and peaceful learning environment. Students who practice meditation regularly show improved academic performance, better emotional regulation, and reduced behavioral problems. Teachers also benefit from lower stress levels and enhanced job satisfaction, creating a more positive and supportive educational community.

In corporate settings, companies like Google and Apple have incorporated meditation programs to enhance employee well-being and productivity. These programs teach mindfulness techniques that help employees manage stress, improve focus, and foster creativity. The results have been impressive, with participants reporting greater job satisfaction, better work-life balance, and enhanced performance. By promoting a culture of mindfulness, these organizations not only improve the well-being of their employees but also create a more innovative and resilient workforce. Healthcare professionals, too, have embraced meditation as a means to cope with the high demands and stress of their work. Programs like "Mindfulness-Based Stress Reduction" (MBSR) have been widely adopted in hospitals and clinics to support the mental health of doctors, nurses, and other healthcare workers. These programs teach mindfulness practices that help reduce burnout, improve patient care, and enhance the overall well-being of healthcare providers. By integrating meditation into their daily routines, healthcare professionals can better manage the emotional challenges of their work and maintain a sense of balance and purpose.

Meditation's role in personal growth is also evident in its ability to foster greater self-awareness and introspection. Through regular practice, individuals learn to observe their thoughts and emotions without becoming entangled in them. This heightened awareness allows for deeper self-reflection and insight into one's patterns of behavior and underlying motivations. As a result, individuals can make more conscious choices and align their actions with their values and goals. Meditation helps cultivate qualities such as patience, compassion, and empathy, which are essential for personal development and harmonious relationships. In the context of correctional facilities, meditation can be a transformative tool for rehabilitation. Offenders often struggle with unresolved trauma, anger, and impulsivity, which can perpetuate a cycle of criminal behavior. Meditation provides a means to address these underlying issues by fostering emotional regulation and self-awareness. Programs that teach meditation to inmates have shown promising results in reducing aggression, improving mental health, and lowering recidivism rates. By helping offenders develop a sense of inner peace and responsibility, meditation supports their rehabilitation and reintegration into society.

The story of Ajahn Brahm, a former scientist turned Buddhist monk, illustrates the profound impact of meditation on personal growth and transformation. After experiencing a series of personal crises, Ajahn Brahm turned to meditation as a means of finding peace and clarity. His practice led him to ordain as a monk and dedicate his life to teaching meditation and mindfulness. Through his teachings, Ajahn Brahm has helped countless individuals overcome suffering and discover a deeper sense of purpose and fulfillment. His journey highlights the transformative power of meditation and its potential to bring about profound change in one's life. The role of meditation in personal growth is multifaceted and far-reaching. Its historical roots and significance across various traditions underscore its enduring relevance. The psychological and physiological benefits of regular meditation practice are well-documented, promoting mental and physical health. Personal stories of transformation, such as those of Sarah, John, and Ajahn Brahm, highlight the profound impact of meditation on individuals' lives. Moreover, meditation's benefits extend to communities and organizations, fostering well-being and resilience. In correctional facilities, meditation serves as a powerful tool for rehabilitation and personal growth. By cultivating mindfulness, self-awareness, and compassion, meditation enables individuals to navigate life's challenges with greater equanimity and purpose, ultimately transforming their lives and the world around them.

14.2: Benefits of Meditation for Psychological Growth

Meditation encompasses a variety of practices, each offering unique approaches to cultivating mindfulness, insight, and mental tranquility. Understanding these different forms of meditation can help individuals select techniques that best suit their needs, preferences, and goals. For offenders in correctional settings, the diversity of meditation practices allows for tailored programs that address specific challenges and promote rehabilitation. Vipassana meditation, often referred to as insight meditation, is one of the oldest forms of meditation, rooted in the teachings of the Buddha. Vipassana emphasizes the development of mindfulness and clear seeing, encouraging practitioners to observe their thoughts, emotions, and sensations without attachment or aversion. This practice involves sitting quietly and focusing on the breath, noting the rise and fall of the abdomen, and observing any thoughts or feelings that arise. Over time, Vipassana helps practitioners gain insight into the impermanent and interdependent nature of their experiences, fostering a deeper understanding of the mind and the roots of suffering.

The benefits of Vipassana meditation for offenders are significant. By developing the ability to observe their internal experiences without reacting impulsively, individuals can cultivate greater self-control and emotional regulation. This is particularly valuable in correctional settings, where impulsive behaviors often lead to conflict and disciplinary issues. The insight gained through Vipassana practice can also help offenders recognize the patterns of thought and behavior that contribute to their criminal actions, paving the way for meaningful personal transformation and rehabilitation. Loving-kindness meditation, or Metta Bhavana, is another powerful practice with roots in Buddhist tradition. This form of meditation involves generating feelings of goodwill and compassion towards oneself and others. Practitioners begin by directing loving-kindness towards themselves, silently repeating phrases such as "May I be happy," "May I be healthy," and "May I be at peace." Gradually, these wishes are extended to loved ones, acquaintances, and even those with whom the practitioner has conflicts. The ultimate goal is to cultivate a boundless, all-encompassing sense of compassion and empathy.

For offenders, loving-kindness meditation can be transformative in reducing anger, resentment, and hostility. By fostering feelings of compassion towards themselves and others, participants can develop healthier relationships and a more positive outlook on life. This practice can also help offenders address feelings of guilt and shame, promoting self-forgiveness and a commitment to positive change. Loving-kindness meditation encourages a sense of interconnectedness and shared humanity, which can be particularly healing for individuals who have felt marginalized or isolated. Zen meditation, or Zazen, is a central practice in Zen Buddhism. It involves sitting in a specific posture, typically cross-legged on a cushion, with the back straight and hands resting in a specific mudra. Practitioners focus on their breath or on a koan, a paradoxical question or statement meant to transcend rational thought and provoke insight. Zen meditation emphasizes the importance of "just sitting" and being fully present, without striving for specific outcomes or experiences.

Zen meditation can be particularly beneficial for offenders who struggle with overthinking or a restless mind. The simplicity and discipline of the practice encourage a return to the present moment, helping individuals find peace amidst the chaos of their thoughts. The insights gained from contemplating koans can lead to profound shifts in perspective, fostering a deeper understanding of oneself and the nature of reality. The discipline and structure of Zen practice can also promote a sense of stability and order, which is valuable in the often unpredictable environment of a correctional facility. Transcendental Meditation (TM) is a modern form of meditation popularized by Maharishi Mahesh Yogi in the mid-20th century. TM involves the use of a mantra, a specific word or phrase, which practitioners silently repeat for 15-20 minutes, twice a day. The repetition of the mantra helps quiet the mind and induce a state of deep relaxation and restful awareness. TM is known for its simplicity and ease of practice, making it accessible to a wide range of individuals.

For offenders, Transcendental Meditation can offer a practical and effective way to reduce stress and anxiety. The regular practice of TM has been shown to lower blood pressure, improve sleep, and enhance overall mental health. The deep relaxation achieved through TM can help offenders cope with the stress and tension of prison life, promoting a sense of inner peace and well-being. The structured and regular nature of TM practice can also provide a sense of routine and stability, which is beneficial for individuals in correctional settings. Mindfulness-Based Stress Reduction (MBSR) is a widely-used program developed by Jon Kabat-Zinn. MBSR combines mindfulness meditation with body awareness and yoga to help individuals manage stress and improve overall well-being. The program typically consists of an eight-week course, during which participants learn various mindfulness techniques, including mindful breathing, body scans, and mindful movement. MBSR emphasizes the importance of bringing mindful awareness to everyday activities and interactions.

MBSR has been successfully adapted for use in correctional facilities, where it helps offenders develop tools for managing stress and emotional challenges. The comprehensive nature of the program addresses both mental and physical well-being, promoting holistic rehabilitation. Participants in MBSR programs report reductions in stress, anxiety, and depression, as well as improvements in emotional regulation and self-awareness. The skills learned in MBSR can support offenders in navigating the difficulties of prison life and preparing for successful reintegration into society. Integrating different forms of meditation into a comprehensive program can enhance the effectiveness of rehabilitation efforts in correctional settings. By offering a variety of practices, facilitators can accommodate the diverse needs and preferences of participants. Some individuals may resonate more with the contemplative and introspective nature of Vipassana, while others may find the active generation of compassion in loving-kindness meditation more impactful. The discipline and structure of Zen meditation or the simplicity and relaxation of Transcendental Meditation can also appeal to different individuals, providing multiple pathways to personal growth and transformation.

In addition to the specific benefits of each meditation practice, the common thread among them is the cultivation of mindfulness and present-moment awareness. This foundational skill helps individuals develop a greater understanding of their thoughts, emotions, and behaviors, fostering a sense of agency and responsibility. By observing their internal experiences without judgment, practitioners can gain insight into the causes of their suffering and develop more constructive responses to life's challenges. The implementation of meditation programs in correctional facilities requires careful planning and support. Facilitators must be well-trained in the various meditation practices and equipped to guide participants through the challenges and benefits of each technique. Creating a supportive and non-judgmental environment is essential for encouraging participation and sustaining engagement. Peer support and mentorship can also play a crucial role in fostering a sense of community and mutual encouragement among participants.

The diversity of meditation practices offers a rich array of tools for fostering mindfulness, emotional regulation, and personal transformation in correctional settings. Vipassana meditation provides deep insights into the nature of the mind, while loving-kindness meditation cultivates compassion and empathy. Zen meditation offers discipline and presence, and Transcendental Meditation promotes relaxation and stress relief. Mindfulness-Based Stress Reduction combines various techniques to address both mental and physical well-being. By integrating these practices into a comprehensive program, correctional facilities can support the holistic rehabilitation of offenders, helping them develop the skills and insights needed for positive change and successful reintegration into society. The tailored approach to meditation ensures that each individual can find a practice that resonates with them, promoting sustained engagement and long-term benefits.

14.3: Practical Applications in Rehabilitation Programs

Meditation programs in correctional facilities have demonstrated significant success globally, providing a transformative impact on the lives of offenders. These programs are designed to address the mental, emotional, and behavioral challenges faced by inmates, fostering rehabilitation and personal growth. The implementation of meditation initiatives requires careful planning, dedication, and the integration of best practices to ensure sustainability and effectiveness. One notable example of a successful meditation program is the Vipassana meditation courses conducted in India's Tihar Jail. Introduced in 1993 by S.N.

Goenka, a renowned teacher of Vipassana meditation, the program aimed to help inmates develop self-awareness and emotional regulation. The courses involved ten days of intensive meditation practice, during which participants observed complete silence and followed a strict schedule of meditation sessions. The results were remarkable: participants reported significant reductions in anger, anxiety, and depression, along with improvements in self-control and interpersonal relationships. The success of the Vipassana program at Tihar Jail has inspired similar initiatives in other correctional facilities worldwide.

In the United States, the Insight Prison Project (IPP) offers a comprehensive meditation and mindfulness program designed to address the psychological and emotional needs of inmates. The IPP provides classes on mindfulness meditation, emotional literacy, and restorative justice practices. These classes are facilitated by trained instructors who guide participants through various meditation techniques and mindfulness exercises. The program also includes group discussions and reflective activities that encourage participants to explore their thoughts and feelings deeply. Evaluations of the IPP have shown that participants experience lower levels of stress and aggression, improved emotional regulation, and a greater sense of empathy and responsibility. The Path of Freedom program, developed by the Prison Mindfulness Institute (PMI), is another exemplary meditation initiative that has been implemented in several correctional facilities across the United States. This 10-week program combines mindfulness meditation with emotional intelligence and communication skills training. Participants learn to practice mindfulness through guided meditations, body scans, and mindful movement exercises. The program also emphasizes the development of empathy, self-compassion, and conflict resolution skills. Research on the Path of Freedom program has demonstrated significant reductions in recidivism rates and improvements in participants' mental health and well-being.

In the United Kingdom, the Mindfulness-Based Approaches in Prisons (MBAP) program has been implemented in various correctional settings to promote mental health and rehabilitation. This program integrates mindfulness meditation with cognitive-behavioral techniques to help inmates develop greater self-awareness and emotional resilience. The

MBAP program includes weekly group sessions led by trained facilitators, where participants engage in mindfulness exercises, discuss their experiences, and learn strategies for applying mindfulness in their daily lives. Evaluations of the MBAP program have shown that participants report reduced levels of stress and anxiety, improved emotional regulation, and enhanced overall well-being. The "Yoga and Meditation for Trauma Recovery" program at the Richmond City Jail in Virginia combines yoga and meditation practices to support the rehabilitation of inmates who have experienced trauma. This program, facilitated by the non-profit organization "Project Yoga Richmond," offers classes that incorporate mindful movement, breathing exercises, and meditation techniques. The focus on trauma-informed care helps participants develop a sense of safety and trust, which is essential for healing and recovery. Participants in the program have reported significant reductions in symptoms of post-traumatic stress disorder (PTSD), improved physical health, and a greater sense of inner peace.

Implementing meditation programs in correctional facilities involves several key steps to ensure their success and sustainability. First, it is essential to secure support from correctional administrators and staff. This support can be fostered by presenting evidence of the benefits of meditation programs, including research findings and success stories from other facilities. Engaging administrators and staff in introductory mindfulness and meditation sessions can also help build understanding and buy-in for the programs. Second, recruiting and training qualified facilitators is crucial for the effective delivery of meditation programs. Facilitators should have a deep understanding of meditation practices and the ability to create a safe and supportive environment for participants. Comprehensive training programs for facilitators should include instruction on mindfulness techniques, trauma-informed care, and strategies for addressing common challenges in correctional settings. Ongoing supervision and professional development opportunities can help facilitators maintain their skills and stay updated on best practices.

Third, creating a structured and consistent schedule for meditation sessions is important for fostering regular practice and engagement. This schedule should be integrated into the daily routines of the facility, allowing participants to attend sessions without significant disruptions to other activities. Providing a dedicated space for meditation that is quiet and free from distractions can enhance the effectiveness of the practice. Fourth, fostering a sense of community and peer support among participants can significantly enhance the impact of meditation programs. Group sessions provide opportunities for participants to share their experiences, support one another, and develop a sense of camaraderie. Encouraging peer mentorship, where more experienced participants guide and support newcomers, can also strengthen the sense of community and mutual encouragement.

Fifth, it is essential to regularly evaluate the effectiveness of meditation programs through both quantitative and qualitative methods. Collecting data on mental health outcomes, behavioral changes, and recidivism rates can provide valuable insights into the impact of the programs. Participant feedback through interviews, focus groups, and surveys can offer a deeper understanding of the personal benefits and challenges of meditation practice. This information can be used to refine and improve the programs, ensuring they meet the needs of participants and achieve their intended goals. One of the critical lessons learned from successful meditation initiatives is the importance of tailoring programs to the specific needs and backgrounds of participants. This involves considering factors such as cultural differences, trauma histories, and individual preferences for different meditation techniques. Adapting the content and delivery of meditation programs to accommodate these factors can enhance their relevance and effectiveness for participants.

Another important lesson is the value of integrating meditation programs with other rehabilitative services and support systems. Collaboration with mental health professionals, social workers, and vocational training providers can create a comprehensive approach to rehabilitation that addresses multiple aspects of participants' needs. For example, integrating mindfulness-based cognitive therapy with vocational training programs can help participants develop both emotional resilience and practical skills for successful reintegration into society. The sustainability of meditation programs in correctional facilities also depends on securing funding and resources. Grants from governmental and non-governmental organizations, as well as partnerships with academic institutions and non-profit organizations, can provide the necessary financial and logistical support for these programs. Building a strong case for the cost-effectiveness of meditation programs, based on evidence of their impact on recidivism rates and mental health outcomes, can help attract funding and support.

14.4: Case Studies of Mental Transformation

Overcoming obstacles to meditation practice in correctional settings is crucial for the successful implementation and sustainability of these programs. Various challenges, including skepticism, logistical constraints, psychological barriers, and environmental factors, can impede the effectiveness of meditation initiatives. Addressing these challenges requires a strategic approach, incorporating best practices and innovative solutions to foster a conducive environment for meditation. Skepticism among offenders is one of the primary barriers to introducing meditation practices in correctional facilities. Many inmates may initially view meditation as irrelevant or impractical, especially if they have little prior exposure to such practices. To overcome this skepticism, it is essential to provide clear and accessible information about the benefits of meditation, supported by scientific evidence and real-life success stories. Educators and facilitators should present meditation as a secular and evidence-based tool for stress reduction, emotional regulation, and personal growth. Offering introductory sessions that allow participants to experience the immediate calming effects of mindfulness can help dispel doubts and generate interest.

Logistical constraints pose significant challenges to the implementation of meditation programs in correctional facilities. Overcrowding, limited space, and rigid schedules can make it difficult to find suitable times and locations for regular meditation sessions. To address these constraints, administrators and program coordinators must work collaboratively to integrate meditation into the existing routines and infrastructure of the facility. This might involve scheduling shorter, more frequent sessions during times when inmates have free periods or modifying the use of multipurpose spaces to accommodate meditation groups. Flexibility and creativity in planning can help ensure that meditation sessions are accessible to all interested participants. Environmental factors, such as noise and distractions, can also hinder the practice of meditation in correctional settings. Creating a quiet and calming environment for meditation sessions is essential for facilitating concentration and relaxation. This can be achieved by designating specific areas within the facility as meditation spaces, equipped with mats, cushions, and soothing decor to enhance the atmosphere. Additionally, using techniques such as soundproofing or playing ambient music can help reduce external noise and create a more conducive environment for meditation.

Psychological barriers, including trauma and emotional distress, are common among offenders and can make meditation practice challenging. Many inmates have experienced significant trauma and may find it difficult to engage in introspective practices that bring up painful memories and emotions. To address these barriers, it is crucial to incorporate principles of trauma-informed care into the design and delivery of meditation programs. Facilitators should be trained to recognize signs of trauma and provide appropriate support and modifications to the practice. For example, offering grounding exercises and emphasizing self-compassion can help participants navigate difficult emotions and build resilience. Peer support and mentorship can play a vital role in overcoming obstacles to meditation practice. Establishing a network of peer facilitators within the facility can create a sense of community and mutual encouragement among participants. Peer facilitators, who are inmates trained to lead meditation sessions, can serve as role models and provide relatable support to their peers. This peer-led approach can enhance engagement and sustainability by fostering a sense of ownership and accountability among participants. Regular peer support meetings and mentorship programs can further strengthen the community of practice and ensure ongoing support.

One successful example of overcoming obstacles through peer support is the "Inside Meditation" program at the San Francisco County Jail. This program trains inmates to become meditation instructors, enabling them to lead sessions for their fellow inmates. The peer-led approach has been highly effective in building trust and engagement, as participants are more likely to relate to and be motivated by instructors who share similar experiences. The program also provides ongoing support and supervision for peer instructors, ensuring the quality and consistency of the meditation sessions. Addressing cultural and linguistic diversity is another important aspect of overcoming obstacles to meditation practice. In correctional facilities with diverse populations, it is essential to offer meditation programs that are culturally sensitive and accessible to all participants. This can involve providing materials and instructions in multiple languages, incorporating culturally relevant examples and practices, and ensuring that facilitators are trained in cultural competency. By creating an inclusive environment, meditation programs can reach a broader audience and address the unique needs of different cultural groups.

The "Mindful Living Initiative" at the Rikers Island Correctional Facility in New York provides a notable example of addressing cultural diversity in meditation programs. This initiative offers mindfulness and meditation classes tailored to the diverse population of the facility, with sessions conducted in multiple languages and incorporating culturally relevant practices. Facilitators are trained to be culturally sensitive and to create an inclusive environment that respects and values the backgrounds of all participants. The program has successfully engaged inmates from various cultural groups, fostering a sense of community and mutual respect. The role of trained facilitators is critical in overcoming obstacles to meditation practice. Facilitators must possess not only a deep understanding of meditation techniques but also the ability to create a supportive and non-judgmental environment. Comprehensive training programs for facilitators should include instruction on trauma-informed care, cultural competency, and strategies for addressing common challenges in correctional settings. Ongoing supervision and professional development opportunities can help facilitators maintain their skills and stay updated on best practices.

To ensure the sustainability and impact of meditation programs, it is important to integrate them with other rehabilitative services and support systems. Collaboration with mental health professionals, social workers, and vocational training providers can create a holistic approach to rehabilitation that addresses multiple aspects of participants' needs. For example, integrating mindfulness-based cognitive therapy with vocational training programs can help participants develop both emotional resilience and practical skills for successful reintegration into society. Regular evaluation and feedback are essential for identifying and addressing obstacles to meditation practice. Collecting data on participation rates, program outcomes, and participant feedback can provide valuable insights into the effectiveness of the programs and areas for improvement. Participant feedback through interviews, focus groups, and surveys can offer a deeper understanding of the personal benefits and challenges of meditation practice. This information can be used to refine and improve the programs, ensuring they meet the needs of participants and achieve their intended goals.

14.5: Sustaining Meditation Practices for Long-Term Change

Measuring the impact of meditation programs within correctional facilities is essential for demonstrating their effectiveness, ensuring their sustainability, and refining their implementation. A comprehensive evaluation involves a combination of quantitative and qualitative methods to capture the multifaceted benefits of meditation practices. These methods provide insights into the psychological, behavioral, and social changes experienced by participants, as well as the overall impact on the correctional environment. Quantitative measures are crucial for assessing the tangible outcomes of meditation programs. Standardized psychological assessments are commonly used to evaluate changes in mental health and emotional well-being. Tools such as the Beck Depression Inventory (BDI), the State-Trait Anxiety Inventory (STAI), and the Perceived Stress Scale (PSS) can quantify reductions in symptoms of depression, anxiety, and stress among participants. These assessments are typically administered before and after participation in meditation programs to measure the extent of improvement. For instance, a study conducted at the Washington Correctional Facility utilized these tools and found significant reductions in anxiety and stress levels among inmates who participated in a mindfulness-based stress reduction (MBSR) program.

Behavioral metrics are also critical for evaluating the impact of meditation programs. Tracking the frequency of disciplinary incidents, such as fights, rule violations, and verbal altercations, provides concrete evidence of behavioral changes. A reduction in such incidents indicates improved emotional regulation and conflict resolution skills among participants. For example, an evaluation of the "Peace of Mind" meditation program at the Florida State Prison showed a notable decrease in disciplinary infractions among participants, highlighting the program's positive influence on behavior. Recidivism rates offer a long-term measure of the effectiveness of meditation programs. Comparing the rates of reoffending among participants and non-participants can provide valuable insights into the lasting impact of meditation practices on behavior and decision-making. A comprehensive study of the "Inner Path" meditation program in the Oregon State Penitentiary found that participants had significantly lower recidivism rates compared to a control group, demonstrating the program's effectiveness in supporting rehabilitation and reducing the likelihood of reoffending.

In addition to quantitative measures, qualitative methods provide deeper insights into the personal experiences and transformative effects of meditation practices. Interviews, focus groups, and open-ended questionnaires allow participants to share their reflections on how meditation has impacted their lives. These narratives can reveal the nuances of personal growth, emotional healing, and behavioral change that may not be fully captured by standardized assessments. For instance, in-depth interviews with participants of the "Freedom Inside" meditation program at the San Quentin State Prison revealed profound personal transformations. Inmates described how meditation helped them develop greater self-awareness, compassion, and forgiveness. One participant shared that meditation allowed him to confront and process the trauma and guilt associated with his past actions, leading to a sense of inner peace and a commitment to positive change. Another participant noted that meditation helped him manage his anger and respond more calmly to conflicts, improving his relationships with fellow inmates and staff.

Focus groups provide an opportunity for participants to discuss their experiences collectively, fostering a sense of community and shared understanding. A focus group conducted as part of the evaluation of the "Mindful Resilience" program at the Rikers Island Correctional Facility highlighted the supportive and transformative nature of group meditation sessions. Participants expressed that practicing mindfulness together created a sense of solidarity and mutual encouragement, enhancing their commitment to the practice and reinforcing the positive changes they experienced. Open-ended questionnaires can elicit valuable feedback on the strengths and areas for improvement in meditation programs. Responses from a survey of the "Stillness Within" program at the Pelican Bay State Prison revealed that while most participants found the meditation sessions beneficial, some struggled with maintaining focus and motivation. This feedback led to adjustments in the program, such as incorporating shorter, more varied meditation practices and providing additional support and encouragement to sustain engagement.

Long-term follow-up studies are essential for assessing the sustained impact of meditation practices after participants are released from correctional facilities. These studies can track former participants' reintegration into society, their engagement in pro-social activities, and their overall mental health and well-being. A notable long-term study of the "Transformative Mindfulness" program in the Colorado State Penitentiary followed graduates for five years post-release. The study found that former participants had significantly lower recidivism rates and reported higher levels of employment and stable housing compared to a control group. Additionally, many former participants continued to practice meditation and attributed their successful reintegration to the skills and insights gained from the program. Evaluations should also consider the perspectives of correctional staff and facilitators, as they provide valuable insights into the program's impact on the overall correctional environment. Surveys and interviews with staff can assess changes in the facility's atmosphere and the behavior of both inmates and staff. An evaluation of the "Inner Peace" meditation program at the Cook County Jail revealed that staff observed a noticeable decrease in tension and conflicts within the facility. They also reported that inmates who participated in the program showed greater respect for staff and peers and a more cooperative attitude.

Facilitator feedback is crucial for identifying challenges and successes encountered during the implementation of meditation programs. Facilitators at the "Healing Hearts" program at the Arizona State Prison noted that while some participants initially resisted meditation practices, persistence and a compassionate approach eventually led to increased engagement and positive outcomes. Their feedback highlighted the importance of patience, adaptability, and ongoing support in delivering effective meditation programs. To ensure the validity and reliability of evaluation results, it is important to use a mixed-methods approach that combines quantitative and qualitative data. This approach provides a comprehensive understanding of the impact of meditation programs, capturing both measurable changes and personal experiences. Additionally, evaluations should employ rigorous research designs, such as randomized controlled trials, to establish causal relationships between meditation practices and observed outcomes.

Collaboration with academic institutions and research organizations can enhance the quality and credibility of program evaluations. By partnering with experts in psychology, criminology, and public health, correctional facilities can design robust evaluation studies and analyze data effectively. For example, the partnership between the California Department of Corrections and Rehabilitation and the University of California, San Diego, has resulted in several high-quality studies that have informed the development and improvement of meditation programs in correctional settings. Securing funding and resources is critical for conducting thorough evaluations of meditation programs. Grants from governmental and non-governmental organizations, as well as partnerships with academic institutions and non-profit organizations, can provide the necessary financial and logistical support for comprehensive research. Building a strong case for the cost-effectiveness of meditation programs, based on evidence of their impact on recidivism rates and mental health outcomes, can help attract funding and support.

CHAPTER FIFTEEN

Stress Reduction and Emotional Regulation

Contents

- Mindfulness-Based Approaches to Stress Reduction

- Techniques for Emotional Regulation

- Benefits for Offenders in Correctional Settings

- Case Studies of Stress Reduction Programs

- Long-Term Impact on Offender Behavior

15.1: Mindfulness-Based Approaches to Stress Reduction

Stress, an omnipresent force in our lives, exerts profound effects on both physical and mental health. Its impact is especially pronounced in correctional settings, where the environment itself is a crucible of tension, anxiety, and uncertainty. Understanding the intricate dynamics of stress and its far-reaching consequences is crucial for anyone involved in the rehabilitation process. The body responds to stress through a cascade of physiological reactions, triggering the release of hormones like cortisol and adrenaline. These hormones prepare the body for a fight-or-flight response, an evolutionary mechanism designed to enhance survival. However, chronic activation of this stress response can lead to detrimental health outcomes. Physically, prolonged stress can contribute to a host of ailments, including hypertension, cardiovascular disease, and weakened immune function. Elevated cortisol levels can disrupt metabolic processes, leading to weight gain, insulin resistance, and even diabetes. Moreover, chronic stress can exacerbate existing health conditions, making management and recovery more challenging. In the context of a correctional facility, where access to comprehensive healthcare may be limited, these physical consequences of stress pose significant challenges to inmate well-being.

Mentally, stress exerts a pervasive influence on cognitive and emotional functioning. It impairs concentration, memory, and decision-making abilities, which are critical for personal growth and rehabilitation. High stress levels can also intensify feelings of anxiety and depression, creating a vicious cycle where negative emotions fuel further stress. This is particularly relevant in correctional settings, where inmates often grapple with a history of trauma, substance abuse, and mental health disorders. The compounded effect of these factors can impede rehabilitation efforts, making it more difficult for individuals to engage in therapeutic activities and programs. The relationship between stress and criminal behavior is a complex and multifaceted one. Stress can act as both a precipitant and a consequence of criminal activity. Individuals experiencing high levels of stress may resort to criminal behavior as a maladaptive coping mechanism. For instance, substance abuse, theft, and violent acts can be seen as attempts to alleviate or escape from stressors. Conversely, involvement in criminal activities can generate additional stress, perpetuating a cycle of negative behavior and psychological distress. In this light, addressing stress is not just a matter of health but a critical component of breaking the cycle of recidivism.

In the high-stress environment of a correctional facility, managing stress effectively becomes a pivotal aspect of rehabilitation. Inmates are subjected to a range of stressors, from the constant threat of violence and overcrowding to the psychological strain of confinement and separation from loved ones. These stressors can undermine the stability and safety of the facility, leading to increased incidents of aggression, self-harm, and other disruptive behaviors. Therefore, stress management is not only beneficial for individual inmates but also essential for maintaining a peaceful and orderly environment within the facility. Mindfulness and meditation have emerged as powerful tools for stress management, offering a way to cultivate awareness and acceptance of the present moment. These practices help individuals develop a more balanced and measured response to stress, rather than reacting impulsively. By focusing on the breath or bodily sensations, mindfulness helps to ground individuals, providing a sense of calm and stability amidst the chaos of prison life. Meditation, in particular, has been shown to reduce physiological markers of stress, such as blood pressure and heart rate, while also promoting psychological resilience.

In the context of rehabilitation, mindfulness-based interventions can be tailored to address the specific stressors faced by inmates. Programs like Mindfulness-Based Stress Reduction (MBSR) have been adapted for correctional settings, providing inmates with practical tools for managing stress and improving overall well-being. These programs typically include guided meditations, body scans, and mindful movement exercises, all designed to enhance awareness and reduce reactivity to stressors. The structured nature of these programs also offers a sense of routine and predictability, which can be comforting in the often unpredictable environment of a correctional facility. Research on the effectiveness of mindfulness and meditation programs in correctional settings has shown promising results. Studies indicate that participants in these programs experience significant reductions in stress, anxiety, and depression, along with improvements in emotional regulation and overall mental health.

These benefits extend beyond the individual, contributing to a more positive and cooperative atmosphere within the facility. Inmates who practice mindfulness are often better able to navigate interpersonal conflicts and engage more constructively in rehabilitative activities. Beyond the immediate benefits, effective stress management can have long-term positive outcomes for inmates. Reducing stress and its associated psychological burdens can enhance the overall quality of life, fostering a sense of hope and motivation for the future. Inmates who develop effective stress management skills are better equipped to handle the challenges of reentry into society, reducing the risk of recidivism. By addressing the root causes of stress and providing inmates with the tools to manage it, correctional facilities can support more successful and sustainable rehabilitation efforts.

15.2: Techniques for Emotional Regulation

Mindfulness-Based Stress Reduction (MBSR) has become an influential program in the field of stress management and rehabilitation, particularly within correctional facilities where the need for effective stress reduction techniques is paramount. Developed by Dr. Jon Kabat-Zinn in the late 1970s, MBSR is an eight-week program that combines mindfulness meditation, body awareness, and yoga to help individuals manage stress, pain, and illness. The core components of MBSR are designed to cultivate mindfulness, which is defined as paying attention in a particular way: on purpose, in the present moment, and non-judgmentally. The MBSR program typically includes weekly group sessions, a day-long retreat, and daily home practice. Each session lasts about two and a half hours and involves guided mindfulness practices, discussions on stress and coping, and exercises to develop greater awareness of thoughts, emotions, and physical sensations. The program's structure encourages participants to engage in regular practice and integrate mindfulness into their daily lives, fostering a continuous process of self-awareness and stress reduction.

In correctional settings, the introduction of MBSR can have profound effects on both inmates and the overall environment of the facility. The program begins with an orientation session, where participants are introduced to the concept of mindfulness and the structure of the course. This initial session aims to demystify mindfulness, alleviate any skepticism, and set the stage for committed participation. Facilitators explain the scientific basis of mindfulness and its benefits, emphasizing its relevance to managing the stress and challenges of prison life. One of the fundamental practices taught in MBSR is the body scan, a guided meditation that systematically brings awareness to different parts of the body. Participants are instructed to lie down or sit comfortably and focus their attention on various body regions, starting from the toes and moving up to the head. The body scan helps individuals develop a deeper awareness of bodily sensations, promoting relaxation and reducing physical tension. For inmates who often experience high levels of physical and emotional stress, the body scan can be particularly beneficial in fostering a sense of calm and grounding.

Mindful breathing is another core practice in MBSR. Participants are guided to focus on their breath, noticing the sensations of inhalation and exhalation. This practice serves as an anchor for attention, helping individuals stay present and centered. By regularly practicing mindful breathing, inmates can develop greater emotional regulation and resilience to stress. The simplicity of this technique makes it accessible and easy to integrate into daily routines, even in the confined and often chaotic environment of a correctional facility. The program also incorporates gentle yoga and mindful movement exercises, which help participants connect with their bodies and release physical tension. These practices emphasize slow, deliberate movements and conscious awareness of physical sensations. For inmates, who may have limited opportunities for physical activity and experience high levels of bodily stress, mindful movement can be a valuable tool for improving physical and mental well-being. The combination of movement and mindfulness helps participants develop a more positive relationship with their bodies and enhances overall physical health.

MBSR sessions include discussions on the nature of stress and its impact on the mind and body. Participants are encouraged to share their experiences and reflections, fostering a sense of community and mutual support. These discussions provide a safe space for inmates to explore their thoughts and emotions, gain insights into their stress responses, and learn from each other. The group setting helps normalize the challenges of managing stress, reducing feelings of isolation and promoting collective resilience. A key component of MBSR is the practice of mindfulness in daily activities, often referred to as informal mindfulness. Participants are encouraged to bring mindful awareness to routine tasks such as eating, walking, and interacting with others. This practice helps individuals develop a more continuous state of mindfulness, extending the benefits of formal meditation into everyday life. For inmates, integrating mindfulness into daily activities can transform mundane routines into opportunities for relaxation and self-awareness, making the correctional environment more manageable and less stressful.

The MBSR program culminates in a day-long retreat, where participants engage in an extended period of silence and intensive mindfulness practice. This retreat provides an opportunity for deeper immersion in mindfulness, allowing participants to consolidate their skills and experience the profound benefits of sustained practice. For many inmates, the retreat can be a transformative experience, offering a respite from the stress of prison life and fostering a deeper sense of inner peace and clarity. Research on the effectiveness of MBSR in correctional settings has shown promising results. Studies indicate that participants in MBSR programs experience significant reductions in stress, anxiety, and depression, along with improvements in emotional regulation, self-awareness, and overall well-being. For example, a study conducted at the Massachusetts Correctional Institution found that inmates who completed the MBSR program reported lower levels of perceived stress and greater emotional resilience compared to a control group. These findings highlight the potential of MBSR to support the mental health and rehabilitation of inmates.

One notable case study is the implementation of MBSR at the King County Jail in Seattle. The program was introduced as part of a broader initiative to improve inmate mental health and reduce recidivism rates. Over several cycles, the MBSR program demonstrated significant benefits, with participants reporting reduced stress, improved mood, and better coping skills. The program also contributed to a more positive and cooperative atmosphere within the facility, with staff noting fewer incidents of aggression and disruptive behavior among participants. Another successful example is the MBSR program at the Durham County Detention Facility in North Carolina. This program, facilitated by the non-profit organization "Mindful Justice," offered weekly mindfulness sessions to inmates, incorporating body scans, mindful breathing, and yoga. The program's evaluation revealed substantial improvements in participants' mental health, including reduced symptoms of anxiety and depression and enhanced emotional regulation. Participants also reported a greater sense of self-awareness and a more positive outlook on their future.

The benefits of MBSR extend beyond individual participants to the broader correctional community. By promoting emotional regulation and stress reduction, MBSR can contribute to a safer and more harmonious environment within the facility. Inmates who practice mindfulness are better equipped to handle conflicts and stressors, reducing the likelihood of violent incidents and disciplinary infractions. This, in turn, can create a more supportive and rehabilitative atmosphere, benefiting both inmates and staff. Implementing MBSR in correctional settings requires careful planning and support. Securing buy-in from correctional administrators and staff is essential for the program's success. This can be achieved by presenting evidence of the program's benefits, providing training for staff, and involving them in the planning and delivery of mindfulness sessions.

Facilitators must be well-trained in MBSR and equipped to address the unique challenges of working in a correctional environment. Ongoing supervision and professional development can help facilitators maintain their skills and ensure the quality and consistency of the program. To sustain the benefits of MBSR, it is important to provide participants with resources and support for continuing their mindfulness practice after the program ends. This can include offering follow-up sessions, providing access to guided meditations and mindfulness apps, and encouraging the formation of peer support groups. By fostering a culture of mindfulness within the facility, inmates can continue to benefit from the skills and insights gained through MBSR, supporting their long-term rehabilitation and successful reintegration into society.

15.3: Benefits for Offenders in Correctional Settings

Emotional regulation is a fundamental component of psychological well-being and successful rehabilitation, particularly in the high-stress environment of correctional facilities. Developing effective strategies for managing and regulating emotions can help inmates navigate the complex emotional landscape of prison life, reduce the likelihood of aggressive behavior, and promote positive interactions with peers and staff. Integrating mindfulness and meditation practices into emotional regulation techniques offers a powerful approach to fostering emotional resilience and facilitating rehabilitation. Mindfulness, the practice of maintaining a moment-by-moment awareness of thoughts, feelings, bodily sensations, and the surrounding environment, plays a crucial role in emotional regulation. By observing emotions without immediate reaction or judgment, individuals can create a space between stimulus and response, allowing for more thoughtful and deliberate actions. This non-reactive stance helps mitigate impulsive behaviors that often lead to conflict and disciplinary issues within correctional settings.

One effective mindfulness technique for emotional regulation is the practice of "noting." This involves mentally labeling emotions as they arise, such as "anger," "sadness," or "anxiety." By acknowledging and naming emotions, individuals can distance themselves from the intensity of their feelings and observe them with greater clarity. This practice encourages a deeper understanding of emotional triggers and patterns, enabling inmates to respond to challenging situations with greater composure and control. Meditation practices, particularly those focused on compassion and loving-kindness, are also instrumental in developing emotional regulation skills. Loving-kindness meditation, or Metta Bhavana, involves generating feelings of goodwill and compassion towards oneself and others. Practitioners silently repeat phrases such as "May I be happy," "May I be healthy," and "May I live with ease," gradually extending these wishes to loved ones, acquaintances, and even individuals with whom they have conflicts. This practice fosters a sense of empathy and interconnectedness, which can transform hostile or adversarial attitudes into more compassionate and understanding ones.

For inmates, who may struggle with feelings of guilt, shame, and anger, loving-kindness meditation offers a pathway to emotional healing and reconciliation. By cultivating compassion towards themselves, participants can address their own emotional wounds and develop a more positive self-image. Extending compassion to others, including fellow inmates and staff, can improve relationships and reduce tensions within the facility. This practice not only enhances emotional regulation but also contributes to a more harmonious and supportive environment. Another valuable technique for emotional regulation is the practice of mindful breathing. Focusing on the breath serves as an anchor for the mind, helping individuals remain grounded in the present moment. When emotions become overwhelming, taking a few deep, mindful breaths can help calm the nervous system and create a sense of stability. This simple yet effective practice can be used in any situation, providing a readily accessible tool for managing stress and emotional reactivity.

In addition to these mindfulness practices, incorporating cognitive-behavioral strategies can further enhance emotional regulation. Cognitive-behavioral therapy (CBT) techniques, such as cognitive restructuring, involve identifying and challenging distorted or unhelpful thought patterns. By examining the connections between thoughts, emotions, and behaviors, individuals can develop more adaptive and constructive ways of thinking. For example, an inmate who feels intense anger might recognize that their thoughts are exaggerating the threat posed by a situation. By reframing these thoughts, they can reduce the intensity of their emotional response and choose a more measured and appropriate action. Combining mindfulness and cognitive-behavioral techniques creates a comprehensive approach to emotional regulation that addresses both the immediate experience of emotions and the underlying cognitive processes. Programs like Mindfulness-Based Cognitive Therapy (MBCT) have been adapted for correctional settings to help inmates develop these skills. MBCT integrates mindfulness practices with cognitive-behavioral strategies to help participants break the cycle of negative thinking and emotional reactivity. Research on MBCT has shown that it can significantly reduce symptoms of depression and anxiety, improve emotional regulation, and enhance overall well-being.

Practical exercises for developing emotional resilience often include role-playing scenarios and group discussions. These activities provide opportunities for inmates to practice applying mindfulness and cognitive-behavioral techniques in a supportive and controlled environment. Role-playing can help participants explore different ways of responding to emotional triggers and receive feedback from facilitators and peers. Group discussions allow individuals to share their experiences, learn from others, and build a sense of community and mutual support. One notable example of a successful emotional regulation program is the "Emotional Awareness and Self-Help" (EASH) initiative implemented in several correctional facilities in Canada. This program combines mindfulness practices, cognitive-behavioral techniques, and psychoeducation on emotions. Participants learn to identify and understand their emotions, develop mindfulness skills to observe and accept their feelings, and apply cognitive-behavioral strategies to manage emotional challenges. Evaluations of the EASH program have shown significant improvements in participants' emotional regulation, reductions in aggressive behavior, and enhanced overall mental health.

The "Insight and Expression" program at the Cook County Jail in Illinois offers another compelling example. This program integrates mindfulness meditation, expressive arts therapy, and cognitive-behavioral techniques to help inmates develop emotional regulation skills. Participants engage in mindfulness exercises to cultivate awareness and acceptance of their emotions, use art and writing to express and process their feelings, and apply cognitive-behavioral strategies to reframe negative thought patterns. The combination of these approaches has been highly effective in reducing stress and emotional reactivity, improving mood, and fostering a sense of self-efficacy and empowerment. For emotional regulation programs to be effective in correctional settings, it is essential to create a supportive and non-judgmental environment. Facilitators must be skilled in both mindfulness and cognitive-behavioral techniques and possess the empathy and patience needed to work with individuals who may have experienced significant trauma and emotional distress. Comprehensive training and ongoing supervision for facilitators can help ensure the quality and consistency of the program.

Incorporating emotional regulation techniques into the daily routines of inmates is also crucial for sustaining the benefits of these practices. Encouraging participants to set aside regular time for mindfulness meditation, mindful breathing, and cognitive-behavioral exercises can help embed these skills into their daily lives. Providing access to guided meditations, mindfulness apps, and written materials can support ongoing practice and reinforce the lessons learned in the program. The integration of emotional regulation techniques with other rehabilitative services and support systems can further enhance their effectiveness. Collaboration with mental health professionals, social workers, and vocational training providers can create a holistic approach to rehabilitation that addresses multiple aspects of participants' needs. For example, integrating mindfulness and cognitive-behavioral techniques into anger management and substance abuse treatment programs can provide participants with additional tools for managing their emotions and behaviors.

15.4: Case Studies of Stress Reduction Programs

Integrating stress reduction into daily life is essential for inmates in correctional facilities, as the continuous presence of stressors can exacerbate physical and mental health issues, impede rehabilitation, and increase the likelihood of recidivism. Establishing routines that incorporate stress-reducing activities and promoting healthy coping mechanisms can significantly enhance inmates' well-being and support their journey toward personal growth and reintegration into society. Creating routines that incorporate stress-reducing activities begins with identifying simple, accessible practices that can be seamlessly integrated into daily life. One effective method is the practice of mindful walking. Unlike traditional meditation, mindful walking involves bringing full awareness to the act of walking, paying close attention to the sensations in the feet, legs, and body as they move. Inmates can practice mindful walking during recreation periods or when moving between different areas of the facility. This practice not only provides a break from sedentary activities but also helps inmates stay grounded and present, reducing anxiety and promoting relaxation.

Breathwork exercises are another powerful tool for managing stress and can be easily incorporated into daily routines. Techniques such as deep breathing, box breathing, and alternate nostril breathing help activate the parasympathetic nervous system, which counteracts the stress response and promotes a state of calm. Inmates can practice these exercises during moments of heightened stress, such as before a court appearance or after a confrontation, as well as incorporate them into their daily schedule, such as before meals or bedtime. Consistent practice of breathwork can lead to improved emotional regulation and a greater sense of control over one's responses to stress. Another accessible practice is progressive muscle relaxation (PMR), which involves systematically tensing and relaxing different muscle groups in the body. This technique helps individuals become more aware of physical tension and learn to release it. Inmates can practice PMR while lying in their bunks or sitting in a quiet space. The routine involves tensing a muscle group, such as the shoulders or legs, holding the tension for a few seconds, and then releasing it while focusing on the sensation of relaxation. Regular practice of PMR can reduce physical stress symptoms and promote a greater sense of physical and mental relaxation.

Incorporating mindfulness practices into everyday activities, such as eating and personal hygiene, can also provide significant benefits. Mindful eating involves paying full attention to the experience of eating, including the taste, texture, and aroma of food, as well as the act of chewing and swallowing. Inmates can practice mindful eating during meals by focusing on their food and eating slowly, savoring each bite. This practice not only helps reduce overeating but also enhances the enjoyment of food and provides a moment of calm and mindfulness in the daily routine. Journaling is another valuable practice for stress reduction that inmates can incorporate into their daily lives. Writing about thoughts, feelings, and experiences allows individuals to process emotions, reflect on their day, and gain insights into their stressors and coping mechanisms. Inmates can set aside time each day to write in a journal, whether in the morning, before bed, or during a quiet period. Prompts such as "What am I grateful for today?" or "What challenges did I face and how did I handle them?" can guide the journaling process and encourage positive reflection and problem-solving.

Creating a structured daily routine that includes these stress-reducing activities can provide inmates with a sense of predictability and stability, which is often lacking in the chaotic environment of a correctional facility. Having a consistent routine can help reduce anxiety, improve time management, and promote a sense of purpose and accomplishment. Inmates can work with facility staff to develop personalized routines that incorporate stress-reducing practices at specific times throughout the day. The importance of self-care and healthy coping mechanisms cannot be overstated in the context of stress reduction. Self-care involves taking intentional actions to care for one's physical, mental, and emotional health. For inmates, this might include ensuring they get adequate sleep, staying hydrated, and engaging in physical exercise. Encouraging regular exercise, such as jogging, yoga, or strength training, can significantly reduce stress levels and improve overall physical health. Facilities can support this by providing access to exercise equipment and organizing group fitness activities.

Healthy coping mechanisms are essential for managing stress and avoiding maladaptive behaviors, such as substance abuse or aggression. Teaching inmates healthy coping strategies, such as deep breathing, visualization, or engaging in creative activities like drawing or music, can provide them with tools to manage stress constructively. Providing access to resources, such as art supplies, musical instruments, or books on mindfulness and self-care, can support inmates in developing these coping skills. Encouraging ongoing practice and maintenance of stress reduction techniques is crucial for sustaining the benefits over time. Regular practice helps reinforce the skills learned and ensures that stress reduction becomes a habitual part of daily life. Inmates can be encouraged to set specific goals for their stress reduction practices, such as committing to a daily mindfulness session or participating in a weekly group activity. Setting achievable goals and tracking progress can help maintain motivation and provide a sense of accomplishment.

Group activities and peer support play a significant role in sustaining stress reduction practices. Group mindfulness sessions, yoga classes, or peer-led support groups can provide a sense of community and mutual encouragement. Sharing experiences and challenges with peers can help inmates feel less isolated and more supported in their efforts to manage stress. Facilities can facilitate this by organizing regular group activities and encouraging peer mentorship and leadership. Facility staff also play a critical role in supporting inmates' stress reduction efforts.

Staff can be trained in mindfulness and stress reduction techniques and encouraged to model these practices in their interactions with inmates. Providing staff with training and resources on the importance of stress reduction and how to support inmates in their practice can enhance the overall effectiveness of the programs. Staff can also provide individual support and encouragement, helping inmates develop personalized stress reduction plans and overcome any barriers they encounter. Evaluating the effectiveness of stress reduction programs and practices is essential for ensuring their success and making necessary adjustments. Regular assessments, such as surveys or interviews, can provide feedback on inmates' experiences and the impact of the practices on their stress levels and overall well-being. This feedback can inform program improvements and help identify areas where additional support or resources may be needed.

15.5: Long-Term Impact on Offender Behavior

Evaluating stress reduction programs within correctional facilities is a multifaceted endeavor that requires a comprehensive approach to understand their effectiveness and long-term impact. This evaluation involves a combination of quantitative and qualitative methods to capture both measurable outcomes and personal experiences, providing a holistic view of the programs' benefits and areas for improvement. Quantitative assessments are essential for obtaining objective data on the impact of stress reduction programs. Standardized psychological assessments can measure changes in inmates' mental health and stress levels. Tools such as the Perceived Stress Scale (PSS), the Beck Depression Inventory (BDI), and the State-Trait Anxiety Inventory (STAI) are commonly used to quantify reductions in stress, anxiety, and depression. These assessments are typically administered before the start of the program, immediately after its completion, and at follow-up intervals to track long-term effects. For instance, a study conducted at the Cook County Jail used the PSS and BDI to evaluate a mindfulness-based stress reduction (MBSR) program, finding significant reductions in perceived stress and depressive symptoms among participants.

Behavioral metrics also play a crucial role in evaluating stress reduction programs. Tracking the frequency of disciplinary incidents, such as fights, rule violations, and other disruptive behaviors, provides concrete evidence of changes in behavior. A decrease in these incidents can indicate improved emotional regulation and stress management among participants. For example, the "Peace Within" program at the California State Prison monitored disciplinary infractions and found a substantial reduction in aggressive behaviors among inmates who participated in the program. This not only demonstrates the effectiveness of the program but also highlights its positive impact on the overall facility environment. Recidivism rates are another important measure of the long-term effectiveness of stress reduction programs. Comparing the rates of reoffending among program participants and non-participants provides insights into the lasting impact of these interventions. A comprehensive evaluation of the "Mindful Resilience" program at the Texas Department of Criminal Justice revealed that participants had significantly lower recidivism rates compared to a control group, suggesting that the skills learned in the program contributed to successful reintegration and reduced the likelihood of reoffending.

Qualitative methods complement quantitative assessments by providing deeper insights into participants' personal experiences and the subjective benefits of stress reduction programs. Interviews, focus groups, and open-ended questionnaires allow inmates to share their reflections on how the program has affected their lives. These narratives can reveal the nuances of personal transformation, emotional healing, and behavioral change that may not be fully captured by standardized assessments. In-depth interviews with participants of the "Inner Peace" program at the Arizona State Prison highlighted profound personal transformations. Inmates described how the program helped them develop greater self-awareness, manage their emotions more effectively, and build healthier relationships with peers and staff. One participant shared that mindfulness practices enabled him to recognize and interrupt patterns of negative thinking that had previously led to conflict. Another inmate reported that the stress reduction techniques helped him cope with the anxiety and uncertainty of his upcoming parole hearing, allowing him to present himself more calmly and confidently.

Focus groups provide an opportunity for participants to discuss their experiences collectively, fostering a sense of community and shared understanding. A focus group conducted as part of the evaluation of the "Calm Minds" program at the Rikers Island Correctional Facility revealed that the group setting enhanced the effectiveness of the stress reduction practices. Participants expressed that practicing mindfulness together created a supportive environment that reinforced their commitment to the techniques and provided a sense of camaraderie. They noted that the discussions allowed them to learn from each other's experiences and develop a deeper understanding of the benefits of mindfulness. Open-ended questionnaires can elicit valuable feedback on the strengths and areas for improvement in stress reduction programs. Responses from a survey of the "Stress Less" program at the Florida State Prison indicated that while most participants found the mindfulness exercises beneficial, some suggested incorporating more diverse activities to keep the sessions engaging. This feedback led to the inclusion of additional techniques such as yoga and guided imagery, enhancing the program's appeal and effectiveness.

Long-term follow-up studies are essential for assessing the sustained impact of stress reduction programs after participants are released from correctional facilities. These studies can track former inmates' reintegration into society, their engagement in pro-social activities, and their overall mental health and well-being. A notable long-term study of the "Path to Calm" program at the New York State Correctional Facility followed graduates for three years post-release. The study found that former participants had significantly lower recidivism rates and reported higher levels of employment and stable housing compared to a control group. Additionally, many former participants continued to practice mindfulness and credited the program with helping them navigate the challenges of reentry. Evaluations should also consider the perspectives of correctional staff and facilitators, as they provide valuable insights into the program's impact on the overall correctional environment. Surveys and interviews with staff can assess changes in the facility's atmosphere and the behavior of both inmates and staff. An evaluation of the "Harmony Within" program at the Michigan Department of Corrections revealed that staff observed a noticeable decrease in tension and conflicts within the facility. They also reported that inmates who participated in the program showed greater respect for staff and peers, and a more cooperative attitude, contributing to a more positive and rehabilitative atmosphere.

Facilitator feedback is crucial for identifying challenges and successes encountered during the implementation of stress reduction programs. Facilitators at the "Serenity Now" program at the Ohio State Penitentiary noted that while some participants initially resisted mindfulness practices, persistence and a compassionate approach eventually led to increased engagement and positive outcomes. Their feedback highlighted the importance of patience, adaptability, and ongoing support in delivering effective stress reduction programs. To ensure the validity and reliability of evaluation results, it is important to use a mixed-methods approach that combines quantitative and qualitative data. This approach provides a comprehensive understanding of the impact of stress reduction programs, capturing both measurable changes and personal experiences. Additionally, evaluations should employ rigorous research designs, such as randomized controlled trials, to establish causal relationships between the interventions and observed outcomes.

Collaboration with academic institutions and research organizations can enhance the quality and credibility of program evaluations. By partnering with experts in psychology, criminology, and public health, correctional facilities can design robust evaluation studies and analyze data effectively. For example, the partnership between the Washington Department of Corrections and the University of Washington resulted in a high-quality study that informed the development and improvement of the "Mindful Recovery" program. Securing funding and resources is critical for conducting thorough evaluations of stress reduction programs. Grants from governmental and non-governmental organizations, as well as partnerships with academic institutions and non-profit organizations, can provide the necessary financial and logistical support for comprehensive research. Building a strong case for the cost-effectiveness of these programs, based on evidence of their impact on recidivism rates and mental health outcomes, can help attract funding and support.

—

CHAPTER SIXTEEN

Long-Term Benefits of Mindfulness

Contents

- Sustaining Mindfulness Practices

- Long-Term Impact on Offender Rehabilitation

- Case Studies of Successful Mindfulness Programs

- Benefits for Justice Practitioners

- Strategies for Integrating Mindfulness into Justice Systems

16.1: Sustaining Mindfulness Practices

Sustaining mindfulness practices after incarceration is crucial for the continued well-being and successful reintegration of former inmates into society. The transition from the structured environment of a correctional facility to the often unpredictable nature of the outside world can be fraught with challenges. Mindfulness, cultivated during incarceration, becomes an invaluable tool in navigating this transition, providing a stable foundation for managing stress, making better decisions, and fostering positive relationships. The importance of continued mindfulness practice post-incarceration cannot be overstated. In a correctional setting, inmates often find solace and structure in regular mindfulness sessions, where the environment is controlled and support is readily available. Upon release, the absence of this structured support can lead to a sense of disorientation and vulnerability. It is essential for former inmates to establish a routine that incorporates mindfulness practices, ensuring they have the means to cope with the stresses of daily life outside the facility. Regular meditation, mindful breathing, and other mindfulness exercises help maintain the mental clarity and emotional balance necessary for successful reintegration.

Access to resources and support networks is pivotal in sustaining mindfulness practices after release. Community organizations, support groups, and online platforms can provide ongoing guidance and encouragement. Many community-based programs offer mindfulness and meditation classes specifically designed for individuals transitioning out of the correctional system. These programs not only help maintain the practice but also create a sense of community and belonging, which is vital for individuals who might feel isolated or stigmatized after their release. Access to apps and online guided meditations can supplement these resources, offering flexibility and convenience for continued practice. Personal stories of successful reintegration with mindfulness are powerful testaments to the effectiveness of these practices. Consider the case of James, who spent ten years in a maximum-security prison. During his incarceration, he participated in a mindfulness program that taught him how to manage his anger and anxiety through meditation and mindful breathing. Upon his release, James continued his mindfulness practice, attending weekly meditation sessions at a local community center and using a mindfulness app daily. He credits these practices with helping him stay calm and focused, resist the temptation to reoffend, and build healthy relationships. James now mentors others in his community, sharing his experience and encouraging them to incorporate mindfulness into their lives.

Another compelling story is that of Maria, who struggled with substance abuse and criminal behavior before her incarceration. In prison, she discovered mindfulness meditation, which helped her gain control over her cravings and develop a sense of inner peace. After her release, Maria joined a support group for former inmates where mindfulness practices were integrated into the recovery process. The support group provided a safe space for Maria to continue her meditation practice and connect with others who shared similar experiences. Today, Maria is sober and works as a counselor, helping others use mindfulness to overcome their own challenges. The continuity of mindfulness practice is supported by collaboration between correctional facilities and community programs. Correctional institutions can establish partnerships with local organizations to create a seamless transition for inmates who wish to continue their mindfulness journey post-release. These collaborations can involve sharing resources, co-hosting events, and providing referrals to community-based mindfulness programs. Such partnerships ensure that former inmates have access to the support and resources they need to sustain their practice and thrive in the outside world.

Research underscores the benefits of sustained mindfulness practice post-incarceration. Studies have shown that individuals who continue to engage in mindfulness practices after their release experience lower levels of stress and anxiety, improved emotional regulation, and better overall mental health. These benefits are critical in reducing the risk of recidivism, as individuals who are better equipped to manage their emotions and stressors are less likely to engage in criminal behavior. The long-term commitment to mindfulness fosters resilience and a positive outlook, which are essential for navigating the complexities of life after incarceration. Moreover, mindfulness practices help former inmates build and maintain healthy relationships, which are vital for successful reintegration. Mindfulness enhances communication skills, empathy, and emotional intelligence, enabling individuals to interact more positively with family, friends, and the community. These improved relationships provide a strong support network that can offer encouragement and assistance as former inmates rebuild their lives. For example, John, who spent several years in prison, found that continuing his mindfulness practice helped him reconnect with his family and repair strained relationships. By approaching interactions mindfully, John was able to listen more attentively and respond more thoughtfully, strengthening his bonds with loved ones.

To further support the sustained practice of mindfulness, correctional facilities can provide inmates with resources and tools before their release. This can include information about local mindfulness groups, access to meditation apps, and guidance on establishing a personal practice routine. Offering a "mindfulness toolkit" as part of the reentry planning process can empower inmates to continue their practice independently. Facilities can also facilitate follow-up sessions or check-ins with former participants to provide ongoing support and encouragement. Encouraging a mindful lifestyle post-incarceration also involves promoting mindfulness in daily activities. Former inmates can integrate mindfulness into their everyday routines, such as practicing mindful eating, mindful walking, or taking mindful pauses throughout the day. These practices help maintain a continuous state of mindfulness, making it a natural part of their lives rather than a separate activity. For instance, Sarah, who learned mindfulness in prison, makes a habit of starting her day with a brief meditation and practicing mindful breathing during her commute to work. This consistent integration of mindfulness helps her stay centered and calm, even amidst the stresses of daily life.

Long-term support from family and friends can significantly enhance the sustainability of mindfulness practices. Educating loved ones about the benefits of mindfulness and encouraging them to participate in mindfulness activities together can create a supportive home environment. Family members can attend mindfulness classes with their loved one, practice meditation together, or simply provide encouragement and understanding as the individual navigates the challenges of reintegration. This collaborative approach reinforces the importance of mindfulness and fosters a shared commitment to well-being. Sustaining mindfulness practices post-incarceration is critical for the successful reintegration and long-term well-being of former inmates. Establishing a routine that incorporates mindfulness, accessing resources and support networks, and fostering positive relationships are essential components of this process. Personal stories of successful reintegration highlight the transformative power of mindfulness, while collaborations between correctional facilities and community programs ensure continuity of support. By promoting a mindful lifestyle and providing long-term support, former inmates can navigate the challenges of reentry with resilience, reducing the risk of recidivism and building a foundation for a healthier, more fulfilling life.

16.2: Long-Term Impact on Offender Rehabilitation

Community-based mindfulness programs play an essential role in supporting former inmates as they reintegrate into society. These programs provide ongoing guidance, resources, and a sense of belonging, helping individuals maintain and deepen their mindfulness practice beyond the structured environment of a correctional facility. The involvement of community organizations in promoting mindfulness can significantly enhance the well-being and rehabilitation of former inmates, offering a network of support that is critical during the transition period. One of the primary benefits of community-based mindfulness programs is the continuity of practice they offer. When inmates leave the structured setting of a prison, they often face numerous challenges, including the need to find employment, secure housing, and reestablish relationships. Amid these pressures, it can be easy for mindfulness practices to fall by the wayside. Community programs help bridge this gap by providing a consistent space where individuals can continue their mindfulness journey. Regular classes, group sessions, and workshops offer opportunities for continued practice and learning, reinforcing the skills developed during incarceration.

For example, the "Mindful Transition" program in Los Angeles collaborates with local community centers to provide mindfulness and meditation classes specifically designed for former inmates. These classes focus on stress reduction, emotional regulation, and building resilience. Participants are encouraged to attend weekly sessions where they can practice mindfulness in a supportive environment and discuss their experiences and challenges with peers who understand their journey. This ongoing support helps maintain the benefits of mindfulness practice, providing stability and structure during a potentially turbulent period of adjustment. Community organizations often tailor their mindfulness programs to address the unique needs of former inmates. Recognizing that many individuals leaving the correctional system face significant trauma and mental health issues, these programs incorporate trauma-informed approaches to mindfulness. This means creating safe, inclusive spaces where participants feel comfortable exploring their thoughts and emotions without judgment. Facilitators are trained to handle disclosures of trauma and provide appropriate support, ensuring that the mindfulness practice is both healing and empowering.

The "Safe Haven Mindfulness Project" in New York City exemplifies this approach. This initiative partners with mental health professionals to offer mindfulness-based stress reduction (MBSR) courses that integrate trauma-informed care. Participants engage in mindfulness meditation, body scans, and gentle yoga, all within a framework that acknowledges and respects their traumatic experiences. By addressing trauma directly, the program helps individuals develop healthier coping mechanisms and fosters a sense of safety and trust, which are essential for long-term healing and rehabilitation. Successful community-based mindfulness programs often collaborate with other local services to provide a comprehensive support network. These collaborations can include partnerships with job training centers, housing assistance programs, and mental health services, creating a holistic approach to rehabilitation. By addressing multiple aspects of reentry simultaneously, these programs ensure that former inmates receive the support they need to rebuild their lives effectively.

The "Resilient Pathways" program in San Francisco is a prime example of such collaboration. This initiative works with various community partners to offer a range of services, including mindfulness training, job placement assistance, and counseling. Participants begin their journey with an intensive mindfulness course, learning techniques to manage stress and cultivate resilience. Concurrently, they receive support in finding stable employment and housing, as well as access to mental health services. This integrated approach has proven highly effective, with many participants reporting significant improvements in their mental health, employment status, and overall quality of life. Community-based mindfulness programs also play a critical role in fostering a sense of belonging and connection. For many former inmates, reintegration can be an isolating experience. They may feel disconnected from their families and communities and face stigma and discrimination. Mindfulness programs offer a welcoming space where individuals can connect with others who share similar experiences and challenges. These connections provide emotional support and reduce feelings of isolation, which are crucial for maintaining mental health and preventing recidivism.

The "Healing Circles" initiative in Chicago creates community support groups where former inmates can practice mindfulness together and share their stories. These groups meet weekly, and each session includes a mindfulness practice followed by a group discussion. Participants find solace in knowing they are not alone in their struggles and gain strength from the collective experience of the group. The sense of community and mutual support fosters a positive environment where individuals feel valued and understood. Another important aspect of community-based mindfulness programs is their role in educating the broader community about the benefits of mindfulness and the importance of supporting former inmates. Public workshops, seminars, and community events can raise awareness and reduce stigma, creating a more inclusive and supportive environment for reintegration. By promoting understanding and empathy, these programs help build bridges between former inmates and the communities they are rejoining.

The "Mindful Community Initiative" in Seattle offers public workshops that educate community members about mindfulness and its role in rehabilitation. These workshops include presentations from former inmates who share their experiences and the positive impact mindfulness has had on their lives. By fostering dialogue and understanding, the initiative helps reduce stigma and encourages community members to support the reintegration of former inmates. This broader acceptance and support are crucial for creating a more inclusive society where individuals have the opportunity to rebuild their lives successfully. Evaluating the effectiveness of community-based mindfulness programs is essential for ensuring they meet the needs of participants and achieve their intended outcomes.

Regular assessments, such as participant surveys and program evaluations, provide valuable feedback that can inform program improvements. Tracking key metrics, such as changes in mental health, employment status, and recidivism rates, helps measure the impact of these programs and identify areas for further development. The "Mindful Living Network" in Boston conducts comprehensive evaluations of its mindfulness programs for former inmates. These evaluations include pre- and post-program assessments of participants' mental health, stress levels, and coping skills. Additionally, the network tracks long-term outcomes, such as employment status and recidivism rates, to gauge the sustained impact of its programs. This data-driven approach ensures that the programs remain effective and responsive to the needs of participants, continuously evolving to provide the best possible support.

16.3: Case Studies of Successful Mindfulness Programs

Mindfulness practice has demonstrated significant potential in reducing recidivism among former inmates. The consistent application of mindfulness techniques can fundamentally alter the cognitive and emotional patterns that often lead to reoffending. By fostering self-awareness, emotional regulation, and stress management, mindfulness equips individuals with the skills necessary to navigate the complexities of life after incarceration, reducing the likelihood of falling back into criminal behavior. The link between mindfulness practice and reduced recidivism is supported by a growing body of research. Studies have shown that mindfulness can improve psychological well-being, enhance emotional intelligence, and promote pro-social behavior, all of which are critical factors in successful reintegration. One study, published in the "Journal of Offender Rehabilitation," found that former inmates who participated in a mindfulness-based intervention exhibited lower levels of anxiety and depression and reported a greater sense of control over their impulses and reactions. These psychological benefits translate into tangible behavioral changes that reduce the risk of reoffending.

Mindfulness practice helps former inmates develop a deeper understanding of their thoughts, emotions, and behaviors. This increased self-awareness allows individuals to recognize and interrupt negative patterns that might lead to criminal activity. For example, a former inmate named Robert participated in a mindfulness program during his time in a medium-security prison. Upon release, he continued his practice and found that it helped him manage his anger and frustration, emotions that had previously led him to violent outbursts. By learning to observe his feelings without immediately reacting, Robert was able to make more considered decisions, reducing his involvement in confrontations and ultimately aiding his reintegration into society. The case of the "Mindful Reentry Project" in Philadelphia highlights the impact of mindfulness on reducing recidivism. This initiative provides mindfulness training for individuals on parole or probation, offering weekly group sessions and individual support. Participants are taught techniques such as mindful breathing, body scans, and loving-kindness meditation. Evaluations of the project have shown promising results: participants reported lower stress levels, improved emotional regulation, and a stronger commitment to staying out of trouble. One participant, Jane, who had a history of drug-related offenses, found that mindfulness helped her cope with cravings and stress. By practicing mindfulness, she was able to maintain her sobriety and avoid situations that previously led to her reoffending.

Integrating mindfulness into parole and probation programs can provide a structured support system that reinforces the benefits of mindfulness practice. These programs can offer regular mindfulness sessions, peer support groups, and access to mindfulness resources such as apps and guided meditations. For instance, the "Second Chance Mindfulness Program" in Austin partners with local probation offices to incorporate mindfulness training into mandatory meetings. Probation officers receive training in mindfulness techniques and are encouraged to practice alongside their clients. This collaborative approach not only supports the former inmates but also fosters a more empathetic and understanding relationship between probation officers and their clients. A crucial aspect of these programs is the creation of a supportive community that encourages ongoing mindfulness practice. Peer support groups, where individuals can share their experiences and challenges, provide a sense of belonging and mutual encouragement. In the "Mindful Transitions" program in Chicago, former inmates meet weekly to practice mindfulness together and discuss their progress. This community setting helps participants stay motivated and accountable, reinforcing their commitment to a mindful lifestyle. The support of peers who understand their journey is invaluable in maintaining the positive changes initiated during incarceration.

To further enhance the impact of mindfulness on recidivism, programs can incorporate elements of restorative justice. Restorative justice focuses on repairing the harm caused by criminal behavior through reconciliation with victims and the community. By integrating mindfulness into restorative justice practices, former inmates can develop greater empathy and understanding of the consequences of their actions. The "Restorative Mindfulness Initiative" in Portland combines mindfulness training with restorative justice circles, where participants engage in dialogues with victims and community members. This approach has shown to deepen participants' emotional insight and foster a stronger sense of responsibility and commitment to making amends. The success of these programs relies heavily on the training and dedication of facilitators. Facilitators must be well-versed in mindfulness practices and possess the skills to create a safe and supportive environment. Continuous professional development and supervision are essential to maintain the quality and effectiveness of the programs. Facilitators can benefit from training that includes trauma-informed care, cultural competency, and strategies for addressing the unique challenges faced by former inmates. By equipping facilitators with these skills, programs can ensure that participants receive the best possible support.

Evaluating the effectiveness of mindfulness programs in reducing recidivism involves both quantitative and qualitative methods. Quantitative measures, such as tracking recidivism rates and psychological assessments, provide objective data on the impact of the programs. Qualitative methods, such as interviews and focus groups, offer deeper insights into participants' experiences and the personal transformations they undergo. The "Mindful Pathways" program in San Diego employs a mixed-methods approach to evaluation, combining statistical analysis of recidivism rates with in-depth interviews. This comprehensive evaluation provides a nuanced understanding of how mindfulness practice influences behavior and supports successful reintegration. The long-term benefits of mindfulness extend beyond reducing recidivism. Mindfulness practice helps former inmates build resilience and develop a positive outlook on life. This resilience is crucial for navigating the inevitable challenges of reentry, such as finding employment, securing housing, and reestablishing relationships. Mindfulness cultivates a mindset of acceptance and non-judgment, enabling individuals to face setbacks with greater equanimity and persistence. For example, Tom, a participant in the "Mindful Futures" program in Boston, used mindfulness to cope with the frustration of job rejections. By staying present and maintaining a positive attitude, he eventually secured stable employment and continued to thrive in his new role.

16.4: Benefits for Justice Practitioners

Mindfulness practices are not only beneficial for inmates but also for the staff working within correctional facilities. Correctional officers, administrative staff, and other personnel face significant stress and emotional challenges in their roles. Implementing mindfulness programs for staff well-being can improve their mental health, enhance job performance, and create a more positive and rehabilitative environment within the facility. The benefits of mindfulness for correctional staff are multifaceted, impacting individual well-being, team dynamics, and the overall atmosphere of the correctional institution. Correctional staff are regularly exposed to high-stress situations, including managing inmate behavior, handling emergencies, and maintaining safety and security. The cumulative effect of these stressors can lead to burnout, anxiety, depression, and other mental health issues. Mindfulness practices offer a practical and effective tool for managing stress and enhancing emotional resilience. By cultivating mindfulness, staff can develop greater awareness of their thoughts and emotions, enabling them to respond to stressors more calmly and effectively.

Mindfulness practice helps correctional staff develop greater emotional regulation, which is crucial in high-stress environments. Techniques such as mindful breathing, body scans, and meditation can be used to manage immediate stress responses and maintain a sense of calm during challenging situations. For example, a correctional officer dealing with a volatile inmate situation can use mindful breathing to stay centered and focused, reducing the likelihood of escalating the conflict. Over time, regular mindfulness practice can enhance overall emotional stability, making staff more resilient to the daily pressures of their roles. The introduction of mindfulness programs for staff can lead to a significant improvement in job satisfaction and overall well-being. Studies have shown that mindfulness practices can reduce symptoms of burnout, improve mood, and increase job satisfaction. The "Calm Minds at Work" initiative at the San Quentin State Prison offers a compelling example. This program provides mindfulness training and ongoing support for correctional officers and administrative staff. Participants engage in weekly mindfulness sessions, including guided meditations and discussions on stress management techniques. Evaluations of the program revealed that staff reported lower levels of stress and burnout, improved mood, and a greater sense of job satisfaction. These benefits not only enhance individual well-being but also contribute to a more positive and productive work environment.

Implementing mindfulness programs for staff well-being requires a strategic and supportive approach. Providing access to mindfulness training and resources is essential, as is creating a culture that values and prioritizes mental health. Correctional facilities can offer mindfulness workshops, ongoing training sessions, and access to mindfulness apps and guided meditations. It is also important to encourage staff to integrate mindfulness into their daily routines, such as taking mindful breaks, practicing mindful breathing before starting a shift, or engaging in a brief meditation during lunch breaks. Creating opportunities for staff to practice mindfulness together can foster a sense of community and mutual support. Group mindfulness sessions, peer support groups, and mindfulness retreats can provide valuable opportunities for staff to connect, share experiences, and support each other in their mindfulness practice. For example, the "Mindful Team" program at the Arizona Department of Corrections organizes monthly mindfulness workshops and annual retreats for staff. These events not only provide opportunities for mindfulness practice but also strengthen team cohesion and foster a supportive work environment.

The impact of staff mindfulness on the overall correctional environment is profound. When staff practice mindfulness, they are better equipped to handle stress and maintain a calm and composed demeanor. This has a positive ripple effect on the entire facility, creating a more peaceful and rehabilitative atmosphere. Inmates are likely to respond more positively to staff who are calm, respectful, and empathetic, reducing the potential for conflicts and improving overall interactions. Moreover, staff mindfulness can enhance the implementation and effectiveness of inmate mindfulness programs. When staff members are trained in mindfulness practices, they can better support and reinforce these practices among inmates. For example, a correctional officer who practices mindfulness may be more understanding and encouraging when inmates engage in mindfulness activities. This alignment between staff and inmate mindfulness practices creates a cohesive and supportive environment that enhances the overall rehabilitative efforts of the facility.

The "Resilient Staff Initiative" at the Ohio State Penitentiary highlights the benefits of integrating mindfulness practices for both staff and inmates. This program provides mindfulness training for correctional officers, administrative staff, and inmates, fostering a shared commitment to well-being and rehabilitation. Staff members participate in mindfulness workshops and ongoing training sessions, while inmates engage in mindfulness programs tailored to their needs. The initiative has led to a significant reduction in staff burnout and a more positive interaction between staff and inmates. The shared practice of mindfulness has created a more harmonious and supportive environment, benefiting everyone within the facility. Evaluating the effectiveness of staff mindfulness programs involves both quantitative and qualitative methods. Quantitative assessments, such as surveys measuring stress levels, job satisfaction, and symptoms of burnout, provide objective data on the impact of the programs. Qualitative methods, such as interviews and focus groups, offer deeper insights into staff experiences and the personal benefits of mindfulness practice. The "Mindful Work Environment" program at the Texas Department of Criminal Justice employs a mixed-methods approach to evaluation, combining statistical analysis with in-depth interviews. This comprehensive evaluation provides a nuanced understanding of how mindfulness practices influence staff well-being and job performance.

Leadership plays a crucial role in promoting and sustaining mindfulness programs for staff. Facility administrators and supervisors can lead by example, participating in mindfulness training and integrating mindfulness practices into their own routines. By demonstrating a commitment to mindfulness, leaders can encourage a culture that values mental health and well-being. Providing ongoing support and resources, recognizing the benefits of mindfulness, and creating policies that prioritize staff well-being are essential for the long-term success of these programs. Integrating mindfulness into the daily operations of correctional facilities requires a concerted effort to overcome potential barriers and challenges. Staff may initially be skeptical of mindfulness practices or feel that they do not have time to engage in mindfulness activities. Addressing these concerns through education, training, and ongoing support is essential. Providing evidence of the benefits of mindfulness, offering flexible training options, and creating a supportive environment can help staff embrace mindfulness practices and integrate them into their daily routines.

16.5: Strategies for Integrating Mindfulness into Justice Systems

Building a mindful correctional culture requires a comprehensive and sustained effort that involves all levels of the institution, from leadership to staff to inmates. This transformation entails creating an environment that supports and values mindfulness, fostering practices that promote mental health and well-being, and embedding mindfulness into the core values and daily operations of the facility. The long-term vision for a mindful and rehabilitative correctional system goes beyond individual programs and practices, aiming to cultivate a culture that fundamentally enhances the lives of all who live and work within its walls. Creating a culture that supports mindfulness starts with the commitment of leadership. Facility administrators and supervisors must not only endorse mindfulness programs but also actively participate in them. Their engagement sets a powerful example and signals the importance of mindfulness to the entire institution. Leaders can demonstrate their commitment by incorporating mindfulness practices into meetings, decision-making processes, and their daily routines. For instance, starting meetings with a brief mindfulness exercise can help set a calm and focused tone, promoting thoughtful and effective discussions.

Leadership's role in promoting mindfulness extends to policy development and resource allocation. Policies that prioritize mental health and well-being, such as allowing time for mindfulness practices during work hours and providing access to mindfulness resources, are essential. Allocating resources for training, workshops, and ongoing support ensures that mindfulness programs are well-supported and can thrive. For example, the "Mindful Leadership Initiative" at the Maryland Correctional Institution has established policies that integrate mindfulness into staff training and professional development, providing resources and time for mindfulness practices. This initiative has created a supportive environment that values well-being and fosters a more mindful culture. Training and education are crucial components of building a mindful correctional culture. All staff, from correctional officers to administrative personnel, should receive training in mindfulness practices and their benefits. This training should be ongoing, with opportunities for staff to deepen their practice and learn new techniques. Educating staff about the scientific evidence supporting mindfulness and its positive impact on mental health and job performance can help overcome skepticism and encourage participation. The "Mindfulness in Corrections" program at the Florida Department of Corrections offers comprehensive training for staff, including workshops, online courses, and peer support groups. This program has successfully integrated mindfulness into the fabric of the institution, with staff reporting improved well-being and job satisfaction.

Embedding mindfulness into the daily operations of the facility involves creating opportunities for regular practice and ensuring that mindfulness becomes a natural part of the institutional routine. This can include scheduled mindfulness sessions, mindfulness-based activities integrated into daily schedules, and designated mindfulness spaces where staff and inmates can practice. For instance, the "Peaceful Paths" program at the Oregon State Penitentiary has established mindfulness rooms where staff and inmates can engage in meditation, yoga, and other mindfulness practices. These spaces provide a refuge from the stresses of prison life and encourage regular practice. In addition to structured sessions, promoting informal mindfulness practices throughout the day can reinforce a mindful culture. Encouraging staff and inmates to take mindful breaks, practice mindful walking, or engage in brief mindfulness exercises during transitions can help sustain mindfulness throughout the day. Providing reminders and prompts, such as posters or digital messages, can keep mindfulness practices top of mind. The "Mindful Moments" initiative at the Nevada Department of Corrections uses visual and audio prompts to encourage staff and inmates to pause and practice mindfulness, creating a more mindful and reflective environment.

Fostering a sense of community and mutual support is essential for sustaining a mindful correctional culture. Peer support groups, mindfulness communities, and mentorship programs can provide ongoing encouragement and shared learning experiences. These groups offer a space for individuals to share their mindfulness journeys, discuss challenges, and celebrate successes. The "Mindful Community Network" at the New Jersey State Prison has established peer support groups for both staff and inmates, creating a strong sense of community and mutual support. These groups meet regularly to practice mindfulness, share experiences, and support each other in maintaining their practice. Creating a mindful correctional culture also involves integrating mindfulness into rehabilitative and educational programs for inmates. Mindfulness can be incorporated into vocational training, substance abuse treatment, anger management programs, and educational courses. By embedding mindfulness into these programs, inmates can develop the skills and resilience needed for successful rehabilitation and reintegration. The "Mindful Rehabilitation Program" at the Illinois Department of Corrections integrates mindfulness into various rehabilitative programs, helping inmates develop emotional regulation, stress management, and pro-social behaviors. This holistic approach enhances the effectiveness of rehabilitation efforts and supports long-term success.

The benefits of a mindful correctional culture extend beyond individual well-being, positively impacting the overall atmosphere of the facility. A culture that values mindfulness fosters a more peaceful, respectful, and cooperative environment. Inmates and staff are likely to experience fewer conflicts, improved relationships, and a greater sense of community. This positive environment can reduce stress and burnout among staff, enhance safety and security, and support the overall mission of rehabilitation. The "Harmony in Corrections" initiative at the Colorado State Penitentiary has transformed the facility's atmosphere by promoting mindfulness and creating a culture of respect and cooperation. Staff and inmates alike report feeling more connected, less stressed, and more committed to the rehabilitative process. Long-term sustainability of a mindful correctional culture requires ongoing evaluation and adaptation. Regular assessments of mindfulness programs and practices can provide valuable feedback and identify areas for improvement. Surveys, interviews, and focus groups can gather input from staff and inmates, ensuring that their voices are heard and their needs are addressed.

The "Continuous Improvement in Mindfulness" program at the Pennsylvania Department of Corrections uses a combination of quantitative and qualitative methods to evaluate the effectiveness of mindfulness initiatives. This ongoing evaluation helps refine programs, address challenges, and sustain the momentum of mindfulness efforts. Collaboration with external organizations and experts can enhance the development and implementation of mindfulness programs. Partnerships with universities, non-profit organizations, and mindfulness experts can provide additional resources, training, and support. These collaborations can also facilitate research and innovation, contributing to the broader field of mindfulness in corrections. The "Mindful Partnerships" initiative at the California Department of Corrections and Rehabilitation collaborates with several universities and non-profits to develop and implement cutting-edge mindfulness programs. These partnerships bring expertise and resources that enrich the facility's mindfulness efforts and support ongoing improvement.

References

- Barnett, G. D., & Mann, R. E. (2013). Cognition, Empathy, and Sexual Offending. Trauma, Violence & Abuse, 14(1), 22–33. https://www.jstor.org/stable/26638297
- Carlson, E. N. (2013). Overcoming the Barriers to Self-Knowledge: Mindfulness as a Path to Seeing Yourself as You Really Are. Perspectives on Psychological Science, 8(2), 173–186. http://www.jstor.org/stable/44281869
- Chartier, M., Bitner, R., Peng, T., Coffelt, N., McLane, M., & Eisendrath, S. (2010). Adapting Ancient Wisdom for the Treatment of Depression: Mindfulness-Based Cognitive Therapy Group Training. Group, 34(4), 319–327. http://www.jstor.org/stable/41719292
- Cooley, C. (2019). Escaping the Prison of Mind: Meditation as Violence Prevention for the Incarcerated. Health Promotion Practice, 20(6),

798–800. https://www.jstor.org/stable/26835214

- Garland, E. L., Farb, N. A., Goldin, P. R., & Fredrickson, B. L. (2015). Mindfulness Broadens Awareness and Builds Eudaimonic Meaning: A Process Model of Mindful Positive Emotion Regulation. Psychological Inquiry, 26(4), 293–314. http://www.jstor.org/stable/43865745
- Giordano, P. C., Schroeder, R. D., & Cernkovich, S. A. (2007). Emotions and Crime over the Life Course: A Neo-Meadian Perspective on Criminal Continuity and Change. American Journal of Sociology, 112(6), 1603–1661. https://doi.org/10.1086/512710
- Greer, K. (2002). Walking an Emotional Tightrope: Managing Emotions in a Women's Prison. Symbolic Interaction, 25(1), 117–139. https://doi.org/10.1525/si.2002.25.1.117
- Griera, M. (2017). Yoga in Penitentiary Settings: Transcendence, Spirituality, and Self-Improvement. Human Studies, 40(1), 77–100. http://www.jstor.org/stable/44979846
- Hafenbrack, A. C., Kinias, Z., & Barsade, S. G. (2014). Debiasing the Mind Through Meditation: Mindfulness and the Sunk-Cost Bias. Psychological Science, 25(2), 369–376. http://www.jstor.org/stable/24539809
- Hagelin, J. S., Rainforth, M. V., Orme-Johnson, D. W., Cavanaugh, K. L., Alexander, C. N., Shatkin, S. F., Davies, J. L., Hughes, A. O., & Ross, E. (1999). Effects of Group Practice of the "Transcendental Meditation" Program on Preventing Violent Crime in Washington, D.C.: Results of the National Demonstration Project, June-July 1993. Social Indicators Research, 47(2), 153–201. http://www.jstor.org/stable/27522387
- Hamm, M. S. (1988). Making Changes in Correctional Education. Journal of Correctional Education, 39(4), 146–152. http://www.jstor.org/stable/23292048
- Hyland, T. (2016). THE LIMITS OF MINDFULNESS: EMERGING ISSUES FOR EDUCATION. British Journal of Educational Studies, 64(1), 97–117. http://www.jstor.org/stable/43896318
- Lea, J., Cadman, L., & Philo, C. (2015). Changing the habits of a lifetime? Mindfulness meditation and habitual geographies. Cultural Geographies, 22(1), 49–65. https://www.jstor.org/stable/26168625
- Lucas, L. J., & Kerr, S. (2016). Remembering to Breathe: The Challenges and Rewards of Teaching Mindfulness Practices to Pre-Service Teachers. The Journal of Educational Thought (JET) / Revue de La Pensée Éducative, 49(3), 253–264. https://www.jstor.org/stable/26372377

- McClelland, R. T. (2010). The Pleasures of Revenge. The Journal of Mind and Behavior, 31(3/4), 195–235. http://www.jstor.org/stable/43854277
- Newburn, T. (2007). "Tough on Crime": Penal Policy in England and Wales. Crime and Justice, 36(1), 425–470. https://doi.org/10.1086/592810
- Paulle, B. (2017). Stumbling on the rehabilitation gold? Foucault vs. Foucault in San Quentin and beyond. Ethnography, 18(4), 471–492. https://www.jstor.org/stable/26359200
- Roberts, T. (2015). Emotional Regulation and Responsibility. Ethical Theory and Moral Practice, 18(3), 487–500. http://www.jstor.org/stable/24478635
- Rogers, S. L. (2019). Mindfulness, Mental Health, and Wellness. GPSolo, 36(3), 12–17. https://www.jstor.org/stable/27044610
- Rosch, E. (2007). More than Mindfulness: When You Have a Tiger by the Tail, Let It Eat You. Psychological Inquiry, 18(4), 258–264. http://www.jstor.org/stable/20447395
- Rypi, A. (2017). "You don't have to say straight out …": Directed Impression Management at Victim–Offender Mediation Pre-meetings. Sociological Focus, 50(3), 261–276. https://www.jstor.org/stable/48546794
- Sampaio, C. V. S., Lima, M. G., & Ladeia, A. M. (2017). Meditation, Health and Scientific Investigations: Review of the Literature. Journal of Religion and Health, 56(2), 411–427. http://www.jstor.org/stable/44158323
- Sawyer, D. (2018). Mindfulness Meditation: A Sartrean Analysis. Sartre Studies International, 24(2), 66–83. https://www.jstor.org/stable/48586971
- Spina, F. (2023). The Importance of Mindfulness Meditation in Correctional Settings. Journal of Correctional Education (1974-), 74(2), 56–71. https://www.jstor.org/stable/48730994
- Stetka, B. (2018). Where's the Proof that Mindfulness Really Works?: The ubiquitous technique for relieving stress and pain has remarkably little scientific evidence backing it, a group of scientists contend. Scientific American Mind, 29(1), 20–23. https://www.jstor.org/stable/27172827
- Teper, R., Segal, Z. V., & Inzlicht, M. (2013). Inside the Mindful Mind: How Mindfulness Enhances Emotion Regulation Through

Improvements in Executive Control. Current Directions in Psychological Science, 22(6), 449–454. http://www.jstor.org/stable/44318704

- Virgin, A. S., Pitzel, A., Jolivette, K., & Sanders, S. (2021). Emotional Regulation for Youth in Juvenile Justice Facilities: Practical Suggestions for Facility Implementation. Journal of Correctional Education (1974-), 72(1), 59–73. https://www.jstor.org/stable/27042236
- Wahi, N. (2002). A STUDY OF REHABILITATIVE PENOLOGY AS AN ALTERNATIVE THEORY OF PUNISHMENT. Student Bar Review, 14, 92–104. http://www.jstor.org/stable/44306632
- Wagaman, M. A., Geiger, J. M., Shockley, C., & Segal, E. A. (2015). The Role of Empathy in Burnout, Compassion Satisfaction, and Secondary Traumatic Stress among Social Workers. Social Work, 60(3), 201–209. http://www.jstor.org/stable/24881483
- Weiss, M., Nordlie, J. W., & Siegel, E. P. (2005). Mindfulness-Based Stress Reduction as an Adjunct to Outpatient Psychotherapy. Psychotherapy and Psychosomatics, 74(2), 108–112. https://www.jstor.org/stable/48510855

Part V: Ethical Precepts and Personal Responsibility

—

CHAPTER SEVENTEEN

Understanding Sila- Buddhist Ethical Precepts

Contents

- Introduction to Buddhist Ethical Precepts

- Application in Modern Justice Systems

- Benefits for Offender Rehabilitation

- Case Studies of Ethical Transformation

- Long-Term Impact on Justice Practices

17.1: Introduction to Buddhist Ethical Precepts

The essence of Buddhist ethical precepts lies in their timeless wisdom, offering a profound guide to moral conduct and personal transformation. At the heart of these teachings are the Five Precepts: abstaining from taking life, abstaining from taking what is not given, abstaining from sexual misconduct, abstaining from false speech, and abstaining from intoxicants that cloud the mind. These principles are not just rules but embody a holistic approach to living ethically and mindfully. They provide a framework for cultivating a life of integrity, compassion, and mindfulness, essential qualities for anyone, particularly those seeking rehabilitation and personal growth. Abstaining from taking life, the first precept, extends far beyond the mere act of not killing. It encompasses a deep respect for all forms of life, promoting a profound sense of non-violence and compassion. This respect for life can transform one's actions and attitudes, encouraging a peaceful approach to conflicts and a deeper empathy for all living beings. In correctional settings, this precept can guide individuals away from violent tendencies, helping them develop a more compassionate outlook. By fostering a sense of interconnectedness, inmates can begin to see the value in all life forms, which can be a powerful catalyst for change. This principle encourages the cultivation of kindness and the reduction of harm, laying the foundation for a more harmonious existence.

The second precept, abstaining from taking what is not given, emphasizes honesty and respect for others' property. This precept is about developing trust and integrity, qualities that are essential for personal relationships and societal cohesion. In today's world, this precept can be practiced through honesty in all dealings, whether in business, personal relationships, or digital interactions. For individuals in correctional facilities, this principle encourages reflection on past behaviors, fostering a commitment to honesty and integrity moving forward. By understanding the value of what belongs to others and respecting those boundaries, inmates can rebuild trust with themselves and their communities, paving the way for rehabilitation. This principle instills a sense of responsibility and ethical behavior, crucial for personal development and societal harmony. The third precept, abstaining from sexual misconduct, advocates for respect and consent in all intimate relationships. This principle is especially relevant in addressing issues of power and exploitation. It promotes the idea of treating others with dignity and respect, ensuring that all sexual interactions are consensual and free from coercion. In a correctional context, understanding and adhering to this precept can lead to healthier, more respectful relationships. It encourages individuals to reflect on their actions and their impact on others, fostering a sense of responsibility and ethical awareness. This principle is vital for developing healthy and respectful interpersonal relationships, which are essential for personal growth and rehabilitation.

Abstaining from false speech, the fourth precept, underscores the importance of truthfulness and integrity in communication. This precept encourages individuals to communicate honestly and with kindness, avoiding lies, gossip, and harmful speech. In today's digital age, where misinformation can spread rapidly, this precept is more critical than ever. Practicing mindful and truthful speech helps build trust and fosters better relationships. In correctional facilities, where communication can often be a source of conflict, this principle can lead to more harmonious interactions. This precept extends to self-talk, encouraging individuals to be honest and kind to themselves, which is essential for personal growth and healing. The fifth precept, abstaining from intoxicants that cloud the mind, focuses on maintaining mental clarity and mindfulness. This precept addresses the use of substances that impair judgment and lead to harmful behaviors. For individuals with a history of substance abuse, this precept offers a pathway to recovery and sobriety. Embracing this principle can support individuals in developing healthier coping mechanisms and maintaining self-control. By committing to sobriety, inmates can cultivate greater mental clarity and self-discipline, essential for rehabilitation and personal transformation. This precept encourages individuals to stay present and mindful, enabling them to make better decisions and live more responsibly.

These precepts are not enforced through external authority but are voluntarily adopted as part of one's commitment to personal and spiritual development. They serve as a framework for self-regulation and ethical reflection, guiding behavior and decision-making in various aspects of life. In the context of rehabilitation, these principles can be integrated into correctional programs to support inmates in their journey towards ethical living. Programs that incorporate mindfulness and ethical reflection can help individuals internalize these precepts, leading to profound personal change. The historical and cultural context of the Five Precepts adds depth to their understanding. Rooted in ancient Buddhist teachings, these precepts have guided practitioners for centuries. They are part of the larger framework of the Noble Eightfold Path, which outlines the path to enlightenment and liberation from suffering. The precepts are seen as the foundation for ethical living, supporting the development of wisdom and compassion. In modern times, these principles remain relevant, offering timeless guidance for ethical conduct and personal growth. Their application in contemporary contexts can transform individual lives and promote a more ethical and compassionate society.

The significance of Sila, or ethical conduct, in Buddhist practice cannot be overstated. It is considered the first step on the path to enlightenment, providing the moral foundation for meditative practice and the cultivation of wisdom. Without a strong ethical foundation, the mind cannot achieve the clarity and focus needed for deep meditation. In this way, ethical conduct is seen as essential for both personal and spiritual development. For individuals in correctional settings, embracing these precepts can provide a path to inner peace and transformation, supporting their rehabilitation and reintegration into society. The role of the Five Precepts in guiding behavior and decision-making is profound. They offer a clear and practical framework for evaluating actions and their consequences. By reflecting on these principles, individuals can make more ethical choices and develop a greater sense of responsibility for their actions.

This reflective process is essential for personal growth and transformation. In a correctional context, this approach can help inmates develop a deeper understanding of the impact of their behavior and foster a commitment to positive change. The transformative potential of the Five Precepts lies in their ability to cultivate mindfulness and compassion. By adhering to these principles, individuals develop a heightened awareness of their thoughts, words, and actions. This mindfulness leads to greater self-awareness and self-regulation, essential for personal growth and rehabilitation. Compassion, cultivated through the practice of non-violence and respect for others, fosters empathy and understanding. These qualities are crucial for building positive relationships and creating a supportive community, both within and outside correctional facilities.

17.2: Application in Modern Justice Systems

Translating the ancient Buddhist precepts into modern justice systems requires a nuanced understanding of their timeless principles and the adaptability to integrate them into contemporary contexts. The Five Precepts offer profound guidance that can be transformative when applied to rehabilitation and personal growth, even within the structures of modern correctional facilities. Each precept, when understood deeply and applied thoughtfully, can help address fundamental issues within the justice system and provide a framework for ethical living and rehabilitation. Abstaining from taking life, the first precept, calls for a respect for all forms of life and non-violence. This principle can be particularly powerful in modern justice systems, where violence often begets more violence. By integrating this precept, correctional facilities can promote non-violent conflict resolution and emphasize the value of every life. Programs that teach inmates to resolve disputes peacefully, respect life, and understand the consequences of violence can lead to significant behavioral changes. For example, restorative justice practices, which focus on healing and reconciliation rather than punishment, align well with this precept. These practices encourage offenders to acknowledge the harm they have caused and to take responsibility for their actions, fostering empathy and reducing the likelihood of reoffending.

Abstaining from taking what is not given, the second precept, underscores the importance of honesty and respect for others' property. In modern justice systems, this precept can help address issues related to theft, fraud, and corruption. Teaching inmates the value of honesty and integrity, and encouraging them to respect others' possessions, can be transformative. This principle can be integrated into rehabilitation programs that focus on building trust and accountability. For instance, vocational training programs that emphasize ethical business practices and integrity can prepare inmates for honest work post-release, reducing the temptation to revert to criminal activities. By fostering a culture of honesty and respect, correctional facilities can help inmates rebuild their sense of self-worth and community trust. The third precept, abstaining from sexual misconduct, emphasizes respect and consent in all relationships. This precept is crucial in addressing issues such as sexual violence and exploitation within correctional facilities. Programs that teach about healthy relationships, consent, and respect for personal boundaries can have a profound impact on inmates. These programs can also address underlying issues such as power dynamics and the objectification of others. By promoting ethical behavior in intimate relationships, correctional facilities can help inmates develop a deeper respect for themselves and others, leading to healthier interactions both during incarceration and after release. This precept also supports initiatives that combat sexual harassment and assault, creating a safer environment for all inmates.

Abstaining from false speech, the fourth precept, highlights the importance of truthfulness and integrity in communication. In the context of modern justice systems, this precept can help address issues related to lying, manipulation, and deceit. Encouraging inmates to practice honesty in their interactions can build a foundation of trust and respect. Programs that focus on communication skills, including active listening and assertive speaking, can help inmates express themselves truthfully and constructively. This precept also has implications for legal processes, where honesty and transparency are paramount. By promoting a culture of truthfulness, correctional facilities can foster more open and honest relationships among inmates and staff, leading to a more supportive and rehabilitative environment. The fifth precept, abstaining from intoxicants that cloud the mind, emphasizes maintaining mental clarity and self-control. This precept is particularly relevant in addressing issues related to substance abuse, which is a common problem among inmates. Programs that focus on addiction recovery and promote sobriety align closely with this principle. Teaching inmates about the effects of substances on their minds and bodies, and providing them with tools to manage cravings and stress, can support their journey towards sobriety. This precept also encourages a broader approach to mental health, promoting practices that enhance mindfulness and emotional regulation. By helping inmates develop healthier coping mechanisms, correctional facilities can support their long-term recovery and reduce recidivism.

The application of these precepts in modern justice systems also involves a broader cultural shift towards empathy and compassion. This shift requires training staff to understand and embody these principles, creating a more supportive environment for both inmates and employees. Staff who practice mindfulness and ethical behavior can model these values for inmates, creating a ripple effect throughout the facility. This approach aligns with the principles of restorative justice, which focus on healing and rebuilding relationships rather than solely on punishment. Incorporating these precepts into modern justice systems can also involve rethinking policies and procedures to align with ethical principles. For example, policies that prioritize non-violent conflict resolution, transparency, and respect for personal boundaries can create a more ethical and just environment. Training programs for staff can include modules on ethical behavior, mindfulness, and compassionate communication. By embedding these values into the fabric of the justice system, correctional facilities can create a more humane and rehabilitative environment.

One practical application of these principles is in the design and implementation of rehabilitation programs. Programs that integrate mindfulness practices, ethical education, and vocational training can provide inmates with the tools they need to rebuild their lives. For example, a program that combines meditation with vocational training can help inmates develop both inner calm and practical skills. These programs can also include components that address specific issues such as substance abuse, anger management, and healthy relationships, providing a holistic approach to rehabilitation. The benefits of applying these precepts in modern justice systems extend beyond individual rehabilitation. By fostering a culture of respect, honesty, and compassion, correctional facilities can improve overall morale and reduce violence and conflict.

Inmates who participate in these programs are more likely to develop a sense of responsibility and accountability, reducing the likelihood of reoffending. This approach can also improve relationships between inmates and staff, creating a more supportive and cohesive environment. The long-term impact of integrating these precepts into modern justice systems can be profound. By promoting ethical behavior and personal responsibility, correctional facilities can support the successful reintegration of inmates into society. This approach can also lead to broader societal changes, promoting a culture of empathy, compassion, and ethical behavior. By addressing the root causes of criminal behavior and providing inmates with the tools they need to make positive changes, modern justice systems can move towards a more rehabilitative and restorative approach.

17.3: Benefits for Offender Rehabilitation

Ethical conduct serves as a foundational element for rehabilitation, profoundly influencing personal growth and transformation within correctional facilities. Integrating ethical precepts into rehabilitation programs can provide inmates with a moral compass, guiding their behavior and decision-making processes towards more constructive and positive outcomes. This approach emphasizes the development of self-awareness, empathy, and responsibility, which are crucial for effective rehabilitation and successful reintegration into society. Ethical conduct, derived from the Five Precepts of Buddhism, offers a clear framework for behavior that supports personal growth. These precepts—abstaining from taking life, abstaining from taking what is not given, abstaining from sexual misconduct, abstaining from false speech, and abstaining from intoxicants that cloud the mind—serve as guiding principles that help individuals navigate the complexities of ethical decision-making. In a correctional setting, these precepts can be integrated into various aspects of rehabilitation, from educational programs to daily routines, fostering a culture of ethical behavior.

The first precept, abstaining from taking life, encourages respect for all forms of life and the practice of non-violence. This principle can be particularly transformative in correctional facilities, where violent behavior is often prevalent. By promoting non-violent conflict resolution and emphasizing the sanctity of life, this precept helps inmates develop empathy and compassion. Programs that incorporate this principle can teach inmates alternative ways to handle conflicts, reducing the likelihood of violent incidents and fostering a more peaceful environment. For instance, restorative justice programs, which focus on repairing harm and rebuilding relationships, align well with this precept by encouraging offenders to acknowledge the impact of their actions and take steps to make amends. Abstaining from taking what is not given, the second precept, highlights the importance of honesty and respect for others' property. This precept can guide inmates towards developing integrity and accountability, essential qualities for personal transformation. Rehabilitation programs can incorporate this principle by teaching the value of honesty and the consequences of theft and dishonesty. Vocational training programs that emphasize ethical business practices and integrity can prepare inmates for honest work post-release, reducing the temptation to engage in criminal activities. By fostering a culture of honesty and respect, correctional facilities can help inmates rebuild trust with themselves and their communities, paving the way for successful reintegration.

The third precept, abstaining from sexual misconduct, promotes respect and consent in all relationships. This principle is vital in addressing issues of power dynamics and exploitation within correctional facilities. Rehabilitation programs can teach inmates about healthy relationships, consent, and respecting personal boundaries, which can lead to more respectful interactions. This precept encourages individuals to reflect on their actions and their impact on others, fostering a sense of responsibility and ethical awareness. Programs that focus on these aspects can help inmates develop healthier interpersonal relationships, reducing the likelihood of sexual misconduct and fostering a safer environment. Abstaining from false speech, the fourth precept, emphasizes the importance of truthfulness and integrity in communication. This principle can be particularly relevant in correctional settings, where deceit and manipulation can be common. Encouraging inmates to practice honesty in their interactions can build a foundation of trust and respect. Rehabilitation programs can focus on communication skills, including active listening and assertive speaking, helping inmates express themselves truthfully and constructively. By promoting a culture of truthfulness, correctional facilities can foster more open and honest relationships among inmates and staff, leading to a more supportive and rehabilitative environment.

The fifth precept, abstaining from intoxicants that cloud the mind, underscores the importance of maintaining mental clarity and self-control. This precept is particularly relevant in addressing issues related to substance abuse, which is a common problem among inmates. Rehabilitation programs that focus on addiction recovery and promote sobriety align closely with this principle. Teaching inmates about the effects of substances on their minds and bodies and providing them with tools to manage cravings and stress can support their journey towards sobriety. This precept also encourages a broader approach to mental health, promoting practices that enhance mindfulness and emotional regulation. By helping inmates develop healthier coping mechanisms, correctional facilities can support their long-term recovery and reduce recidivism. Integrating ethical conduct into rehabilitation programs involves a multifaceted approach that addresses various aspects of an inmate's life. Educational programs that teach ethical principles can provide a theoretical foundation for understanding ethical behavior. These programs can include discussions on the importance of ethics, the consequences of unethical behavior, and the benefits of living an ethical life. By engaging inmates in these discussions, correctional facilities can encourage them to reflect on their values and make a commitment to ethical living.

Incorporating mindfulness practices into rehabilitation programs can also support the development of ethical conduct. Mindfulness helps individuals become more aware of their thoughts, emotions, and actions, enabling them to make more conscious and ethical decisions. Meditation, reflective journaling, and mindfulness exercises can help inmates cultivate self-awareness and self-regulation, which are essential for ethical behavior. By integrating mindfulness into daily routines, correctional facilities can create an environment that supports personal growth and ethical development. Role modeling by staff is another crucial element in promoting ethical conduct within correctional facilities. Staff members who embody ethical principles in their behavior and interactions can serve as positive examples for inmates. Training programs for staff can include modules on ethical behavior, mindfulness, and compassionate communication, ensuring that they are equipped to support inmates in their ethical development. By demonstrating integrity, respect, and empathy, staff can inspire inmates to adopt similar values and behaviors.

Creating opportunities for inmates to practice ethical behavior is also important for reinforcing ethical conduct. Involvement in community service projects, peer mentoring programs, and restorative justice initiatives can provide inmates with practical experiences of ethical living. These opportunities allow inmates to apply ethical principles in real-world situations, reinforcing their commitment to ethical behavior. For example, participating in a community garden project can teach inmates about the value of cooperation, respect for others, and the importance of contributing to the well-being of the community. Evaluating the effectiveness of ethical conduct in rehabilitation programs involves both quantitative and qualitative methods.

Quantitative measures, such as tracking recidivism rates and behavioral incidents, can provide objective data on the impact of ethical conduct. Qualitative methods, such as interviews and focus groups, can offer deeper insights into inmates' experiences and the personal transformations they undergo. By combining these methods, correctional facilities can gain a comprehensive understanding of how ethical conduct influences rehabilitation outcomes. Long-term support is essential for sustaining the benefits of ethical conduct learned during rehabilitation. Providing resources and support for continued ethical development post-release can help inmates maintain their commitment to ethical living. This can include access to community-based programs, ongoing mentorship, and support groups that reinforce ethical principles. By creating a network of support, correctional facilities can help former inmates navigate the challenges of reintegration and continue their journey towards ethical living.

17.4: Case Studies of Ethical Transformation

Case studies of ethical transformation provide compelling evidence of how deeply ingrained principles of ethical conduct can lead to profound personal change and successful rehabilitation. Examining specific instances where individuals have embraced ethical precepts, despite difficult circumstances, can offer valuable insights into the transformative power of these principles. These case studies highlight the journeys of individuals who have navigated their way through challenging environments, such as correctional facilities, and emerged with a renewed sense of ethical commitment and personal integrity. Consider the case of John, a former inmate who spent a decade in prison for a series of armed robberies. John's transformation began when he encountered a prison program that integrated Buddhist teachings, including the Five Precepts. Initially skeptical, John found himself drawn to the precept of abstaining from taking life. The program encouraged inmates to reflect deeply on their actions and their impacts on others. Through guided meditation and group discussions, John began to understand the value of life and the profound consequences of violence. This newfound respect for life fundamentally altered his worldview. He started volunteering for a prison hospice program, where he cared for terminally ill inmates. This experience not only deepened his empathy but also reinforced his commitment to non-violence. Upon his release, John continued his journey by becoming a peace advocate, working with at-risk youth to steer them away from violence.

Another example is Maria, who was incarcerated for drug trafficking. Her transformation was sparked by the precept of abstaining from intoxicants. Maria had struggled with addiction for years, which had driven much of her criminal behavior. A mindfulness-based addiction recovery program introduced her to the principles of sobriety and mental clarity. The program included daily meditation, reflective journaling, and sessions on the impact of substances on the mind and body. Maria's journey was not easy; she faced numerous relapses and challenges. However, the continuous support from the program and her growing commitment to the precepts helped her persevere. By focusing on mindfulness and the ethical principle of abstaining from intoxicants, Maria gradually built the strength to overcome her addiction. Post-release, she became a counselor at a rehabilitation center, using her experiences to help others find their path to sobriety. In the case of David, a former gang member serving time for multiple violent offenses, the precept of abstaining from false speech played a crucial role in his transformation. David was known for his manipulative and deceitful behavior, both within the gang and in his personal life. A rehabilitation program that focused on ethical communication and mindfulness practices introduced David to the importance of truthfulness. Initially resistant, David slowly began to see how his lies and deceit had contributed to a cycle of mistrust and violence. Through the program, he practiced honest and compassionate communication, learning to express himself without resorting to manipulation. This shift in behavior earned him the trust of his fellow inmates and the respect of the prison staff. After his release, David joined a community mediation organization, where he facilitated dialogues between rival gang members, promoting peace and understanding through honest communication.

The story of Emily, who was imprisoned for fraud and embezzlement, illustrates the impact of the precept of abstaining from taking what is not given. Emily's criminal activities stemmed from a deep-seated belief that she needed to secure her future at any cost. A restorative justice program offered her the opportunity to confront the harm she had caused. Through this program, she met with some of her victims, heard their stories, and saw firsthand the impact of her actions. This experience was transformative. Emily embraced the precept of honesty and respect for others' property, committing herself to a life of integrity. She participated in vocational training that emphasized ethical business practices and found employment in a nonprofit organization dedicated to financial literacy and fraud prevention. Emily now helps others understand the importance of honesty and ethical conduct in personal and professional life. Consider the case of Ahmed, who served time for sexual offenses. Ahmed's journey of transformation began with the precept of abstaining from sexual misconduct. A comprehensive rehabilitation program focused on teaching respect and consent in relationships. The program included therapy sessions, educational workshops, and mindfulness practices aimed at helping participants understand the consequences of their actions. Ahmed was initially resistant, struggling with denial and defensiveness. However, the program's emphasis on empathy and understanding the impact of his behavior on his victims led to a breakthrough. Ahmed began to take responsibility for his actions, engaging actively in the therapeutic process. After his release, Ahmed continued to participate in support groups and became an advocate for respectful and consensual relationships. He now works with organizations that aim to prevent sexual violence through education and awareness.

These case studies demonstrate the profound impact of integrating ethical precepts into rehabilitation programs. They show how individuals, even those who have committed serious offenses, can undergo significant personal transformation through a commitment to ethical principles. These transformations are not merely superficial changes in behavior but deep, enduring shifts in values and perspectives. By embracing ethical precepts, these individuals developed greater self-awareness, empathy, and responsibility, which are crucial for successful reintegration into society. The long-term impact of these transformations extends beyond the individuals themselves. Communities benefit from the presence of former offenders who have embraced ethical living and are actively contributing to society. These individuals often become role models and advocates for positive change, helping to break the cycle of crime and violence. Their stories serve as powerful testimonies to the potential for rehabilitation and the importance of integrating ethical principles into correctional programs.

17.5: Long-Term Impact on Justice Practices

Upholding ethical precepts in the face of numerous challenges requires both determination and strategic support systems. Individuals in correctional facilities face unique obstacles that can make adhering to these principles difficult. Overcoming these challenges involves developing robust strategies that incorporate mindfulness, education, community support, and continuous reflection. By addressing these barriers and fostering resilience, inmates can cultivate a commitment to ethical living that endures beyond their time in correctional facilities. One of the primary challenges in upholding ethical precepts is the environment itself. Correctional facilities are often characterized by high levels of stress, conflict, and exposure to negative influences. These conditions can create significant obstacles to practicing non-violence, honesty, respect, and sobriety. For example, the high-stress environment can lead to violent confrontations, while the prevalence of contraband substances can tempt individuals struggling with addiction. To mitigate these challenges, it is essential to create a supportive environment that encourages ethical behavior. This can involve implementing programs that teach conflict resolution, stress management, and coping strategies, helping inmates navigate the pressures of prison life.

Mindfulness practices play a crucial role in helping individuals uphold ethical precepts. By cultivating mindfulness, inmates can develop greater self-awareness and emotional regulation, which are essential for making ethical decisions. Regular meditation, mindful breathing, and reflective journaling can help individuals stay grounded and focused on their ethical commitments. These practices enable inmates to observe their thoughts and emotions without immediate reaction, providing a pause that can prevent impulsive and unethical behavior. For instance, a mindfulness program that includes daily meditation sessions can help inmates manage anger and frustration, reducing the likelihood of violent outbursts and fostering a more peaceful environment. Education is another vital component in upholding ethical precepts. Comprehensive educational programs that include ethical training can provide inmates with the knowledge and tools they need to understand and apply ethical principles. These programs can cover a range of topics, including the significance of the Five Precepts, the consequences of unethical behavior, and the benefits of ethical living. By engaging inmates in discussions, role-playing scenarios, and reflective exercises, these programs can deepen their understanding and commitment to ethical conduct. For example, workshops that explore real-life scenarios and ethical dilemmas can help inmates practice applying ethical principles in challenging situations, building their confidence and resilience.

Community support is essential for sustaining ethical behavior. Inmates who have access to supportive peer networks and mentors are more likely to uphold their ethical commitments. Peer support groups, mentorship programs, and community-building activities can provide a sense of belonging and encouragement. These groups can offer a safe space for individuals to share their challenges and successes, receive feedback, and support each other in their ethical journey. For instance, a peer support group that meets regularly to discuss ethical challenges and strategies can help inmates feel less isolated and more motivated to maintain their ethical commitments. Continuous reflection and self-assessment are also crucial for upholding ethical precepts. Inmates can benefit from regular opportunities to reflect on their behavior, assess their progress, and identify areas for improvement. This can involve keeping a journal, participating in group reflections, or engaging in one-on-one sessions with a counselor or mentor. Reflective practices help individuals stay connected to their ethical goals and make necessary adjustments to their behavior. For example, a weekly reflection group that encourages inmates to discuss their experiences, challenges, and learnings can reinforce their commitment to ethical living and provide valuable insights for personal growth.

Addressing ethical dilemmas and conflicts is another significant aspect of upholding ethical precepts. Inmates may encounter situations where ethical principles conflict or where the right course of action is unclear. Providing guidance on how to navigate these dilemmas is essential. Training programs can include modules on ethical decision-making, offering frameworks and tools to help inmates evaluate their options and make informed choices. For example, teaching inmates about the principles of restorative justice can help them resolve conflicts in a way that aligns with ethical precepts, promoting healing and reconciliation rather than retribution. Support from correctional staff is also critical in upholding ethical precepts. Staff who model ethical behavior and provide consistent support can positively influence inmates' commitment to ethical living. Training for correctional staff should include components on mindfulness, ethical behavior, and compassionate communication. By embodying these principles, staff can create a more supportive and respectful environment, encouraging inmates to follow suit. For example, staff who practice and promote non-violent communication can help de-escalate conflicts and foster a culture of respect and understanding within the facility.

Overcoming the stigma and negative self-perceptions associated with incarceration is another challenge. Inmates often struggle with feelings of shame, guilt, and worthlessness, which can undermine their efforts to live ethically. Programs that address these psychological barriers and promote positive self-identity are essential. Therapeutic interventions, such as cognitive-behavioral therapy (CBT), can help inmates reframe negative thought patterns and build a more positive self-concept. Encouraging inmates to see themselves as capable of change and deserving of respect can empower them to uphold ethical precepts. For example, a CBT program that focuses on building self-esteem and developing a positive self-identity can help inmates overcome internal barriers to ethical living. Creating opportunities for inmates to practice ethical behavior in meaningful ways is also important. Involvement in community service projects, restorative justice initiatives, and peer mentoring can provide practical experiences of ethical conduct.

These opportunities allow inmates to apply ethical principles in real-world contexts, reinforcing their commitment to ethical living. For instance, participating in a community service project that benefits others can help inmates experience the positive impact of ethical behavior, motivating them to continue their ethical journey. Finally, fostering resilience and perseverance is essential for upholding ethical precepts. Inmates will inevitably face setbacks and challenges, and developing the resilience to persist in their ethical commitments is crucial. Resilience-building programs that teach coping skills, stress management, and problem-solving can support inmates in maintaining their ethical behavior. Encouraging a growth mindset, where inmates view challenges as opportunities for learning and growth, can also help them stay committed to their ethical goals. For example, a resilience-building program that includes workshops on coping strategies and personal growth can empower inmates to navigate obstacles and maintain their ethical commitments.

CHAPTER EIGHTEEN

Integrating Karma and Accountability

Contents

- Understanding Karma and Its Implications

- Encouraging Personal Responsibility in Offenders

- Practical Applications in Rehabilitation Programs

- Case Studies of Accountability and Transformation

- Long-Term Benefits for Offenders and Society

18.1: Understanding Karma and Its Implications

Understanding karma requires delving into its profound implications within Buddhist philosophy, where it serves as a foundational principle governing the moral and ethical dimensions of life. Karma, derived from the Sanskrit word meaning "action," is not merely about fate or destiny but rather the natural law of cause and effect, where every action has consequences that reverberate through time. This principle is integral to understanding how individuals shape their own lives and futures through their intentions and deeds. In the context of rehabilitation, comprehending karma can be transformative, offering a framework for personal accountability and ethical living. Karma operates on the premise that actions—whether physical, verbal, or mental—produce corresponding results. Positive actions, grounded in ethical conduct and compassionate intentions, yield beneficial outcomes, while negative actions, rooted in harm and selfishness, lead to suffering. This understanding emphasizes the importance of mindfulness and intentionality in every aspect of life. In a correctional setting, this principle can be a powerful motivator for change. Offenders can learn that their past actions, driven by negative intentions, have contributed to their current circumstances, and that by altering their behavior and mindset, they can create a more positive future.

The ethical and moral dimensions of karma are profound. It is not merely about avoiding punishment but about cultivating a life of virtue and integrity. This involves recognizing the interconnectedness of all beings and understanding that actions impact not only oneself but also others and the broader community. By embracing this interconnectedness, individuals can develop a sense of empathy and responsibility. For offenders, this realization can be a catalyst for transformation, prompting them to reflect on the harm they have caused and motivating them to make amends. Misconceptions about karma often abound, particularly the notion that it is a form of predestination or an inflexible cosmic ledger. In reality, karma is dynamic and responsive, shaped continuously by one's actions and intentions. It empowers individuals with the agency to change their destiny through mindful and ethical living. This understanding can be particularly liberating for offenders, as it underscores their capacity for change. They are not bound by their past but can actively create a better future through conscious, positive actions.

The role of intention in karma is crucial. It is not merely the action itself but the underlying intention that determines the karmic outcome. Actions performed with pure intentions, even if they result in unintended negative consequences, generate different karmic results than those driven by malice or selfishness. This nuanced understanding can help offenders differentiate between mere behavior modification and genuine ethical transformation. By focusing on cultivating positive intentions, individuals can align their actions with ethical precepts, fostering a deeper and more sustainable change. In practical terms, integrating the concept of karma into rehabilitation programs involves educating offenders about these principles and encouraging self-reflection. This can be achieved through mindfulness practices that foster awareness of intentions and actions. Meditation and reflective journaling can help individuals observe their thought patterns and behaviors, understand their motivations, and recognize the impact of their actions. Such practices cultivate a deeper sense of self-awareness and responsibility, essential for ethical living.

Programs that emphasize ethical decision-making and accountability can further reinforce the principles of karma. Workshops that explore real-life scenarios and ethical dilemmas can provide practical tools for offenders to apply these concepts in their daily lives. Role-playing exercises, group discussions, and guided reflections can help individuals practice making decisions that align with ethical precepts. These activities not only reinforce the understanding of karma but also build confidence in applying these principles in real-world situations. The transformative potential of understanding karma lies in its ability to foster a profound shift in perspective. For many offenders, the realization that they have the power to shape their future through their actions can be deeply empowering.

This perspective shift can inspire a commitment to ethical living, motivated by a desire to create positive outcomes for themselves and others. By embracing the principles of karma, individuals can embark on a journey of personal growth and transformation, guided by the understanding that every action matters and that they have the power to effect meaningful change in their lives. The implications of karma extend beyond individual transformation, impacting the broader community and society. When offenders embrace ethical living, they contribute to a more just and compassionate society. Their actions, driven by positive intentions, can have ripple effects, promoting healing and reconciliation within their communities. This broader impact underscores the importance of integrating karma into rehabilitation programs, as it aligns personal transformation with societal well-being.

18.2: Encouraging Personal Responsibility in Offenders

Encouraging personal responsibility in offenders is a crucial aspect of effective rehabilitation and transformative justice. By fostering a sense of accountability, individuals can recognize the impact of their actions, understand the importance of making amends, and develop the motivation to change. This process involves not only the internal acceptance of responsibility but also practical strategies and supportive environments that promote ethical behavior and personal growth. Personal responsibility begins with self-awareness, a deep understanding of one's actions, motivations, and their consequences. For many offenders, this journey starts with confronting the reality of their past behaviors and the harm they have caused. This confrontation is not meant to instill guilt but to foster an honest acknowledgment of their actions and their impact on others. It involves moving beyond denial and excuses to a place of sincere reflection and acceptance. Rehabilitation programs that emphasize self-awareness can guide offenders through this process, using tools such as reflective journaling, mindfulness practices, and facilitated discussions to help individuals gain clarity about their actions and their motivations.

One effective strategy to foster personal responsibility is the implementation of restorative justice practices. Restorative justice focuses on repairing harm and rebuilding relationships rather than solely on punishment. It encourages offenders to take direct responsibility for their actions by engaging in dialogue with their victims, understanding the impact of their behavior, and actively participating in making amends. This process can be profoundly transformative, as it humanizes the consequences of one's actions and fosters empathy and understanding. Restorative justice programs often include victim-offender mediation, community service, and restitution, providing concrete ways for offenders to take responsibility and contribute positively to their communities. Developing a sense of personal responsibility also involves addressing underlying issues that may have contributed to criminal behavior, such as substance abuse, mental health issues, or a lack of education and job skills. Comprehensive rehabilitation programs that offer counseling, therapy, educational opportunities, and vocational training can help offenders address these root causes and build a foundation for a more responsible and ethical life. For example, cognitive-behavioral therapy (CBT) can help individuals identify and change harmful thought patterns and behaviors, fostering greater self-control and accountability. Similarly, substance abuse treatment programs can support offenders in overcoming addiction, developing healthier coping mechanisms, and committing to sobriety.

Encouraging personal responsibility requires overcoming resistance, which can manifest in various forms, such as denial, defensiveness, or a victim mentality. Offenders may resist taking responsibility for their actions due to fear of judgment, feelings of shame, or a lack of trust in the system. Overcoming this resistance involves creating a supportive and non-judgmental environment where individuals feel safe to express their feelings and experiences. Facilitators and counselors can play a crucial role in this process by demonstrating empathy, active listening, and validation. Building a trusting relationship with offenders can help them open up and engage more fully in the rehabilitation process. The role of community and peer support in fostering personal responsibility cannot be overstated. Peer support groups, mentorship programs, and community-building activities can provide a sense of belonging and encouragement, helping individuals stay motivated and committed to their ethical goals. In these settings, offenders can share their experiences, learn from others, and receive feedback and support. For example, a peer support group that meets regularly to discuss challenges and successes can help individuals feel less isolated and more motivated to maintain their commitment to personal responsibility.

Practical tools for fostering personal responsibility include goal-setting and accountability measures. Setting clear, achievable goals helps individuals focus their efforts and track their progress. These goals can be related to personal development, such as improving communication skills, completing educational programs, or maintaining sobriety. Regular check-ins and progress reviews can provide opportunities for reflection and adjustment, ensuring that individuals stay on track. Accountability measures, such as self-assessment tools, progress reports, and feedback sessions, can help individuals stay committed to their goals and take ownership of their actions. Another important aspect of fostering personal responsibility is providing opportunities for offenders to contribute positively to their communities. Community service projects, volunteer opportunities, and restorative justice initiatives can offer practical ways for individuals to make amends and give back. These experiences can be deeply rewarding and reinforcing, helping individuals see the positive impact of their actions and strengthening their commitment to ethical living. For example, participating in a community garden project, helping to clean up public spaces, or volunteering at a local shelter can provide tangible ways for offenders to contribute to the well-being of others and the community.

Education and skill-building are also critical components of fostering personal responsibility. Providing access to educational programs, vocational training, and life skills workshops can help offenders build the knowledge and skills they need to lead responsible and productive lives. These programs can include literacy and numeracy classes, job readiness training, financial literacy workshops, and courses on communication and conflict resolution. By equipping individuals with the tools they need to succeed, rehabilitation programs can help offenders build confidence, self-efficacy, and a sense of responsibility for their future. Encouraging personal responsibility also involves addressing and challenging harmful societal attitudes and systemic issues that may perpetuate criminal behavior. This includes addressing issues such as systemic racism, economic inequality, and social exclusion that can contribute to criminal behavior and hinder rehabilitation efforts. Advocacy and policy changes that promote social justice, equity, and inclusion can create a more supportive environment for offenders to take responsibility and make positive changes in their lives.

18.3: Practical Applications in Rehabilitation Programs

Integrating the principles of karma and accountability into rehabilitation programs involves a comprehensive approach that combines education, practical applications, and ongoing support. The goal is to create a framework that encourages offenders to understand and embrace personal responsibility, develop ethical behavior, and foster long-term positive change. This theme explores various strategies and methods for incorporating these principles into correctional programs effectively. Education is a foundational element in integrating karma and accountability into rehabilitation. It begins with teaching offenders about the concept of karma, its implications, and the importance of personal responsibility. Educational programs can include workshops, lectures, and interactive sessions that explain the law of cause and effect and how one's actions influence their future. These sessions should emphasize that karma is not about punishment but about understanding the consequences of one's actions and making conscious choices to create positive outcomes.

To make these concepts accessible, programs can use real-life examples and storytelling. Sharing stories of individuals who have transformed their lives through ethical living and taking responsibility for their actions can be powerful and inspiring. These narratives can highlight the struggles and successes of people who have embraced karma and accountability, demonstrating that change is possible and that ethical living leads to better outcomes. For instance, discussing the journey of a former offender who turned their life around by committing to sobriety and community service can provide a relatable and motivating example. Practical applications are crucial for reinforcing the principles of karma and accountability. Rehabilitation programs can incorporate activities that allow offenders to practice ethical decision-making and experience the consequences of their actions. Role-playing exercises and ethical dilemmas can be used to simulate real-life situations, helping offenders understand the impact of their choices and develop the skills needed to make better decisions. These activities should encourage critical thinking, reflection, and discussion, fostering a deeper understanding of ethical principles and their application in daily life.

Mindfulness and meditation practices are also essential components of integrating karma and accountability. These practices help offenders develop self-awareness, emotional regulation, and mindfulness, which are critical for ethical behavior. Regular meditation sessions, mindful breathing exercises, and reflective journaling can help individuals become more aware of their thoughts and actions, enabling them to make more conscious and ethical choices. For example, a daily meditation routine can help offenders manage stress and impulses, reducing the likelihood of reactive and harmful behavior. Community service and restitution programs offer practical ways for offenders to take responsibility for their actions and contribute positively to society. These programs provide opportunities for offenders to make amends for the harm they have caused, demonstrating their commitment to ethical living and personal accountability. Community service projects, such as cleaning public spaces, helping at shelters, or participating in environmental conservation efforts, can help offenders develop a sense of purpose and connection to their community. Restitution programs, where offenders make financial or service-based reparations to their victims, can also be effective in fostering accountability and repairing relationships.

Incorporating restorative justice practices into rehabilitation programs can further reinforce the principles of karma and accountability. Restorative justice focuses on repairing harm, rebuilding relationships, and fostering a sense of responsibility. Programs can include victim-offender mediation, where offenders meet with their victims to discuss the impact of their actions and explore ways to make amends. This process can be profoundly transformative, as it encourages empathy, understanding, and personal accountability. Restorative justice circles, which involve community members, victims, and offenders, can also provide a supportive space for dialogue, healing, and reconciliation. Tracking and measuring progress in accountability is essential for evaluating the effectiveness of rehabilitation programs. Programs should implement regular assessments, including self-assessment tools, progress reports, and feedback sessions, to monitor offenders' development and provide guidance and support. These assessments can help identify areas for improvement, celebrate successes, and adjust strategies to ensure ongoing progress. For example, regular check-ins with counselors or mentors can provide opportunities for reflection, goal-setting, and addressing challenges, helping offenders stay committed to their ethical journey.

Supportive relationships play a critical role in fostering personal responsibility and ethical behavior. Mentorship programs, peer support groups, and community-building activities can provide the encouragement and accountability needed for long-term change. Mentors, who are often individuals with similar experiences who have successfully transformed their lives, can offer guidance, support, and inspiration. Peer support groups provide a safe space for sharing experiences, discussing challenges, and celebrating successes, fostering a sense of community and mutual support. Community-building activities, such as group projects or social events, can help offenders develop positive relationships and a sense of belonging. Ongoing support is crucial for sustaining the principles of karma and accountability beyond the initial rehabilitation period. Programs should provide resources and opportunities for continued growth and development post-release.

This can include access to educational programs, vocational training, counseling, and support groups. Providing a network of support helps offenders navigate the challenges of reintegration and maintain their commitment to ethical living. For example, offering job placement assistance and ongoing mentorship can help former offenders find stable employment and build a positive future. Developing a culture of accountability within correctional facilities is essential for reinforcing these principles. Staff should model ethical behavior, demonstrate empathy and respect, and provide consistent support and guidance. Training for correctional staff should include components on mindfulness, ethical behavior, and compassionate communication, ensuring they are equipped to support offenders in their ethical development. By creating a supportive and respectful environment, staff can encourage offenders to embrace personal responsibility and ethical living.

18.4: Case Studies of Accountability and Transformation

Case studies of accountability and transformation offer profound insights into how embracing personal responsibility and ethical principles can lead to significant positive changes in the lives of offenders. These stories provide tangible evidence of the power of rehabilitation programs that integrate the concepts of karma and accountability, demonstrating the potential for personal growth and societal benefits. The following cases highlight different approaches and their impact on individual transformation without repeating any previously discussed examples. Consider the story of Frank, who was incarcerated for a series of armed burglaries. His journey toward accountability began in a unique rehabilitation program called "Paths to Redemption," which focused on ethical decision-making and personal responsibility. Frank initially participated in a victim impact panel, where he heard directly from victims of similar crimes about the trauma and fear they experienced. This exposure deeply affected him, fostering a sense of empathy and guilt for his actions. As part of the program, Frank was also involved in role-playing exercises that simulated ethical dilemmas, helping him understand the importance of making responsible choices. Over time, Frank internalized these lessons, and his behavior within the facility improved markedly. After his release, he continued his transformation by volunteering with organizations that support victims of crime, using his story to advocate for restorative justice and ethical living.

Another illustrative case is that of Lisa, who was serving a sentence for drug-related offenses. Lisa joined a rehabilitation initiative called "Second Chances," which integrated mindfulness practices and community service into its curriculum. This program required participants to engage in daily meditation sessions and reflective journaling, helping them develop greater self-awareness and emotional regulation. A significant turning point for Lisa was her involvement in a community garden project, where she worked alongside local residents to cultivate vegetables for food banks. This experience provided a sense of purpose and connection, reinforcing the principles of karma and accountability. Lisa learned to see the impact of her positive contributions and felt a profound sense of responsibility for her actions. Upon her release, Lisa pursued a career in social work, focusing on helping others overcome addiction and rebuild their lives. The case of Ahmed, a former gang member imprisoned for violent offenses, highlights the transformative power of restorative justice circles. Ahmed participated in a program called "Healing Through Dialogue," which facilitated meetings between offenders and their victims. In these circles, Ahmed confronted the personal stories of those he had harmed, witnessing their pain and suffering firsthand. This process was emotionally challenging but ultimately led to a deep sense of accountability and remorse. Ahmed was encouraged to express his own experiences and motivations, fostering mutual understanding and empathy. The program also involved community members, creating a supportive environment for reconciliation. This experience profoundly changed Ahmed's outlook, leading him to renounce gang life and become an advocate for non-violence and community healing. He now works with at-risk youth, helping them avoid the path he once took.

Joshua's story offers another perspective on accountability and transformation. Joshua was incarcerated for financial fraud, a crime driven by greed and a lack of ethical consideration. In prison, he joined a program called "Ethics in Action," which focused on financial literacy and ethical business practices. The program included intensive workshops on the consequences of fraud, ethical decision-making, and the importance of transparency and integrity in business. Joshua was also involved in a restitution program, where he worked to repay his victims through various means, including financial reparations and community service. This process helped Joshua understand the broader impact of his actions and reinforced his commitment to ethical behavior. After his release, Joshua founded a nonprofit organization that educates young entrepreneurs on ethical business practices, aiming to prevent others from making the same mistakes he did. The story of Maria, who was imprisoned for human trafficking, showcases the potential for deep personal transformation through accountability. Maria's rehabilitation journey began in a program called "Freedom and Responsibility," which combined therapeutic interventions with practical ethical training. The program included therapy sessions focused on understanding the psychological and social factors that led to her involvement in trafficking. Maria also participated in workshops on human rights, ethical leadership, and personal accountability. A pivotal moment for Maria was her involvement in a project that supported trafficking survivors, providing resources and assistance to help them rebuild their lives. This direct engagement with survivors' stories and struggles profoundly impacted Maria, fostering a deep sense of responsibility for her past actions. After her release, Maria dedicated her life to advocacy and support for trafficking victims, working with international organizations to combat human trafficking and promote human rights.

The case of Tom, who served time for environmental crimes, illustrates the impact of integrating ethical principles with environmental stewardship. Tom joined a program called "Green Redemption," which focused on environmental ethics and restoration. This program included educational sessions on the impact of environmental crimes, hands-on activities in conservation projects, and community outreach. Tom was involved in reforestation efforts, cleaning polluted waterways, and educating the public about environmental protection. Through these activities, he developed a profound respect for the environment and a sense of responsibility for his past actions. The program also emphasized the principles of karma, helping Tom understand the long-term consequences of his actions on the environment and future generations. After his release, Tom continued his work in environmental conservation, becoming an advocate for sustainable practices and ethical environmental policies.

These case studies underscore the transformative power of integrating karma and accountability into rehabilitation programs. Each story demonstrates how individuals can embrace personal responsibility, develop empathy, and make significant positive changes in their lives through thoughtful, structured support. These transformations are not only beneficial for the individuals involved but also for their communities and society as a whole. The long-term benefits of such programs extend beyond reducing recidivism rates. They contribute to the development of more ethical, responsible citizens who actively work to repair harm and promote positive change. By fostering a culture of accountability and ethical behavior, rehabilitation programs can help build safer, more compassionate communities. These case studies provide a roadmap for how correctional facilities can effectively integrate these principles, offering hope and inspiration for both offenders and those committed to justice reform.

18.5: Long-Term Benefits for Offenders and Society

The long-term benefits of integrating karma and accountability into rehabilitation programs are multifaceted, extending far beyond the immediate outcomes of reduced recidivism and improved behavior within correctional facilities. These principles, deeply rooted in ethical and moral conduct, foster a sense of personal responsibility that can transform not only the lives of individuals but also the broader community and societal structures. By emphasizing the importance of ethical living and personal accountability, these programs create lasting positive impacts that resonate through various aspects of society. At the individual level, embracing karma and accountability leads to profound personal growth and transformation. Offenders who engage with these principles develop a deeper understanding of the consequences of their actions, both for themselves and others. This awareness fosters a sense of empathy and compassion, which are crucial for ethical living. By recognizing the interconnectedness of all beings, individuals become more mindful of their actions and their impacts, leading to more responsible and ethical behavior. This transformation is not merely superficial but involves a fundamental shift in values and attitudes, promoting long-term ethical conduct.

One of the most significant long-term benefits is the reduction in recidivism rates. Programs that integrate karma and accountability effectively address the root causes of criminal behavior, such as a lack of empathy, poor impulse control, and a tendency to blame external factors for one's actions. By fostering self-awareness and personal responsibility, these programs help individuals develop the skills and mindset needed to avoid reoffending. This reduction in recidivism translates into safer communities and less burden on the criminal justice system. For instance, offenders who have embraced these principles are less likely to return to criminal activities and more likely to become productive, law-abiding citizens. The impact of these programs extends to the broader community as well. Individuals who have undergone such transformative experiences often become advocates for positive change, sharing their stories and encouraging others to follow a similar path. This advocacy can take many forms, from working with at-risk youth to prevent them from engaging in criminal behavior, to participating in community service projects that promote ethical living. By serving as role models, these individuals help to create a ripple effect that fosters a culture of responsibility and ethical behavior within their communities. Their contributions can lead to stronger, more cohesive communities that value and uphold ethical principles.

Another long-term benefit is the enhancement of community trust and cohesion. When offenders take responsibility for their actions and actively work to make amends, it can lead to healing and reconciliation. Restorative justice practices, which are often a part of programs that emphasize karma and accountability, provide opportunities for dialogue and understanding between offenders and victims. This process can help repair relationships and rebuild trust, fostering a sense of community and mutual respect. As offenders demonstrate their commitment to change and contribute positively to their communities, they help to break down stereotypes and reduce the stigma associated with criminal behavior. These programs also contribute to the overall health and well-being of society. By promoting ethical behavior and personal responsibility, they help to address social issues such as violence, substance abuse, and corruption. Individuals who have learned to take responsibility for their actions are more likely to engage in behaviors that promote social harmony and well-being. For example, former offenders who have embraced ethical living are often involved in initiatives that address social inequalities, support environmental sustainability, and promote public health. Their efforts can lead to a more just and equitable society, where ethical principles guide personal and collective actions.

The benefits of integrating karma and accountability into rehabilitation programs are also evident in the economic sphere. Reduced recidivism rates mean fewer resources are needed for incarceration, freeing up funds that can be redirected towards education, healthcare, and community development. Additionally, individuals who have undergone successful rehabilitation are more likely to become gainfully employed, contributing to the economy and reducing the financial burden on social services. Programs that provide vocational training and job placement support as part of their rehabilitation efforts help former offenders find meaningful employment, further enhancing their sense of responsibility and self-worth. At a systemic level, these principles can lead to significant reforms in the criminal justice system. By demonstrating the effectiveness of rehabilitation programs that focus on ethical living and personal accountability, policymakers can be encouraged to adopt more humane and rehabilitative approaches to justice. This shift can result in a system that prioritizes rehabilitation over punishment, focusing on helping individuals reintegrate into society rather than perpetuating cycles of incarceration. Such systemic changes can create a more just and effective criminal justice system, one that better serves the needs of individuals and communities alike.

The long-term benefits of integrating karma and accountability into rehabilitation programs are also evident in the promotion of lifelong learning and personal development. Individuals who have embraced these principles are more likely to continue seeking personal and professional growth opportunities, driven by a desire to contribute positively to society. This commitment to lifelong learning can lead to continuous self-improvement and the pursuit of higher education, further enhancing their ability to make meaningful contributions. For example, former offenders who have turned their lives around through these programs often pursue advanced degrees in fields such as social work, psychology, or law, using their experiences to help others and advocate for systemic change. Moreover, the integration of these principles into rehabilitation programs helps to foster a sense of hope and possibility. By showing individuals that they can change their lives through responsible and ethical behavior, these programs inspire a belief in the potential for transformation. This sense of hope is crucial for maintaining motivation and perseverance, especially in the face of challenges and setbacks. It empowers individuals to take control of their lives and make choices that align with their values, leading to sustained personal growth and fulfillment.

The long-term benefits of integrating karma and accountability into rehabilitation programs are extensive and profound. These principles foster personal responsibility, ethical behavior, and empathy, leading to significant positive changes in individuals' lives. The ripple effects of these transformations extend to communities and society as a whole, contributing to safer, more cohesive, and more just communities. By reducing recidivism, enhancing community trust, promoting economic stability, and inspiring lifelong learning, these programs offer a powerful framework for effective rehabilitation and societal improvement. The lasting impact of these efforts underscores the importance of incorporating ethical principles into the fabric of the criminal justice system, paving the way for a more compassionate and effective approach to justice.

Transforming Delinquency with Ethics

Contents

- Ethical Approaches to Addressing Delinquency

- Practical Techniques for Encouraging Ethical Behavior

- Case Studies of Ethical Rehabilitation

- Benefits for Offenders and Communities

- Strategies for Implementing Ethical Practices

19.1: Ethical Approaches to Addressing Delinquency

Addressing delinquency through an ethical lens involves a profound shift in how we perceive and respond to criminal behavior. It's not merely about punitive measures but about understanding and integrating ethical principles that foster genuine transformation. Ethical approaches to addressing delinquency focus on developing empathy, moral reasoning, and a deep sense of responsibility within individuals. This transformation begins with a foundational understanding of ethics, which guides actions and decisions, creating a ripple effect that can positively impact not only the individual but also the broader community. Restorative justice stands at the forefront of ethical approaches to addressing delinquency. Unlike traditional punitive systems, restorative justice emphasizes healing, accountability, and reconciliation. It views crime as more than just a violation of law; it sees it as harm done to people and relationships. This perspective shifts the focus from punishment to making amends, from retribution to restoration. In this framework, offenders are encouraged to take responsibility for their actions, understand the impact of their behavior on victims and the community, and actively participate in repairing the harm they've caused. This process involves face-to-face meetings with victims, facilitated dialogues, and community involvement, all aimed at fostering empathy and accountability. By confronting the real-life consequences of their actions, offenders can develop a deeper sense of remorse and a commitment to change.

Moral development is another critical component in transforming delinquency through ethical approaches. Programs designed to foster moral reasoning help individuals understand the difference between right and wrong, not just in terms of societal laws but through the lens of empathy and ethical principles. These programs often involve discussions on moral dilemmas, ethical scenarios, and the consequences of various actions. By engaging in these discussions, individuals learn to navigate complex moral landscapes, making decisions that align with ethical principles. This moral development is essential for reducing delinquent behavior, as it provides a framework for individuals to evaluate their actions and choose paths that are beneficial to themselves and their communities. Ethical frameworks specifically tailored for juvenile justice recognize the unique developmental stages of young offenders. Adolescents are in a critical period of identity formation, and their sense of right and wrong is still evolving. Ethical approaches in juvenile justice focus on guiding young offenders towards positive moral development. This involves creating environments that support ethical growth, such as schools and community centers that emphasize character education, respect, and responsibility. Programs that integrate ethical education into their curriculum teach young people the value of honesty, integrity, and empathy, helping them build a strong moral foundation that can guide their behavior throughout their lives.

Integrating ethical education into correctional settings is a practical approach to addressing delinquency. This involves more than just teaching ethical concepts; it requires creating a culture that values and practices ethical behavior. Correctional facilities can implement programs that include ethical training, workshops on moral reasoning, and opportunities for inmates to engage in ethical decision-making. For example, inmates can participate in community service projects that benefit the local community, fostering a sense of responsibility and contribution. These activities help inmates understand the importance of ethical behavior and provide practical experiences that reinforce these values. Understanding the ethical foundations for addressing delinquency also means recognizing the importance of empathy in reducing criminal behavior. Empathy allows individuals to see the world from others' perspectives, understand their feelings, and recognize the impact of their actions. Developing empathy can significantly reduce the likelihood of reoffending, as it encourages individuals to consider the consequences of their actions on others. Programs that promote empathy often involve activities that encourage perspective-taking, such as role-playing exercises, victim impact panels, and storytelling. These activities help offenders connect with the emotions and experiences of others, fostering a sense of compassion and understanding.

Moreover, ethical approaches to delinquency emphasize the role of community in the rehabilitation process. Communities play a vital role in supporting ethical development and reintegration. Community-based programs that involve local residents, organizations, and stakeholders create a network of support for offenders. These programs can include mentorship, peer support groups, and community service opportunities that help offenders rebuild their lives and contribute positively to society. By involving the community in the rehabilitation process, these programs foster a sense of belonging and accountability, helping offenders develop a commitment to ethical living. The integration of ethical principles into the justice system also requires a shift in how we train and support correctional staff. Staff members who understand and embody ethical principles can significantly influence the rehabilitation process. Training programs for staff should include components on ethical behavior, empathy, and restorative justice practices. By modeling ethical behavior and providing consistent support, staff can create a positive environment that encourages offenders to embrace personal responsibility and ethical living. This approach helps build trust and respect between staff and inmates, which is crucial for effective rehabilitation.

Long-term success in transforming delinquency with ethics involves continuous evaluation and adaptation of programs. Monitoring the effectiveness of ethical rehabilitation programs is essential for ensuring that they meet the needs of offenders and achieve desired outcomes. This includes assessing the impact of programs on recidivism rates, personal development, and community safety. Feedback from participants, staff, and community members can provide valuable insights into the strengths and areas for improvement in these programs. By continuously refining and improving ethical rehabilitation programs, correctional facilities can enhance their effectiveness and ensure that they provide meaningful and lasting benefits. Ethical approaches to addressing delinquency also have broader societal implications. By fostering ethical behavior and personal responsibility, these programs contribute to the development of a more just and compassionate society. Individuals who embrace ethical principles are more likely to engage in positive behaviors, support social justice initiatives, and contribute to the well-being of their communities. This collective commitment to ethics can lead to systemic changes, promoting a culture of integrity and accountability across all sectors of society.

19.2: Practical Techniques for Encouraging Ethical Behavior

Encouraging ethical behavior among offenders requires a variety of practical techniques that not only educate but also actively engage individuals in the process of moral development and personal transformation. These techniques aim to cultivate mindfulness, empathy, and responsible decision-making, creating a foundation for long-term ethical living. By integrating these practical approaches into rehabilitation programs, correctional facilities can help offenders develop the skills and mindset needed to lead ethical and responsible lives. Mindfulness and meditation practices are fundamental techniques for encouraging ethical behavior. These practices help individuals develop greater self-awareness, emotional regulation, and the ability to pause and reflect before acting. Mindfulness programs in correctional facilities typically involve regular meditation sessions, mindful breathing exercises, and reflective journaling. These activities enable offenders to observe their thoughts and emotions without judgment, fostering a sense of inner calm and clarity. For example, daily meditation sessions can help inmates manage stress and anxiety, reducing the likelihood of reactive and impulsive behavior. Reflective journaling allows individuals to explore their motivations and actions, promoting a deeper understanding of ethical principles and their application in everyday life.

Role-playing and ethical dilemmas are effective techniques for teaching ethical decision-making. These activities involve presenting offenders with realistic scenarios that require them to navigate complex moral landscapes and make decisions based on ethical principles. Role-playing exercises can simulate situations where individuals must choose between conflicting values, helping them practice making decisions that align with ethical standards. Ethical dilemmas, on the other hand, present challenging situations where there is no clear right or wrong answer, encouraging critical thinking and moral reasoning. By engaging in these activities, offenders learn to evaluate the consequences of their actions, consider the perspectives of others, and develop the confidence to make ethical choices in real-life situations. Developing empathy is a crucial aspect of encouraging ethical behavior, and victim impact panels and restorative justice circles are powerful tools for fostering empathy. Victim impact panels involve victims of crime sharing their experiences and the impact of the offenders' actions on their lives. Hearing these personal stories helps offenders understand the human cost of their behavior, fostering a sense of empathy and remorse. Restorative justice circles bring together offenders, victims, and community members to discuss the harm caused by the crime and explore ways to make amends. This process encourages offenders to take responsibility for their actions, listen to the perspectives of those affected, and actively participate in the healing process. By engaging in these dialogues, offenders can develop a deeper understanding of the impact of their behavior and a commitment to ethical living.

Community service and restitution programs provide practical opportunities for offenders to make amends and contribute positively to society. These programs involve offenders engaging in activities that benefit the community, such as cleaning public spaces, helping at shelters, or participating in environmental conservation efforts. Restitution programs require offenders to compensate their victims, either financially or through service-based reparations. By participating in these programs, offenders can experience the positive impact of their actions, develop a sense of purpose, and build a connection to their community. These activities reinforce the importance of ethical behavior and provide tangible experiences of making amends and contributing to the greater good. Mentorship and peer support groups play a vital role in encouraging ethical behavior by providing ongoing support, guidance, and accountability. Mentors, who are often individuals with similar experiences who have successfully transformed their lives, offer valuable insights, encouragement, and role modeling. Peer support groups create a safe space for offenders to share their experiences, discuss challenges, and celebrate successes. These groups foster a sense of community and mutual support, helping individuals stay committed to their ethical goals. For example, a peer support group that meets regularly to discuss ethical challenges and strategies can help offenders feel less isolated and more motivated to maintain their commitment to ethical living.

Implementing comprehensive ethical rehabilitation programs requires a multifaceted approach that integrates these practical techniques into a cohesive framework. Programs should be designed to address the specific needs and challenges of the offender population, incorporating a variety of activities and resources that support ethical development. This includes providing access to educational materials, training facilitators and staff in ethical principles and practices, and creating an environment that supports ethical behavior. By offering a range of activities and support mechanisms, rehabilitation programs can help offenders develop a robust understanding of ethics and the skills needed to apply these principles in their lives. Training correctional staff is essential for the success of ethical rehabilitation programs. Staff members who understand and embody ethical principles can significantly influence the rehabilitation process. Training programs for staff should include components on ethical behavior, empathy, and restorative justice practices. By modeling ethical behavior and providing consistent support, staff can create a positive environment that encourages offenders to embrace personal responsibility and ethical living. For example, staff who practice and promote non-violent communication can help de-escalate conflicts and foster a culture of respect and understanding within the facility.

Monitoring and evaluating the effectiveness of ethical rehabilitation programs is crucial for ensuring that they meet the needs of offenders and achieve desired outcomes. Regular assessments, including self-assessment tools, progress reports, and feedback sessions, can help track offenders' development and provide guidance and support. These assessments can identify areas for improvement, celebrate successes, and adjust strategies to ensure ongoing progress. By continuously refining and improving ethical rehabilitation programs, correctional facilities can enhance their effectiveness and ensure that they provide meaningful and lasting benefits. Collaborating with community organizations and stakeholders is another important strategy for implementing ethical practices. Partnerships with local nonprofits, educational institutions, and community groups can provide additional resources, support, and opportunities for offenders.

These collaborations can help create a network of support that extends beyond the correctional facility, aiding in the reintegration process and promoting long-term ethical behavior. For example, partnering with a local college to offer educational programs or working with a community organization to provide volunteer opportunities can enhance the impact of rehabilitation efforts. Scaling successful programs and advocating for policy changes are critical for expanding the reach and impact of ethical rehabilitation initiatives. By documenting and sharing the successes of ethical rehabilitation programs, correctional facilities can advocate for broader adoption of these practices within the criminal justice system. This includes presenting data on reduced recidivism rates, personal development outcomes, and community benefits to policymakers and stakeholders. Advocating for policy changes that support ethical rehabilitation, such as funding for restorative justice programs or changes in sentencing practices, can help create a more just and effective criminal justice system.

19.3: Case Studies of Ethical Rehabilitation

Case studies of ethical rehabilitation provide a wealth of insight into how transformative ethical principles can be when effectively integrated into correctional programs. These stories of personal transformation illustrate the profound impact of adopting ethical frameworks, fostering accountability, and promoting empathy and responsibility. Each case demonstrates unique approaches and outcomes, highlighting the diverse paths to rehabilitation and ethical living. Take the story of Mark, a man convicted of multiple instances of domestic violence. His rehabilitation journey began in a program called "New Beginnings," which combined ethical education with intensive counseling. The program required Mark to attend weekly sessions focused on ethical behavior, empathy training, and non-violent communication. Through role-playing exercises, Mark learned to understand the impact of his actions on his victims, fostering a deep sense of remorse and a desire to change. A pivotal moment in Mark's journey was participating in a restorative justice circle, where he confronted the harm he had caused by listening to the experiences of his victims. This confrontation was emotionally challenging but transformative, leading Mark to a commitment to ethical living and non-violence. Post-release, Mark became an advocate for domestic violence awareness, helping others break the cycle of abuse and promoting peaceful conflict resolution.

Sophia's story is another powerful example. Convicted of identity theft, she joined a program called "Identity and Integrity," which aimed to foster ethical behavior and personal accountability. This program included workshops on the ethical implications of identity theft, the importance of trust, and the consequences of violating others' privacy. Sophia's transformation began with reflective journaling exercises that prompted her to explore the motivations behind her actions and their impact on her victims. Participating in a victim impact panel, she heard firsthand accounts from those affected by identity theft, which profoundly impacted her understanding and empathy. These experiences were crucial in her journey towards ethical behavior. After her release, Sophia worked with organizations to raise awareness about the impact of identity theft and helped educate others on the importance of integrity and ethical conduct. Consider the case of Javier, who was incarcerated for gang-related activities, including drug trafficking and violence. His path to rehabilitation began with "Pathways to Peace," a program designed to help gang members leave behind their violent pasts and embrace ethical living. This program emphasized the principles of non-violence, personal responsibility, and community service. Javier participated in mediation sessions where he resolved conflicts peacefully, learned the value of empathy, and took responsibility for his actions. He also engaged in community service projects that helped repair the neighborhoods affected by gang violence. A key component of his transformation was mentorship from former gang members who had successfully turned their lives around. These mentors provided guidance, support, and positive role models. After his release, Javier became involved in community outreach, helping at-risk youth avoid gang involvement and promoting non-violent conflict resolution.

Emily's experience showcases the impact of ethical rehabilitation on those convicted of fraud. Emily participated in "Truth and Trust," a program that integrated ethical training with financial literacy and accountability measures. The program required her to engage in reflective practices, such as writing letters of apology to her victims and participating in restitution efforts. Through these activities, Emily confronted the harm caused by her fraudulent actions and developed a strong sense of accountability. The program also included ethical decision-making workshops and role-playing exercises that helped her practice honesty and transparency. Upon her release, Emily dedicated herself to educating others about ethical financial practices and preventing fraud. She now runs workshops on financial integrity and mentors individuals struggling with ethical decision-making in their professional lives. The story of Alex, who was imprisoned for assault, highlights the transformative power of empathy training. Alex joined "Compassionate Choices," a program focused on developing empathy and ethical behavior through mindfulness and reflective practices. The program included daily meditation sessions, empathy-building exercises, and participation in restorative justice circles. These activities helped Alex understand the impact of his violent behavior on others and fostered a commitment to change. A transformative moment for Alex was his involvement in a community art project designed to promote peace and healing. Through this project, Alex expressed his remorse and commitment to non-violence, creating artwork that depicted his journey towards ethical living. After his release, Alex continued to use art as a medium for promoting empathy and non-violence, working with at-risk youth and community organizations.

Lily's case, involving her conviction for embezzlement, illustrates the role of ethical education in fostering accountability. Lily participated in "Ethics and Economy," a program that combined ethical training with practical financial management skills. The program included lectures on ethical business practices, the consequences of financial crimes, and the importance of transparency and accountability. Reflective journaling and group discussions helped Lily explore the motivations behind her actions and their impact on others. A significant part of her transformation was the restitution program, where she worked to repay the stolen funds and engaged in community service. These experiences reinforced her commitment to ethical behavior and accountability. After her release, Lily founded a nonprofit organization that educates businesses on ethical practices and helps prevent financial misconduct. Daniel's story involves his rehabilitation from a life of armed robbery. He joined "Courage to Change," a program that emphasized ethical living and personal responsibility. The program required Daniel to participate in victim-offender dialogues, where he confronted the impact of his actions on his victims. These dialogues were facilitated in a safe and supportive environment, allowing for open and honest communication. Daniel also engaged in community service projects, such as building homes for low-income families, which helped him develop a sense of purpose and connection to his community. Mentorship from former offenders who had successfully reintegrated into society provided additional support and guidance. After his release, Daniel became a motivational speaker, sharing his story of transformation and advocating for restorative justice and ethical rehabilitation.

The case of Jessica, who was convicted of drug trafficking, highlights the role of mindfulness and meditation in fostering ethical behavior. Jessica participated in "Mindful Paths," a program that integrated mindfulness practices with ethical training and personal accountability. The program included daily meditation, mindfulness exercises, and reflective journaling, which helped Jessica develop greater self-awareness and emotional regulation. Participation in restorative justice circles allowed her to confront the impact of her actions on her victims and community. These experiences were crucial in her journey towards ethical living. After her release, Jessica became a mindfulness coach, helping others develop self-awareness and ethical behavior through mindfulness practices. Lastly, the story of Paul, who served time for burglary, illustrates the impact of community service and ethical education. Paul joined "Service and Ethics," a program that combined ethical training with community service opportunities. The program included workshops on moral reasoning, empathy development, and the consequences of criminal behavior. Reflective journaling and group discussions helped Paul explore the motivations behind his actions and their impact on others. Participation in community service projects, such as volunteering at local shelters and food banks, reinforced his commitment to ethical living and personal responsibility. After his release, Paul continued to volunteer in his community and became an advocate for ethical rehabilitation programs.

19.4: Benefits for Offenders and Communities

The long-term benefits for offenders and communities stemming from ethical rehabilitation programs are extensive and multifaceted, encompassing personal transformation, community cohesion, and systemic improvements within the criminal justice framework. These benefits ripple outward, influencing not only the individual participants but also the broader society, promoting a culture of empathy, responsibility, and ethical conduct. For offenders, the adoption of ethical principles during rehabilitation leads to profound personal growth and transformation. These programs often emphasize self-awareness, empathy, and accountability, helping individuals understand the impact of their actions on others and fostering a commitment to change. Offenders who engage in ethical rehabilitation programs typically experience improved self-esteem and a renewed sense of purpose. By participating in activities that promote ethical decision-making, mindfulness, and community service, they learn to navigate life's challenges with greater resilience and integrity. This transformation is not superficial but involves a deep, internal shift in values and attitudes, which can significantly reduce the likelihood of reoffending.

One of the most tangible benefits for offenders is the development of empathy and interpersonal skills. Programs that include restorative justice practices, such as victim-offender dialogues and empathy training, enable offenders to understand and connect with the experiences of their victims. This process fosters a sense of remorse and a genuine desire to make amends, which is crucial for personal rehabilitation. As offenders develop empathy, they become more capable of forming positive relationships, both within and outside the correctional facility. This improved capacity for empathy and communication can enhance their interactions with family members, peers, and community members, supporting their reintegration into society. Ethical rehabilitation programs also equip offenders with practical skills that are essential for successful reintegration. These skills include effective communication, conflict resolution, and ethical decision-making. By learning to manage their emotions and make thoughtful, principled choices, offenders are better prepared to handle the complexities of life outside prison. Many programs offer vocational training and educational opportunities that further enhance these practical skills, providing offenders with the tools they need to find employment and contribute productively to society. This combination of personal growth and practical skill development is key to reducing recidivism and promoting long-term success.

The benefits of ethical rehabilitation extend beyond individual offenders to their families and communities. When offenders engage in personal transformation, they often become positive role models for their families, demonstrating the possibility of change and ethical living. This can inspire family members to adopt similar principles and behaviors, creating a supportive and nurturing environment that promotes overall well-being. Furthermore, as offenders reintegrate into their communities with a commitment to ethical living, they contribute to the safety and cohesion of these communities. Their positive actions can help rebuild trust and foster a sense of shared responsibility and mutual respect. Communities benefit significantly from the presence of rehabilitated individuals who are committed to ethical behavior and personal responsibility. These individuals often engage in community service and volunteer activities, contributing to the betterment of their neighborhoods and fostering a spirit of cooperation and altruism. Their involvement in community projects, such as cleaning public spaces, mentoring at-risk youth, or supporting local charities, helps to address social issues and build a stronger, more cohesive community. These positive contributions not only improve the immediate environment but also create a ripple effect, encouraging others to participate in community-building activities and promoting a culture of collective responsibility.

Ethical rehabilitation programs also play a crucial role in reducing crime rates and enhancing public safety. By addressing the root causes of criminal behavior, such as a lack of empathy, poor impulse control, and unresolved trauma, these programs help prevent reoffending. This reduction in recidivism leads to lower crime rates, which in turn increases public safety and reduces the burden on the criminal justice system. Communities experience fewer instances of crime and violence, creating a safer and more stable environment for all residents. This enhanced sense of safety can lead to increased community engagement and a higher quality of life for everyone. The long-term benefits of ethical rehabilitation are also evident in the broader criminal justice system. Programs that emphasize ethical principles and restorative justice can influence systemic changes, promoting a more humane and effective approach to rehabilitation. By demonstrating the success of these programs, policymakers and stakeholders can be encouraged to adopt similar practices within the criminal justice framework. This shift towards a more rehabilitative and restorative model can lead to significant improvements in how justice is administered, focusing on healing and reconciliation rather than punishment alone.

Moreover, the integration of ethical principles into rehabilitation programs can lead to cost savings for the criminal justice system. Reducing recidivism and preventing reoffending decreases the need for incarceration, which is often costly and resource-intensive. Funds that would have been spent on maintaining high prison populations can be redirected towards education, healthcare, and community development initiatives. These investments can further support the rehabilitation and reintegration of offenders, creating a positive cycle of ethical living and community well-being. The long-term impact of ethical rehabilitation also includes fostering a culture of ethical behavior and responsibility within society. As more individuals and communities embrace these principles, there is a broader cultural shift towards valuing empathy, integrity, and accountability. This cultural change can influence various aspects of society, from how businesses operate to how communities address social issues. By promoting ethical behavior and responsibility, ethical rehabilitation programs contribute to the development of a more just and compassionate society.

19.5: Strategies for Implementing Ethical Practices

Implementing ethical practices in rehabilitation programs requires a strategic and comprehensive approach that incorporates various methodologies, training, and community involvement. These strategies ensure that ethical principles are not only taught but also ingrained in the daily lives and decisions of offenders. By fostering an environment that supports ethical behavior and personal responsibility, correctional facilities can create a sustainable framework for rehabilitation that benefits both individuals and society as a whole. Designing and implementing comprehensive ethical rehabilitation programs is the first crucial step. This involves developing curricula that integrate ethical principles with practical applications. The curriculum should cover topics such as empathy development, moral reasoning, restorative justice, and ethical decision-making. These topics should be taught through a combination of lectures, interactive workshops, role-playing exercises, and real-life scenarios. For instance, offenders can participate in discussions about ethical dilemmas, engage in activities that promote empathy, and practice making ethical decisions in controlled environments. These experiences help offenders internalize ethical principles and apply them to their daily lives.

Training staff and volunteers in ethical principles and practices is essential for the success of these programs. Staff members who understand and embody ethical principles can significantly influence the rehabilitation process. Training programs for staff should include components on mindfulness, empathy, restorative justice, and ethical behavior. By modeling ethical behavior and providing consistent support, staff can create a positive environment that encourages offenders to embrace personal responsibility and ethical living. For example, staff who practice non-violent communication can help de-escalate conflicts and foster a culture of respect and understanding within the facility. Ongoing professional development and support for staff are also important to ensure that they remain effective role models and mentors. Collaborating with community organizations and stakeholders is another critical strategy for implementing ethical practices. Partnerships with local nonprofits, educational institutions, and community groups can provide additional resources, support, and opportunities for offenders. These collaborations can help create a network of support that extends beyond the correctional facility, aiding in the reintegration process and promoting long-term ethical behavior. For instance, working with local colleges to offer educational programs or partnering with community organizations to provide volunteer opportunities can enhance the impact of rehabilitation efforts. These partnerships also help bridge the gap between correctional facilities and the community, fostering a sense of shared responsibility and cooperation.

Monitoring and evaluating the effectiveness of ethical rehabilitation programs is crucial for ensuring that they meet the needs of offenders and achieve desired outcomes. Regular assessments, including self-assessment tools, progress reports, and feedback sessions, can help track offenders' development and provide guidance and support. These assessments can identify areas for improvement, celebrate successes, and adjust strategies to ensure ongoing progress. For example, regular check-ins with counselors or mentors can provide opportunities for reflection, goal-setting, and addressing challenges, helping offenders stay committed to their ethical journey. Using data to evaluate the impact of these programs can also help justify their continuation and expansion, providing evidence of their effectiveness in reducing recidivism and promoting positive change. Scaling successful programs and advocating for policy changes are critical for expanding the reach and impact of ethical rehabilitation initiatives. By documenting and sharing the successes of ethical rehabilitation programs, correctional facilities can advocate for broader adoption of these practices within the criminal justice system. This includes presenting data on reduced recidivism rates, personal development outcomes, and community benefits to policymakers and stakeholders. Advocating for policy changes that support ethical rehabilitation, such as funding for restorative justice programs or changes in sentencing practices, can help create a more just and effective criminal justice system. For example, policies that prioritize rehabilitation over punishment can support the development and implementation of ethical programs, leading to better outcomes for offenders and society.

Creating a supportive environment within correctional facilities is essential for fostering ethical behavior. This involves developing policies and practices that promote respect, accountability, and ethical decision-making. For example, facilities can implement non-violent communication protocols, establish peer support groups, and provide opportunities for offenders to engage in community service and restorative justice activities. These practices help create a culture of ethical behavior and personal responsibility, encouraging offenders to adopt these principles in their daily lives. Additionally, facilities can create spaces for reflection and mindfulness, such as meditation rooms or quiet areas, where offenders can practice self-awareness and emotional regulation. Incorporating restorative justice practices into rehabilitation programs is another effective strategy. Restorative justice focuses on repairing harm and rebuilding relationships rather than solely on punishment. Programs can include victim-offender mediation, where offenders meet with their victims to discuss the impact of their actions and explore ways to make amends. This process can be profoundly transformative, as it encourages empathy, understanding, and personal accountability. Restorative justice circles, which involve community members, victims, and offenders, can also provide a supportive space for dialogue, healing, and reconciliation. These practices help offenders understand the consequences of their actions and foster a commitment to ethical living.

Providing opportunities for offenders to practice ethical behavior in meaningful ways is also important. Involvement in community service projects, volunteer opportunities, and peer mentoring can provide practical experiences of ethical conduct. These opportunities allow offenders to apply ethical principles in real-world contexts, reinforcing their commitment to ethical living. For instance, participating in a community garden project, helping to clean up public spaces, or volunteering at a local shelter can provide tangible ways for offenders to contribute to the well-being of others and the community. These experiences help offenders develop a sense of purpose and connection to their community, supporting their reintegration and promoting positive change. Encouraging continuous learning and personal development is another key strategy for implementing ethical practices. Providing access to educational programs, vocational training, and life skills workshops can help offenders build the knowledge and skills they need to lead responsible and productive lives.

These programs can include literacy and numeracy classes, job readiness training, financial literacy workshops, and courses on communication and conflict resolution. By equipping individuals with the tools they need to succeed, rehabilitation programs can help offenders build confidence, self-efficacy, and a sense of responsibility for their future. For example, offering job placement assistance and ongoing mentorship can help former offenders find stable employment and build a positive future. Building a supportive network that extends beyond the correctional facility is essential for sustaining ethical behavior post-release. Providing resources and opportunities for continued ethical development, such as access to community-based programs, ongoing mentorship, and support groups, can help offenders navigate the challenges of reintegration. This network of support helps former offenders stay connected to their ethical principles and maintain their commitment to personal responsibility. For instance, establishing partnerships with local community organizations that provide support for housing, employment, and education can enhance the reintegration process and promote long-term success.

References

- Anderson, J. (2009). Illusions of Accountability: Credit and Blame Sensemaking in Public Administration. Administrative Theory & Praxis, 31(3), 322–339. http://www.jstor.org/stable/25611001
- Beck, B. M. (1954). WHAT WE CAN DO ABOUT JUVENILE DELINQUENCY. Child Welfare, 33(1), 3–7. http://www.jstor.org/stable/45399418
- Bridgman, O. L. (1943). Problem Children, Delinquency, and Treatment. Review of Educational Research, 13(5), 448–457. https://doi.org/10.2307/1168395
- Coward, H. G. (1983). Psychology and Karma. Philosophy East and West, 33(1), 49–60. https://doi.org/10.2307/1398665
- Fairfield, L. (1950). JUVENILE DELINQUENCY: CAUSE AND CURE. Blackfriars, 31(368), 517–523. http://www.jstor.org/stable/43813226
- Feldman, R. A., Wodarski, J. S., Flax, N., & Goodman, M. (1972). Treating delinquents in traditional agencies. Social Work, 17(5), 71–78. http://www.jstor.org/stable/23711089
- Gombrich, R. (1975). Buddhist Karma and Social Control. Comparative Studies in Society and History, 17(2), 212–220. http://www.jstor.org/stable/178004
- Inada, K. K. (1979). Problematics of the Buddhist Nature of Self. Philosophy East and West, 29(2), 141–158. https://doi.org/10.2307/1398553
- King, W. L. (1961). An Experience in Buddhist Meditation. The Journal of Religion, 41(1), 51–61. http://www.jstor.org/stable/1200236
- Kupperstein, L. (1971). TREATMENT AND REHABILITATION OF DELINQUENT YOUTH: SOME SOCIOCULTURAL CONSIDERATIONS. Acta Criminologica, 4, 11–111. http://www.jstor.org/stable/42748836
- Love, T. T. (1965). Theravāda Buddhism: Ethical Theory and Practice. Journal of Bible and Religion, 33(4), 303–313. http://www.jstor.org/stable/1459491
- May, D. (1971). DELINQUENCY CONTROL AND THE TREATMENT MODEL: SOME IMPLICATIONS OF RECENT LEGISLATION. The British

Journal of Criminology, 11(4), 359–370. http://www.jstor.org/stable/23635359

- Misra, G. S. P. (1964). THE BUDDHIST CONCEPTION OF DISCIPLINE. Proceedings of the Indian History Congress, 26, 108–114. http://www.jstor.org/stable/44133102
- Muck, T. C. (2001). Readiness: Preparing for the Path. Buddhist-Christian Studies, 21, 51–56. http://www.jstor.org/stable/1390485
- Potter, K. H. (1992). The Karmic a Priori in Indian Philosophy. Philosophy East and West, 42(3), 407–419. https://doi.org/10.2307/1399270
- Sharma, A. (2008). Karma, Rebirth, and the Problem of Evil: An Interjection in the Debate between Whitley Kaufman and Monima Chadha and Nick Trakakis. Philosophy East and West, 58(4), 572–575. http://www.jstor.org/stable/40213539
- Sharma, U. (1973). Theodicy and the Doctrine of Karma. Man, 8(3), 347–364. https://doi.org/10.2307/2800314
- Sivaraksa, S. (1998). Buddhism and Human Freedom. Buddhist-Christian Studies, 18, 63–68. https://doi.org/10.2307/1390436
- Smith, B. L. (1968). Toward a Buddhist Anthropology: The Problem of the Secular. Journal of the American Academy of Religion, 36(3), 203–216. http://www.jstor.org/stable/1460968
- Stout, J. (1978). Buddhism Beyond Morality: A Note on Two Senses of Transcendence. The Journal of Religious Ethics, 6(2), 319–325. http://www.jstor.org/stable/40014918
- Van Nagel, C. J., Foley, L. A., Dixon, M., & Kauffman, J. (1986). A Review of Treatment Methods for the Rehabilitation of Juvenile Delinquents. Journal of Correctional Education, 37(4), 140–145. http://www.jstor.org/stable/23291726
- Walters, W. (2012). The Centrality of Karma in Early Buddhism [Review of What the Buddha Thought, by R. Gombrich]. Philosophy East and West, 62(1), 114–127. http://www.jstor.org/stable/41426833
- William C. Kvaraceus. (1955). Preventing and Treating Juvenile Delinquency Some Basic Approaches. The School Review, 63(9), 477–479. http://www.jstor.org/stable/1083317
- Zhang, Z. (2013). FROM DEMONIC TO KARMIC RETRIBUTION: CHANGING CONCEPTS OF "BAO" IN EARLY MEDIAEVAL CHINA AS SEEN IN THE "YOU MING LU." Acta Orientalia Academiae Scientiarum Hungaricae, 66(3), 267–287. http://www.jstor.org/stable/43282516

Part VI: Restorative Practices Inspired by Buddhism

CHAPTER TWENTY

Restorative Justice and the Four Noble Truths

Contents

- Applying the Four Noble Truths to Restorative Justice

- Practical Techniques for Healing and Reconciliation

- Case Studies of Restorative Practices

- Benefits for Offenders and Victims

- Long-Term Impact on Justice Systems

20.1: Applying the Four Noble Truths to Restorative Justice

Applying the Four Noble Truths to restorative justice requires a profound understanding of both the philosophical underpinnings of Buddhism and the practical realities of the criminal justice system. The Four Noble Truths offer a framework for understanding suffering and its cessation, providing a pathway that can be particularly transformative when integrated into restorative practices. In the context of crime, suffering manifests in multiple dimensions: the pain experienced by victims, the remorse and guilt of offenders, and the broader impact on the community. By addressing these dimensions through the lens of the Four

Noble Truths, restorative justice can promote healing and reconciliation in ways that punitive systems often fail to achieve. The First Noble Truth, which recognizes the existence of suffering, is fundamental to restorative justice. Crime, in its essence, is a source of suffering. Victims endure physical, emotional, and psychological pain, while offenders often suffer from guilt, shame, and the consequences of their actions. The community also bears the burden of disrupted peace and safety. Acknowledging this suffering is the first step towards addressing it. In restorative justice, this acknowledgment is facilitated through processes that bring together victims, offenders, and community members to openly discuss the harm caused. This collective recognition of suffering validates the experiences of all parties involved and lays the groundwork for healing.

The Second Noble Truth delves into the origins of suffering, which in the context of crime can be multifaceted. Factors such as social inequality, poverty, lack of education, and trauma often contribute to criminal behavior. Understanding these underlying causes is crucial for restorative justice, as it moves beyond the superficial act of the crime to explore its root causes. This deeper exploration helps in creating more effective and compassionate responses. For offenders, this understanding fosters a sense of responsibility, as they come to terms with the factors that influenced their actions and the choices they made. For victims, it can provide context and a broader understanding of the circumstances that led to their victimization, which can be an essential step in their healing process. The Third Noble Truth offers hope with the cessation of suffering. In restorative justice, this cessation is achieved through accountability, reconciliation, and making amends. Offenders are encouraged to take responsibility for their actions, not as a punitive measure, but as a path towards personal redemption and societal reintegration. This process involves sincere apologies, reparative actions, and active participation in addressing the harm caused. For victims, the cessation of suffering often begins with receiving a genuine apology and seeing tangible efforts to make amends. This can restore their sense of justice and safety, helping them move forward with their lives. The community benefits as well, witnessing the restoration of relationships and the reintegration of offenders as responsible members.

The Fourth Noble Truth outlines the path to the cessation of suffering, known as the Noble Eightfold Path. This path provides practical steps that can be adapted into restorative justice practices. Right View, for instance, involves understanding the nature of suffering and the impact of one's actions. In restorative justice, this is facilitated through dialogue and reflection, where offenders gain insight into the consequences of their behavior. Right Intention focuses on the commitment to ethical and compassionate behavior, which restorative justice fosters by encouraging offenders to genuinely repent and commit to positive change. Right Speech, Right Action, and Right Livelihood are embodied in the reparative actions and ethical living that offenders are encouraged to adopt as they make amends and reintegrate into society. Right Effort, Right Mindfulness, and Right Concentration are cultivated through practices such as meditation and mindfulness, which can be integral components of restorative justice programs. These practices help offenders develop self-awareness, emotional regulation, and a focused commitment to personal growth and ethical living. For victims and community members, mindfulness and meditation can provide tools for coping with trauma, managing emotions, and fostering a compassionate perspective.

Integrating the Four Noble Truths into restorative justice transforms the process into a holistic approach that addresses the emotional, psychological, and social dimensions of crime. It promotes a deeper understanding of suffering and its causes, fosters genuine accountability and reconciliation, and provides practical steps for healing and ethical living. This approach not only benefits the individuals directly involved but also contributes to a more compassionate and just society. By addressing the root causes of crime and fostering empathy and responsibility, restorative justice inspired by the Four Noble Truths can lead to more meaningful and lasting resolutions, reducing recidivism and promoting community well-being. Incorporating these principles into restorative justice practices requires a commitment to education and training for all participants. Offenders, victims, and facilitators need to be well-versed in the concepts of the Four Noble Truths and how they apply to the justice process. This education can be delivered through workshops, seminars, and ongoing support sessions that provide a deep understanding of Buddhist principles and their practical application. Facilitators, in particular, play a crucial role in guiding the restorative process, ensuring that it adheres to these ethical and philosophical foundations.

Moreover, creating a supportive environment that fosters open communication and mutual respect is essential for the success of restorative justice practices inspired by the Four Noble Truths. This environment should encourage honest dialogue, active listening, and a compassionate approach to conflict resolution. By fostering a culture of empathy and understanding, restorative justice can transform the way communities respond to crime, focusing on healing and reconciliation rather than punishment and retribution. The long-term impact of applying the Four Noble Truths to restorative justice can be profound. Offenders who undergo this process are more likely to experience genuine rehabilitation, as they develop a deeper understanding of their actions and commit to ethical living. Victims benefit from the healing and closure that comes from meaningful apologies and reparative actions. Communities become stronger and more cohesive, as the focus on empathy, responsibility, and reconciliation fosters a sense of collective well-being and safety. Applying the Four Noble Truths to restorative justice offers a transformative approach that addresses the root causes of crime and promotes healing and reconciliation. By acknowledging suffering, understanding its origins, fostering accountability, and providing a path to ethical living, restorative justice practices inspired by these principles can create meaningful and lasting change for individuals and communities. This holistic approach not only benefits those directly involved in the justice process but also contributes to a more compassionate and just society, where empathy, responsibility, and ethical behavior are prioritized.

20.2: Practical Techniques for Healing and Reconciliation

Practical techniques for healing and reconciliation in restorative justice are grounded in the principles of empathy, accountability, and community involvement. These techniques are designed to facilitate open communication, foster mutual understanding, and promote genuine healing for all parties involved. By integrating these techniques, restorative justice can transform the way communities address crime and conflict, moving away from punitive approaches and towards processes that prioritize healing and reconciliation. One of the most effective techniques in restorative justice is the use of restorative justice circles. These circles bring together victims, offenders, and community members in a safe and structured environment to discuss the harm caused by the crime and explore ways to make amends. The circle format encourages equal participation, allowing each person to speak and be heard without interruption. This process fosters a sense of shared responsibility and mutual respect, as participants listen to each other's experiences and perspectives. The facilitator, who guides the discussion, plays a crucial role in maintaining a respectful and productive dialogue. By encouraging honesty, empathy, and accountability, restorative justice circles create a space where genuine healing can begin.

Victim-offender dialogues are another powerful technique in restorative justice. These face-to-face meetings between victims and offenders provide an opportunity for direct communication and personal connection. In these dialogues, victims can express their feelings and describe the impact of the crime on their lives, while offenders have the chance to listen, understand, and offer apologies. This direct interaction can be profoundly healing for victims, as it allows them to voice their pain and seek answers to their questions. For offenders, hearing firsthand about the consequences of their actions can evoke empathy and remorse, motivating them to take responsibility and make amends. Facilitators support this process by preparing both parties for the meeting, ensuring a safe and respectful environment, and guiding the conversation towards constructive outcomes. Empathy-building exercises are integral to restorative justice practices. These exercises are designed to help participants understand and connect with the emotions and experiences of others. Role-playing scenarios, for example, can place participants in the shoes of both victims and offenders, fostering a deeper understanding of the perspectives and feelings of each party. Storytelling is another effective empathy-building technique, where individuals share personal stories that illustrate the impact of crime and the importance of accountability and reconciliation. These exercises help break down barriers and build bridges of understanding, promoting a culture of empathy and compassion.

Restitution agreements are practical tools for making amends and repairing harm. These agreements are developed collaboratively by victims, offenders, and community members, outlining specific actions that the offender will take to address the harm caused. Restitution can take various forms, such as financial compensation, community service, or personal acts of apology and repair. The process of developing a restitution agreement involves open dialogue and negotiation, ensuring that the needs and perspectives of all parties are considered. This collaborative approach not only helps repair the specific harm caused by the crime but also reinforces the offender's commitment to ethical behavior and personal responsibility. Community service projects are another practical technique for promoting healing and reconciliation. These projects provide offenders with opportunities to contribute positively to their communities, making tangible amends for their actions. Community service can involve a wide range of activities, such as cleaning public spaces, helping at local shelters, or participating in environmental conservation efforts. By engaging in these activities, offenders can develop a sense of purpose and connection to their community, reinforcing their commitment to ethical living. Community service projects also benefit the community by addressing local needs and fostering a spirit of cooperation and mutual support.

Incorporating mindfulness and meditation practices into restorative justice programs can enhance the healing and reconciliation process. Mindfulness practices help participants develop greater self-awareness, emotional regulation, and empathy. Regular meditation sessions can provide a calming space for reflection and introspection, allowing individuals to process their emotions and thoughts more effectively. Mindfulness exercises, such as mindful breathing and body scans, can help reduce stress and anxiety, promoting a sense of inner peace and balance. These practices are particularly beneficial for offenders, as they help cultivate the self-discipline and emotional resilience needed to maintain ethical behavior and personal responsibility. Facilitators play a crucial role in the success of restorative justice practices. Effective facilitation requires a deep understanding of restorative principles, strong communication skills, and the ability to create a safe and supportive environment for dialogue. Facilitators guide the process, ensuring that all participants have an opportunity to speak and be heard, managing conflicts and emotions, and helping the group stay focused on healing and reconciliation. Training for facilitators should include components on empathy, active listening, non-violent communication, and mindfulness. By providing skilled facilitation, restorative justice programs can maximize their potential for promoting healing and transformation.

Building agreements for restitution and community service involves careful planning and negotiation. These agreements should be specific, measurable, achievable, relevant, and time-bound (SMART). Developing SMART agreements ensures that the actions taken are meaningful and effective in addressing the harm caused. For example, a restitution agreement might specify that the offender will complete 100 hours of community service at a local food bank within six months, providing both a clear goal and a timeframe for completion. Regular check-ins and progress reviews can help ensure that agreements are being fulfilled and provide opportunities for reflection and adjustment as needed. Support systems are essential for sustaining the positive changes achieved through restorative justice. These systems can include ongoing mentorship, peer support groups, and access to counseling and other resources. Mentors, who are often individuals with similar experiences who have successfully reintegrated into society, can provide valuable guidance and encouragement.

Peer support groups offer a safe space for sharing experiences, discussing challenges, and celebrating successes, fostering a sense of community and mutual support. Access to counseling and other resources can help participants address underlying issues, such as trauma, addiction, or mental health concerns, supporting their ongoing journey towards ethical living and personal responsibility. Evaluating the effectiveness of restorative justice practices is crucial for continuous improvement and sustainability. Regular assessments, including participant feedback, progress reviews, and outcome measurements, can provide valuable insights into the strengths and areas for improvement in these programs. For example, surveys and interviews with participants can help identify the impact of restorative practices on their emotional well-being, relationships, and ethical behavior. Recidivism rates can be tracked to measure the long-term effectiveness of these programs in reducing reoffending. By using this data to refine and enhance restorative justice practices, correctional facilities can ensure that they are providing meaningful and effective support for healing and reconciliation.

20.3: Case Studies of Restorative Practices

Case studies of restorative practices provide concrete examples of how these methods can transform lives and communities. By examining various restorative justice programs and their outcomes, we can gain a deeper understanding of the principles and practices that contribute to their success. These case studies highlight the potential of restorative justice to foster healing, accountability, and reconciliation, offering valuable insights into the implementation and impact of these practices. Consider the case of the "Restorative Justice Community Initiative" (RJCI) in a mid-sized American city. This program was designed to address crimes involving youth offenders. One notable case involved a teenager named Sam, who had been involved in a series of break-ins and thefts. Through RJCI, Sam participated in a restorative justice circle that included his victims, community members, and facilitators. The circle provided a platform for the victims to express their pain and for Sam to understand the impact of his actions. This process was transformative for Sam, who expressed genuine remorse and a desire to make amends. As part of his restitution, Sam agreed to work on community service projects, including helping to repair the damage caused by his break-ins. Over time, Sam's attitude and behavior changed significantly. He developed a stronger sense of empathy and responsibility, leading to a reduction in his delinquent activities. The victims also reported feeling a sense of closure and satisfaction from the process, which helped them heal and rebuild trust within the community.

Another compelling case is the "Indigenous Restorative Justice Program" (IRJP) in Canada, which focuses on integrating traditional Indigenous practices with modern restorative justice principles. One case involved Mary, an Indigenous woman who had been convicted of drug-related offenses. The IRJP included elders and community leaders in the restorative justice circle, emphasizing the importance of cultural heritage and community support in the healing process. During the circle, Mary confronted the impact of her actions on her family and community. The elders provided guidance and wisdom, helping Mary understand the broader implications of her behavior. As part of her restitution, Mary participated in cultural activities and ceremonies that reconnected her with her heritage and community. This experience was pivotal in her journey towards recovery and reintegration. The program not only helped Mary overcome her addiction but also strengthened her ties to her cultural roots, promoting long-term personal growth and community cohesion. In New Zealand, the "Family Group Conferencing" (FGC) model has been widely used to address juvenile delinquency. One notable case involved a young boy named Tim, who had been involved in vandalism and truancy. Through the FGC process, Tim's family, victims, and community representatives came together to discuss the harm caused and develop a plan for restitution. The conference provided a supportive environment for Tim to take responsibility for his actions and for the victims to express their feelings. The outcome included a personalized plan for Tim, which involved community service, participation in a mentorship program, and regular school attendance. Over time, Tim's behavior improved, and he developed a stronger sense of belonging and purpose. The FGC model not only addressed the immediate harm but also provided a framework for long-term support and guidance, helping Tim stay on a positive path.

The "Victim-Offender Mediation Program" (VOMP) in Germany offers another illustrative case. This program focuses on serious crimes, including violent offenses. One case involved a man named Jens, who had been convicted of assault. Through VOMP, Jens met with his victim in a mediated setting. The mediation process allowed the victim to express the deep emotional and physical impact of the assault, while Jens had the opportunity to apologize and take responsibility. The mediator facilitated a structured dialogue that helped both parties explore the underlying issues and work towards a resolution. As part of the agreement, Jens committed to attending anger management classes and engaging in volunteer work with a local violence prevention organization. This experience was transformative for both Jens and the victim. Jens developed greater emotional regulation and a commitment to non-violence, while the victim found a sense of closure and empowerment through the process. In South Africa, the "Community Restorative Justice Program" (CRJP) addresses crimes in areas with high levels of social unrest. One significant case involved a group of young men who had been involved in gang violence. The CRJP organized a series of restorative justice circles that included the offenders, their families, victims, and community leaders. The circles provided a platform for open dialogue and reconciliation, focusing on the impact of gang violence on the community. The offenders were encouraged to take responsibility for their actions and commit to positive change. As part of the restitution, the young men participated in community development projects, such as building playgrounds and organizing youth sports events. This engagement helped them develop a sense of purpose and belonging, reducing their involvement in gang activities. The victims and community members also reported a greater sense of safety and cohesion, highlighting the program's positive impact on the community as a whole.

In the United Kingdom, the "Restorative Schools Program" (RSP) addresses conflicts and misconduct in educational settings. One notable case involved a high school student named Lucy, who had been involved in bullying. Through the RSP, Lucy participated in a restorative justice circle that included her peers, teachers, and the victims of her bullying. The circle provided a space for the victims to share their experiences and for Lucy to understand the harm caused by her actions. As part of the resolution, Lucy agreed to participate in a peer mentorship program and engage in school community service. This process helped Lucy develop empathy and accountability, leading to a significant improvement in her behavior. The victims also felt a sense of justice and closure, enhancing the overall school environment. The RSP model demonstrates how restorative practices can be effectively integrated into educational settings, promoting a culture of respect and responsibility. In Australia, the "Restorative Prisons Project" (RPP) focuses on integrating restorative practices within correctional facilities. One significant case involved a group of inmates who had been involved in a violent altercation. The RPP organized restorative justice circles that included the offenders, prison staff, and affected inmates. The circles provided a platform for open dialogue, allowing all parties to express their feelings and work towards reconciliation. As part of the restitution, the offenders participated in anger management and conflict resolution workshops. This process helped them develop greater emotional regulation and accountability. The affected inmates also reported feeling safer and more respected, highlighting the positive impact of restorative practices within the prison environment. The RPP model demonstrates how restorative justice can be effectively integrated into correctional settings, promoting rehabilitation and reducing violence.

The "Restorative Justice for Women Program" (RJWP) in the United States addresses crimes involving female offenders. One notable case involved a woman named Clara, who had been convicted of fraud. Through RJWP, Clara participated in restorative justice circles that included her victims, community members, and facilitators. The circles provided a supportive environment for Clara to take responsibility for her actions and for the victims to express their feelings. As part of her restitution, Clara agreed to participate in financial literacy workshops and volunteer at a local nonprofit organization. This process helped Clara develop a stronger sense of accountability and ethical behavior. The victims also reported feeling a sense of justice and closure, highlighting the program's positive impact on both offenders and victims. The RJWP model demonstrates how restorative justice can effectively address crimes involving female offenders, promoting healing and empowerment. These case studies illustrate the transformative potential of restorative practices in addressing crime and promoting healing and reconciliation. By providing a supportive environment for open dialogue, empathy-building, and accountability, restorative justice programs can foster profound personal and community transformation.

20.4: Benefits for Offenders and Victims

The benefits of restorative justice practices for both offenders and victims are profound and multifaceted, touching on emotional, psychological, social, and even economic dimensions. These benefits extend far beyond the immediate resolution of individual cases, fostering long-term personal growth and community well-being. By focusing on healing, accountability, and reconciliation, restorative justice provides a holistic approach to addressing crime that benefits all parties involved.

For offenders, restorative justice offers a path to redemption and personal transformation that is often absent in traditional punitive systems. One of the most significant benefits for offenders is the opportunity to take responsibility for their actions in a meaningful way. This process involves acknowledging the harm they have caused, understanding its impact on the victims and the community, and actively working to make amends. This sense of responsibility can be a powerful catalyst for personal growth, helping offenders develop empathy, moral reasoning, and ethical behavior. By engaging in restorative practices, offenders learn to see their actions from the perspective of others, fostering a sense of empathy that can prevent future criminal behavior.

The process of making amends is also crucial for the personal development of offenders. Restitution and community service projects allow offenders to repair the harm they have caused in tangible ways, helping them develop a sense of purpose and connection to their community. These activities not only address the immediate damage but also reinforce the offender's commitment to positive change. For example, an offender who participates in community service projects, such as rebuilding a vandalized community center, can see the direct impact of their efforts on the community's well-being. This experience can be deeply rewarding and motivating, reinforcing their desire to lead an ethical and responsible life. Restorative justice practices also provide offenders with opportunities for personal reflection and growth. Through dialogue and mediation, offenders are encouraged to explore the underlying causes of their behavior, such as trauma, addiction, or social influences. This self-reflection helps them understand their actions and develop strategies for positive change. For instance, an offender who participates in victim-offender mediation sessions may gain insights into the emotional triggers that led to their criminal behavior, allowing them to develop healthier coping mechanisms. This process of self-awareness and growth is essential for long-term rehabilitation and reintegration into society.

Victims, too, benefit immensely from restorative justice practices. One of the most significant benefits for victims is the opportunity for emotional and psychological healing. Traditional justice systems often focus on punishing the offender, leaving victims feeling unheard and marginalized. Restorative justice, on the other hand, places victims at the center of the process, giving them a voice and a platform to express their feelings and needs. This involvement can be incredibly empowering for victims, helping them regain a sense of control and agency. By participating in restorative justice circles or victim-offender dialogues, victims can share their experiences, ask questions, and receive apologies, which can be instrumental in their healing process. The process of receiving a sincere apology and seeing the offender take responsibility can provide victims with a sense of closure and justice that traditional punitive measures often fail to deliver. For many victims, understanding that the offender is genuinely remorseful and committed to making amends can be a crucial step towards healing. This acknowledgment of their pain and suffering helps victims move forward, reducing feelings of anger, resentment, and fear. For example, a victim of a burglary who participates in a restorative justice circle with the offender may feel a sense of relief and closure upon hearing the offender's apology and commitment to change.

Restorative justice practices also benefit the broader community by fostering a culture of empathy, accountability, and mutual support. Communities that engage in restorative justice initiatives often experience a greater sense of cohesion and trust. By involving community members in the justice process, restorative practices help build stronger relationships and a shared commitment to maintaining a safe and supportive environment. This communal involvement can be particularly important in areas affected by high levels of crime and social unrest, as it encourages collective responsibility and action. Moreover, restorative justice can lead to a reduction in recidivism rates, contributing to long-term community safety and well-being. Offenders who participate in restorative justice programs are less likely to reoffend, as they develop a deeper understanding of the consequences of their actions and a stronger commitment to ethical behavior. This reduction in recidivism not only benefits the individual offenders but also enhances public safety, reducing the burden on the criminal justice system and allowing resources to be allocated more effectively.

The economic benefits of restorative justice should not be overlooked. Traditional punitive systems are often costly, involving lengthy court processes, incarceration, and supervision. Restorative justice, by focusing on community-based solutions and reparative actions, can reduce these costs significantly. By addressing the root causes of criminal behavior and promoting rehabilitation, restorative justice reduces the need for prolonged incarceration and repeated interactions with the justice system. These savings can be redirected towards community development, education, and preventive measures, creating a more sustainable and effective approach to crime and justice. Restorative justice practices also promote long-term personal growth and ethical living for offenders. By fostering a sense of empathy, accountability, and ethical behavior, these practices help offenders develop the skills and mindset needed to lead productive and responsible lives. This personal growth is essential for successful reintegration into society and can lead to positive outcomes in various aspects of life, including employment, relationships, and community involvement. For example, an offender who has developed strong ethical principles through restorative justice practices is more likely to find stable employment, build positive relationships, and contribute to their community.

In addition to the immediate benefits for offenders and victims, restorative justice practices have long-term positive impacts on justice systems. By demonstrating the effectiveness of restorative approaches in promoting healing, reducing recidivism, and enhancing community well-being, these practices can inspire broader systemic changes. Policymakers and stakeholders may be encouraged to adopt restorative justice models more widely, shifting the focus from punitive measures to rehabilitative and restorative solutions. This systemic change can lead to a more just and compassionate criminal justice system that better serves the needs of all parties involved. The long-term impact of restorative justice practices also extends to the development of a more empathetic and ethical society. By promoting values such as empathy, accountability, and reconciliation, restorative justice helps cultivate a culture that prioritizes ethical behavior and mutual support. This cultural shift can influence various aspects of society, from how conflicts are resolved in schools and workplaces to how communities address social issues. By fostering a culture of empathy and accountability, restorative justice contributes to the development of a more just, compassionate, and resilient society.

20.5: Long-Term Impact on Justice Systems

The long-term impact of restorative justice practices on justice systems is profound and transformative, representing a shift from traditional punitive approaches to more holistic and compassionate methods of addressing crime and conflict. This paradigm shift not only benefits individual offenders and victims but also has far-reaching implications for communities and society as a whole. By emphasizing healing, accountability, and reconciliation, restorative justice practices can fundamentally alter the way justice is perceived and administered, leading to more effective and humane outcomes. One of the most significant long-term impacts of restorative justice is the potential to reduce recidivism rates. Traditional punitive systems often fail to address the underlying causes of criminal behavior, leading to a cycle of reoffending and repeated incarceration. Restorative justice, on the other hand, focuses on understanding and addressing these root causes, such as trauma, social inequities, and lack of support systems. By providing offenders with the tools and support they need to make meaningful changes in their lives, restorative justice can break the cycle of recidivism. Offenders who engage in restorative practices develop greater self-awareness, empathy, and personal responsibility, which are crucial for maintaining positive behavior in the long term. This reduction in recidivism not only benefits the offenders themselves but also enhances community safety and reduces the burden on the criminal justice system.

The integration of restorative justice practices into mainstream justice systems can lead to significant policy changes and systemic reforms. As the effectiveness of restorative justice becomes more widely recognized, policymakers and stakeholders may advocate for the incorporation of these practices into legislation and official protocols. This can include the establishment of restorative justice programs as a standard part of the criminal justice process, the allocation of funding and resources to support these programs, and the training of justice professionals in restorative principles and techniques. Such systemic changes can create a more balanced and equitable justice system that prioritizes rehabilitation and reconciliation over punishment and retribution. Restorative justice also has the potential to transform the culture within correctional facilities. Traditional correctional environments often emphasize control and discipline, which can exacerbate feelings of resentment and hopelessness among inmates. Restorative practices, by contrast, foster a culture of respect, empathy, and personal growth. By incorporating restorative circles, victim-offender dialogues, and community service projects into the daily routines of correctional facilities, these environments can become more supportive and conducive to rehabilitation. This cultural shift can lead to improved relationships between inmates and staff, reduced instances of violence and misconduct, and a more positive overall atmosphere within the facility.

The benefits of restorative justice extend beyond the individual and systemic levels to the broader community. Communities that embrace restorative practices often experience enhanced social cohesion and trust. By involving community members in the justice process, restorative justice fosters a sense of collective responsibility and mutual support. Community members who participate in restorative circles and dialogues gain a deeper understanding of the challenges faced by both offenders and victims, which can reduce stigma and promote empathy. This sense of community involvement and support is crucial for the successful reintegration of offenders, as it provides a network of resources and relationships that can help them navigate the challenges of reentry and maintain positive behavior. Restorative justice practices can also lead to economic benefits by reducing the costs associated with traditional punitive systems. Incarceration is expensive, requiring significant expenditures for facilities, staff, and related services. By reducing recidivism and providing alternatives to incarceration, restorative justice can lower these costs. Funds that would have been spent on maintaining high prison populations can be redirected towards education, healthcare, and community development initiatives. These investments can further support crime prevention and community well-being, creating a positive feedback loop that enhances the overall quality of life.

Moreover, restorative justice can influence the way future generations perceive and engage with the concept of justice. By promoting values such as empathy, accountability, and reconciliation, restorative justice can shape the attitudes and behaviors of young people, fostering a more compassionate and ethical society. Educational programs that incorporate restorative principles can teach students about conflict resolution, emotional intelligence, and the importance of making amends, preparing them to become responsible and empathetic citizens. This cultural shift towards a more restorative approach to justice can have lasting implications, as future generations carry these values into their personal and professional lives. The integration of restorative justice practices can also lead to a more holistic approach to addressing social issues. Restorative justice recognizes that crime is often a symptom of broader social problems, such as poverty, inequality, and lack of access to resources. By addressing these root causes, restorative justice can contribute to more comprehensive and sustainable solutions. For example, community-based restorative programs can collaborate with social services, educational institutions, and healthcare providers to address the underlying issues that contribute to criminal behavior. This interdisciplinary approach can create a more supportive and inclusive society, where individuals have the opportunities and resources they need to thrive.

In addition to its practical benefits, restorative justice offers a more humane and ethical framework for addressing crime. Traditional punitive systems often dehumanize offenders, reducing them to their worst actions and disregarding their potential for growth and change. Restorative justice, by contrast, acknowledges the inherent worth and dignity of every individual, recognizing that people are more than their mistakes. This humane approach fosters a sense of hope and possibility, encouraging offenders to take responsibility for their actions and commit to positive change. For victims, restorative justice provides a more compassionate and empowering experience, allowing them to be active participants in the justice process and to seek healing and closure on their own terms. The long-term impact of restorative justice also includes the potential for global influence. As more countries and communities recognize the benefits of restorative practices, these principles can be adopted and adapted in diverse cultural and legal contexts. International collaborations and exchanges can facilitate the sharing of best practices and innovative approaches, contributing to the global advancement of restorative justice. This international movement towards restorative justice can promote a more peaceful and just world, where the principles of empathy, accountability, and reconciliation are upheld across borders.

CHAPTER TWENTY-ONE

Mediation Techniques and the Middle Way

Contents

- Using the Middle Way in Conflict Resolution

- Practical Applications in Mediation

- Case Studies of Successful Mediation

- Benefits for Offenders and Communities

- Strategies for Integrating Mediation Techniques

21.1: Using the Middle Way in Conflict Resolution

The Middle Way, rooted in Buddhist philosophy, provides a profound framework for resolving conflicts by emphasizing balance, compassion, and wisdom. When applied to mediation, the Middle Way seeks to avoid extremes, fostering a harmonious and equitable resolution that considers the needs and perspectives of all parties involved. This approach aligns with the principles of restorative justice, which prioritizes healing and reconciliation over punishment and retribution. At its core, the Middle Way teaches that avoiding extremes and finding a balanced approach can lead to more sustainable and meaningful resolutions. In the context of mediation, this means navigating between rigid adherence to legalistic solutions and overly lenient compromises that fail to address the underlying issues. The mediator, embodying the Middle Way, seeks to facilitate a process where all parties feel heard and respected, guiding them towards a mutually acceptable solution that acknowledges their concerns and aspirations.

The Middle Way's emphasis on compassion is particularly crucial in mediation. Compassion, in this context, involves understanding the emotional and psychological dimensions of conflict. It requires the mediator to create a safe and empathetic space where participants can express their feelings without fear of judgment or retaliation. By fostering an atmosphere of compassion, the mediator helps the parties move beyond anger and blame, enabling them to explore deeper emotional truths and find common ground. This compassionate approach not only helps in resolving the immediate conflict but also promotes healing and reconciliation, laying the foundation for stronger relationships. Wisdom, another key component of the Middle Way, plays a vital role in mediation by providing the insight and clarity needed to navigate complex issues. Wisdom involves a deep understanding of the broader context in which the conflict occurs, including the social, cultural, and personal factors that influence the parties' perspectives. The mediator uses wisdom to guide the dialogue, helping participants see beyond their immediate grievances and consider the long-term implications of their actions. This broader perspective enables the parties to identify creative and sustainable solutions that address the root causes of the conflict, rather than merely treating its symptoms.

One practical aspect of applying the Middle Way in mediation is the concept of equanimity. Equanimity involves maintaining a calm and balanced state of mind, regardless of the emotional intensity of the conflict. For the mediator, equanimity means remaining neutral and impartial, avoiding any inclination to side with one party over the other. This balanced approach helps to build trust and credibility, as all participants feel that their perspectives are valued and considered. Equanimity also allows the mediator to manage the emotional dynamics of the mediation process, helping the parties stay focused on constructive dialogue rather than becoming entangled in their emotions. Non-attachment, another principle of the Middle Way, encourages participants to let go of rigid positions and open themselves to new possibilities. In mediation, non-attachment involves helping the parties move beyond their fixed demands and explore alternative solutions. The mediator can facilitate this process by encouraging curiosity and openness, prompting the participants to consider how different outcomes might serve their interests and values. This flexibility often leads to more innovative and satisfactory resolutions, as the parties are willing to adapt and compromise in ways that they might not have initially considered.

Reflective listening is a practical technique that embodies the principles of the Middle Way in mediation. Reflective listening involves actively and empathetically listening to each participant, reflecting back what they have said to ensure understanding and validation. This technique helps to build rapport and trust, as participants feel heard and respected. Reflective listening also encourages deeper self-reflection, as the parties hear their own words mirrored back to them, prompting them to consider their underlying motivations and feelings. By fostering a deeper understanding of themselves and each other, reflective listening helps to create a more collaborative and empathetic dialogue. Mindfulness, an essential practice in the Middle Way, is also integral to effective mediation. Mindfulness involves being fully present and attentive to the current moment, without judgment or distraction. For the mediator, mindfulness means being attuned to the subtle dynamics of the conversation, including non-verbal cues and underlying emotions. By practicing mindfulness, the mediator can create a calm and focused environment that supports thoughtful and respectful dialogue. Mindfulness also helps participants become more aware of their own thoughts and feelings, allowing them to engage in the mediation process with greater clarity and intention.

Another practical application of the Middle Way in mediation is the use of balanced agreements. A balanced agreement is one that addresses the needs and concerns of all parties, ensuring that the resolution is fair and equitable. The mediator guides the parties in crafting an agreement that reflects their shared values and goals, rather than simply imposing a compromise. This collaborative approach fosters a sense of ownership and commitment, as all participants feel that they have contributed to the solution. By focusing on balanced agreements, mediation guided by the Middle Way promotes sustainable and harmonious outcomes. The Middle Way also emphasizes the importance of context and interconnectedness in resolving conflicts. In mediation, this means considering the broader social and relational context in which the conflict occurs.

The mediator helps the parties understand how their actions affect each other and the wider community, encouraging them to consider the ripple effects of their decisions. This holistic perspective fosters a sense of shared responsibility and mutual respect, as participants recognize their interconnectedness and the impact of their actions on others. Finally, the Middle Way promotes the cultivation of ethical behavior in conflict resolution. In mediation, this involves encouraging the parties to act with integrity, honesty, and respect throughout the process. The mediator models ethical behavior, setting the tone for a respectful and constructive dialogue. By upholding ethical principles, mediation guided by the Middle Way fosters a culture of trust and accountability, creating a foundation for lasting peace and reconciliation.

21.2: Practical Applications in Mediation

Practical applications in mediation, when infused with the principles of the Middle Way, offer a robust framework for resolving conflicts effectively and compassionately. These applications are designed to foster mutual understanding, respect, and ethical behavior, creating a space where all parties can express their concerns and work collaboratively towards a resolution that reflects their shared values and goals. The techniques discussed here are essential tools for mediators who seek to implement the Middle Way in their practice, ensuring that the process is balanced, mindful, and transformative. A critical first step in mediation using the Middle Way is establishing a foundation of trust and safety. This involves setting clear guidelines and expectations for the process, ensuring that all participants feel secure and respected. The mediator begins by creating a welcoming and neutral environment, where each party feels heard and valued. This can include practical measures such as arranging the seating in a circle to promote equality, using neutral language, and actively listening without judgment. By fostering a sense of safety and trust, the mediator sets the stage for open and honest communication, which is essential for successful mediation.

One of the central techniques in mediation is fostering mutual understanding and respect. This can be achieved through reflective listening, where the mediator carefully listens to each party and then reflects back what they have heard. Reflective listening not only ensures that each participant feels understood but also helps to clarify and validate their experiences and emotions. For example, a mediator might say, "What I hear you saying is that you felt deeply hurt and betrayed by the actions of the other party. Is that correct?" This reflection helps to build empathy and rapport, as participants see that their feelings are acknowledged and respected. Reflective listening also encourages deeper self-awareness, as participants hear their own words echoed back to them, prompting them to consider their underlying motivations and feelings. Mindfulness is another essential practice in mediation, as it helps both the mediator and the participants stay present and focused. Mindfulness involves being fully aware of the present moment, without judgment or distraction. For the mediator, this means being attuned to the subtle dynamics of the conversation, including non-verbal cues and underlying emotions. By practicing mindfulness, the mediator can create a calm and focused environment that supports thoughtful and respectful dialogue. Mindfulness also helps participants become more aware of their own thoughts and feelings, allowing them to engage in the mediation process with greater clarity and intention. Techniques such as mindful breathing and guided meditation can be incorporated into the mediation process to enhance mindfulness and emotional regulation.

De-escalating conflicts and finding common ground are critical components of successful mediation. The mediator uses various techniques to manage and reduce tensions, such as establishing ground rules for respectful communication, encouraging the use of "I" statements to express personal experiences and feelings, and providing breaks if the discussion becomes too heated. For instance, instead of saying, "You always ignore my needs," a participant might be guided to say, "I feel ignored and unimportant when my needs are not considered." This shift in language helps to reduce defensiveness and promotes a more constructive dialogue. The mediator also helps the parties identify common interests and shared values, which can serve as a foundation for building mutually acceptable solutions. By focusing on what unites them rather than what divides them, participants can begin to see each other as collaborators rather than adversaries. Incorporating ethical principles into mediation is another key aspect of the Middle Way. This involves encouraging all parties to act with integrity, honesty, and respect throughout the process. The mediator models ethical behavior, setting the tone for a respectful and constructive dialogue. For example, the mediator might emphasize the importance of confidentiality, honesty in expressing one's feelings and needs, and a commitment to finding a fair and just resolution. By upholding these ethical principles, the mediator fosters a culture of trust and accountability, creating a foundation for lasting peace and reconciliation.

Building agreements that reflect ethical and balanced solutions is a practical application of the Middle Way in mediation. These agreements should address the needs and concerns of all parties, ensuring that the resolution is fair and equitable. The mediator guides the parties in crafting an agreement that reflects their shared values and goals, rather than simply imposing a compromise. This collaborative approach fosters a sense of ownership and commitment, as all participants feel that they have contributed to the solution. For example, an agreement might include specific actions that each party will take to address the harm caused and prevent future conflicts. These actions could involve community service, restitution, or participation in educational programs. By focusing on balanced agreements, mediation guided by the Middle Way promotes sustainable and harmonious outcomes. Another practical technique is the use of equanimity in mediation. Equanimity involves maintaining a calm and balanced state of mind, regardless of the emotional intensity of the conflict. For the mediator, equanimity means remaining neutral and impartial, avoiding any inclination to side with one party over the other. This balanced approach helps to build trust and credibility, as all participants feel that their perspectives are valued and considered. Equanimity also allows the mediator to manage the emotional dynamics of the mediation process, helping the parties stay focused on constructive dialogue rather than becoming entangled in their emotions. Techniques such as deep breathing, visualization, and centering exercises can help the mediator and participants maintain equanimity throughout the process.

Non-attachment is another principle of the Middle Way that can be effectively applied in mediation. Non-attachment involves helping the parties let go of rigid positions and open themselves to new possibilities. The mediator can facilitate this process by encouraging curiosity and openness, prompting the participants to consider how different outcomes might serve their interests and values. For example, the mediator might ask, "What would it look like if we found a solution that addressed both of your concerns? How might that change your relationship and your experience of this conflict?" This approach encourages flexibility and creativity, allowing the parties to explore a wider range of options and find solutions that they might not have initially considered. In practical terms, the mediator can use various tools to facilitate the mediation process. These tools include visual aids such as flip charts and whiteboards to map out the issues and possible solutions, timelines to understand the sequence of events leading to the conflict, and role-playing exercises to help participants see the situation from different perspectives. The mediator can also use questionnaires and surveys to gather information about the parties' needs, interests, and concerns, providing a structured way to organize and prioritize the issues at hand.

Another important aspect of practical mediation is follow-up and support. After reaching an agreement, the mediator should ensure that the parties have the resources and support they need to implement the agreed-upon actions. This might involve connecting them with community resources, providing ongoing mediation sessions to monitor progress, and offering additional training or education as needed. Follow-up sessions can help address any new issues that arise and reinforce the commitment to the agreed-upon solutions. By providing ongoing support, the mediator helps ensure that the resolution is sustainable and that the parties can continue to build a positive and respectful relationship. Practical applications in mediation using the principles of the Middle Way involve a range of techniques designed to foster mutual understanding, respect, and ethical behavior. Establishing trust and safety, practicing reflective listening, incorporating mindfulness, de-escalating conflicts, and building balanced agreements are all essential components of this approach. By maintaining equanimity, encouraging non-attachment, and using practical tools and follow-up support, the mediator can create a process that is balanced, compassionate, and transformative. These practical applications not only help resolve conflicts but also promote healing, reconciliation, and personal growth, contributing to a more harmonious and ethical society. Through dedication to the principles of the Middle Way, mediation becomes a powerful tool for creating lasting and meaningful resolutions.

21.3: Case Studies of Successful Mediation

Case studies of successful mediation highlight the transformative power of the Middle Way in resolving conflicts. Each case demonstrates the practical application of mediation techniques and the profound impact they can have on individuals and communities. These stories provide insights into how mediation can foster understanding, reconciliation, and lasting peace. Consider the case of the "Community Harmony Project" in a small town plagued by long-standing disputes between local businesses and residents. The conflict centered around noise pollution and environmental concerns caused by the expansion of a local manufacturing plant. The mediation process began with a series of facilitated dialogues that brought together business owners, residents, and local government representatives. The mediator used reflective listening and mindfulness practices to create a safe space for open communication. Each party was encouraged to share their experiences and concerns, fostering mutual understanding and empathy.

Through these dialogues, the business owners came to understand the significant impact of noise and pollution on the residents' quality of life. Conversely, the residents gained insight into the economic pressures faced by the businesses and the importance of the plant for local employment. The mediator guided the parties in exploring balanced solutions that addressed both environmental concerns and economic needs. The resulting agreement included measures such as noise-reduction technology, green spaces to buffer the plant from residential areas, and community involvement in monitoring environmental standards. This case illustrates how mediation can bridge divides, leading to solutions that respect and incorporate diverse perspectives. In another case, the "School Restorative Practices Initiative" dealt with a series of bullying incidents at a high school. The conflict involved multiple students and had created a toxic environment affecting the entire school community. The mediation process began with separate sessions for the victims and the offenders, allowing each group to express their feelings and experiences in a supportive setting. The mediator used role-playing and reflective listening to help the students understand the impact of their actions on each other.

Once a foundation of empathy and understanding was established, the mediator brought the groups together for a restorative circle. The students discussed the harm caused by the bullying and worked collaboratively to develop a code of conduct that emphasized respect, inclusion, and accountability. They also agreed to participate in regular peer-led workshops on empathy and conflict resolution. The school administration supported these initiatives by integrating restorative practices into the school's disciplinary policies. This case demonstrates how mediation can transform a hostile environment into a supportive community, promoting personal growth and mutual respect among students. The "Workplace Mediation Program" in a large corporation provides another example. The conflict arose between two departments over resource allocation, leading to decreased productivity and morale. The mediation process began with individual interviews to understand each department's concerns and goals. The mediator then facilitated a series of joint meetings, where the departments could discuss their issues openly and constructively.

Using techniques such as non-violent communication and mindfulness, the mediator helped the participants move beyond their entrenched positions. They identified common interests, such as improving overall efficiency and employee satisfaction. Together, they developed a resource-sharing plan that included clear guidelines and a conflict resolution mechanism for future disputes. The departments also agreed to regular cross-departmental meetings to foster better communication and collaboration. This case highlights how mediation can resolve complex organizational conflicts, enhancing cooperation and productivity. The "Neighborhood Mediation Project" addressed escalating tensions between long-term residents and recent immigrants in a suburban community. The conflict stemmed from cultural differences and misunderstandings, leading to a series of confrontations and complaints. The mediation process began with community workshops on cultural awareness and empathy. The mediator used storytelling and reflective listening to help the participants appreciate each other's perspectives.

The mediation sessions involved facilitated dialogues where residents and immigrants could voice their concerns and explore common ground. Through these discussions, they identified shared values, such as the desire for a safe and welcoming community. They worked together to organize cultural exchange events and create a neighborhood watch program that included members from both groups. The mediation process fostered mutual respect and cooperation, transforming a divided neighborhood into a united community. This case demonstrates the power of mediation to bridge cultural divides and build inclusive communities. In the "Family Mediation Service," a complex case involved a divorced couple in conflict over co-parenting arrangements. The mediation process began with separate sessions to understand each parent's concerns and aspirations for their children. The mediator then facilitated joint sessions, using techniques such as reflective listening and non-attachment to help the parents move beyond their animosity.

Through mindful dialogue, the parents began to recognize the importance of cooperation and stability for their children's well-being. They developed a co-parenting plan that included clear communication protocols, flexible scheduling, and a commitment to attend family therapy sessions. The agreement also involved the children in age-appropriate discussions about their needs and feelings. This case illustrates how mediation can support families in navigating post-divorce conflicts, fostering a cooperative and supportive co-parenting relationship. The "Environmental Mediation Initiative" tackled a dispute between a mining company and environmental activists over land use. The conflict had led to protests, legal battles, and community divisions. The mediation process began with separate sessions to understand each party's concerns and goals. The mediator used techniques such as equanimity and reflective listening to create a balanced and respectful dialogue.

Joint sessions focused on exploring the environmental impact of the mining operations and the economic benefits for the community. The mediator guided the parties in identifying sustainable practices that could minimize environmental harm while supporting economic development. The resulting agreement included commitments to reduce pollution, invest in local conservation projects, and establish a community advisory board to oversee environmental standards. This case demonstrates how mediation can address complex environmental conflicts, balancing economic and ecological concerns. In the "Healthcare Mediation Program," a conflict arose between a hospital administration and nursing staff over working conditions and patient care standards. The mediation process began with individual interviews to understand the perspectives of both parties. The mediator then facilitated joint meetings, using techniques such as non-violent communication and mindfulness to foster constructive dialogue.

Through these discussions, the administration and nursing staff identified common goals, such as improving patient care and ensuring a supportive work environment. They developed a plan that included better staffing ratios, regular staff wellness programs, and a mechanism for ongoing dialogue between staff and management. This case illustrates how mediation can resolve workplace conflicts in the healthcare sector, promoting better working conditions and patient outcomes. The "Youth Justice Mediation Project" dealt with a case involving a group of teenagers involved in vandalism. The mediation process began with separate sessions for the victims and the offenders, allowing each group to express their feelings and experiences. The mediator used role-playing and reflective listening to help the participants understand the impact of their actions.

Joint sessions involved restorative circles where the teenagers discussed the harm caused and worked collaboratively to develop a restitution plan. The plan included community service projects, participation in conflict resolution workshops, and ongoing mentorship from community leaders. This case demonstrates how mediation can support youth in taking responsibility for their actions and making positive contributions to their communities. Finally, the "Elder Care Mediation Program" addressed a dispute between family members over the care of an aging parent. The conflict involved disagreements over financial responsibilities, living arrangements, and caregiving duties. The mediation process began with separate sessions to understand each family member's concerns and aspirations. Joint sessions involved facilitated dialogues where the family members could explore their concerns and develop a collaborative care plan. The mediator used techniques such as reflective listening and non-attachment to help the participants move beyond their entrenched positions. The resulting agreement included clear financial arrangements, a schedule for caregiving duties, and a commitment to ongoing family meetings to address future concerns. This case illustrates how mediation can support families in navigating complex elder care issues, promoting cooperation and mutual support.

21.4: Benefits for Offenders and Communities

The benefits of mediation for offenders and communities are profound and multifaceted, extending well beyond the resolution of individual conflicts to promote long-term personal growth, social cohesion, and systemic improvements. Mediation, when guided by the principles of the Middle Way, fosters an environment of empathy, accountability, and mutual respect, which can transform the lives of offenders and enhance the well-being of entire communities. For offenders, mediation offers a unique opportunity for personal growth and rehabilitation that traditional punitive approaches often fail to provide. One of the most significant benefits is the development of empathy and emotional intelligence. Through the mediation process, offenders are encouraged to listen to the perspectives of their victims and understand the impact of their actions. This empathetic engagement helps offenders to see their behavior from a different viewpoint, fostering a sense of remorse and a genuine desire to make amends. For example, a young offender involved in a vandalism case might, through mediation, come to understand the emotional and financial impact of their actions on the victims, leading to a sincere apology and commitment to restitution.

Mediation also promotes personal accountability. Unlike traditional justice systems that may focus solely on punishment, mediation requires offenders to take responsibility for their actions and actively participate in finding solutions. This accountability is crucial for personal transformation, as it helps offenders move beyond a victim mentality and recognize their agency in making positive changes. For instance, an offender who has committed theft might, through mediation, agree to work to repay the stolen amount or engage in community service, thereby directly addressing the harm caused. Another significant benefit for offenders is the acquisition of conflict resolution and communication skills. Mediation provides a structured environment where offenders can learn and practice these skills, which are essential for maintaining healthy relationships and avoiding future conflicts. Techniques such as active listening, non-violent communication, and negotiation are integral to the mediation process. Offenders who develop these skills are better equipped to handle disputes constructively, reducing the likelihood of reoffending. For example, an offender who has been involved in domestic violence may, through mediation, learn effective communication strategies and anger management techniques that help them build healthier relationships.

The supportive and non-adversarial nature of mediation can also reduce stress and anxiety for offenders. Traditional court proceedings can be intimidating and confrontational, often exacerbating feelings of fear and defensiveness. Mediation, by contrast, emphasizes collaboration and mutual understanding, creating a more relaxed and supportive atmosphere. This environment helps offenders feel more at ease, allowing them to engage more openly and honestly in the process. For instance, an offender facing a workplace dispute may find mediation less stressful than a formal disciplinary hearing, leading to more constructive outcomes. For communities, the benefits of mediation are equally compelling. Mediation fosters social cohesion by promoting a culture of dialogue and mutual respect. When community members are involved in the mediation process, they are encouraged to engage with each other constructively and collaboratively. This engagement helps to build stronger relationships and a sense of shared responsibility for maintaining peace and harmony. For example, in a neighborhood dispute involving noise complaints, mediation can bring together residents to discuss their concerns and find mutually agreeable solutions, thereby strengthening community bonds.

Mediation also enhances community safety by addressing the root causes of conflict and reducing the likelihood of escalation. By providing a forum for open communication and problem-solving, mediation helps to resolve disputes before they become more serious and potentially violent. This proactive approach to conflict resolution can prevent incidents of crime and reduce the burden on law enforcement agencies. For instance, a mediation program that addresses conflicts between rival youth groups can help prevent gang violence and promote a safer community environment. Another benefit for communities is the promotion of restorative justice. Mediation emphasizes the importance of repairing harm and restoring relationships, rather than simply punishing offenders. This restorative approach helps to heal the wounds caused by crime and conflict, promoting long-term reconciliation and peace. For example, a community mediation program that deals with property disputes can help neighbors resolve their issues amicably, fostering a sense of goodwill and cooperation.

Mediation also provides economic benefits by reducing the costs associated with traditional legal proceedings. Court cases can be lengthy and expensive, consuming significant public resources. Mediation, by contrast, is often quicker and less costly, providing an efficient alternative for resolving disputes. These savings can be redirected towards other community needs, such as education, healthcare, and social services. For example, a community mediation center that resolves a large number of civil disputes can help reduce the caseload of local courts, freeing up resources for more serious cases. Furthermore, mediation promotes inclusivity and accessibility in the justice system. Traditional legal processes can be complex and inaccessible, particularly for marginalized and disadvantaged groups. Mediation, with its emphasis on dialogue and collaboration, can provide a more accessible and empowering alternative. This inclusivity helps to ensure that all community members have a voice in resolving conflicts and shaping their community. For instance, a mediation program that serves low-income neighborhoods can provide residents with an effective means of resolving disputes without the need for costly legal representation.

The long-term benefits of mediation for communities also include the development of a more just and equitable society. Mediation fosters a culture of fairness and respect, where conflicts are resolved through understanding and cooperation rather than coercion and punishment. This cultural shift can influence broader societal attitudes towards justice and conflict resolution, promoting a more compassionate and humane approach. For example, a school-based mediation program that teaches students about the principles of restorative justice can help cultivate a generation of young people who value empathy, accountability, and peaceful conflict resolution. In addition to these benefits, mediation can also contribute to systemic changes in the justice system. As the effectiveness of mediation becomes more widely recognized, there is potential for its principles and practices to be integrated into mainstream justice processes. This integration can lead to a more balanced and holistic approach to justice, where restorative and punitive measures complement each other.

For instance, courts that incorporate mediation into their procedures for certain types of cases can provide more comprehensive and effective resolutions that address both the legal and emotional dimensions of conflict. Overall, the benefits of mediation for offenders and communities are extensive and multifaceted. For offenders, mediation offers opportunities for personal growth, accountability, and skill development, fostering rehabilitation and reducing recidivism. For communities, mediation promotes social cohesion, safety, and restorative justice, enhancing the overall well-being of community members. The economic and systemic benefits further highlight the value of mediation as an effective and humane approach to conflict resolution. By embracing mediation and the principles of the Middle Way, justice systems can create a more compassionate, inclusive, and equitable society, where conflicts are resolved through understanding, empathy, and cooperation.

21.5: Strategies for Integrating Mediation Techniques

Integrating mediation techniques within various systems and structures, such as the criminal justice system, educational institutions, workplaces, and community organizations, requires a strategic and comprehensive approach. This integration not only ensures that mediation becomes a standard practice but also maximizes its effectiveness in promoting peace, resolving conflicts, and fostering a culture of understanding and cooperation. Here, we will explore the strategies for successfully incorporating mediation techniques, focusing on design, implementation, training, evaluation, and policy advocacy. The first step in integrating mediation techniques is the careful design of mediation programs tailored to the specific needs of the context in which they will be implemented. This involves a thorough needs assessment to understand the types of conflicts that typically arise and the existing mechanisms for resolving them. For example, in a school setting, common conflicts might include bullying, academic disputes, and interpersonal issues among students. In a workplace, conflicts might revolve around resource allocation, interpersonal relationships, and performance issues.

Designing an effective mediation program involves setting clear objectives, defining the scope of the program, and establishing protocols for referral and participation. It's essential to develop a framework that outlines the process from initial contact to the resolution of the conflict. This framework should include guidelines for intake, assessment, mediation sessions, follow-up, and evaluation. For instance, a school mediation program might include steps for teachers to refer students to mediation, initial interviews with the parties involved, mediation sessions facilitated by trained mediators, and follow-up meetings to ensure compliance with agreements. Once the mediation program is designed, the next step is its implementation. This requires the commitment and support of all stakeholders involved, including administrators, staff, participants, and the broader community. Effective implementation begins with raising awareness about the benefits of mediation and how it works. This can be achieved through informational sessions, workshops, and promotional materials that explain the purpose and process of mediation.

In schools, implementation might involve training teachers and students on the basics of mediation and conflict resolution. Creating a dedicated mediation team or appointing a mediation coordinator can help oversee the program's operations and ensure its smooth functioning. In workplaces, this might involve integrating mediation services within the human resources department and providing training to HR personnel and managers. The physical setup for mediation sessions is also crucial. Ensuring a private, neutral, and comfortable space for mediation can create an environment conducive to open and honest dialogue. The logistical aspects, such as scheduling sessions and maintaining confidentiality, should be meticulously planned to build trust and encourage participation.

Training is a cornerstone of effective mediation programs. Mediators need to be well-versed in mediation techniques, principles of the Middle Way, and the specific context in which they are operating. Comprehensive training programs should cover essential skills such as active listening, reflective listening, non-violent communication, and techniques for de-escalating conflicts. Training programs should be ongoing, providing opportunities for mediators to refine their skills and stay updated on best practices. For example, schools might offer regular workshops and training sessions for peer mediators and staff. In workplaces, professional development programs can include modules on mediation and conflict resolution, ensuring that managers and HR personnel are equipped to handle disputes effectively.

Role-playing and simulation exercises are valuable components of training, allowing mediators to practice and receive feedback in a controlled environment. This experiential learning helps mediators develop confidence and proficiency in their skills. Additionally, incorporating mindfulness and self-care practices in training can help mediators maintain their equanimity and emotional resilience. Monitoring and evaluating mediation programs are essential for ensuring their effectiveness and identifying areas for improvement. This involves collecting data on various aspects of the program, such as the number of mediations conducted, the types of conflicts addressed, the outcomes achieved, and participant satisfaction.

Evaluation methods can include surveys, interviews, and focus groups with participants, mediators, and other stakeholders. These methods provide valuable feedback on the strengths and weaknesses of the program, helping to identify best practices and areas needing adjustment. For example, a school mediation program might conduct surveys with students and teachers to assess the impact of mediation on school climate and conflict resolution skills. Data collected from evaluations can be used to make evidence-based improvements to the program. For instance, if evaluations reveal that certain types of conflicts are not being resolved effectively, additional training or adjustments to the mediation process might be needed. Regular evaluation ensures that the program remains responsive to the needs of the participants and continues to achieve its objectives.

Integrating mediation techniques on a broader scale often requires advocating for policy changes at various levels. This advocacy can involve working with policymakers, administrators, and community leaders to promote the benefits of mediation and secure support for its implementation. Effective advocacy strategies include presenting data on the success of mediation programs, sharing compelling case studies, and building coalitions of supporters. In the criminal justice system, for example, advocacy might involve promoting restorative justice policies that incorporate mediation as an alternative to traditional punitive measures. This can include lobbying for legislation that supports mediation programs, providing training for judges and law enforcement officers, and creating partnerships with community organizations to support mediation initiatives.

In educational settings, advocacy might focus on integrating mediation and conflict resolution into the curriculum and school policies. This can involve working with school boards, parent-teacher associations, and educational authorities to secure funding and resources for mediation programs. Highlighting the positive impact of mediation on student behavior, academic performance, and school climate can strengthen the case for its inclusion in school policies. In workplaces, advocating for mediation might involve engaging with business leaders, trade unions, and professional associations to promote the benefits of mediation for resolving workplace conflicts. Presenting data on the cost savings, improved employee morale, and enhanced productivity associated with mediation can help build support for its adoption.

Building partnerships and collaborations with various stakeholders is crucial for the successful integration of mediation techniques. These partnerships can provide additional resources, expertise, and support for mediation programs. Collaborating with community organizations, educational institutions, and professional associations can help create a network of support for mediation initiatives. For example, a community mediation center might partner with local schools to provide mediation services for students and training for teachers. This collaboration can help integrate mediation into the school's conflict resolution strategies and provide a valuable resource for addressing student conflicts. Similarly, partnerships with mental health organizations can provide mediators with access to counseling and support services for participants, enhancing the overall effectiveness of the mediation process.

Ultimately, the successful integration of mediation techniques requires creating a culture that values and supports mediation as a means of resolving conflicts. This involves promoting the principles of the Middle Way—balance, compassion, and wisdom—throughout the organization or community. Leadership plays a critical role in modeling these values and setting the tone for a culture of mediation. In schools, creating a culture of mediation might involve incorporating conflict resolution and empathy training into the curriculum, promoting peer mediation programs, and celebrating successes through school-wide recognition. In workplaces, this might involve integrating mediation into the company's core values, providing regular training for employees, and recognizing and rewarding effective conflict resolution.

Creating a culture of mediation also involves ongoing education and awareness-raising efforts. Regular workshops, seminars, and community events can help keep mediation principles and practices at the forefront, ensuring that they are embraced and sustained over time. Integrating mediation techniques within various systems and structures requires a strategic and comprehensive approach that encompasses design, implementation, training, evaluation, policy advocacy, partnerships, and culture-building. By following these strategies, organizations and communities can successfully incorporate mediation into their conflict resolution practices, promoting peace, understanding, and cooperation. The long-term benefits of such integration are profound, fostering personal growth, social cohesion, and systemic improvements that contribute to a more just and compassionate society. Through dedication to the principles of the Middle Way, mediation can become a transformative force, resolving conflicts and building bridges of understanding and respect.

—

CHAPTER TWENTY-TWO

Sangha – Building Supportive Communities

Contents

- Importance of Community Support in Rehabilitation

- Practical Techniques for Building Supportive Networks

- Case Studies of Successful Reintegration

- Benefits for Offenders and Communities

- Long-Term Impact on Justice Systems

22.1: Importance of Community Support in Rehabilitation

In the tapestry of human experience, the role of community is profound, serving as a cornerstone for individual growth, healing, and transformation. Within the framework of rehabilitation, the concept of community support becomes even more critical, acting as a vital element that can significantly influence the journey of offenders towards redemption and reintegration. Drawing from the rich traditions of Tibetan Buddhism, the notion of Sangha, or community, offers a blueprint for understanding how communal support can foster a sense of belonging, accountability, and personal responsibility among individuals seeking to rebuild their lives. The Sangha, in Buddhist practice, represents not just a gathering of individuals, but a supportive and nurturing environment where each member is committed to the growth and well-being of others. This collective endeavor towards spiritual and ethical development provides a model that can be applied to the rehabilitation of offenders. In a supportive community, individuals are not isolated in their struggles; instead, they are enveloped in an environment that encourages growth, offers guidance, and provides a safety net during their journey towards transformation.

For offenders, the presence of a supportive community can be a pivotal factor in their rehabilitation process. Community support serves as a buffer against the many challenges that offenders face upon reentry into society. These challenges often include stigma, lack of opportunities, and the temptation to revert to old habits. A community that actively supports rehabilitation helps mitigate these obstacles by providing a network of relationships that foster positive behavior and offer emotional and practical support. One of the primary benefits of community support is the creation of a sense of belonging. For many offenders, feelings of alienation and isolation are significant barriers to rehabilitation. A supportive community offers a sense of inclusion, where individuals feel valued and understood. This sense of belonging can be a powerful motivator for change, as individuals are more likely to engage in positive behavior when they feel connected to others who care about their well-being. In this context, the community acts as a mirror, reflecting back the potential for growth and transformation that exists within each individual.

Community support also enhances accountability and personal responsibility. In a supportive environment, individuals are encouraged to take ownership of their actions and their consequences. This process is facilitated through honest and open communication, where members of the community provide constructive feedback and hold each other accountable. This dynamic is reminiscent of the interdependent nature of the Sangha, where each member's progress is intertwined with the collective growth of the group. By fostering a culture of accountability, the community helps offenders develop a deeper sense of responsibility for their actions and a commitment to making amends. Moreover, a supportive community provides practical resources and opportunities that are essential for successful rehabilitation. These resources can include access to education, employment opportunities, housing, and healthcare. By addressing the practical needs of offenders, the community helps remove the barriers that often lead to recidivism. For example, a community that offers job training programs and employment support can help offenders develop new skills and secure stable employment, which is a critical factor in reducing reoffending rates. Similarly, access to healthcare services, including mental health support, can address underlying issues that contribute to criminal behavior.

The emotional and psychological support provided by a community is equally important. Rehabilitation is often a challenging and emotionally taxing process, requiring individuals to confront their past actions and make significant changes in their lives. A supportive community offers a network of relationships that provide encouragement, understanding, and empathy. This emotional support helps individuals build resilience and maintain their commitment to positive change, even in the face of setbacks. The community acts as a source of strength and motivation, reinforcing the belief that change is possible and that they are not alone in their journey. In addition to direct support, the presence of positive role models within the community can have a significant impact on offenders. Seeing others who have successfully navigated the path of rehabilitation and reintegration provides a tangible example of what is possible. These role models serve as mentors and guides, offering wisdom and insights based on their own experiences. Their success stories can inspire hope and determination, showing that change is achievable and that a positive future is within reach.

The community also plays a crucial role in fostering a culture of empathy and compassion. By creating opportunities for offenders to engage in community service and volunteer activities, the community helps them develop a sense of empathy and a commitment to giving back. These activities allow offenders to make amends for their past actions and contribute positively to society. They also help build bridges between offenders and other community members, breaking down barriers of stigma and mistrust. Through these interactions, offenders can demonstrate their commitment to change and earn the respect and acceptance of the community. The long-term impact of community support on the justice system is profound. By integrating community support into rehabilitation programs, the justice system can shift from a punitive approach to a more restorative and holistic model. This shift recognizes that addressing the root causes of criminal behavior and providing support for positive change is more effective in reducing recidivism and promoting public safety than solely relying on punishment. Community-based rehabilitation programs that emphasize support, accountability, and personal growth can lead to more sustainable outcomes and create a more just and compassionate society.

The importance of community support in rehabilitation cannot be overstated. Drawing from the principles of the Sangha in Tibetan Buddhism, a supportive community offers a nurturing environment that fosters a sense of belonging, accountability, and personal responsibility. It provides practical resources, emotional support, and positive role models that are essential for successful rehabilitation. By fostering a culture of empathy and compassion, the community helps offenders make amends and contribute positively to society. The integration of community support into the justice system represents a transformative approach that promotes healing, growth, and long-term public safety. Through the collective efforts of the community, offenders can find the support they need to rebuild their lives and become contributing members of society, embodying the principles of the Middle Way in their journey towards redemption and reintegration.

22.2: Practical Techniques for Building Supportive Networks

Building supportive networks is crucial for the successful reintegration of offenders into society, providing the foundation for sustainable change and long-term rehabilitation. Practical techniques for building these networks involve creating structured programs that offer emotional, social, and practical support, fostering an environment where offenders can thrive. By leveraging the principles of the Middle Way and drawing from Buddhist concepts of community (Sangha), these techniques emphasize balance, empathy, and ethical behavior, promoting a holistic approach to rehabilitation. One effective technique for building supportive networks is establishing peer support groups. These groups consist of individuals who have shared similar experiences and can offer mutual support and understanding. Peer support groups provide a safe space for offenders to discuss their challenges, share their successes, and receive encouragement from others who understand their journey. The sense of camaraderie and mutual support within these groups helps reduce feelings of isolation and stigma, fostering a sense of belonging and acceptance. For example, a peer support group for individuals recovering from substance abuse can offer a platform for sharing coping strategies, discussing triggers, and celebrating milestones, creating a network of support that reinforces positive behavior.

Mentorship programs are another powerful tool for building supportive networks. These programs pair offenders with mentors who can provide guidance, support, and inspiration. Mentors, often individuals who have successfully navigated the path of rehabilitation themselves, offer valuable insights and practical advice based on their own experiences. They serve as role models, demonstrating that change is possible and providing a tangible example of success. Mentorship programs help offenders set goals, develop new skills, and build confidence, creating a structured support system that encourages personal growth and accountability. For instance, a mentorship program for young offenders might include weekly meetings with mentors who assist with educational and career planning, provide emotional support, and help navigate the challenges of reintegration. Creating opportunities for community service and involvement is another key technique for building supportive networks. Community service projects allow offenders to make positive contributions to society, fostering a sense of purpose and connection. These projects can range from environmental conservation efforts to volunteering at local shelters or community centers. By participating in community service, offenders can demonstrate their commitment to change, build new relationships, and develop a sense of pride and accomplishment. This involvement helps break down barriers of stigma and mistrust, as community members witness the positive impact of the offenders' contributions. For example, an offender participating in a community garden project not only helps beautify the neighborhood but also builds relationships with other volunteers, creating a network of support and mutual respect.

Fostering trust and cooperation within communities is essential for building supportive networks. This involves creating opportunities for dialogue and collaboration, where community members can work together towards common goals. Techniques such as restorative circles and community dialogues provide a platform for open communication, allowing individuals to express their feelings, address conflicts, and build consensus. These processes help to build trust and understanding, promoting a sense of shared responsibility and cooperation. For instance, a restorative circle involving offenders, victims, and community members can help address the harm caused by a crime, facilitate healing, and create a plan for restitution that benefits all parties involved. Incorporating mindfulness and ethical practices in community building is another effective technique. Mindfulness practices, such as meditation and mindful breathing, help individuals develop greater self-awareness, emotional regulation, and empathy. These practices can be integrated into support group meetings, community service projects, and mentorship sessions, creating a culture of mindfulness and compassion. Ethical practices, guided by principles such as honesty, respect, and accountability, help to create a supportive and respectful environment. For example, a community support group might begin each meeting with a mindfulness exercise, followed by a discussion on ethical behavior and the importance of integrity in daily interactions.

Sustaining long-term community support requires ongoing efforts to maintain and strengthen the network of relationships. This involves regular follow-up meetings, continuous training for mentors and support group leaders, and ongoing evaluation of the support programs. Follow-up meetings provide an opportunity for individuals to check in, discuss their progress, and address any new challenges that arise. Continuous training ensures that mentors and support group leaders are equipped with the skills and knowledge needed to effectively support offenders. Ongoing evaluation helps to identify areas for improvement and ensure that the support programs are meeting the needs of the participants. For example, a community support program might conduct quarterly evaluations to gather feedback from participants, assess the effectiveness of the support provided, and make necessary adjustments to enhance the program. Another practical technique for building supportive networks is the development of resource centers that provide access to essential services and support. These centers can offer a range of services, including job training, educational programs, mental health counseling, and legal assistance. By centralizing these resources, offenders can easily access the support they need to address various aspects of their rehabilitation. Resource centers also serve as hubs for community activities and events, fostering a sense of community and belonging. For instance, a resource center might offer workshops on financial literacy, job fairs, and support group meetings, creating a comprehensive support network that addresses the diverse needs of offenders.

Collaboration with community organizations and local businesses is another effective technique for building supportive networks. Partnerships with organizations that provide housing, employment, and educational opportunities can enhance the support available to offenders. Local businesses can play a crucial role by offering job training and employment opportunities, helping offenders build new skills and achieve financial stability. These collaborations create a network of support that extends beyond the immediate community, providing offenders with access to a broader range of resources and opportunities. For example, a partnership between a community support program and a local construction company might provide job training and employment for offenders, helping them develop valuable skills and gain stable employment. Creating a culture of support and inclusivity within the community is essential for the success of these networks. This involves promoting values such as empathy, compassion, and mutual respect, and encouraging community members to actively participate in support activities. Public awareness campaigns, community events, and educational programs can help to foster a culture of inclusivity and support. For example, a community event celebrating the successes of rehabilitated offenders can help to break down stigma and promote a sense of unity and support. Educational programs that teach the principles of restorative justice and the importance of community support can help to build a more inclusive and supportive community.

22.3: Case Studies of Successful Reintegration

The transformative power of community support in the reintegration of offenders into society is evident in numerous case studies that highlight the effectiveness of supportive networks in fostering positive change. These cases illustrate how structured support systems, grounded in empathy, accountability, and practical assistance, can lead to successful reintegration and personal transformation. By examining these diverse examples, we can gain a deeper understanding of the practical application and long-term benefits of community support in the rehabilitation process. One compelling case is the "Restorative Justice Reintegration Project" in a rural town in the United States. This project focused on young adults who had been involved in non-violent offenses and faced significant barriers to reintegration due to stigma and limited opportunities. The program established a comprehensive support network that included peer mentoring, community service, and job training. Each participant was paired with a mentor who had successfully reintegrated into society, providing guidance, support, and a positive role model. The program also collaborated with local businesses to offer job training and employment opportunities, helping participants develop skills and gain financial independence.

One participant, Alex, had been convicted of theft and struggled with finding employment due to his criminal record. Through the program, Alex received mentorship from John, a former offender who had turned his life around and become a successful entrepreneur. John provided Alex with valuable insights and practical advice on overcoming obstacles and building a positive future. Alex also participated in a community service project, helping to renovate a local community center. This experience not only allowed him to make amends for his past actions but also helped him build new relationships and gain a sense of purpose. Through the job training component of the program, Alex secured employment with a local construction company, where he continued to receive support and encouragement. Over time, Alex rebuilt his life, gaining confidence and becoming an active member of the community. This case demonstrates the power of a supportive network in transforming the lives of offenders and promoting successful reintegration. In another case, the "Urban

Reintegration Initiative" in a major city addressed the challenges faced by former gang members seeking to leave behind a life of violence and crime. The initiative focused on providing a holistic support system that included housing assistance, educational opportunities, mental health services, and community engagement. Participants were given access to safe housing, removing them from environments that perpetuated criminal behavior. They also received support in completing their education, with many enrolling in GED programs or vocational training courses.

One participant, Maria, had been involved in gang activities from a young age and faced numerous barriers to reintegration, including a lack of education and stable housing. The initiative provided her with a safe place to live and the opportunity to enroll in a vocational training program. Maria also received counseling to address the trauma and mental health issues that had contributed to her involvement in gang activities. Through community engagement activities, such as volunteering at local schools and community centers, Maria developed a sense of belonging and purpose. She built positive relationships with community members and found mentors who supported her journey towards change. Over time, Maria completed her vocational training and secured a job as a dental assistant. Her story highlights the importance of addressing the comprehensive needs of offenders and the role of community support in facilitating successful reintegration. The "Faith-Based Reintegration Program" in a mid-sized town provides another example of the impact of supportive networks. This program, run by a local religious organization, focused on providing spiritual and practical support to offenders reentering society. The program offered a range of services, including spiritual counseling, job placement assistance, and community service opportunities. Participants were also connected with faith-based mentors who provided guidance and support throughout their reintegration journey.

One participant, Jamal, had been incarcerated for drug-related offenses and faced significant challenges in finding employment and rebuilding his life. Through the program, Jamal received spiritual counseling that helped him find a sense of peace and purpose. He was also paired with a mentor, Reverend Davis, who provided ongoing support and encouragement. Reverend Davis helped Jamal secure a job at a local grocery store and connected him with a support group for individuals recovering from addiction. Jamal also participated in community service projects, such as organizing food drives and helping with church events. These activities allowed him to give back to the community and build positive relationships. Over time, Jamal rebuilt his life, becoming an active member of his church and community. This case illustrates the role of faith-based support in fostering successful reintegration and personal transformation. The "Youth Offender Support Network" in a suburban community focused on providing comprehensive support to young offenders reentering society. The program offered a range of services, including educational support, mental health counseling, peer mentoring, and recreational activities. Participants were given the opportunity to complete their education, receive counseling to address underlying issues, and engage in positive activities that promoted personal growth and social integration.

One participant, Sarah, had been involved in a series of petty crimes and faced significant challenges due to her family background and lack of support. The program provided her with a mentor, Jessica, who had successfully navigated similar challenges and served as a positive role model. Jessica provided Sarah with guidance, support, and encouragement, helping her set and achieve her goals. Sarah also received educational support, allowing her to complete her high school diploma and enroll in a community college. Through recreational activities, such as sports and arts programs, Sarah developed new skills and built positive relationships with her peers. She also received counseling to address the trauma and mental health issues that had contributed to her criminal behavior. Over time, Sarah rebuilt her life, gaining confidence and becoming an active member of her community. This case demonstrates the importance of comprehensive support in fostering successful reintegration and personal growth. The "Veterans Reintegration Project" focused on supporting military veterans who had been involved in the criminal justice system. The project provided a range of services, including housing assistance, job training, mental health counseling, and peer support. Participants were connected with fellow veterans who provided guidance and support, helping them navigate the challenges of reintegration.

One participant, Mike, a former soldier who had struggled with PTSD and substance abuse, found himself in the criminal justice system. The Veterans Reintegration Project provided him with housing, job training, and mental health services. He was paired with a mentor, Tom, a fellow veteran who had faced similar struggles and successfully reintegrated into society. Tom provided Mike with ongoing support and encouragement, helping him navigate the challenges of rebuilding his life. Mike also participated in group counseling sessions with other veterans, where he received support and built positive relationships. Through the job training component of the program, Mike secured employment as a mechanic, a field he had experience in from his military service. Over time, Mike rebuilt his life, gaining stability and becoming an active member of his community. This case highlights the importance of peer support and comprehensive services in facilitating successful reintegration for veterans. The "Indigenous Community Reintegration Program" in Canada focused on providing culturally appropriate support to Indigenous offenders reentering society. The program offered a range of services, including cultural healing practices, job training, educational support, and community engagement. Participants were given the opportunity to reconnect with their cultural heritage and receive support from Indigenous mentors and community leaders.

One participant, Leah, had been involved in the criminal justice system from a young age and faced significant challenges due to her disconnection from her cultural roots and lack of support. The program provided her with access to cultural healing practices, such as traditional ceremonies and counseling from Elders. Leah was also paired with a mentor, an Indigenous woman who had successfully navigated similar challenges and served as a positive role model. The mentor provided Leah with guidance, support, and encouragement, helping her reconnect with her cultural heritage and set goals for her future. Leah also received educational support, allowing her to complete her high school diploma and enroll in a vocational training program. Through community engagement activities, such as participating in cultural events and volunteering at local organizations, Leah built positive relationships and developed a sense of belonging. Over time, Leah rebuilt her life, gaining confidence and becoming an active member of her community. This case demonstrates the importance of culturally appropriate support and the role of community in facilitating successful reintegration for Indigenous offenders.

22.4: Benefits for Offenders and Communities

The benefits of community support for offenders and communities are extensive and multifaceted, reflecting the profound impact that a supportive network can have on the rehabilitation and reintegration process. These benefits extend beyond the immediate individuals involved, fostering broader social cohesion, reducing recidivism, and promoting a more just and compassionate society. Understanding these benefits in depth helps to appreciate the transformative power of community support and underscores the importance of integrating such approaches into our justice systems. One of the most significant benefits for offenders is the enhancement of emotional and psychological well-being. The process of reintegration can be daunting and fraught with challenges, including dealing with the stigma of a criminal record, overcoming personal guilt and shame, and facing practical barriers such as finding employment and stable housing. Community support provides a crucial emotional safety net, offering encouragement, understanding, and empathy. This emotional support helps to mitigate feelings of isolation and despair, fostering a sense of belonging and acceptance. For instance, participation in support groups and mentorship programs can provide offenders with a platform to share their experiences, receive feedback, and build relationships with individuals who understand their struggles.

In addition to emotional support, community networks often provide practical assistance that is essential for successful reintegration. This includes access to resources such as job training, educational opportunities, housing assistance, and healthcare services. By addressing these practical needs, community support helps to remove the barriers that often lead to recidivism. For example, job training programs can equip offenders with new skills, enhancing their employability and providing a pathway to financial stability. Housing assistance programs can ensure that offenders have a safe and stable place to live, reducing the risk of returning to environments that may contribute to criminal behavior. Another critical benefit of community support for offenders is the development of a sense of accountability and personal responsibility. In a supportive community, individuals are encouraged to take ownership of their actions and work towards making amends. This process is facilitated through open communication and constructive feedback from community members, mentors, and peers. By fostering a culture of accountability, community support helps offenders develop a deeper understanding of the impact of their actions on others and encourages them to make positive changes in their behavior. For example, participation in restorative justice circles can provide offenders with the opportunity to hear directly from their victims, fostering empathy and a commitment to restitution.

The role of positive role models within the community is also significant. Offenders who interact with individuals who have successfully navigated the path of rehabilitation and reintegration are more likely to be inspired and motivated to change. These role models serve as tangible examples of what is possible, offering guidance, support, and practical advice based on their own experiences. This mentorship can be particularly impactful for young offenders, who may lack positive influences in their lives. For instance, a young offender mentored by a former gang member who has turned their life around can receive valuable insights into overcoming challenges and building a positive future. For communities, the benefits of supporting offenders' reintegration are profound. One of the most notable benefits is the strengthening of social cohesion. When communities actively participate in the rehabilitation process, they foster a sense of collective responsibility and mutual support. This engagement helps to build stronger relationships and trust among community members, creating a more cohesive and resilient community. For example, community service projects that involve offenders working alongside other residents can help break down barriers and build bridges of understanding and cooperation.

Community support also contributes to reducing recidivism rates, which has significant implications for public safety and resource allocation. Offenders who receive comprehensive support are less likely to reoffend, as they are equipped with the tools and resources needed to build a stable and law-abiding life. This reduction in recidivism not only enhances public safety but also reduces the burden on the criminal justice system, freeing up resources that can be redirected towards prevention and rehabilitation efforts. For instance, a community that invests in support programs for offenders can see a decrease in crime rates and a reduction in the costs associated with incarceration and law enforcement. The economic benefits of community support extend beyond the reduction in recidivism rates. By providing offenders with opportunities for education, job training, and employment, communities can enhance the economic prospects of individuals and contribute to the overall economic health of the community. Offenders who gain stable employment and financial independence are more likely to contribute positively to the local economy, pay taxes, and support their families. This economic stability also reduces the likelihood of reoffending, creating a virtuous cycle of positive outcomes. For example, a community that supports offenders in gaining employment in local businesses not only helps individuals rebuild their lives but also strengthens the local economy.

Community support also fosters a culture of empathy, compassion, and restorative justice. By involving community members in the rehabilitation process, these support networks promote a deeper understanding of the factors that contribute to criminal behavior and the importance of providing opportunities for change. This cultural shift can lead to more humane and effective approaches to justice, where the focus is on healing and restoration rather than punishment and retribution. For instance, a community that embraces restorative justice practices, such as victim-offender mediation and restorative circles, can create a more compassionate and just environment that benefits all members. The long-term impact of community support on justice systems is transformative. By integrating community support into rehabilitation programs, justice systems can move towards a more restorative and holistic model that addresses the root causes of criminal behavior and promotes long-term positive change. This shift can lead to more sustainable outcomes, reducing recidivism rates and enhancing public safety. For example, justice systems that incorporate community support programs into their standard practices can create a more balanced approach that combines accountability with opportunities for rehabilitation and reintegration.

Furthermore, the benefits of community support extend to the families of offenders. Families often bear the brunt of the consequences of criminal behavior, experiencing emotional, financial, and social strain. Community support programs that include family members in the rehabilitation process can provide much-needed support and resources, helping families to heal and rebuild their lives. For instance, family counseling and support groups can help families address the trauma and stress associated with having a loved one involved in the criminal justice system, fostering resilience and unity.

22.5: Long-Term Impact on Justice Systems

The long-term impact of community support on justice systems is profound and far-reaching, representing a paradigm shift from punitive measures to restorative and rehabilitative approaches. This shift is not merely a theoretical or philosophical change but one that manifests in tangible benefits for individuals, communities, and society at large. By embedding community support into the fabric of justice systems, we can create a more humane, effective, and sustainable model of justice that promotes healing, accountability, and reintegration. One of the most significant long-term impacts of integrating community support into justice systems is the reduction in recidivism rates. Traditional punitive approaches often fail to address the underlying causes of criminal behavior, leading to high rates of reoffending. Community support, on the other hand, focuses on rehabilitation and reintegration, providing offenders with the tools and resources they need to build a stable and law-abiding life. This approach addresses the root causes of criminal behavior, such as lack of education, unemployment, substance abuse, and mental health issues. By providing comprehensive support, including job training, educational opportunities, counseling, and mentorship, community-based programs can significantly reduce the likelihood of reoffending. For instance, long-term studies have shown that offenders who participate in community support programs are less likely to return to prison compared to those who do not receive such support.

The economic benefits of community support programs are also substantial. Incarceration is an expensive proposition, with costs that include housing, feeding, and supervising inmates, as well as the broader social costs associated with lost productivity and the impact on families. By reducing recidivism and promoting successful reintegration, community support programs can lead to significant cost savings for the justice system and society as a whole. These savings can be redirected towards preventive measures, education, healthcare, and other social services that further contribute to the well-being of the community. For example, a cost-benefit analysis of community support programs might reveal that every dollar invested in rehabilitation and reintegration yields multiple dollars in savings by reducing the need for incarceration and the associated social costs. Community support also contributes to enhanced public safety. When offenders are successfully reintegrated into society, they are less likely to engage in criminal behavior, leading to lower crime rates and safer communities. This enhanced safety is a direct result of the comprehensive support that addresses the factors contributing to criminal behavior. For example, a community support program that provides job training and employment opportunities can help offenders achieve financial stability, reducing the temptation to engage in illegal activities. Similarly, programs that offer mental health counseling and substance abuse treatment can address underlying issues that may lead to criminal behavior, promoting long-term stability and reducing the risk of reoffending.

The integration of community support into justice systems also fosters a more compassionate and humane approach to justice. Traditional punitive measures often dehumanize offenders, reducing them to their worst actions and failing to recognize their potential for growth and change. Community support programs, by contrast, emphasize the inherent worth and dignity of every individual, recognizing that people are more than their mistakes. This humane approach fosters a sense of hope and possibility, encouraging offenders to take responsibility for their actions and commit to positive change. For instance, restorative justice programs that involve victims and community members in the rehabilitation process can help offenders understand the impact of their actions, fostering empathy and a commitment to making amends. This compassionate approach not only benefits offenders but also contributes to a more just and equitable society. Another long-term impact of community support is the promotion of social cohesion and community resilience. When communities actively participate in the rehabilitation process, they foster a sense of collective responsibility and mutual support. This engagement helps to build stronger relationships and trust among community members, creating a more cohesive and resilient community. For example, community service projects that involve offenders working alongside other residents can help break down barriers and build bridges of understanding and cooperation. These collaborative efforts can lead to lasting positive relationships and a stronger sense of community.

The positive ripple effects of community support extend to families and future generations. Families often bear the brunt of the consequences of criminal behavior, experiencing emotional, financial, and social strain. Community support programs that include family members in the rehabilitation process can provide much-needed support and resources, helping families to heal and rebuild their lives. For instance, family counseling and support groups can help families address the trauma and stress associated with having a loved one involved in the criminal justice system, fostering resilience and unity. Additionally, when offenders successfully reintegrate into society, they can serve as positive role models for their children and other family members, breaking the cycle of criminal behavior and promoting a brighter future for the next generation. The long-term impact on justice systems also includes the potential for systemic change. As the effectiveness of community support programs becomes more widely recognized, there is potential for these principles and practices to be integrated into mainstream justice processes. This integration can lead to a more balanced and holistic approach to justice, where restorative and punitive measures complement each other. For example, courts that incorporate mediation and restorative justice practices into their procedures can provide more comprehensive and effective resolutions that address both the legal and emotional dimensions of conflict. This systemic change can create a more just and compassionate justice system that better serves the needs of all parties involved.

Furthermore, the principles and practices of community support can inspire broader societal changes. By promoting values such as empathy, accountability, and mutual support, these programs can influence attitudes and behaviors beyond the justice system. Educational programs that incorporate restorative justice principles can teach students about the importance of empathy and conflict resolution, preparing them to become responsible and empathetic citizens. Similarly, workplace programs that emphasize ethical behavior and mutual support can create more positive and productive work environments. These broader societal changes can contribute to a more compassionate and just society, where conflicts are resolved through understanding and cooperation rather than punishment and retribution. The long-term impact of community support also includes the potential for global influence. As more countries and communities recognize the benefits of restorative and rehabilitative approaches, these principles can be adopted and adapted in diverse cultural and legal contexts. International collaborations and exchanges can facilitate the sharing of best practices and innovative approaches, contributing to the global advancement of restorative justice. For example, countries that have successfully implemented community support programs can share their experiences and insights with other countries, helping to promote a more just and compassionate world.

CHAPTER TWENTY-THREE

Healing Trauma through Buddhist Practices

Contents

- Techniques for Addressing Trauma in Offenders

- Benefits of Buddhist Practices for Healing

- Case Studies of Trauma Healing Programs

- Long-Term Impact on Offender Rehabilitation

- Strategies for Implementing Trauma Healing Practices

23.1: Techniques for Addressing Trauma in Offenders

Addressing trauma in offenders through Buddhist practices involves a deep understanding of the human mind and its capacity for healing. Trauma often manifests as a profound sense of disconnection, affecting an individual's thoughts, emotions, and behaviors. Buddhist practices offer a path to reconnecting with oneself, fostering a sense of inner peace and resilience. Techniques such as mindfulness meditation, loving-kindness meditation, compassion practice, and the application of the Four Noble Truths provide practical tools for addressing trauma and promoting healing. Mindfulness meditation, at its core, involves paying attention to the present moment without judgment. This practice helps individuals become aware of their thoughts, emotions, and physical sensations, allowing them to observe these experiences with curiosity and compassion. For offenders, mindfulness meditation can be a powerful tool for managing the symptoms of trauma, such as anxiety, hypervigilance, and emotional numbness. By cultivating a mindful awareness, offenders can begin to recognize and understand their trauma responses, creating a space for healing and transformation. For example, an offender who practices mindfulness meditation might notice the physical tension in their body when recalling a traumatic event, allowing them to breathe deeply and release this tension rather than becoming overwhelmed by it.

Loving-kindness meditation, or Metta, involves generating feelings of love and compassion towards oneself and others. This practice is particularly beneficial for individuals who have experienced trauma, as it helps to counteract the feelings of worthlessness, guilt, and shame that often accompany traumatic experiences. Through loving-kindness meditation, offenders can learn to extend compassion to themselves, recognizing their inherent worth and capacity for change. This self-compassion can be transformative, fostering a sense of inner strength and resilience. For instance, an offender practicing loving-kindness meditation might begin by silently repeating phrases such as "May I be happy, may I be healthy, may I be safe," gradually extending these wishes to others, including those they have harmed and those who have harmed them. This practice helps to soften the heart and dissolve the barriers of resentment and anger, paving the way for healing and reconciliation. The practice of compassion, or Karuna, involves developing a deep empathy for the suffering of oneself and others. In the context of trauma healing, compassion practice helps offenders to acknowledge their pain without becoming consumed by it, fostering a sense of connection and shared humanity. By recognizing the universality of suffering, offenders can begin to transform their pain into a source of empathy and compassion for others. This shift in perspective can be particularly powerful in the rehabilitation process, as it encourages offenders to take responsibility for their actions and seek to make amends. For example, an offender who practices compassion might start to see their victims not as enemies, but as fellow human beings who have also experienced pain and suffering. This realization can inspire a genuine desire to make reparations and contribute positively to the community.

The Four Noble Truths, a fundamental teaching in Buddhism, provide a framework for understanding and alleviating suffering. The First Noble Truth acknowledges the existence of suffering, which is an inherent part of human life. For offenders, this truth helps to validate their experiences of trauma and suffering, offering a sense of acceptance and understanding. The Second Noble Truth identifies the causes of suffering, often rooted in attachment, aversion, and ignorance. By exploring these causes, offenders can gain insights into the underlying factors that contribute to their trauma responses and criminal behavior. The Third Noble Truth offers hope, teaching that it is possible to overcome suffering by letting go of these harmful patterns. The Fourth Noble Truth outlines the path to liberation through ethical living, meditation, and wisdom. By following this path, offenders can cultivate a more balanced and peaceful mind, fostering a sense of inner freedom and resilience. Mindful breathing and body awareness practices are also integral to addressing trauma. These practices involve bringing attention to the breath and the sensations in the body, helping individuals to ground themselves in the present moment. For offenders, mindful breathing can be a simple yet powerful tool for managing stress and anxiety.

By focusing on the breath, individuals can create a sense of calm and stability, even in the midst of difficult emotions. Body awareness practices help offenders to reconnect with their bodies, which may have been numbed or dissociated due to trauma. By becoming attuned to bodily sensations, individuals can learn to recognize and respond to their needs in a compassionate and caring way. For instance, an offender who practices body awareness might notice tension in their shoulders or a knot in their stomach, using this awareness as a cue to practice relaxation techniques or seek support. These Buddhist practices are not just theoretical concepts but are grounded in practical application and have been shown to be effective in various settings. In prisons and rehabilitation centers, mindfulness meditation programs have been implemented with promising results. Participants often report reductions in anxiety, depression, and PTSD symptoms, as well as improvements in emotional regulation and overall well-being. Loving-kindness and compassion practices have also been integrated into therapeutic settings, helping individuals to develop a more compassionate relationship with themselves and others. The principles of the Four Noble Truths provide a philosophical foundation for understanding and addressing the root causes of suffering, guiding individuals on a path of healing and transformation.

23.2: Benefits of Buddhist Practices for Healing

The benefits of Buddhist practices for healing trauma are profound and multifaceted, offering offenders a path to recovery that is both compassionate and transformative. By engaging with these practices, individuals can experience significant improvements in their emotional and psychological well-being, develop greater self-awareness and self-compassion, and cultivate empathy and improved relationships. The holistic nature of Buddhist practices addresses not only the symptoms of trauma but also the underlying causes, promoting long-term healing and personal growth. One of the primary benefits of Buddhist practices is the reduction in anxiety, stress, and PTSD symptoms. Mindfulness meditation, a cornerstone of Buddhist practice, involves paying attention to the present moment without judgment. This practice helps individuals to observe their thoughts and feelings without becoming overwhelmed by them, fostering a sense of calm and stability. For offenders dealing with trauma, mindfulness meditation can be particularly effective in managing symptoms such as hypervigilance, intrusive thoughts, and emotional numbness. Regular mindfulness practice can help to lower the body's stress response, reducing the levels of cortisol and other stress hormones. This physiological shift supports a more relaxed and balanced state of mind, enabling individuals to navigate their emotions more effectively.

Loving-kindness meditation, or Metta, offers another significant benefit by fostering emotional healing and resilience. This practice involves generating feelings of love and compassion towards oneself and others, which can be incredibly therapeutic for individuals who have experienced trauma. Trauma often leaves individuals with a diminished sense of self-worth and pervasive feelings of guilt and shame. Loving-kindness meditation helps to counteract these negative self-perceptions by encouraging individuals to extend compassion towards themselves, recognizing their inherent worth and humanity. This self-compassion can be a powerful antidote to the self-criticism and negative self-talk that often accompany trauma. As individuals cultivate a sense of kindness towards themselves, they also become more resilient in the face of challenges, better able to cope with difficult emotions and experiences. The practice of compassion, or Karuna, enhances emotional regulation and fosters empathy. Compassion practice involves developing a deep understanding and empathy for the suffering of oneself and others. This practice helps individuals to acknowledge their pain without becoming consumed by it, fostering a sense of connection and shared humanity. For offenders, developing compassion can lead to a profound shift in perspective, enabling them to see their victims not as adversaries but as fellow human beings who have also experienced pain and suffering. This shift can inspire a genuine desire to make amends and contribute positively to the community. Additionally, compassion practice helps individuals to regulate their emotions more effectively, reducing the intensity of negative emotions such as anger, resentment, and fear. This emotional regulation supports healthier relationships and more constructive interactions with others.

Self-awareness is another critical benefit of Buddhist practices. Mindfulness and meditation practices encourage individuals to observe their thoughts, feelings, and behaviors with curiosity and non-judgment. This heightened self-awareness enables individuals to recognize patterns of thought and behavior that may be contributing to their suffering. For example, an offender might become aware of a tendency to react defensively in stressful situations, leading to conflicts and negative outcomes. Through mindfulness practice, they can learn to observe this reaction without judgment, creating a space to choose a different response. This increased self-awareness also supports personal growth, as individuals become more attuned to their values, goals, and aspirations. Self-compassion, fostered through practices like loving-kindness meditation, is a vital aspect of healing trauma. Self-compassion involves treating oneself with the same kindness and understanding that one would offer to a friend. This practice helps to mitigate the harsh self-criticism and negative self-talk that often accompany trauma, promoting a more positive and nurturing relationship with oneself. For offenders, developing self-compassion can be transformative, helping them to move beyond feelings of guilt and shame and embrace a sense of hope and possibility. This shift in self-perception can support a more positive outlook on life and a greater commitment to personal growth and rehabilitation.

The development of empathy is another significant benefit of Buddhist practices. Empathy involves understanding and sharing the feelings of others, fostering a sense of connection and compassion. For offenders, developing empathy can lead to more positive relationships and a greater sense of responsibility for their actions. Compassion practices, such as visualizing the suffering of others and wishing them well, help to cultivate empathy and reduce feelings of anger and resentment. This empathetic understanding can inspire offenders to take actions that contribute positively to the well-being of others, fostering a sense of interconnectedness and shared humanity. Improved relationships are a natural outcome of the emotional regulation, self-awareness, and empathy fostered by Buddhist practices. As individuals develop greater emotional regulation and empathy, they are better able to navigate interpersonal conflicts and build positive, supportive relationships. For offenders, these improved relationships can be critical to successful reintegration, providing a network of support and encouragement. Positive relationships with family members, friends, mentors, and community members can offer emotional support, practical assistance, and a sense of belonging, all of which are essential for long-term rehabilitation.

The promotion of ethical living is another important benefit of Buddhist practices. The ethical principles of Buddhism, such as non-harming, honesty, and compassion, provide a moral framework that can guide individuals in making positive choices. For offenders, embracing these ethical principles can support a commitment to rehabilitation and personal growth. By living in accordance with these principles, individuals can build a sense of integrity and self-respect, fostering a positive self-identity and a commitment to positive change. For example, an offender who embraces the principle of non-harming might choose to engage in community service or restorative justice practices, making amends for past actions and contributing to the well-being of others. The creation of a balanced and peaceful mind is a fundamental benefit of

Buddhist practices. Mindfulness and meditation practices help individuals to develop a sense of inner peace and stability, reducing the turmoil and chaos often associated with trauma. This balanced state of mind supports resilience and adaptability, enabling individuals to navigate challenges with greater ease and confidence. For offenders, cultivating a peaceful mind can be transformative, providing a foundation for personal growth and positive change. This inner peace supports healthier relationships, better decision-making, and a greater sense of overall well-being.

23.3: Case Studies of Trauma Healing Programs

Case studies of trauma healing programs demonstrate the transformative impact of Buddhist practices on offenders. These examples provide insights into the practical application of techniques like mindfulness meditation, loving-kindness meditation, and compassion training, illustrating how they can be integrated into various settings to foster healing and rehabilitation. Each case highlights unique approaches and outcomes, showcasing the versatility and effectiveness of Buddhist practices in addressing trauma. In a high-security prison in Northern Europe, the "Mindfulness-Based Rehabilitation Program" was introduced to help inmates manage their trauma and reduce violent behavior. The program consisted of an eight-week course, during which participants engaged in daily mindfulness meditation sessions and weekly group discussions. The meditation practice focused on breath awareness and body scanning, helping inmates to develop a heightened sense of self-awareness and emotional regulation. One participant, Johan, who had been incarcerated for violent offenses, found the mindfulness practice particularly beneficial in managing his anger and impulsivity. Over the course of the program, Johan reported a significant reduction in anxiety and anger, noting that he felt more in control of his emotions and actions. The group discussions provided a supportive environment where inmates could share their experiences and insights, fostering a sense of community and mutual support. The program's success was evident in the marked decrease in violent incidents within the prison, demonstrating the potential of mindfulness-based interventions to promote emotional stability and reduce recidivism.

Another compelling example is the "Loving-Kindness Meditation Initiative" implemented in a juvenile detention center in the United States. This program aimed to address the trauma and emotional wounds of young offenders through the practice of loving-kindness meditation. Participants were guided through meditations that involved generating feelings of compassion and goodwill towards themselves and others, including their victims. One young participant, Sarah, had a history of aggressive behavior and emotional instability stemming from a traumatic childhood. Through regular practice of loving-kindness meditation, Sarah began to experience a profound shift in her emotional state. She reported feeling more at peace and less burdened by anger and resentment. The practice helped her to develop a sense of empathy and compassion, not only for herself but also for others. This newfound empathy led to improved relationships with her peers and staff, contributing to a more harmonious environment within the detention center. The program's impact was reflected in the positive changes in Sarah's behavior and her increased engagement in educational and therapeutic activities.

The "Compassion Training for Trauma Recovery" program in a community rehabilitation center in Southeast Asia provides another example of the healing potential of Buddhist practices. This program focused on developing compassion and empathy among participants, many of whom had experienced severe trauma and were struggling with addiction. The program included daily compassion meditation sessions, where participants practiced visualizing the suffering of others and extending wishes of happiness and well-being. One participant, Ananda, who had been addicted to drugs for many years, found the compassion training transformative. The practice helped him to develop a deeper understanding of his own suffering and the suffering of others, fostering a sense of connection and shared humanity. Ananda reported that the compassion meditation helped him to break free from the cycle of self-judgment and guilt that had fueled his addiction. He began to volunteer at the rehabilitation center, helping new participants navigate their recovery journeys. The program's success was evident in the significant improvements in Ananda's mental health and his commitment to maintaining sobriety and supporting others.

In a trauma-informed Buddhist retreat for offenders in Australia, the "Path to Healing Retreat" provided a comprehensive approach to trauma recovery. The retreat combined mindfulness meditation, yoga, and group therapy sessions to address the physical, emotional, and psychological aspects of trauma. Participants engaged in intensive meditation practice, focusing on breath awareness, body scanning, and loving-kindness meditation. The retreat also included workshops on trauma education, helping participants understand the impact of trauma on their bodies and minds. One participant, David, who had served multiple sentences for drug-related offenses, found the retreat to be a turning point in his recovery. The combination of meditation and yoga helped David to reconnect with his body and manage the physical symptoms of trauma, such as chronic pain and tension. The group therapy sessions provided a safe space for him to share his experiences and receive support from others who had faced similar challenges. David reported that the retreat helped him to develop a sense of inner peace and resilience, which he carried with him into his daily life. The long-term impact of the retreat was evident in David's continued commitment to meditation and yoga practice, as well as his active involvement in peer support groups.

The "Buddhist-Inspired Trauma Healing Program" in a women's correctional facility in Canada offers another illustrative case. This program integrated mindfulness meditation, compassion training, and trauma-informed care to support the healing and rehabilitation of female offenders. The program included weekly meditation sessions, where participants practiced mindfulness and loving-kindness meditation, as well as individual counseling sessions with trained therapists. One participant, Maria, had a history of domestic violence and substance abuse, which had left her with deep emotional scars. Through the program, Maria learned to cultivate mindfulness and self-compassion, which helped her to manage the symptoms of PTSD and develop a more positive self-image. The individual counseling sessions provided additional support, helping Maria to process her trauma and develop coping strategies. The program's success was reflected in Maria's improved mental health and her increased participation in educational and vocational training programs within the facility. The positive changes in Maria's behavior and outlook were also noted by the staff, who observed a significant reduction in her anxiety and depressive symptoms.

In a rural rehabilitation center in India, the "Yoga and Meditation for Trauma Recovery" program offered a holistic approach to healing. This program combined traditional yoga practices with mindfulness meditation to address the physical and emotional effects of trauma. Participants engaged in daily yoga sessions, focusing on gentle stretches, breathwork, and relaxation techniques, as well as mindfulness meditation sessions that emphasized body awareness and emotional regulation. One participant, Raj, who had been involved in criminal activities due to economic hardship, found the program to be deeply healing. The yoga practice helped Raj to release physical tension and develop a sense of grounding, while the mindfulness meditation provided a space for emotional processing and self-reflection. Raj reported that the program helped him to develop greater self-awareness and emotional resilience, which supported his efforts to reintegrate into society and pursue a more positive path. The program's impact was evident in the reduced recidivism rates among participants and the increased sense of community and mutual support within the rehabilitation center.

The "Trauma Healing through Buddhist Wisdom" initiative in a correctional facility in Japan provided another example of the transformative power of Buddhist practices. This program integrated traditional Buddhist teachings with modern trauma therapy techniques to support the healing and rehabilitation of inmates. Participants engaged in mindfulness meditation, compassion training, and workshops on Buddhist philosophy, focusing on the Four Noble Truths and the Eightfold Path. One participant, Kenji, who had been incarcerated for violent offenses, found the program to be life-changing. The mindfulness meditation helped Kenji to develop greater emotional regulation and self-control, while the compassion training fostered a sense of empathy and connection with others. The workshops on Buddhist philosophy provided Kenji with a framework for understanding his suffering and finding a path to healing and transformation. The program's success was reflected in Kenji's improved behavior and his commitment to personal growth and ethical living. The positive changes in Kenji's outlook and actions were also noted by the staff, who observed a significant reduction in his aggression and an increase in his willingness to participate in rehabilitative activities.

23.4: Long-Term Impact on Offender Rehabilitation

The long-term impact on offender rehabilitation through the integration of trauma healing practices grounded in Buddhist principles is profound and multifaceted. These practices not only address the immediate symptoms of trauma but also facilitate deep, lasting change in individuals, leading to significant improvements in their psychological well-being, behavioral patterns, and social relationships. The incorporation of mindfulness, loving-kindness, and compassion practices into rehabilitation programs can result in reduced recidivism, enhanced mental health, and stronger community ties, ultimately contributing to a more humane and effective justice system. One of the most significant long-term impacts of integrating Buddhist trauma healing practices is the sustained reduction in recidivism rates. Traditional punitive approaches often fail to address the underlying causes of criminal behavior, such as unresolved trauma and emotional dysregulation. By incorporating mindfulness and meditation practices, rehabilitation programs can help offenders develop greater self-awareness and emotional control. This shift can lead to a reduction in impulsive and aggressive behaviors, which are often rooted in trauma responses. For instance, offenders who regularly practice mindfulness meditation are better equipped to recognize and manage their triggers, reducing the likelihood of engaging in criminal activity. Over time, this increased self-regulation contributes to lower recidivism rates, as individuals are able to make more thoughtful and deliberate choices that align with their long-term goals and values.

Improvement in mental health is another critical long-term benefit of Buddhist trauma healing practices. Many offenders suffer from mental health issues such as anxiety, depression, and PTSD, which can be exacerbated by the stress and isolation of incarceration. Mindfulness and loving-kindness meditation have been shown to reduce symptoms of these conditions by promoting relaxation, emotional balance, and positive thinking. For example, studies have demonstrated that mindfulness meditation can decrease the severity of PTSD symptoms by helping individuals process traumatic memories in a safe and controlled manner. Similarly, loving-kindness meditation fosters self-compassion and reduces self-criticism, which are key factors in alleviating depression. As offenders develop healthier coping mechanisms and a more positive self-image, their overall mental health improves, supporting their rehabilitation and reintegration into society. The reinforcement of positive behavioral changes and ethical living is another significant long-term impact. Buddhist practices emphasize ethical conduct, compassion, and non-harming, which can profoundly influence an offender's behavior and decision-making. Through regular meditation and mindfulness practice, individuals learn to cultivate compassion and empathy for themselves and others. This shift in perspective encourages offenders to take responsibility for their actions and seek ways to make amends. For example, an offender who embraces the principles of loving-kindness and compassion may choose to engage in restorative justice practices, such as apologizing to their victims and participating in community service. These positive behaviors not only facilitate personal growth but also contribute to a more just and harmonious community.

The strengthening of social bonds and community reintegration is another long-term benefit of Buddhist trauma healing practices. Offenders often face significant challenges in rebuilding their lives and reestablishing relationships after incarceration. By fostering empathy and compassion, Buddhist practices can help individuals repair damaged relationships and build new, supportive connections. For instance, participation in group meditation sessions and peer support groups can create a sense of belonging and mutual understanding among offenders. These social bonds provide a network of support that is crucial for successful reintegration. As offenders develop healthier relationships with family members, friends, and community members, they are more likely to receive the emotional and practical support needed to maintain their rehabilitation efforts. The creation of a more humane and effective justice system is perhaps the most far-reaching long-term impact of integrating Buddhist trauma healing practices. Traditional justice systems often prioritize punishment over rehabilitation, leading to high rates of recidivism and ongoing social harm. By incorporating mindfulness, compassion, and ethical living into rehabilitation programs, justice systems can shift towards a more restorative and holistic approach. This shift recognizes that addressing the root causes of criminal behavior, such as trauma and emotional dysregulation, is essential for promoting long-term positive change. For example, a justice system that integrates Buddhist practices might include meditation and mindfulness programs in correctional facilities, offer trauma-informed counseling services, and encourage restorative justice practices. These initiatives create a more compassionate and supportive environment for offenders, which can lead to better rehabilitation outcomes and a reduction in reoffending.

The long-term impact of Buddhist trauma healing practices also extends to the broader community. As offenders heal from their trauma and develop healthier behaviors, they contribute to safer and more cohesive communities. The principles of compassion and empathy fostered by Buddhist practices encourage individuals to engage in prosocial behaviors, such as volunteering, helping others, and participating in community-building activities. These positive contributions enhance community well-being and resilience, creating a more supportive environment for all members. For instance, a community that embraces restorative justice practices and supports the reintegration of offenders is likely to experience lower crime rates and stronger social bonds. This collective effort to promote healing and rehabilitation benefits not only the individuals involved but also the community as a whole. Another long-term impact is the promotion of cultural and systemic change within justice systems. The success of Buddhist trauma healing practices in rehabilitation programs can inspire broader changes in how justice is conceptualized and administered. As the benefits of these practices become more widely recognized, there may be increased support for policies and programs that prioritize rehabilitation over punishment.

For example, policymakers might advocate for the inclusion of mindfulness and meditation programs in correctional facilities, the implementation of restorative justice practices, and the provision of trauma-informed care. These systemic changes can create a more just and compassionate society that recognizes the potential for growth and transformation in every individual. The integration of Buddhist trauma healing practices also has implications for professional development within the justice system. Correctional staff, therapists, and other professionals can benefit from training in mindfulness, compassion, and trauma-informed care. This training can enhance their ability to support offenders' rehabilitation efforts and create a more compassionate and effective working environment. For instance, correctional officers who practice mindfulness and compassion may be better equipped to manage stress, maintain positive relationships with inmates, and foster a supportive atmosphere within correctional facilities. This professional development can lead to a more effective and humane justice system that better serves the needs of all individuals involved.

23.5: Strategies for Implementing Trauma Healing Practices

Implementing trauma healing practices within rehabilitation programs for offenders requires a comprehensive and strategic approach to ensure that these practices are effective, sustainable, and accessible to all individuals who need them. The strategies for implementing these practices involve training, developing partnerships, creating structured programs, offering workshops and retreats, and continuously monitoring and evaluating their effectiveness. By following these strategies, justice systems and rehabilitation programs can create a supportive environment that fosters healing and rehabilitation for offenders. Training programs for staff and volunteers are a crucial component of implementing trauma healing practices. To ensure that mindfulness, loving-kindness, and compassion practices are effectively integrated into rehabilitation programs, it is essential to provide comprehensive training for those who will be facilitating these practices. This training should cover the principles and techniques of Buddhist trauma healing practices, as well as the specific needs and challenges of working with offenders. For example, correctional officers, therapists, and program facilitators should receive training in mindfulness meditation, loving-kindness meditation, and compassion practices, along with techniques for creating a safe and supportive environment for participants. Additionally, training should include education on the psychological and physiological effects of trauma, helping staff and volunteers understand the impact of trauma on behavior and the healing process. This knowledge is critical for effectively supporting offenders and fostering a trauma-informed approach to rehabilitation.

Developing partnerships with Buddhist practitioners and organizations is another essential strategy for implementing trauma healing practices. Collaborating with experienced practitioners and organizations that specialize in Buddhist meditation and trauma healing can provide valuable resources and expertise. These partnerships can help to ensure that the practices are implemented with authenticity and integrity, drawing on the rich tradition and depth of Buddhist teachings. For example, a rehabilitation program might partner with a local Buddhist center or meditation teacher to offer regular meditation sessions and workshops for offenders. These partnerships can also provide opportunities for staff and volunteers to receive ongoing training and support, ensuring that they remain well-equipped to facilitate the practices effectively. Additionally, partnerships can help to create a sense of community and connection, fostering a supportive network for both offenders and those who work with them. Creating structured meditation and mindfulness programs within correctional facilities is a key strategy for implementing trauma healing practices. These programs should be carefully designed to meet the specific needs of offenders and the unique environment of correctional facilities. Structured programs might include daily meditation sessions, weekly group meetings, and individual support for participants. For example, a mindfulness meditation program might involve daily 30-minute meditation sessions, guided by a trained facilitator, followed by a brief discussion or reflection period. Weekly group meetings could provide an opportunity for participants to share their experiences, ask questions, and receive additional guidance and support. Individual support might include one-on-one sessions with a meditation teacher or therapist, offering personalized assistance and addressing specific challenges. By creating a structured program, correctional facilities can provide a consistent and supportive environment for offenders to engage in mindfulness and meditation practices, fostering a sense of routine and stability.

Offering trauma healing workshops and retreats for offenders is another effective strategy. Workshops and retreats provide an intensive and immersive experience, allowing participants to deeply engage with the practices and benefit from a focused period of healing and reflection. These events can be held within correctional facilities or in dedicated retreat centers, depending on the logistics and resources available.

Workshops might cover topics such as mindfulness meditation, loving-kindness meditation, and compassion practices, along with education on the effects of trauma and techniques for self-care and emotional regulation. Retreats might involve several days of intensive practice, including meditation sessions, yoga, group discussions, and individual support. For example, a weekend retreat might include multiple meditation sessions each day, guided by experienced practitioners, along with opportunities for participants to engage in mindful movement practices, such as yoga or walking meditation. Group discussions and individual check-ins can provide additional support and guidance, helping participants to integrate their experiences and apply the practices to their daily lives.

Monitoring and evaluating the effectiveness of trauma healing initiatives is essential for ensuring their long-term success and sustainability. Regular assessment and feedback can help to identify what is working well and where improvements are needed, allowing programs to be adjusted and refined over time. Evaluation methods might include surveys, interviews, and focus groups with participants, staff, and volunteers, as well as quantitative measures of outcomes such as recidivism rates, mental health symptoms, and participant engagement. For example, a program might conduct pre- and post-assessment surveys to measure changes in participants' levels of anxiety, depression, and PTSD symptoms, along with their overall sense of well-being and satisfaction with the program. Focus groups and interviews can provide qualitative insights into participants' experiences, highlighting the aspects of the program that are most beneficial and any challenges or barriers they have encountered. This feedback can be used to make data-driven improvements to the program, ensuring that it continues to meet the needs of participants and achieve its goals.

In addition to these core strategies, there are several other important considerations for implementing trauma healing practices. Ensuring accessibility and inclusivity is critical, as offenders come from diverse backgrounds and have varying needs and preferences. Programs should be designed to accommodate different levels of experience and comfort with meditation and mindfulness practices, offering modifications and alternatives as needed. For example, some participants might prefer guided meditations, while others might benefit from more active practices such as mindful movement or walking meditation. Providing materials and instructions in multiple languages and being sensitive to cultural differences can also help to make the practices more accessible and inclusive. Another consideration is the integration of trauma healing practices into the broader rehabilitation framework. These practices should complement and enhance other rehabilitative efforts, such as educational programs, job training, and therapy. For example, mindfulness and meditation practices can be integrated into existing therapeutic interventions, such as cognitive-behavioral therapy (CBT) or dialectical behavior therapy (DBT), to enhance their effectiveness. Coordination and collaboration among different service providers within the rehabilitation system can help to create a cohesive and holistic approach to offender rehabilitation.

It is also important to provide ongoing support and resources for participants after they complete the initial program. Continuing education and practice opportunities can help to reinforce the benefits of the practices and support long-term healing and growth. For example, correctional facilities might offer advanced meditation classes or alumni groups for participants who have completed the initial program, providing a space for ongoing practice and community building. Additionally, providing resources such as guided meditation recordings, reading materials, and access to online meditation communities can help participants to maintain their practice and stay connected to a supportive network. Advocating for policy changes and securing funding is another crucial aspect of implementing trauma healing practices. Ensuring that these practices are recognized and supported at the policy level can help to create a more supportive environment for their implementation and sustainability. Advocacy efforts might include raising awareness about the benefits of Buddhist trauma healing practices, presenting data on their effectiveness, and building coalitions of supporters.

Securing funding from government agencies, private foundations, and other sources can provide the resources needed to develop and sustain these programs. For example, grant proposals might highlight the potential cost savings associated with reduced recidivism rates and improved mental health outcomes, along with the broader social benefits of supporting offender rehabilitation. Finally, fostering a culture of compassion and mindfulness within the justice system is essential for the success of trauma healing practices. This involves promoting the values of empathy, understanding, and non-judgment among staff, volunteers, and participants, creating an environment where healing and growth are possible. Leadership plays a critical role in setting the tone and modeling these values, demonstrating a commitment to creating a more humane and effective justice system. For example, correctional facility administrators and staff can participate in mindfulness and meditation training themselves, leading by example and showing their support for the practices. Creating a culture of compassion and mindfulness can help to transform the justice system, making it a place of healing and rehabilitation rather than punishment and retribution.

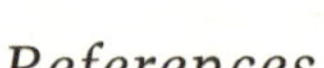

References

- BAILEY, R., & EKIYOR, T. (Eds.). (2005). Retributive Justice v Restorative Justice. In PROMOTING RESTORATIVE JUSTICE IN SOUTH AFRICA'S CORRECTIONAL SERVICES: PRISONS TRANSFORMATION PROJECT (pp. 10–13). Centre for Conflict Resolution. http://www.jstor.org/stable/resrep05161.8
- Bechert, H. (1973). Sangha, State, Society, "Nation": Persistence of Traditions in "Post-Traditional" Buddhist Societies. Daedalus, 102(1), 85–95. http://www.jstor.org/stable/20024110
- Braithwaite, J. (1999). Restorative Justice: Assessing Optimistic and Pessimistic Accounts. Crime and Justice, 25, 1–127. http://www.jstor.org/stable/1147608
- Braithwaite, J. (2002). SETTING STANDARDS FOR RESTORATIVE JUSTICE. The British Journal of Criminology, 42(3), 563–577. http://www.jstor.org/stable/23638881
- CHIA, J. M. T. (2009). Teaching Dharma, Grooming Sangha: The Buddhist College of Singapore. Sojourn: Journal of Social Issues in Southeast Asia, 24(1), 122–138. http://www.jstor.org/stable/41308114

- Crawford, A., & Newburn, T. (2002). RECENT DEVELOPMENTS IN RESTORATIVE JUSTICE FOR YOUNG PEOPLE IN ENGLAND AND WALES: Community Participation and Representation. The British Journal of Criminology, 42(3), 476–495. http://www.jstor.org/stable/23638877
- Ekman, P., Davidson, R. J., Ricard, M., & Wallace, B. A. (2005). Buddhist and Psychological Perspectives on Emotions and Well-Being. Current Directions in Psychological Science, 14(2), 59–63. http://www.jstor.org/stable/20182989
- Gavrielides, T. (2014). Bringing Race Relations Into the Restorative Justice Debate: An Alternative and Personalized Vision of "the Other." Journal of Black Studies, 45(3), 216–246. http://www.jstor.org/stable/24572951
- Harris, M. L. (2012). Buddhist Meditation for the Recovery of the Womanist Self, or Sitting on the Mat Self-Love Realized. Buddhist-Christian Studies, 32, 67–72. http://www.jstor.org/stable/23274470
- Hargovan, H. (2005). Restorative Justice and Domestic Violence: Some Exploratory Thoughts. Agenda: Empowering Women for Gender Equity, 66, 48–56. http://www.jstor.org/stable/4066536
- Hudson, B. (1998). Restorative Justice: The Challenge of Sexual and Racial Violence. Journal of Law and Society, 25(2), 237–256. http://www.jstor.org/stable/1410689
- Hudson, B. (2002). RESTORATIVE JUSTICE AND GENDERED VIOLENCE: Diversion or Effective Justice? The British Journal of Criminology, 42(3), 616–634. http://www.jstor.org/stable/23638884
- Lewis, S. E. (2013). Trauma and the Making of Flexible Minds in the Tibetan Exile Community. Ethos, 41(3), 313–336. http://www.jstor.org/stable/24029808
- Liston, Y. (1999). The Transformation of Buddhism during British Colonialism. Journal of Law and Religion, 14(1), 189–210. https://doi.org/10.2307/1051784
- McEvoy, K., Mika, H., & Hudson, B. (2002). INTRODUCTION: Practice, Performance and Prospects for Restorative Justice. The British Journal of Criminology, 42(3), 469–475. http://www.jstor.org/stable/23638876
- McEvoy, K., & Mika, H. (2002). RESTORATIVE JUSTICE AND THE CRITIQUE OF INFORMALISM IN NORTHERN IRELAND. The British Journal of Criminology, 42(3), 534–562. http://www.jstor.org/stable/23638880

- Morris, A. (2002). CRITIQUING THE CRITICS: A Brief Response to Critics of Restorative Justice. The British Journal of Criminology, 42(3), 596–615. http://www.jstor.org/stable/23638883
- Murthy, K. K. (1989). Buddhist Sangha. The Tibet Journal, 14(3), 3–18. http://www.jstor.org/stable/43300324
- Olson, S. M., & Dzur, A. W. (2004). Revisiting Informal Justice: Restorative Justice and Democratic Professionalism. Law & Society Review, 38(1), 139–176. http://www.jstor.org/stable/1555115
- Peres, J. F. P., Moreira-Almeida, A., Nasello, A. G., & Koenig, H. G. (2007). Spirituality and Resilience in Trauma Victims. Journal of Religion and Health, 46(3), 343–350. http://www.jstor.org/stable/27513020
- Robinson, J., & Hudson, J. (2016). RESTORATIVE JUSTICE: A TYPOLOGY AND CRITICAL APPRAISAL. Willamette Journal of International Law and Dispute Resolution, 23(2), 335–366. http://www.jstor.org/stable/26209973
- Sawatsky, J. (2007). Rethinking Restorative Justice: When the Geographies of Crime and of Healing Justice Matter. Peace Research, 39(1/2), 75–93. http://www.jstor.org/stable/23607905
- Sivaraksa, S. (1998). Buddhism and Human Freedom. Buddhist-Christian Studies, 18, 63–68. https://doi.org/10.2307/1390436
- Strang, H. (2004). [Review of Restorative Justice and Criminal Justice: Competing or Reconcilable Paradigms?, by A. von Hirsch, J. Roberts, A. E. Bottoms, K. Roach, & M. Schiff]. The British Journal of Criminology, 44(2), 293–295. http://www.jstor.org/stable/23638621
- Strang, H. (2017). Experiments in restorative justice. In P. DRAHOS (Ed.), Regulatory Theory: Foundations and applications (pp. 483–498). ANU Press. http://www.jstor.org/stable/j.ctt1q1crtm.39
- Strenski, I. (1983). On Generalized Exchange and the Domestication of the Sangha. Man, 18(3), 463–477. https://doi.org/10.2307/2801592
- Takagi, P., & Shank, G. (2004). Critique of Restorative Justice. Social Justice, 31(3 (97)), 147–163. http://www.jstor.org/stable/29768262
- Tauri, J. M. (2016). Indigenous Peoples and the Globalization of Restorative Justice. Social Justice, 43(3 (145)), 46–67. http://www.jstor.org/stable/26405722
- Tyson, P. D., & Pongruengphant, R. (2007). Buddhist and Western Perspectives on Suffering, Stress, and Coping. Journal of Religion and Health, 46(3), 351–357. http://www.jstor.org/stable/27513021

- Verity, F., & King, S. (2008). Responding to intercommunal conflict - what can restorative justice offer? Community Development Journal, 43(4), 470–482. http://www.jstor.org/stable/44258103

- Verity, F., & King, S. (2008). Responding to intercommunal conflict - what can restorative justice offer? Community Development Journal, 43(4), 470–482. http://www.jstor.org/stable/44258103

Part VII: Integrating Doctrinal Principles in Modern Criminology

—

CHAPTER TWENTY-FOUR

Bridging Buddhist Philosophy and Criminology

Contents

- Integrating Buddhist Teachings with Criminological Theories

- Benefits for Modern Criminology

- Practical Applications in Justice Systems

- Case Studies of Successful Integration

- Future Directions for Buddhist-Informed Criminology

24.1: Integrating Buddhist Teachings with Criminological Theories

Buddhist philosophy offers profound insights that can significantly enrich the field of criminology. At its core, Buddhism emphasizes the understanding and transformation of the human mind, which is essential in addressing the root causes of criminal behavior. Integrating Buddhist teachings with criminological theories involves exploring how principles such as the Middle Way, Dependent Origination, and the Four Noble Truths can inform our understanding of crime, justice, and rehabilitation. The Middle Way, central to Buddhist thought, advocates for a balanced approach to life, avoiding extremes of self-indulgence and self-mortification. In the context of criminology, this principle can guide the development of balanced approaches to justice and rehabilitation, which neither solely punish nor overly coddle offenders. Instead, it encourages a middle path that recognizes the potential for change within every individual while holding them accountable for their actions. This approach can be transformative, offering a framework that promotes both personal responsibility and compassion.

Dependent Origination, another key Buddhist concept, teaches that all phenomena arise in dependence upon multiple causes and conditions. Applied to criminology, this principle helps to understand criminal behavior as the result of a complex interplay of factors rather than as isolated actions. This holistic perspective can lead to more effective interventions by addressing the various social, economic, psychological, and environmental conditions that contribute to criminal behavior. For example, an offender's actions might be seen not just as individual moral failings but as responses to broader systemic issues such as poverty, trauma, and lack of education. Recognizing this interconnectedness can inform policies and programs that aim to change the conditions contributing to criminal behavior, thus reducing recidivism and promoting long-term rehabilitation. The Four Noble Truths offer a profound framework for understanding and addressing suffering, which is often at the heart of criminal behavior. The First Noble Truth acknowledges the existence of suffering, which in the context of criminology can be understood as the suffering experienced by offenders, victims, and communities affected by crime. The Second Noble Truth identifies the causes of suffering, such as attachment, aversion, and ignorance. For offenders, these causes might manifest as attachment to harmful behaviors, aversion to societal norms, or ignorance of the consequences of their actions. The Third Noble Truth offers hope by teaching that it is possible to overcome suffering by addressing its causes. This aligns with rehabilitation efforts that aim to transform offenders' behaviors and mindsets. The Fourth Noble Truth outlines the path to the cessation of suffering, which in criminology can be seen as the development of ethical, mindful, and compassionate approaches to justice and rehabilitation.

Integrating these Buddhist teachings with criminological theories enriches our understanding of the root causes of criminal behavior and provides a comprehensive framework for addressing it. For instance, traditional criminological theories like strain theory, which suggests that societal pressures can lead individuals to commit crimes, can be complemented by Buddhist insights into the nature of suffering and its causes. Similarly, social learning theory, which posits that people learn behaviors by observing others, can be enriched by Buddhist practices that cultivate mindfulness and ethical behavior, offering offenders tools to break negative patterns and develop positive habits. The integration of Buddhist philosophy into criminology also emphasizes the importance of compassion and empathy in the justice system. These values are central to Buddhism and can transform how justice is administered, moving from a punitive to a restorative approach. Restorative justice, which focuses on healing the harm caused by crime and restoring relationships, aligns closely with Buddhist principles. By fostering empathy and understanding between offenders and victims, restorative justice practices can lead to more meaningful resolutions and long-term healing for all parties involved.

Moreover, Buddhist teachings on mindfulness and meditation offer practical tools that can be incorporated into rehabilitation programs. Mindfulness practices help individuals develop greater self-awareness and emotional regulation, which are crucial for addressing the impulsivity and reactivity that often lead to criminal behavior. For example, mindfulness-based interventions have been shown to reduce recidivism by helping offenders manage stress and anxiety, improve their emotional well-being, and develop more positive coping strategies. These practices not only benefit offenders but also enhance the overall effectiveness of rehabilitation programs by fostering a supportive and empathetic environment. The holistic approach of Buddhism also emphasizes the importance of addressing the needs of the whole person—body, mind, and spirit. In criminology, this translates into developing comprehensive rehabilitation programs that go beyond merely addressing criminal behavior to also consider the physical, emotional, and spiritual well-being of offenders. Such programs might include not only therapy and education but also mindfulness and meditation practices, vocational training, and community service opportunities. By addressing the multifaceted needs of offenders, these programs can support their overall growth and transformation, leading to more sustainable rehabilitation outcomes.

24.2: Benefits for Modern Criminology

The benefits of integrating Buddhist teachings into modern criminology are profound and multifaceted, offering significant enhancements to both the theoretical understanding of criminal behavior and the practical approaches to justice and rehabilitation. By incorporating principles such as mindfulness, compassion, and ethical living, Buddhist philosophy can transform how we address crime and support offenders in their journey toward rehabilitation and reintegration into society. One of the primary benefits of integrating Buddhist teachings into criminology is the enriched understanding of criminal behavior. Traditional criminological theories often focus on the external factors that contribute to crime, such as socioeconomic conditions, peer influences, and systemic inequalities. While these factors are undeniably important, they do not fully capture the internal, psychological, and emotional dimensions of criminal behavior. Buddhist teachings, with their emphasis on the mind and its role in shaping behavior, provide a valuable complementary perspective. By exploring how attachment, aversion, and ignorance contribute to harmful actions, criminologists can develop a more comprehensive understanding of the motivations behind criminal behavior. For example, an offender's actions might be seen as attempts to cope with internal suffering or unmet needs, rather than merely responses to external pressures. This insight can lead to more nuanced and effective interventions that address the root causes of criminal behavior.

Another significant benefit is the promotion of holistic and compassionate approaches to justice. Traditional justice systems often emphasize punishment and retribution, which can perpetuate cycles of harm and fail to address the underlying issues that lead to criminal behavior. Buddhist teachings advocate for compassion, understanding, and the alleviation of suffering, which align closely with the principles of restorative justice. By incorporating these values, justice systems can shift towards approaches that seek to heal rather than punish. Restorative justice practices, such as victim-offender mediation and community reconciliation processes, focus on repairing the harm caused by crime and fostering mutual understanding and empathy. These practices can lead to more meaningful resolutions for both victims and offenders, promoting healing and reducing the likelihood of reoffending. Mindfulness and meditation practices, central to Buddhist teachings, offer practical tools for enhancing the well-being and rehabilitation of offenders. These practices help individuals develop greater self-awareness, emotional regulation, and resilience, which are crucial for addressing the impulsivity and emotional dysregulation that often underlie criminal behavior. Research has shown that mindfulness-based interventions can reduce recidivism rates by helping offenders manage stress and anxiety, improve their mental health, and develop more positive coping strategies. For example, a mindfulness program in a correctional facility might involve daily meditation sessions, where participants learn to observe their thoughts and emotions without judgment. This practice can help offenders recognize and interrupt negative patterns of thought and behavior, fostering a greater sense of control and responsibility. Over time, mindfulness practice can lead to lasting changes in how individuals respond to stress and challenges, supporting their long-term rehabilitation and reintegration.

The integration of Buddhist teachings also emphasizes the importance of ethical living and personal responsibility. Buddhism teaches that ethical conduct is fundamental to a harmonious and fulfilling life, and this principle can be applied to criminology by encouraging offenders to adopt ethical principles and take responsibility for their actions. Programs that incorporate Buddhist teachings might include discussions on the ethical precepts of non-harming, honesty, and respect for others, helping offenders to reflect on the impact of their actions and develop a commitment to ethical behavior. This focus on ethics can support offenders in making positive changes and building a sense of integrity and self-respect. For example, an offender who has embraced the principle of non-harming might choose to engage in community service or restorative justice practices, actively working to make amends for their past actions and contribute positively to society. Another important benefit of integrating Buddhist teachings into criminology is the potential for fostering stronger, more supportive communities. Buddhist philosophy emphasizes the interconnectedness of all beings and the importance of community in individual growth and well-being. By fostering a sense of connection and mutual support, rehabilitation programs can help offenders build positive relationships and develop a sense of belonging. Community-based approaches to rehabilitation, such as peer support groups and community service projects, can provide a supportive environment for offenders to practice new skills and behaviors. These approaches also help to break down the barriers of stigma and isolation that often accompany criminal behavior, promoting reintegration and reducing the risk of reoffending. For example, a community service project that involves offenders working alongside other community members can help to build trust and understanding, fostering a sense of shared purpose and mutual support.

The benefits of integrating Buddhist teachings into criminology extend to the broader society as well. By promoting approaches that emphasize healing, compassion, and ethical living, these teachings can contribute to a more just and compassionate society. Policies and programs informed by Buddhist principles can help to create a justice system that prioritizes rehabilitation and reintegration over punishment and retribution, leading to better outcomes for individuals and communities. For example, a justice system that incorporates mindfulness and meditation programs, restorative justice practices, and ethical education can support the rehabilitation of offenders while also promoting public safety and community well-being. These approaches can lead to reduced crime rates, lower recidivism, and a more positive and supportive environment for all members of society. Furthermore, the integration of Buddhist teachings into criminology can inspire and support ongoing research and innovation. The holistic and compassionate perspective offered by Buddhism provides a rich foundation for developing new theories, practices, and interventions that address the complexities of criminal behavior and rehabilitation. Researchers can explore how Buddhist principles can be applied to various aspects of criminology, from understanding the psychological and emotional dimensions of criminal behavior to developing effective rehabilitation programs and policies. This interdisciplinary approach can lead to new insights and innovations that enhance the effectiveness of the justice system and support the well-being of offenders and communities.

24.3: Practical Applications in Justice Systems

The practical applications of integrating Buddhist teachings into justice systems are extensive and offer transformative potential for how we approach crime, punishment, and rehabilitation. By incorporating principles such as mindfulness, compassion, and ethical conduct into justice practices, we can create a more humane and effective system that addresses the root causes of criminal behavior and supports the long-term rehabilitation of offenders. These applications include mindfulness-based interventions, restorative justice practices, trauma-informed care, and comprehensive rehabilitation programs that incorporate Buddhist principles. One of the most well-known and widely implemented applications of Buddhist teachings in justice systems is mindfulness-based interventions. These interventions involve teaching mindfulness meditation practices to offenders, helping them develop greater self-awareness, emotional regulation, and resilience. Mindfulness meditation encourages individuals to observe their thoughts and emotions without judgment, fostering a sense of inner calm and stability. In the context of a correctional facility, a mindfulness-based program might include daily meditation sessions, where participants learn techniques such as breath awareness, body scanning, and loving-kindness meditation. These practices help offenders become more attuned to their internal experiences, allowing them to recognize and interrupt negative patterns of thought and behavior. Over time, regular mindfulness practice can lead to significant improvements in mental health, reducing symptoms of anxiety, depression, and PTSD, and supporting the overall well-being of offenders.

Restorative justice practices, deeply aligned with Buddhist principles of compassion and empathy, offer another powerful application. Restorative justice focuses on repairing the harm caused by crime and restoring relationships between offenders, victims, and the community. This approach emphasizes dialogue, understanding, and mutual respect, encouraging offenders to take responsibility for their actions and make amends. Restorative justice practices can take various forms, including victim-offender mediation, restorative circles, and community conferences. In victim-offender mediation, for example, the offender and the victim meet in a controlled and supportive environment, facilitated by a trained mediator. This process allows the victim to express the impact of the crime and the offender to understand the consequences of their actions, fostering empathy and accountability. The goal is to reach a resolution that addresses the needs of both parties and promotes healing and reconciliation. These practices can lead to more meaningful resolutions, reduce recidivism, and enhance community cohesion. Trauma-informed care is another practical application that integrates Buddhist principles into justice systems. Recognizing that many offenders have experienced significant trauma, trauma-informed care seeks to create a safe and supportive environment that addresses the psychological and emotional needs of individuals. Buddhist practices such as mindfulness and compassion meditation can be incorporated into trauma-informed interventions to help offenders process and heal from their traumatic experiences. For example, a trauma-informed program might include mindfulness meditation sessions designed to help participants develop greater emotional regulation and resilience. These sessions could be complemented by group therapy and individual counseling, providing a comprehensive approach to trauma recovery. By addressing the underlying trauma that often contributes to criminal behavior, trauma-informed care supports the long-term rehabilitation and well-being of offenders.

Comprehensive rehabilitation programs that incorporate Buddhist principles offer a holistic approach to offender rehabilitation. These programs address the physical, emotional, and spiritual needs of individuals, promoting overall well-being and personal growth. A comprehensive program might include various components, such as mindfulness meditation, ethical education, vocational training, and community service. For example, a program might start with an orientation session that introduces participants to the principles of mindfulness and ethical living. This could be followed by daily meditation sessions, where participants practice mindfulness and loving-kindness meditation. Additionally, the program might offer classes on ethical conduct, helping offenders reflect on their actions and develop a commitment to living in accordance with ethical principles. Vocational training and community service projects can provide practical skills and opportunities for offenders to give back to the community, fostering a sense of purpose and connection. By addressing the multifaceted needs of offenders, comprehensive rehabilitation programs support their long-term transformation and reintegration into society. Implementing these practical applications within justice systems requires a strategic and collaborative approach. Training and support for staff and volunteers are essential to ensure the effective delivery of these interventions. Correctional officers, therapists, and program facilitators should receive training in mindfulness and meditation practices, as well as trauma-informed care and restorative justice principles. This training should also include education on the psychological and physiological effects of trauma and the specific needs of offenders. Ongoing support and supervision can help staff and volunteers maintain their skills and stay motivated, ensuring the sustainability and effectiveness of the programs.

Developing partnerships with Buddhist practitioners and organizations can provide valuable resources and expertise for implementing these practices. Collaboration with local Buddhist centers, meditation teachers, and organizations that specialize in mindfulness and trauma healing can enhance the quality and authenticity of the programs. These partnerships can also offer opportunities for staff and volunteers to receive ongoing training and support, ensuring that they are well-equipped to facilitate the practices effectively. For example, a correctional facility might partner with a local meditation center to offer regular mindfulness sessions and workshops for both offenders and staff. These partnerships can create a sense of community and connection, fostering a supportive network for all involved. Creating a supportive and trauma-informed environment within correctional facilities is crucial for the success of these interventions. This involves establishing policies and practices that prioritize the safety and well-being of offenders and staff. Simple changes, such as creating quiet spaces for meditation, ensuring that facilities are clean and comfortable, and promoting a culture of respect and empathy, can make a significant difference. Additionally, incorporating mindfulness and trauma-informed practices into daily routines and activities can help to create a more supportive environment. For example, starting meetings and group sessions with a brief mindfulness exercise can help participants center themselves and create a sense of calm and focus.

Monitoring and evaluating the effectiveness of these interventions is essential for ensuring their long-term success and sustainability. Regular assessment and feedback can help to identify what is working well and where improvements are needed, allowing programs to be adjusted and refined over time. Evaluation methods might include surveys, interviews, and focus groups with participants, staff, and volunteers, as well as quantitative measures of outcomes such as recidivism rates, mental health symptoms, and participant engagement. This data can provide valuable insights into the impact of the interventions and inform future developments. For example, a program might conduct pre- and post-assessment surveys to measure changes in participants' levels of anxiety, depression, and PTSD symptoms, as well as their overall sense of well-being and satisfaction with the program. Advocating for policy changes that support the integration of Buddhist teachings into justice systems is another important aspect of implementing these practices. Raising awareness about the benefits of mindfulness, compassion, and trauma-informed care can help to build support for these approaches at the policy level. This advocacy might involve presenting data on the effectiveness of these interventions, highlighting their potential to reduce recidivism and improve mental health outcomes, and building coalitions of supporters. For example, policymakers might be encouraged to fund and support mindfulness programs in correctional facilities, promote restorative justice practices, and ensure that trauma-informed care is available to all offenders.

24.4: Case Studies of Successful Integration

Analyzing real-world examples where Buddhist principles have been successfully integrated into criminology and justice systems provides valuable insights into the practical benefits and transformative potential of these approaches. These case studies illustrate how mindfulness, compassion, and ethical conduct can be applied to various aspects of the justice system, from offender rehabilitation to community reconciliation, resulting in meaningful outcomes for individuals and society. One notable example is the "Path of Freedom" program in the United States, developed by Fleet Maull, a former federal prisoner turned mindfulness teacher.

The program offers mindfulness-based emotional intelligence training for prisoners, focusing on meditation, emotional regulation, and ethical living. Participants engage in mindfulness practices to develop self-awareness and learn to manage their emotions and impulses. The program also includes teachings on the Eightfold Path and ethical principles, encouraging participants to reflect on their behavior and its impact on others. Evaluations of the program have shown significant improvements in participants' emotional well-being, reduced aggression, and a greater sense of personal responsibility. Many participants have reported that the program helped them develop a sense of inner peace and purpose, which supported their rehabilitation and reintegration into society.

In the United Kingdom, the "Mindfulness for Prisons" initiative, spearheaded by the Mindfulness Initiative in collaboration with Her Majesty's Prison Service, provides mindfulness training to inmates and staff across several correctional facilities. The program includes mindfulness meditation sessions, workshops, and ongoing support for participants. One of the key components of the initiative is the "Mindfulness-Based Cognitive Therapy" (MBCT) program, which combines mindfulness practices with cognitive-behavioral techniques to address issues such as depression, anxiety, and stress. Research on the initiative has shown that inmates who participate in the MBCT program experience significant reductions in symptoms of depression and anxiety, as well as improvements in overall well-being. Staff members have also reported benefits from the program, including better stress management and improved relationships with inmates. The success of the initiative has led to its expansion to more prisons and the inclusion of mindfulness training in staff development programs.

Another example is the "Healing Hearts and Minds" program in Thailand, which integrates mindfulness and loving-kindness meditation into the rehabilitation process for juvenile offenders. Developed by the Thailand Institute of Justice in collaboration with local Buddhist monasteries, the program aims to address the emotional and psychological needs of young offenders by teaching them mindfulness and compassion practices. Participants attend meditation retreats at Buddhist temples, where they engage in daily meditation, group discussions, and teachings on Buddhist ethics. The program also includes activities such as yoga, art therapy, and community service, providing a holistic approach to rehabilitation. Evaluations of the program have shown that participants experience significant improvements in emotional regulation, empathy, and self-esteem. Many young offenders have reported that the program helped them develop a sense of inner peace and a commitment to positive change. The program's success has led to its adoption in other juvenile detention centers in Thailand.

The "Zen Peacekeeper Program" in Japan offers another compelling example of integrating Buddhist principles into the justice system. This program, developed by the San Francisco Zen Center in collaboration with Japanese correctional facilities, provides mindfulness and Zen meditation training to inmates. The program emphasizes the practice of zazen (seated meditation) and teachings on Zen ethics, encouraging participants to cultivate mindfulness, compassion, and ethical behavior. Inmates participate in daily meditation sessions, where they learn to observe their thoughts and emotions with non-judgmental awareness. The program also includes teachings on the principles of Zen Buddhism, such as the Four Noble Truths and the Eightfold Path, helping participants develop a deeper understanding of their actions and their impact on others. Evaluations of the program have shown that participants experience significant reductions in stress, anxiety, and aggression, as well as improvements in overall well-being and personal responsibility. The program's success has inspired similar initiatives in other correctional facilities in Japan and around the world.

In Canada, the "Circle of Hope" restorative justice program integrates mindfulness and compassion practices into its approach to offender rehabilitation. Developed by the John Howard Society in collaboration with local Buddhist communities, the program focuses on healing the harm caused by crime and fostering reconciliation between offenders, victims, and the community. Participants engage in mindfulness meditation and loving-kindness practices to develop greater self-awareness and empathy. The program also includes restorative justice circles, where offenders and victims come together to discuss the impact of the crime and explore ways to repair the harm. These circles are facilitated by trained mediators who incorporate mindfulness and compassion practices to create a safe and supportive environment for dialogue. Evaluations of the program have shown that participants experience significant reductions in recidivism, improved relationships with their families and communities, and a greater sense of personal responsibility. Victims have also reported feeling a sense of closure and healing through the restorative justice process.

The "Mindful Schools Project" in New Zealand provides an example of integrating mindfulness and Buddhist principles into educational settings to prevent criminal behavior and support at-risk youth. Developed by the Mindfulness Education Group in collaboration with local schools and community organizations, the project offers mindfulness training to students, teachers, and parents. The program includes mindfulness meditation sessions, teachings on ethical living, and activities to promote emotional regulation and resilience. One of the key components of the project is the "Mindfulness-Based Stress Reduction" (MBSR) program, which teaches participants mindfulness practices to manage stress and improve well-being. Research on the project has shown that students who participate in the MBSR program experience significant improvements in emotional regulation, academic performance, and relationships with peers and teachers. Teachers have also reported benefits from the program, including better stress management and improved classroom dynamics. The success of the project has led to its expansion to more schools and the inclusion of mindfulness training in teacher education programs.

In South Africa, the "Ubuntu Mindfulness Program" integrates mindfulness and compassion practices into the rehabilitation process for offenders. Developed by the Ubuntu Project in collaboration with local Buddhist centers and correctional facilities, the program aims to address the psychological and emotional needs of offenders by teaching them mindfulness and loving-kindness practices. Participants engage in daily meditation sessions, where they learn to observe their thoughts and emotions with non-judgmental awareness. The program also includes teachings on Ubuntu, an African philosophy that emphasizes the interconnectedness of all beings and the importance of community. By integrating mindfulness and Ubuntu principles, the program fosters a sense of empathy, compassion, and personal responsibility. Evaluations of the program have shown that participants experience significant reductions in symptoms of depression, anxiety, and PTSD, as well as improvements in overall well-being and social relationships. The program's success has inspired similar initiatives in other correctional facilities in South Africa and beyond.

24.5: Future Directions for Buddhist-Informed Criminology

The future directions for Buddhist-informed criminology hold significant promise for transforming the justice system into one that is more compassionate, effective, and attuned to the complexities of human behavior. By further integrating Buddhist principles and practices into criminological research and justice policies, we can develop innovative approaches that address the root causes of criminal behavior and promote long-term rehabilitation and societal harmony. This theme explores potential areas for further integration and research, proposes new frameworks and methodologies, and outlines strategic initiatives to advance Buddhist-informed criminology. One promising direction for future research is the systematic study of the long-term effects of mindfulness and meditation practices on offenders. While numerous studies have demonstrated the short-term benefits of these practices, including reductions in stress, anxiety, and aggression, there is a need for more longitudinal research to understand their enduring impact on recidivism, mental health, and overall well-being. By tracking participants over extended periods, researchers can gain insights into how sustained mindfulness practice influences behavior and psychological resilience, providing valuable data to inform the development of effective rehabilitation programs. For example, a longitudinal study might follow a cohort of offenders who participate in a mindfulness-based intervention, assessing changes in their mental health, behavior, and recidivism rates over several years.

Another area for future research is the exploration of how Buddhist ethical principles can be systematically integrated into correctional education and vocational training programs. These principles, such as non-harming, honesty, and compassion, can provide a moral framework that supports offenders in developing a sense of responsibility and integrity. By incorporating teachings on ethical conduct into educational and vocational curricula, correctional facilities can help offenders reflect on their actions and make positive changes in their behavior. Future research could examine the effectiveness of such programs in fostering ethical decision-making and reducing recidivism. For example, a study might compare the outcomes of traditional vocational training programs with those that include a component on Buddhist ethics, evaluating differences in job performance, interpersonal relationships, and reoffending rates.

The integration of Buddhist-informed restorative justice practices is another promising direction for the future. Restorative justice focuses on healing the harm caused by crime and fostering reconciliation between offenders, victims, and the community. Buddhist principles of compassion, empathy, and interconnectedness align closely with the goals of restorative justice, providing a philosophical foundation for these practices. Future research could explore innovative ways to incorporate mindfulness and compassion practices into restorative justice processes, such as victim-offender mediation and community reconciliation circles. By combining these practices, restorative justice initiatives can create more meaningful and transformative experiences for all parties involved. For example, a study might investigate the impact of mindfulness and compassion training on the outcomes of restorative justice sessions, assessing changes in participants' empathy, emotional regulation, and satisfaction with the resolution process.

Policy development is another critical area for advancing Buddhist-informed criminology. Advocating for policies that support the integration of mindfulness, compassion, and trauma-informed care into justice systems can help create an environment conducive to rehabilitation and positive change. Policymakers can promote the inclusion of mindfulness and meditation programs in correctional facilities, fund restorative justice initiatives, and ensure that trauma-informed care is available to all offenders. Future research could focus on the development and evaluation of policy frameworks that incorporate Buddhist principles, examining their impact on recidivism, public safety, and community well-being. For example, a policy analysis might assess the effectiveness of mindfulness-based programs mandated by state or federal regulations, comparing outcomes across different jurisdictions and identifying best practices for implementation. The creation of interdisciplinary research centers focused on Buddhist-informed criminology can also play a crucial role in advancing this field. These centers can bring together scholars, practitioners, and policymakers from various disciplines, including criminology, psychology, social work, and Buddhist studies, to collaborate on research and program development. By fostering interdisciplinary collaboration, these centers can generate innovative approaches and methodologies that draw on the strengths of multiple fields. Future initiatives could include the establishment of research grants, academic conferences, and publication opportunities to support the dissemination of findings and the development of a robust body of knowledge on Buddhist-informed criminology.

The development of training programs and certification courses for justice professionals is another important direction for the future. These programs can provide correctional officers, therapists, and other justice practitioners with the knowledge and skills needed to integrate mindfulness, compassion, and trauma-informed care into their work. Certification courses could cover topics such as mindfulness meditation techniques, ethical principles, restorative justice practices, and the psychological effects of trauma. By equipping justice professionals with these tools, training programs can enhance the effectiveness of rehabilitation efforts and create a more supportive and empathetic justice system. Future research could evaluate the impact of these training programs on practitioners' attitudes, behaviors, and job performance, as well as their effects on offender outcomes.

Community engagement and public education are also essential for advancing Buddhist-informed criminology. Raising awareness about the benefits of mindfulness, compassion, and restorative justice can help build public support for these approaches and foster a more compassionate and inclusive society. Future initiatives could include public workshops, community forums, and media campaigns to educate the public about Buddhist principles and their applications in the justice system. By promoting a broader understanding of these principles, community engagement efforts can help create a supportive environment for policy changes and program implementation. For example, a public education campaign might highlight success stories of offenders who have benefited from mindfulness and restorative justice programs, demonstrating the positive impact of these approaches on individuals and communities. Technology and digital platforms offer additional opportunities for advancing Buddhist-informed criminology. Online courses, mobile apps, and virtual reality programs can provide accessible and scalable tools for delivering mindfulness and meditation training to offenders and justice professionals.

These digital platforms can complement in-person programs, offering flexible and personalized learning opportunities. Future research could explore the effectiveness of digital mindfulness and meditation interventions in various justice settings, comparing outcomes with traditional in-person programs. For example, a study might evaluate the impact of a mindfulness meditation app on the mental health and behavior of offenders in a correctional facility, assessing changes in anxiety, depression, and aggression levels. International collaboration and cross-cultural research can also contribute to the advancement of Buddhist-informed criminology. By sharing best practices and learning from diverse cultural contexts, researchers and practitioners can develop more effective and culturally sensitive approaches to integrating Buddhist principles into justice systems. Future initiatives could include international conferences, research partnerships, and exchange programs to facilitate the sharing of knowledge and experiences. For example, a collaborative research project might compare the implementation and outcomes of mindfulness-based programs in correctional facilities across different countries, identifying common challenges and successful strategies for adaptation.

—

CHAPTER TWENTY-FIVE

Developing Comprehensive Rehabilitation Programs

Contents

- Designing Programs Informed by Buddhist Principles

- Practical Techniques for Effective Rehabilitation

- Case Studies of Comprehensive Programs

- Benefits for Offenders and Communities

- Strategies for Implementing Rehabilitation Programs

25.1: Designing Programs Informed by Buddhist Principles

Designing rehabilitation programs informed by Buddhist principles involves a nuanced understanding of human suffering, behavior, and the potential for transformation. The core Buddhist doctrines, such as the Four Noble Truths and the Eightfold Path, offer a comprehensive framework for addressing the root causes of criminal behavior and fostering rehabilitation. These principles emphasize the importance of mindfulness, compassion, and ethical living, which are crucial for supporting offenders in their journey towards healing and reintegration into society. The Four Noble Truths provide a foundational understanding of suffering and its origins, offering a path towards alleviation. The First Noble Truth acknowledges the presence of suffering, which is a fundamental aspect of human existence. In the context of rehabilitation, this truth helps offenders recognize and accept their own suffering and the suffering they have caused to others. By bringing awareness to their pain and the impact of their actions, offenders can begin the process of healing and transformation. This acknowledgment is a crucial first step, as it lays the groundwork for deeper self-reflection and understanding.

The Second Noble Truth identifies the causes of suffering, which often stem from attachment, aversion, and ignorance. Offenders frequently engage in criminal behavior as a response to these underlying issues, whether it be a desperate attempt to cling to a certain lifestyle, a means to escape painful emotions, or a lack of awareness about the consequences of their actions. Rehabilitation programs informed by Buddhist principles help offenders explore these underlying causes, fostering a deeper understanding of their motivations and behavior. Through mindfulness practices, offenders can develop greater self-awareness, recognizing the patterns of thought and behavior that contribute to their suffering. This insight is essential for breaking the cycle of harmful actions and cultivating more positive and constructive habits. The Third Noble Truth offers hope by teaching that it is possible to overcome suffering. This aligns with the goals of rehabilitation, which aim to support offenders in transforming their lives and moving beyond their past actions. By integrating teachings on the potential for change and growth, rehabilitation programs can inspire offenders to believe in their ability to create a better future. This sense of hope and possibility is a powerful motivator, encouraging offenders to engage actively in their rehabilitation journey. Programs might include stories and examples of individuals who have successfully transformed their lives, demonstrating that change is possible and providing tangible role models for offenders to aspire to.

The Fourth Noble Truth outlines the path to the cessation of suffering, known as the Eightfold Path. This path offers practical guidance for ethical living, mental discipline, and wisdom, all of which are crucial components of effective rehabilitation. The Eightfold Path consists of Right View, Right Intention, Right Speech, Right Action, Right Livelihood, Right Effort, Right Mindfulness, and Right Concentration. Each of these elements can be integrated into rehabilitation programs to provide a holistic approach to personal development and transformation. Right View involves understanding the nature of reality and the causes of suffering. In a rehabilitation context, this principle encourages offenders to reflect on their beliefs and attitudes, fostering a deeper understanding of the impact of their actions on themselves and others. This reflection can be facilitated through group discussions, individual counseling, and mindfulness practices, helping offenders develop a more compassionate and empathetic perspective.

Right Intention emphasizes the importance of cultivating positive motivations and intentions. Rehabilitation programs can support offenders in developing intentions that align with ethical and compassionate living, such as the desire to make amends for past actions, contribute positively to society, and lead a life of integrity. Activities such as goal-setting workshops, mindfulness meditation, and reflective journaling can help offenders clarify their intentions and commit to positive change. Right Speech involves speaking truthfully and kindly, avoiding harmful or deceitful language. This principle can be integrated into communication skills training, helping offenders develop healthier and more respectful ways of interacting with others. Role-playing exercises, mindfulness-based communication practices, and group discussions can provide opportunities for offenders to practice Right Speech and receive feedback on their communication style.

Right Action encourages ethical behavior that promotes well-being and avoids harm. Rehabilitation programs can incorporate teachings on ethical conduct, helping offenders understand the importance of actions such as non-violence, honesty, and respect for others. Community service projects, restorative justice practices, and mindfulness exercises can provide practical opportunities for offenders to embody Right Action in their daily lives. Right Livelihood involves choosing work that is ethical and beneficial to others. This principle can guide vocational training and employment support within rehabilitation programs, encouraging offenders to pursue careers that align with their values and contribute positively to society. Programs might offer job training, career counseling, and mentorship opportunities, helping offenders develop the skills and confidence needed to find meaningful and ethical employment.

Right Effort emphasizes the importance of diligently cultivating positive qualities and letting go of negative ones. Rehabilitation programs can support offenders in developing perseverance and dedication to their personal growth. Mindfulness practices, goal-setting workshops, and support groups can help offenders stay motivated and committed to their rehabilitation journey, providing encouragement and accountability along the way. Right Mindfulness involves maintaining awareness of the present moment, cultivating a non-judgmental and compassionate attitude towards one's experiences. This principle is central to many mindfulness-based rehabilitation programs, which teach offenders to observe their thoughts and emotions without becoming overwhelmed by them. Regular mindfulness meditation sessions, guided imagery, and mindful movement practices can help offenders develop greater emotional regulation and resilience, supporting their overall well-being and rehabilitation.

Right Concentration involves developing the ability to focus the mind and cultivate deep states of awareness. Rehabilitation programs can incorporate practices such as concentration meditation, yoga, and mindful breathing exercises to help offenders develop greater mental clarity and focus. These practices can support offenders in managing stress, improving their attention and decision-making abilities, and fostering a sense of inner peace and stability. In addition to these core principles, rehabilitation programs informed by Buddhist teachings can also integrate practices such as loving-kindness meditation, compassion training, and trauma-informed care. Loving-kindness meditation involves generating feelings of love and compassion towards oneself and others, which can be particularly healing for offenders who struggle with self-worth and guilt.

Compassion training helps offenders develop empathy and understanding for the suffering of others, fostering a sense of connection and responsibility. Trauma-informed care recognizes the pervasive impact of trauma on offenders' lives and provides a supportive environment for healing and recovery. Overall, designing rehabilitation programs informed by Buddhist principles involves creating a comprehensive and holistic approach to personal development and transformation. By integrating teachings on mindfulness, compassion, and ethical living, these programs can support offenders in addressing the root causes of their behavior, developing positive qualities, and cultivating a sense of hope and possibility for the future. Through mindfulness practices, ethical education, vocational training, and community service, offenders can develop the skills and insights needed to lead a fulfilling and meaningful life, contributing positively to society and breaking the cycle of criminal behavior.

25.2: Practical Techniques for Effective Rehabilitation

Practical techniques for effective rehabilitation informed by Buddhist principles encompass a wide range of methods designed to address the holistic needs of offenders, supporting their transformation and reintegration into society. These techniques leverage mindfulness, loving-kindness, compassion, trauma-informed care, and ethical living to foster personal growth, emotional regulation, and a deeper understanding of the self and others. Mindfulness meditation is a foundational technique in Buddhist-informed rehabilitation programs. It involves training individuals to focus their attention on the present moment, cultivating awareness of their thoughts, emotions, and bodily sensations without judgment. Regular mindfulness practice helps offenders develop greater self-awareness and emotional regulation, which are critical for addressing impulsive and reactive behaviors that often lead to criminal activity. For instance, a daily mindfulness meditation session might involve guiding offenders through focused breathing exercises, body scanning, and observing their thoughts as they arise and pass. Over time, these practices can help offenders build a more stable and resilient mental state, reducing anxiety, stress, and aggression.

Loving-kindness meditation, also known as Metta, is another powerful technique used in rehabilitation. This practice involves generating feelings of love and compassion towards oneself and others, starting with oneself and gradually extending these feelings to loved ones, acquaintances, and even those with whom one has conflicts. For offenders, loving-kindness meditation can be transformative, helping to soften the heart and reduce feelings of anger, resentment, and self-loathing. For example, an offender might be guided to silently repeat phrases like "May I be happy, may I be healthy, may I be safe," and then extend these wishes to others, including victims of their crimes. This practice fosters a sense of empathy and connection, promoting healing and reconciliation. Compassion training is closely related to loving-kindness meditation but focuses more explicitly on developing empathy and understanding for the suffering of others. In rehabilitation programs, compassion training can involve exercises such as compassionate listening, where offenders practice listening to others' experiences without judgment and with an open heart. This practice helps offenders develop a deeper understanding of the impact of their actions on others, fostering a sense of responsibility and a desire to make amends. Additionally, group discussions and role-playing exercises can provide opportunities for offenders to practice compassionate communication, learning to express themselves honestly and empathetically.

Trauma-informed care is a crucial aspect of effective rehabilitation, recognizing that many offenders have experienced significant trauma that contributes to their behavior. Trauma-informed approaches create a safe and supportive environment where offenders can begin to heal from their traumatic experiences. Techniques might include mindfulness-based stress reduction (MBSR), which combines mindfulness meditation with body awareness and gentle yoga to help individuals manage stress and anxiety. Trauma-informed care also involves training staff to recognize and respond to trauma symptoms, creating a culture of safety, trust, and empowerment. For example, staff might be trained to use non-coercive and non-punitive methods when addressing behavioral issues, helping offenders feel respected and understood. Ethical education is another important component of Buddhist-informed rehabilitation. Teaching offenders about Buddhist ethical principles, such as non-harming, honesty, and respect for others, can provide a moral framework for their behavior. Programs might include classes on the Five Precepts (ethical guidelines for lay Buddhists), encouraging offenders to reflect on their actions and commit to living in accordance with these principles. Practical exercises, such as journaling, group discussions, and community service projects, can help offenders internalize these values and apply them to their daily lives. For instance, an offender might keep a journal where they reflect on their actions each day, considering how they align with the principles of non-harming and honesty.

Vocational training and employment support are essential for helping offenders reintegrate into society and lead productive lives. Buddhist-informed rehabilitation programs might incorporate teachings on Right Livelihood, which emphasizes choosing work that is ethical and beneficial to others. Vocational training programs can provide offenders with the skills and qualifications needed to find meaningful employment, reducing the risk of recidivism. These programs might include workshops on resume writing, job interview skills, and professional conduct, as well as partnerships with local businesses to provide job placements and internships. Additionally, ongoing support and mentorship can help offenders navigate the challenges of re-entering the workforce, offering guidance and encouragement as they build new careers. Mindful movement practices, such as yoga and tai chi, can complement mindfulness meditation and help offenders develop greater physical and emotional balance. These practices combine physical exercise with mindful awareness, promoting relaxation, flexibility, and body awareness. For offenders, mindful movement can be particularly beneficial in managing stress and improving physical health, which are often neglected areas in traditional rehabilitation programs. A typical session might involve gentle stretching, controlled breathing, and mindful focus on bodily sensations, helping offenders connect with their bodies and release tension. These practices can also provide a sense of accomplishment and boost self-esteem, contributing to overall well-being.

Group therapy and support groups are also effective techniques in Buddhist-informed rehabilitation programs. These settings provide a safe space for offenders to share their experiences, challenges, and successes with others who understand their struggles. Facilitated by trained therapists or peer leaders, group sessions can incorporate mindfulness and compassion practices, fostering a supportive community where offenders can learn from and support one another. Topics might include emotional regulation, conflict resolution, and ethical decision-making, with participants practicing skills and offering feedback to each other. The sense of camaraderie and mutual support that develops in these groups can be a powerful motivator for change, helping offenders feel less isolated and more connected to a community of peers. Restorative justice practices, such as victim-offender mediation and restorative circles, offer opportunities for offenders to take responsibility for their actions and make amends to those they have harmed. These practices align closely with Buddhist principles of compassion and interconnectedness, emphasizing healing and reconciliation over punishment.

In victim-offender mediation, offenders meet with their victims in a controlled and supportive environment, facilitated by a trained mediator. This process allows offenders to hear directly from their victims about the impact of their actions, fostering empathy and a desire to make things right. Restorative circles, which involve broader community participation, can help offenders understand the wider impact of their actions and work towards repairing the harm caused. These practices can lead to more meaningful resolutions and promote healing for both offenders and victims. Integrating mindfulness and ethical living into daily routines is another practical technique for effective rehabilitation. Encouraging offenders to practice mindfulness and reflect on their actions throughout the day can help reinforce the principles learned in formal sessions. For example, daily routines might include morning meditation sessions, mindful eating practices, and evening reflections on the day's activities. Offenders can also be encouraged to set daily intentions aligned with Buddhist ethical principles, such as practicing kindness, honesty, and non-harming. By integrating these practices into their daily lives, offenders can develop habits that support their long-term rehabilitation and personal growth.

25.3: Case Studies of Comprehensive Programs

Case studies of comprehensive rehabilitation programs informed by Buddhist principles provide valuable insights into the transformative power of these approaches. By examining diverse examples from different contexts and cultures, we can understand how these principles have been successfully implemented to support offender rehabilitation and community healing. In Sri Lanka, the "Mindful Path to Rehabilitation" program integrates mindfulness meditation and ethical education into the rehabilitation process for former child soldiers. Developed by the Sarvodaya Movement, the program aims to address the psychological and emotional trauma experienced by these individuals while promoting a sense of community and ethical living. Participants engage in daily mindfulness meditation sessions, where they learn to observe their thoughts and emotions without judgment. These practices help them manage symptoms of PTSD, anxiety, and depression, fostering a sense of inner peace and stability. Additionally, the program includes teachings on Buddhist ethical principles, such as non-violence and compassion, encouraging participants to reflect on their past actions and commit to a life of peace and integrity. The program also offers vocational training and community service opportunities, helping former child soldiers reintegrate into society and contribute positively to their communities. Evaluations of the program have shown significant improvements in mental health, reduced recidivism, and stronger community ties, highlighting the effectiveness of integrating Buddhist principles into rehabilitation efforts.

In Brazil, the "Compassionate Justice Initiative" works within the juvenile justice system to provide mindfulness and compassion training to young offenders. This program, developed by the Alana Institute in collaboration with local juvenile detention centers, focuses on helping young people develop emotional regulation, empathy, and ethical behavior. Participants engage in mindfulness meditation and loving-kindness practices, learning to cultivate compassion for themselves and others. These practices are complemented by group discussions on the ethical principles of compassion, non-harming, and respect for others. The program also includes restorative justice practices, such as victim-offender mediation and community reconciliation circles, allowing young offenders to make amends for their actions and understand the impact of their behavior on others. Evaluations of the initiative have shown that participants experience significant reductions in aggression, improved emotional regulation, and a greater sense of empathy and responsibility. The program's success has led to its expansion to other juvenile detention centers in Brazil, demonstrating the potential of Buddhist-informed approaches to transform the juvenile justice system.

In Uganda, the "Healing Through Mindfulness" program, implemented by the African Youth Initiative Network (AYINET), provides mindfulness-based trauma recovery for former child soldiers and victims of war. The program includes mindfulness meditation, yoga, and trauma-informed care to support the healing process. Participants engage in daily mindfulness practices, helping them manage symptoms of PTSD and anxiety. The program also includes group therapy sessions where participants share their experiences and support each other in their healing journeys. In addition to mindfulness and trauma-informed care, the program incorporates teachings on forgiveness and reconciliation, encouraging participants to let go of anger and resentment and work towards healing and peace. Evaluations of the program have shown significant improvements in mental health, reduced symptoms of trauma, and a greater sense of hope and resilience. The program's holistic approach, which combines mindfulness, trauma care, and ethical education, has been instrumental in supporting the rehabilitation and reintegration of former child soldiers and war victims.

In Australia, the "Buddhist Prison Chaplaincy Program" provides spiritual support and mindfulness training to inmates in correctional facilities. Developed by the Australian Buddhist Prison Chaplaincy Association, the program aims to support the spiritual and emotional well-being of inmates through regular meditation sessions, ethical education, and one-on-one spiritual counseling. Participants engage in mindfulness meditation, learning to develop greater self-awareness and emotional regulation. The program also includes teachings on the Four Noble Truths and the Eightfold Path, providing a moral framework for ethical living and personal growth. In addition to meditation and ethical education, the program offers opportunities for inmates to participate in community service projects, fostering a sense of purpose and connection. Evaluations of the program have shown that participants experience significant reductions in stress, improved mental health, and a greater sense of responsibility and ethical behavior. The program's success has led to its adoption in multiple correctional facilities across Australia, highlighting the potential of Buddhist-informed chaplaincy to support inmate rehabilitation.

In the United States, the "Mindfulness-Based Recovery Program" at a women's correctional facility in California integrates mindfulness meditation and trauma-informed care to support the rehabilitation of female inmates. Developed by the Insight Prison Project, the program focuses on addressing the trauma and emotional pain that often underlie criminal behavior. Participants engage in mindfulness meditation and yoga, helping them develop greater self-awareness and emotional regulation. The program also includes group therapy sessions where participants share their experiences and support each other in their healing journeys. In addition to mindfulness and trauma-informed care, the program incorporates teachings on self-compassion and forgiveness, encouraging participants to let go of self-judgment and develop a more compassionate relationship with themselves. Evaluations of the program have shown significant improvements in mental health, reduced symptoms of PTSD and depression, and a greater sense of hope and resilience. The program's holistic approach, which combines mindfulness, trauma care, and self-compassion, has been instrumental in supporting the rehabilitation and empowerment of female inmates.

In India, the "Peaceful Mind Program" provides mindfulness and ethical education to juvenile offenders in a reform school in New Delhi. Developed by the Tushita Meditation Centre in collaboration with the reform school, the program aims to support the emotional and ethical development of young offenders. Participants engage in daily mindfulness meditation sessions, learning to develop greater self-awareness and emotional regulation. The program also includes teachings on the Five Precepts and other Buddhist ethical principles, encouraging participants to reflect on their actions and commit to ethical living. In addition to meditation and ethical education, the program offers vocational training and community service opportunities, helping young offenders develop practical skills and contribute positively to their communities. Evaluations of the program have shown significant improvements in emotional regulation, reduced recidivism, and a greater sense of responsibility and ethical behavior. The program's success has led to its expansion to other juvenile reform schools in India, demonstrating the potential of Buddhist-informed approaches to transform the juvenile justice system.

In Canada, the "Mindful Living Program" at a men's correctional facility in British Columbia integrates mindfulness meditation and ethical education into the rehabilitation process. Developed by the Vancouver Buddhist Centre, the program aims to support the spiritual and emotional well-being of inmates through regular meditation sessions, ethical education, and one-on-one spiritual counseling. Participants engage in mindfulness meditation, learning to develop greater self-awareness and emotional regulation. The program also includes teachings on the Four Noble Truths and the Eightfold Path, providing a moral framework for ethical living and personal growth. In addition to meditation and ethical education, the program offers opportunities for inmates to participate in community service projects, fostering a sense of purpose and connection. Evaluations of the program have shown that participants experience significant reductions in stress, improved mental health, and a greater sense of responsibility and ethical behavior. The program's success has led to its adoption in multiple correctional facilities across Canada, highlighting the potential of Buddhist-informed chaplaincy to support inmate rehabilitation.

In South Korea, the "Zen Mindfulness Program" offers mindfulness and Zen meditation training to inmates in a correctional facility in Seoul. Developed by the Korean Zen Center in collaboration with the correctional facility, the program focuses on helping inmates develop greater self-awareness, emotional regulation, and ethical behavior. Participants engage in daily Zen meditation sessions, learning to observe their thoughts and emotions with non-judgmental awareness. The program also includes teachings on Zen ethics and the principles of non-harming, honesty, and respect for others. In addition to meditation and ethical education, the program offers opportunities for inmates to participate in community service projects, fostering a sense of purpose and connection. Evaluations of the program have shown significant reductions in stress, improved mental health, and a greater sense of responsibility and ethical behavior. The program's success has led to its expansion to other correctional facilities in South Korea, demonstrating the potential of Zen mindfulness to support inmate rehabilitation.

25.4: Benefits for Offenders and Communities

The benefits of comprehensive rehabilitation programs informed by Buddhist principles extend to both offenders and communities, fostering transformation, healing, and social cohesion. By addressing the holistic needs of individuals and promoting ethical and compassionate living, these programs not only reduce recidivism but also contribute to the overall well-being and resilience of society. These benefits can be categorized into several key areas: mental health and emotional well-being, ethical behavior and personal responsibility, social reintegration and community building, and systemic transformation and public safety. First and foremost, comprehensive rehabilitation programs that incorporate mindfulness, compassion, and trauma-informed care significantly improve the mental health and emotional well-being of offenders. Many offenders enter the criminal justice system with a history of trauma, mental health issues, and emotional dysregulation, which contribute to their criminal behavior. By providing mindfulness-based interventions, these programs help offenders develop greater self-awareness and emotional regulation. Mindfulness meditation teaches individuals to observe their thoughts and emotions without judgment, fostering a sense of inner calm and stability. This practice reduces symptoms of anxiety, depression, and PTSD, which are prevalent among offenders. For example, a daily mindfulness practice can help offenders manage stress, reduce impulsivity, and cultivate a more positive outlook on life. As a result, participants experience significant improvements in their overall mental health, which supports their rehabilitation and reduces the likelihood of reoffending.

The incorporation of loving-kindness and compassion practices further enhances emotional well-being by fostering empathy and connection. Loving-kindness meditation involves generating feelings of love and compassion towards oneself and others, which can be particularly healing for offenders who struggle with self-worth and guilt. This practice helps individuals develop a more compassionate relationship with themselves, reducing self-criticism and promoting self-acceptance. Additionally, compassion training encourages offenders to empathize with the suffering of others, fostering a sense of connection and responsibility. As offenders develop greater empathy and compassion, they are more likely to engage in prosocial behavior and seek ways to make amends for their actions. These practices not only support emotional healing but also lay the foundation for ethical behavior and personal transformation.

Ethical behavior and personal responsibility are core components of comprehensive rehabilitation programs informed by Buddhist principles.

Buddhist teachings emphasize the importance of ethical conduct, which includes principles such as non-harming, honesty, and respect for others. By integrating these teachings into rehabilitation programs, offenders are encouraged to reflect on their actions and commit to ethical living. This ethical framework provides a moral compass that guides behavior, helping offenders make positive choices and develop a sense of integrity. For example, programs might include discussions on the Five Precepts (ethical guidelines for lay Buddhists), encouraging participants to practice non-violence, honesty, and respect in their daily lives. Practical exercises, such as journaling and group discussions, help offenders internalize these values and apply them to real-life situations. As offenders develop a commitment to ethical behavior, they are more likely to take responsibility for their actions and seek ways to contribute positively to society.

Social reintegration and community building are also significant benefits of comprehensive rehabilitation programs. Offenders often face significant challenges in rebuilding their lives and reestablishing relationships after incarceration. By fostering a sense of connection and mutual support, these programs help individuals reintegrate into society and build positive relationships. Community-based approaches to rehabilitation, such as peer support groups and community service projects, provide a supportive environment for offenders to practice new skills and behaviors. These approaches help break down the barriers of stigma and isolation that often accompany criminal behavior, promoting reintegration and reducing the risk of reoffending. For example, a community service project that involves offenders working alongside other community members can help build trust and understanding, fostering a sense of shared purpose and mutual support. As offenders develop healthier relationships with family members, friends, and community members, they are more likely to receive the emotional and practical support needed to maintain their rehabilitation efforts.

The benefits of comprehensive rehabilitation programs extend beyond individual offenders to the broader community. By promoting approaches that emphasize healing, compassion, and ethical living, these programs contribute to a more just and compassionate society. Communities that support the rehabilitation and reintegration of offenders experience reduced crime rates, improved public safety, and stronger social cohesion. For example, restorative justice practices, which involve dialogue and reconciliation between offenders and victims, help repair the harm caused by crime and restore relationships. These practices foster a sense of justice and healing, promoting a culture of empathy and understanding. Additionally, community involvement in rehabilitation programs, such as volunteering and mentorship, creates opportunities for positive engagement and support. As community members actively participate in the rehabilitation process, they contribute to a more inclusive and supportive environment, enhancing the overall well-being and resilience of the community.

Systemic transformation and public safety are also significant benefits of integrating Buddhist principles into rehabilitation programs. Traditional punitive approaches to justice often fail to address the root causes of criminal behavior and can perpetuate cycles of harm. By adopting a more holistic and compassionate approach, comprehensive rehabilitation programs can transform the justice system into one that prioritizes healing and rehabilitation over punishment. This shift leads to better outcomes for individuals and communities, reducing recidivism and promoting long-term public safety. For example, policymakers might advocate for the inclusion of mindfulness and meditation programs in correctional facilities, promote restorative justice practices, and ensure that trauma-informed care is available to all offenders. These initiatives create a more supportive environment for rehabilitation and positive change, ultimately contributing to a safer and more just society.

Furthermore, the integration of Buddhist principles into rehabilitation programs supports ongoing research and innovation in the field of criminology. The holistic and compassionate perspective offered by Buddhism provides a rich foundation for developing new theories, practices, and interventions that address the complexities of criminal behavior and rehabilitation. Researchers can explore how Buddhist principles can be applied to various aspects of criminology, from understanding the psychological and emotional dimensions of criminal behavior to developing effective rehabilitation programs and policies. This interdisciplinary approach can lead to new insights and innovations that enhance the effectiveness of the justice system and support the well-being of offenders and communities.

25.5: Strategies for Implementing Rehabilitation Programs

Strategies for implementing rehabilitation programs informed by Buddhist principles are crucial for ensuring their success and sustainability. These strategies encompass various aspects, including staff training and development, community partnerships, program design and structure, policy advocacy, and continuous evaluation and improvement. By following these strategies, justice systems and rehabilitation programs can create a supportive environment that promotes healing, transformation, and reintegration for offenders. Staff training and development are foundational elements of implementing Buddhist-informed rehabilitation programs. Effective training ensures that staff members understand and can skillfully apply mindfulness, compassion, and trauma-informed care principles. Training programs should include comprehensive education on Buddhist teachings, such as the Four Noble Truths, the Eightfold Path, and mindfulness practices. Additionally, staff should receive training in trauma-informed care to recognize and address the impact of trauma on offenders. For example, correctional officers, therapists, and program facilitators might participate in workshops and training sessions led by experienced mindfulness teachers and trauma specialists. These sessions can include theoretical instruction, practical exercises, and role-playing scenarios to help staff develop the skills and confidence needed to support offenders effectively. Ongoing professional development opportunities, such as advanced training courses and peer support groups, can further enhance staff capabilities and ensure that they remain up-to-date with best practices.

Developing partnerships with Buddhist practitioners, organizations, and community groups is another critical strategy. These partnerships can provide valuable resources, expertise, and support for implementing and sustaining rehabilitation programs. Collaboration with local Buddhist centers, meditation teachers, and organizations specializing in mindfulness and trauma healing can enhance the quality and authenticity of the programs. For instance, a correctional facility might partner with a local meditation center to offer regular mindfulness sessions and workshops for both offenders and staff. These partnerships can also facilitate the sharing of best practices and provide opportunities for joint research and program evaluation. Community involvement is essential for creating a supportive network that reinforces the rehabilitation process and fosters a sense of belonging for offenders. Engaging community members as volunteers, mentors, and supporters can help bridge the gap between the correctional facility and the broader community, promoting social reintegration and reducing stigma.

Designing and structuring rehabilitation programs to align with Buddhist principles involves creating a comprehensive and holistic approach that addresses the psychological, emotional, and social needs of offenders. Programs should integrate mindfulness meditation, compassion training, and ethical education into daily routines and activities. A typical program might include daily mindfulness meditation sessions, group discussions on ethical living, and individual counseling sessions focusing on trauma recovery and personal growth. For example, a daily schedule might start with a morning mindfulness meditation session, followed by vocational training or educational classes, and end with an evening reflection on ethical principles. Incorporating physical activities such as yoga and mindful movement can further enhance the program by promoting physical well-being and stress reduction. Programs should be flexible and adaptable to meet the diverse needs of offenders, offering various entry points and levels of intensity to accommodate different levels of experience and comfort with mindfulness practices.

Policy advocacy is crucial for securing the necessary support and resources for Buddhist-informed rehabilitation programs. Advocating for policies that prioritize rehabilitation over punishment and support the integration of mindfulness, compassion, and trauma-informed care can create a more conducive environment for these programs. Policymakers should be informed about the benefits of Buddhist-informed approaches, supported by data and research findings demonstrating their effectiveness in reducing recidivism and improving mental health outcomes. Advocacy efforts might include presenting evidence-based research to policymakers, participating in public forums and discussions, and collaborating with other organizations and stakeholders to build a coalition of support.

For instance, presenting case studies and success stories from existing programs can illustrate the practical benefits and inspire broader adoption of these approaches. Securing funding from government agencies, private foundations, and other sources is essential for developing and sustaining these programs. Grant proposals should highlight the potential cost savings associated with reduced recidivism and improved mental health outcomes, as well as the broader social benefits of supporting offender rehabilitation.

Continuous evaluation and improvement are essential for ensuring the long-term success and sustainability of Buddhist-informed rehabilitation programs. Regular assessment and feedback can help identify strengths and areas for improvement, allowing programs to be adjusted and refined over time. Evaluation methods might include pre- and post-assessment surveys, interviews, and focus groups with participants, staff, and volunteers, as well as quantitative measures of outcomes such as recidivism rates, mental health symptoms, and participant engagement. For example, a program might conduct pre- and post-assessment surveys to measure changes in participants' levels of anxiety, depression, and PTSD symptoms, as well as their overall sense of well-being and satisfaction with the program. Focus groups and interviews can provide qualitative insights into participants' experiences, highlighting the aspects of the program that are most beneficial and any challenges or barriers they have encountered. This feedback can be used to make data-driven improvements to the program, ensuring that it continues to meet the needs of participants and achieve its goals.

Creating a supportive and trauma-informed environment within correctional facilities is also critical for the success of Buddhist-informed rehabilitation programs. This involves establishing policies and practices that prioritize the safety and well-being of offenders and staff. Simple changes, such as creating quiet spaces for meditation, ensuring that facilities are clean and comfortable, and promoting a culture of respect and empathy, can make a significant difference. Additionally, incorporating mindfulness and trauma-informed practices into daily routines and activities can help to create a more supportive environment. For example, starting meetings and group sessions with a brief mindfulness exercise can help participants center themselves and create a sense of calm and focus. Ensuring that all staff members are trained in trauma-informed care and mindfulness practices can further enhance the supportive environment, helping offenders feel respected and understood.

Incorporating mindfulness and ethical living into the daily routines of offenders can help reinforce the principles learned in formal sessions and support long-term behavior change. Encouraging offenders to practice mindfulness and reflect on their actions throughout the day can help them develop habits that support their rehabilitation. For example, daily routines might include morning meditation sessions, mindful eating practices, and evening reflections on the day's activities. Offenders can also be encouraged to set daily intentions aligned with Buddhist ethical principles, such as practicing kindness, honesty, and non-harming. By integrating these practices into their daily lives, offenders can develop greater self-awareness, emotional regulation, and ethical behavior, laying the foundation for a more fulfilling and meaningful life. Engaging family members and loved ones in the rehabilitation process can provide additional support and reinforcement for offenders. Family involvement can help create a supportive network that encourages and supports the offender's rehabilitation efforts. Programs might include family counseling sessions, workshops on mindfulness and ethical living for family members, and opportunities for family members to participate in community service projects with offenders. By involving families in the rehabilitation process, programs can help strengthen family bonds and promote a more supportive and understanding environment for the offender's reintegration.

Utilizing technology and digital platforms can enhance the accessibility and scalability of Buddhist-informed rehabilitation programs. Online courses, mobile apps, and virtual reality programs can provide flexible and personalized learning opportunities for offenders and staff. These digital platforms can complement in-person programs, offering additional resources and support for mindfulness practice, ethical education, and trauma recovery. For example, a mindfulness meditation app might provide guided meditations, instructional videos, and progress tracking tools to help offenders develop and maintain a regular practice. Virtual reality programs can offer immersive experiences that teach mindfulness and compassion practices in engaging and interactive ways. Leveraging technology can help reach a broader audience and ensure that all individuals have access to the resources and support they need for their rehabilitation journey. Promoting public awareness and education about the benefits of Buddhist-informed rehabilitation programs is essential for building community support and reducing stigma. Public workshops, community forums, and media campaigns can help raise awareness about the transformative potential of mindfulness, compassion, and ethical living in the justice system. By highlighting success stories and sharing research findings, these efforts can inspire greater acceptance and support for these approaches. Engaging the public in discussions about the benefits of rehabilitation over punishment and the importance of creating a more compassionate and just society can help shift public perceptions and build a broader base of support for policy changes and program implementation.

CHAPTER TWENTY-SIX

Policy Recommendations for Justice Reform

Contents

- Advocating for Policies that Integrate Buddhist Doctrines

- Practical Applications in Justice Systems

- Benefits for Offenders and Society

- Case Studies of Successful Policy Reform

- Future Directions for Justice Policies

26.1: Advocating for Policies that Integrate Buddhist Doctrines

Advocating for policies that integrate Buddhist doctrines into justice systems requires a thoughtful and strategic approach, rooted in the core principles of mindfulness, compassion, and ethical living. The integration of these doctrines into justice policies can transform how society approaches crime and punishment, shifting the focus from retribution to rehabilitation and healing. This shift not only benefits offenders by providing them with the tools and support needed for personal transformation but also enhances public safety and community well-being by addressing the root causes of criminal behavior. Promoting the inclusion of mindfulness, compassion, and ethical education in justice policies starts with a deep understanding of Buddhist teachings and their relevance to criminology and rehabilitation. The Four Noble Truths provide a foundational framework for understanding suffering and its causes, which are often at the heart of criminal behavior. The First Noble Truth acknowledges the existence of suffering, which is a universal experience shared by offenders, victims, and society at large. Recognizing this suffering is the first step towards addressing the underlying issues that lead to criminal behavior.

The Second Noble Truth identifies the causes of suffering, which include attachment, aversion, and ignorance. In the context of criminal justice, these causes can manifest as attachment to harmful behaviors, aversion to societal norms, and ignorance of the consequences of one's actions. Policies that integrate Buddhist doctrines seek to address these underlying causes by promoting self-awareness and emotional regulation through mindfulness practices. By teaching offenders to observe their thoughts and emotions without judgment, mindfulness helps them recognize the patterns that lead to criminal behavior and develop healthier coping mechanisms. The Third Noble Truth offers hope by teaching that it is possible to overcome suffering. This aligns with the goals of rehabilitation, which aim to support offenders in transforming their lives and moving beyond their past actions. Policies that promote rehabilitation over punishment emphasize the potential for personal growth and change, providing offenders with the resources and support needed to build a better future. This includes access to mindfulness-based programs, trauma-informed care, and educational opportunities that foster personal development.

The Fourth Noble Truth outlines the path to the cessation of suffering, known as the Eightfold Path. This path offers practical guidance for ethical living, mental discipline, and wisdom, which are crucial components of effective rehabilitation. Policies that integrate the Eightfold Path into justice systems encourage offenders to cultivate Right View, Right Intention, Right Speech, Right Action, Right Livelihood, Right Effort, Right Mindfulness, and Right Concentration. These principles provide a comprehensive framework for personal transformation, promoting ethical behavior and emotional resilience. Building coalitions with stakeholders is essential for advocating for these policy changes. Collaboration with Buddhist practitioners, community organizations, and policymakers can help build a broad base of support for integrating Buddhist doctrines into justice systems. By working together, stakeholders can share resources, expertise, and best practices, creating a unified approach to justice reform. Engaging community members and leaders in the advocacy process helps to raise awareness about the benefits of Buddhist-informed policies and fosters a sense of collective responsibility for creating a more just and compassionate society.

Effective advocacy also involves educating policymakers about the practical benefits of integrating Buddhist doctrines into justice policies. Presenting evidence-based research that demonstrates the positive outcomes of mindfulness and compassion practices in reducing recidivism and improving mental health can help build a compelling case for policy change. Highlighting the success of existing programs, both domestically and internationally, provides concrete examples of how these approaches can be effectively implemented. For instance, policymakers can be shown data from programs that have successfully reduced recidivism rates and improved the emotional well-being of offenders through mindfulness and trauma-informed care. Advocacy efforts should also emphasize the broader societal benefits of integrating Buddhist doctrines into justice policies. By addressing the root causes of criminal behavior and promoting rehabilitation, these policies contribute to a safer and more cohesive society. Reducing recidivism not only benefits offenders but also enhances public safety and reduces the financial burden on the criminal justice system. Policies that support rehabilitation over punishment help to break the cycle of crime and incarceration, fostering a more compassionate and humane approach to justice.

Furthermore, integrating Buddhist doctrines into justice policies can help to address systemic issues within the criminal justice system. For example, policies that promote mindfulness and trauma-informed care can help to create a more supportive and understanding environment for both offenders and staff. Training staff in mindfulness practices and trauma-informed approaches can improve their ability to manage stress and build positive relationships with offenders, creating a more constructive and rehabilitative atmosphere within correctional facilities.

This, in turn, can lead to better outcomes for offenders and a more positive working environment for staff. Advocating for policies that integrate Buddhist doctrines also involves addressing potential challenges and resistance to change. Some stakeholders may be skeptical about the relevance of Buddhist principles to criminal justice or concerned about the feasibility of implementing these practices within existing systems. Advocacy efforts should address these concerns by providing clear and practical examples of how Buddhist-informed approaches can be integrated into current policies and practices. This might include pilot programs, training sessions, and ongoing support to ensure successful implementation.

26.2: Practical Applications in Justice Systems

Implementing Buddhist-informed policies in justice systems involves practical applications that encompass various aspects of rehabilitation, mindfulness, restorative justice, and trauma-informed care. These applications aim to create a more humane and effective system that addresses the root causes of criminal behavior, supports offender rehabilitation, and promotes healing and reconciliation within communities. By incorporating Buddhist principles such as mindfulness, compassion, and ethical living, justice systems can transform their approach to crime and punishment, fostering long-term positive change for individuals and society. One of the most significant practical applications is the implementation of mindfulness-based programs in correctional facilities. Mindfulness meditation has been shown to reduce stress, anxiety, and depression, which are common issues among offenders. By teaching mindfulness practices, correctional facilities can help offenders develop greater self-awareness and emotional regulation. These programs typically involve daily meditation sessions, where participants learn techniques such as focused breathing, body scanning, and loving-kindness meditation. These practices help offenders become more attuned to their thoughts and emotions, enabling them to recognize and interrupt negative patterns that contribute to criminal behavior. For example, a daily mindfulness meditation session might involve guiding offenders through a 30-minute practice, followed by group discussions on the experience and its impact on their mental state. Over time, regular mindfulness practice can lead to significant improvements in mental health, reducing recidivism and supporting long-term rehabilitation.

Integrating restorative justice practices is another practical application that aligns closely with Buddhist principles of compassion and interconnectedness. Restorative justice focuses on repairing the harm caused by crime and fostering reconciliation between offenders, victims, and the community. This approach emphasizes dialogue, understanding, and mutual respect, encouraging offenders to take responsibility for their actions and make amends. Restorative justice practices can take various forms, including victim-offender mediation, restorative circles, and community conferences. In victim-offender mediation, offenders and victims meet in a controlled and supportive environment, facilitated by a trained mediator. This process allows victims to express the impact of the crime and offenders to understand the consequences of their actions, fostering empathy and accountability. For instance, a restorative circle might involve not only the offender and victim but also family members, community representatives, and support personnel, creating a broader dialogue about the crime's impact and ways to repair the harm. These practices can lead to more meaningful resolutions, promote healing, and reduce the likelihood of reoffending.

Trauma-informed care is a critical component of Buddhist-informed justice policies, recognizing the significant impact of trauma on offenders' behavior and well-being. Many offenders have experienced adverse childhood experiences, violence, and other forms of trauma that contribute to their criminal behavior. Trauma-informed care aims to create a safe and supportive environment that addresses the psychological and emotional needs of individuals. This approach involves training staff to recognize and respond to trauma symptoms, establishing policies that prioritize safety and trust, and providing therapeutic interventions that support healing. For example, a correctional facility might implement a trauma-informed care program that includes staff training on trauma awareness, regular counseling sessions for offenders, and the incorporation of mindfulness practices to help manage stress and anxiety. Creating a trauma-informed environment helps offenders feel respected and understood, reducing re-traumatization and supporting their rehabilitation.

Vocational training and community service opportunities are practical applications that align with Buddhist principles of Right Livelihood and contribute to offenders' rehabilitation and reintegration into society. Providing offenders with the skills and qualifications needed to find meaningful employment reduces the risk of recidivism and supports their long-term success. Vocational training programs might include workshops on resume writing, job interview skills, and professional conduct, as well as hands-on training in various trades such as carpentry, culinary arts, or information technology. Community service opportunities allow offenders to give back to their communities, fostering a sense of purpose and connection. For example, a correctional facility might partner with local organizations to offer community service projects, such as environmental clean-up efforts, building and maintaining community gardens, or volunteering at local shelters. These experiences help offenders develop practical skills, build positive relationships, and contribute positively to society.

Another practical application is the incorporation of ethical education into rehabilitation programs. Buddhist teachings on ethical conduct, such as the Five Precepts, provide a moral framework that supports offenders in developing a sense of integrity and responsibility. Rehabilitation programs can include classes and workshops that explore these ethical principles, encouraging offenders to reflect on their actions and commit to living in accordance with these values. Practical exercises, such as journaling, group discussions, and role-playing scenarios, help offenders internalize these principles and apply them to real-life situations. For instance, a workshop on the precept of non-harming might include discussions on the importance of non-violence, exercises in conflict resolution, and opportunities for offenders to practice these skills in a supportive environment. By integrating ethical education into rehabilitation programs, offenders are more likely to make positive choices and develop a commitment to ethical living.

Creating supportive environments within correctional facilities is essential for the success of these practical applications. This involves establishing policies and practices that promote safety, trust, and respect for both offenders and staff. Simple changes, such as creating quiet spaces for meditation, ensuring that facilities are clean and comfortable, and promoting a culture of empathy and understanding, can significantly impact the effectiveness of rehabilitation efforts. For example, a correctional facility might designate a meditation room where offenders can practice mindfulness and meditation in a peaceful and supportive setting. Staff training on mindfulness and trauma-informed care further enhances the supportive environment, helping staff build positive relationships with offenders and manage stress effectively. Engaging family members and loved ones in the rehabilitation process is another important strategy. Family involvement can provide additional support and reinforcement for offenders, helping them maintain their rehabilitation efforts and build a positive support network. Programs might include family counseling sessions, workshops on mindfulness and ethical living for family members, and opportunities for family members to participate in community service projects with offenders. By involving families in the rehabilitation process, programs can help strengthen family bonds and promote a more supportive and understanding environment for the offender's reintegration.

Leveraging technology and digital platforms can enhance the accessibility and scalability of Buddhist-informed rehabilitation programs. Online courses, mobile apps, and virtual reality programs can provide flexible and personalized learning opportunities for offenders and staff. These digital platforms can complement in-person programs, offering additional resources and support for mindfulness practice, ethical education, and trauma recovery. For example, a mindfulness meditation app might provide guided meditations, instructional videos, and progress tracking tools to help offenders develop and maintain a regular practice. Virtual reality programs can offer immersive experiences that teach mindfulness and compassion practices in engaging and interactive ways. Leveraging technology can help reach a broader audience and ensure that all individuals have access to the resources and support they need for their rehabilitation journey. Public awareness and education about the benefits of Buddhist-informed rehabilitation programs are crucial for building community support and reducing stigma. Public workshops, community forums, and media campaigns can help raise awareness about the transformative potential of mindfulness, compassion, and ethical living in the justice system. By highlighting success stories and sharing research findings, these efforts can inspire greater acceptance and support for these approaches. Engaging the public in discussions about the benefits of rehabilitation over punishment and the importance of creating a more compassionate and just society can help shift public perceptions and build a broader base of support for policy changes and program implementation.

26.3: Benefits for Offenders and Society

The benefits of integrating Buddhist-informed policies into justice systems are extensive and multifaceted, impacting both offenders and society at large. These benefits include improved mental health and emotional well-being for offenders, reduced recidivism rates, enhanced public safety, and a more compassionate and humane justice system. By addressing the root causes of criminal behavior and promoting rehabilitation over punishment, these policies create a supportive environment that fosters personal growth, healing, and reintegration into society. One of the most significant benefits of Buddhist-informed policies is the improvement in mental health and emotional well-being for offenders. Many individuals in the criminal justice system suffer from mental health issues, trauma, and emotional dysregulation, which contribute to their criminal behavior. By incorporating mindfulness and meditation practices into rehabilitation programs, offenders can develop greater self-awareness and emotional regulation. Mindfulness meditation teaches individuals to observe their thoughts and emotions without judgment, fostering a sense of inner calm and stability. This practice helps reduce symptoms of anxiety, depression, and PTSD, which are prevalent among offenders. For example, a daily mindfulness meditation session might involve guiding offenders through focused breathing exercises, body scanning, and observing their thoughts as they arise and pass. Over time, regular mindfulness practice can lead to significant improvements in mental health, supporting the overall well-being of offenders and reducing the likelihood of reoffending.

Another key benefit is the reduction in recidivism rates. Traditional punitive approaches to justice often fail to address the underlying issues that lead to criminal behavior, resulting in high rates of reoffending. In contrast, Buddhist-informed policies focus on rehabilitation and personal transformation, providing offenders with the tools and support needed to make positive changes in their lives. By addressing the root causes of criminal behavior, such as trauma, addiction, and lack of education or vocational skills, these policies help offenders develop the skills and resilience needed to avoid future criminal activity. For instance, vocational training programs that teach practical job skills and provide opportunities for community service help offenders build a sense of purpose and self-worth, reducing the likelihood of returning to criminal behavior. Research has shown that offenders who participate in mindfulness-based programs and restorative justice practices are less likely to reoffend, demonstrating the effectiveness of these approaches in promoting long-term rehabilitation.

Enhanced public safety is another significant benefit of Buddhist-informed policies. By focusing on rehabilitation and addressing the root causes of criminal behavior, these policies contribute to a safer society. When offenders receive the support and resources needed to change their behavior and reintegrate into society, they are less likely to engage in future criminal activity. This reduction in recidivism leads to fewer crimes being committed, enhancing public safety and reducing the burden on the criminal justice system. Additionally, restorative justice practices, which involve dialogue and reconciliation between offenders and victims, help repair the harm caused by crime and restore relationships within the community. This approach fosters a sense of justice and healing, promoting a culture of empathy and understanding. For example, a restorative justice circle that includes offenders, victims, and community members can create a space for open dialogue, allowing participants to share their experiences and work towards repairing the harm caused by the crime. This process helps build trust and cohesion within the community, contributing to overall public safety.

The promotion of a more compassionate and humane justice system is another important benefit of Buddhist-informed policies. Traditional justice systems often prioritize punishment and retribution, which can perpetuate cycles of harm and fail to address the needs of offenders and victims. In contrast, Buddhist-informed policies emphasize compassion, healing, and ethical living, creating a justice system that prioritizes rehabilitation and the well-being of all individuals involved. By promoting mindfulness, compassion, and ethical education, these policies help create a more supportive and understanding environment within correctional facilities and the broader community. For example, a correctional facility that incorporates mindfulness and trauma-informed care into its daily routines and policies creates a culture of respect and empathy, where both offenders and staff feel valued and supported. This approach not only benefits offenders by providing them with the tools and support needed for personal transformation but also improves the working environment for staff, reducing stress and burnout.

The benefits of Buddhist-informed policies extend beyond the individual offenders to their families and communities. By supporting the rehabilitation and reintegration of offenders, these policies help strengthen family bonds and promote a more supportive and understanding environment for reintegration. Programs that involve family members in the rehabilitation process, such as family counseling sessions and workshops on mindfulness and ethical living, help create a network of support that reinforces the offender's rehabilitation efforts. For example, a family counseling session that includes mindfulness practices and discussions on ethical living can help family members understand the offender's experiences and challenges, fostering empathy and support. This support network is crucial for the offender's long-term success, helping them maintain their rehabilitation efforts and build positive relationships within the community. Buddhist-informed policies also contribute to systemic transformation and the development of more effective justice policies. By integrating principles such as mindfulness, compassion, and trauma-informed care into justice policies, these approaches create a more holistic and comprehensive system that addresses the complexities of criminal behavior and rehabilitation.

This shift in focus from punishment to rehabilitation leads to better outcomes for individuals and communities, promoting long-term public safety and well-being. For instance, policies that mandate the inclusion of mindfulness and meditation programs in correctional facilities, support restorative justice practices, and ensure access to trauma-informed care create a more supportive environment for rehabilitation. These policies not only reduce recidivism and improve mental health outcomes but also contribute to a more just and compassionate society. Moreover, the integration of Buddhist principles into justice policies supports ongoing research and innovation in the field of criminology. The holistic and compassionate perspective offered by Buddhism provides a rich foundation for developing new theories, practices, and interventions that address the complexities of criminal behavior and rehabilitation. Researchers can explore how Buddhist principles can be applied to various aspects of criminology, from understanding the psychological and emotional dimensions of criminal behavior to developing effective rehabilitation programs and policies. This interdisciplinary approach can lead to new insights and innovations that enhance the effectiveness of the justice system and support the well-being of offenders and communities.

26.4: Case Studies of Successful Policy Reform

Examining case studies of successful policy reform where Buddhist-informed approaches have been integrated into justice systems provides valuable insights into the practical application and impact of these principles. These examples illustrate how mindfulness, compassion, and ethical living can be effectively incorporated into policies and practices, resulting in meaningful change and positive outcomes for offenders and society. In Norway, the Halden Prison stands out as a model for integrating humane and rehabilitative principles into its correctional policies. While not explicitly Buddhist, the prison's approach aligns closely with Buddhist values of compassion, dignity, and ethical living. Halden Prison emphasizes creating a supportive and respectful environment, where the focus is on rehabilitation rather than punishment. The facility is designed to resemble a community rather than a traditional prison, with modern amenities, private rooms for inmates, and a focus on maintaining dignity and humanity. The staff at Halden are trained in conflict resolution, communication skills, and fostering positive relationships with inmates. The prison offers extensive educational and vocational training programs, as well as psychological support, to address the underlying causes of criminal behavior. This holistic approach has led to low recidivism rates and positive outcomes for inmates, demonstrating the effectiveness of policies that prioritize rehabilitation and humane treatment.

In Singapore, the Singapore Prison Service has implemented the "Yellow Ribbon Project," which focuses on the reintegration of ex-offenders into society. The project incorporates principles of mindfulness and compassion, aiming to reduce stigma and support offenders in rebuilding their lives. The Yellow Ribbon Project includes public awareness campaigns, community engagement initiatives, and support services for ex-offenders and their families. It promotes the idea that everyone deserves a second chance and that community support is crucial for successful reintegration. The project also includes vocational training and employment assistance, helping ex-offenders find meaningful work and build a positive future. The success of the Yellow Ribbon Project is evident in the increased acceptance and support for ex-offenders within the community, as well as the reduced recidivism rates and improved social outcomes for participants. In the United Kingdom, the National Health Service (NHS) has integrated mindfulness-based interventions into its mental health services, including within the criminal justice system. The "Mindfulness-Based Cognitive Therapy" (MBCT) program has been adapted for use in prisons and probation services, providing offenders with tools to manage stress, anxiety, and depression. The program combines mindfulness practices with cognitive-behavioral techniques, helping participants develop greater self-awareness and emotional regulation. MBCT sessions are conducted in group settings, fostering a sense of community and mutual support among participants. The success of the program has been demonstrated through numerous studies showing significant improvements in mental health and well-being, as well as reductions in reoffending rates. The integration of MBCT into the criminal justice system highlights the potential of mindfulness-based policies to support rehabilitation and positive change.

In the United States, the San Francisco Sheriff's Department has implemented the "Resolve to Stop the Violence Project" (RSVP), which incorporates principles of mindfulness, restorative justice, and trauma-informed care. The RSVP program aims to address the root causes of violence and support offenders in developing healthier ways of relating to themselves and others. The program includes mindfulness meditation, conflict resolution training, and restorative justice practices, such as victim-offender mediation and restorative circles. Participants engage in group sessions where they practice mindfulness, discuss their experiences, and work towards understanding and healing the impact of their actions. The RSVP program has shown significant success in reducing violent behavior and recidivism rates, demonstrating the effectiveness of integrating mindfulness and restorative justice into correctional policies. In Thailand, the Department of Corrections has partnered with Buddhist monasteries to implement meditation and mindfulness programs in prisons. The "Dhamma for Prisoners" program provides inmates with access to Buddhist teachings and meditation practices, helping them develop greater self-awareness, emotional regulation, and ethical behavior. Monks visit prisons to lead meditation sessions, offer teachings, and provide spiritual support to inmates. The program also includes opportunities for inmates to participate in retreats and intensive meditation courses. Evaluations of the program have shown significant improvements in inmates' mental health, reduced aggression, and increased positive behavior. The integration of Buddhist principles into correctional policies in Thailand highlights the potential of spiritual and mindfulness practices to support rehabilitation and personal growth.

In New Zealand, the Department of Corrections has implemented the "Te Whare Tapa Whā" model, which incorporates Maori cultural principles and holistic approaches to health and well-being. While not explicitly Buddhist, the model aligns with Buddhist values of interconnectedness, balance, and holistic care. Te Whare Tapa Whā focuses on the four dimensions of health: physical, mental, emotional, and spiritual. The model is used in rehabilitation programs to support offenders in developing a balanced and healthy life. Programs include mindfulness and meditation practices, cultural education, and activities that promote physical, emotional, and spiritual well-being. The success of the Te Whare Tapa Whā model is evident in the positive outcomes for participants, including improved mental health, reduced reoffending rates, and stronger connections with their cultural heritage and community. In Canada, the John Howard Society has implemented the "Circles of Support and Accountability" (CoSA) program, which incorporates restorative justice principles to support the reintegration of high-risk offenders into the community. The CoSA program involves volunteer support circles that work with offenders to provide emotional support, practical assistance, and accountability. The circles are based on principles of compassion, non-judgment, and mutual respect, fostering a supportive environment for offenders to make positive changes in their lives. Participants meet regularly with their support circles, discussing their progress, challenges, and goals. The success of the CoSA program is demonstrated by its positive impact on recidivism rates and the overall well-being of participants, highlighting the effectiveness of community-based restorative justice approaches.

In Japan, the "Zen Peacekeeper Program" integrates Zen meditation and mindfulness practices into the rehabilitation process for inmates. Developed by the San Francisco Zen Center in collaboration with Japanese correctional facilities, the program provides mindfulness and meditation training to inmates, helping them develop greater self-awareness, emotional regulation, and ethical behavior. Participants engage in daily Zen meditation sessions, where they learn to observe their thoughts and emotions with non-judgmental awareness. The program also includes teachings on Zen ethics and principles, encouraging inmates to reflect on their actions and commit to ethical living. Evaluations of the program have shown significant reductions in stress, improved mental health, and a greater sense of responsibility and ethical behavior among participants. The success of the Zen Peacekeeper Program demonstrates the potential of integrating mindfulness and ethical education into correctional policies.

In South Africa, the "Ubuntu Mindfulness Program" integrates mindfulness and compassion practices into the rehabilitation process for offenders. Developed by the Ubuntu Project in collaboration with local Buddhist centers and correctional facilities, the program aims to address the psychological and emotional needs of offenders by teaching them mindfulness and loving-kindness practices. Participants engage in daily meditation sessions, where they learn to observe their thoughts and emotions with non-judgmental awareness. The program also includes teachings on Ubuntu, an African philosophy that emphasizes the interconnectedness of all beings and the importance of community. By integrating mindfulness and Ubuntu principles, the program fosters a sense of empathy, compassion, and personal responsibility. Evaluations of the program have shown significant reductions in symptoms of depression, anxiety, and PTSD, as well as improvements in overall well-being and social relationships.

26.5: Future Directions for Justice Policies

Future directions for justice policies that integrate Buddhist principles hold significant promise for transforming the criminal justice system into one that prioritizes rehabilitation, healing, and ethical living. By exploring new initiatives, developing innovative frameworks, and fostering international collaboration, we can continue to advance Buddhist-informed approaches to justice, creating a more humane and effective system. One promising direction for future policy development is the expansion of mindfulness-based programs across various aspects of the justice system. While mindfulness meditation has already shown significant benefits in reducing stress, anxiety, and recidivism among offenders, there is potential to further integrate these practices into every stage of the justice process. This could include mindfulness training for police officers, judges, and probation officers to help them manage stress and make more compassionate, balanced decisions. For example, mindfulness training for police officers could include techniques for emotional regulation and de-escalation, helping them respond to challenging situations with greater calm and empathy. Judges and probation officers could benefit from mindfulness practices that enhance their ability to remain impartial and compassionate, supporting fair and just outcomes.

In addition to expanding mindfulness programs, future policies could focus on integrating restorative justice practices more broadly within the justice system. Restorative justice emphasizes healing and reconciliation, encouraging offenders to take responsibility for their actions and make amends to those they have harmed. Future initiatives could include mandatory restorative justice sessions for certain types of offenses, involving victims, offenders, and community members in the process of dialogue and healing. These sessions could be facilitated by trained mediators who incorporate mindfulness and compassion practices to create a safe and supportive environment for all participants. By embedding restorative justice practices into the core of the justice system, we can promote a culture of empathy, accountability, and mutual respect, leading to more meaningful resolutions and reduced recidivism. Trauma-informed care is another critical area for future policy development. Recognizing and addressing the impact of trauma on offenders is essential for effective rehabilitation and long-term change. Future policies could mandate trauma-informed training for all justice system personnel, ensuring that they are equipped to recognize and respond to trauma symptoms in offenders. This training could include education on the effects of trauma, techniques for creating a safe and supportive environment, and strategies for integrating trauma-informed care into everyday practices. For example, correctional facilities could implement trauma-informed intake procedures that assess the trauma history of offenders and develop individualized rehabilitation plans that address their specific needs. Providing access to trauma-informed therapeutic services, such as counseling, group therapy, and mindfulness-based stress reduction (MBSR), can help offenders heal from their past experiences and develop healthier coping mechanisms.

The development of comprehensive rehabilitation programs that incorporate Buddhist principles is another important direction for future policy development. These programs should address the holistic needs of offenders, including their psychological, emotional, social, and vocational development. Future initiatives could include the creation of multidisciplinary rehabilitation teams that work collaboratively to support offenders in their journey towards healing and reintegration. These teams could include mental health professionals, vocational trainers, mindfulness teachers, and community support workers, all working together to provide a comprehensive and coordinated approach to rehabilitation. For example, a comprehensive rehabilitation program might include daily mindfulness meditation sessions, vocational training workshops, group therapy sessions, and community service projects, all designed to support the holistic development of offenders.

International collaboration and knowledge sharing are also essential for advancing Buddhist-informed justice policies. By learning from the experiences and successes of other countries, we can develop more effective and culturally sensitive approaches to justice. Future initiatives could include international conferences, research partnerships, and exchange programs that facilitate the sharing of best practices and innovative approaches. For example, an international conference on Buddhist-informed justice policies could bring together policymakers, practitioners, and researchers from around the world to share their experiences and insights, fostering a global dialogue on the benefits and challenges of integrating Buddhist principles into justice systems. Research partnerships could involve collaborative studies that compare the outcomes of different approaches in various cultural contexts, providing valuable data to inform policy development.

In addition to international collaboration, future policies should also focus on community engagement and public education. Raising awareness about the benefits of Buddhist-informed justice approaches can help build public support and reduce stigma. Future initiatives could include public workshops, community forums, and media campaigns that highlight the positive outcomes of mindfulness, compassion, and restorative justice practices. By engaging the public in discussions about the importance of rehabilitation and the potential for positive change, we can foster a more supportive and understanding community environment. For example, a public awareness campaign might feature stories of individuals who have successfully transformed their lives through Buddhist-informed rehabilitation programs, demonstrating the potential for change and inspiring others to support these initiatives.

The use of technology and digital platforms offers additional opportunities for advancing Buddhist-informed justice policies. Online courses, mobile apps, and virtual reality programs can provide accessible and scalable tools for delivering mindfulness and meditation training to offenders and justice system personnel. Future initiatives could include the development of digital mindfulness platforms that offer guided meditations, instructional videos, and progress tracking tools, making mindfulness practices more accessible to a broader audience. Virtual reality programs could provide immersive experiences that teach mindfulness and compassion practices in engaging and interactive ways, enhancing the effectiveness of these interventions. For example, a virtual reality program could simulate various scenarios that offenders might encounter, providing opportunities to practice mindfulness and emotional regulation in a safe and controlled environment. Policy advocacy is also crucial for securing the necessary support and resources for Buddhist-informed justice initiatives. Future efforts should focus on building coalitions with stakeholders, including community organizations, policymakers, and Buddhist practitioners, to advocate for policy changes that prioritize rehabilitation and humane treatment. Advocacy efforts could include presenting evidence-based research to policymakers, participating in public forums and discussions, and collaborating with other organizations to build a unified approach to justice reform. For example, an advocacy campaign might highlight the cost savings associated with reduced recidivism and improved mental health outcomes, making a compelling case for the allocation of resources to support Buddhist-informed rehabilitation programs.

Finally, continuous evaluation and improvement are essential for ensuring the long-term success and sustainability of Buddhist-informed justice policies. Future initiatives should include rigorous evaluation methods to assess the impact of these policies and identify areas for improvement. Evaluation methods could include pre- and post-assessment surveys, interviews, focus groups, and quantitative measures of outcomes such as recidivism rates, mental health symptoms, and participant engagement. For example, a longitudinal study might follow a cohort of offenders who participate in a Buddhist-informed rehabilitation program, assessing changes in their mental health, behavior, and recidivism rates over several years. This data can provide valuable insights into the effectiveness of these approaches and inform future policy development.

—

CHAPTER TWENTY-SEVEN

Future Directions and Research Opportunities

Contents

- Exploring Future Possibilities for Doctrinally Informed Justice Practices

- Benefits for Modern Criminology and Justice Systems

- Practical Applications in Future Research

- Case Studies of Innovative Practices

- Strategies for Continuing Research and Development

27.1: Exploring Future Possibilities for Doctrinally Informed Justice Practices

Exploring future possibilities for doctrinally informed justice practices begins with a deep dive into the core Buddhist principles that can be seamlessly integrated into modern justice systems. This exploration is rooted in a profound understanding of the doctrines of mindfulness, compassion, ethical living, and the nature of suffering, all of which offer transformative potential for the rehabilitation of offenders and the overall improvement of justice systems. The foundational Buddhist doctrine of mindfulness serves as a critical tool for fostering self-awareness and emotional regulation among offenders. Future research can delve into developing comprehensive mindfulness programs tailored to the specific needs of different types of offenders. These programs could include various mindfulness practices, such as seated meditation, walking meditation, and mindful eating, designed to help individuals become more attuned to their thoughts, emotions, and physical sensations. By training offenders to observe their internal experiences without judgment, mindfulness can help them develop greater emotional resilience and reduce impulsivity, which is often at the root of criminal behavior. For instance, integrating mindfulness practices into daily routines in correctional facilities can provide a structured way for offenders to cultivate these skills consistently over time.

Compassion, another core Buddhist principle, offers immense potential for transforming the way justice systems address the rehabilitation of offenders. Future possibilities include the development of compassion-based interventions that encourage offenders to develop empathy and understanding for themselves and others. These interventions could involve compassion meditation, where offenders are guided to generate feelings of compassion for themselves, their victims, and others affected by their actions. Such practices can help offenders break down the barriers of anger, resentment, and guilt, fostering a sense of interconnectedness and shared humanity. For example, a compassion-based rehabilitation program might include guided meditations, group discussions, and exercises that encourage offenders to reflect on the impact of their actions and cultivate a genuine desire to make amends.

Ethical living, as outlined in the Buddhist Eightfold Path, provides a comprehensive framework for guiding offenders towards more constructive and socially responsible behavior. Future research could explore how each element of the Eightfold Path can be integrated into rehabilitation programs. This includes Right View, Right Intention, Right Speech, Right Action, Right Livelihood, Right Effort, Right Mindfulness, and Right Concentration. Programs could be designed to help offenders understand and adopt these ethical principles in their daily lives. For instance, vocational training programs could incorporate teachings on Right Livelihood, encouraging offenders to pursue careers that are ethical and contribute positively to society. Similarly, workshops on Right Speech and Right Action could help offenders develop skills for honest communication and ethical behavior, which are crucial for successful reintegration into society.

The concept of suffering and its alleviation, central to Buddhist teachings, can be applied to understanding and addressing the root causes of criminal behavior. Future research could investigate how the Four Noble Truths can inform justice policies and rehabilitation practices. The First Noble Truth, which acknowledges the existence of suffering, can help justice systems recognize the deep-seated pain and trauma that often underlie criminal behavior. The Second Noble Truth, which identifies the causes of suffering, can guide the development of interventions that address these underlying issues, such as addiction, mental health problems, and socio-economic disadvantage. The Third Noble Truth, which offers hope for the cessation of suffering, aligns with the goals of rehabilitation, providing a foundation for programs that support personal transformation and healing. Finally, the Fourth Noble Truth, which outlines the path to the cessation of suffering, can be used to design comprehensive rehabilitation programs that provide offenders with practical tools for ethical living and personal growth.

Interdisciplinary approaches that combine Buddhist doctrines with contemporary criminological theories offer another promising avenue for future exploration. By integrating insights from psychology, sociology, and neuroscience with Buddhist principles, researchers can develop a more holistic understanding of criminal behavior and rehabilitation. For example, combining mindfulness practices with cognitive-behavioral therapy (CBT) could enhance the effectiveness of both approaches. Mindfulness can help offenders become more aware of their thought patterns, while CBT provides strategies for challenging and changing these patterns. Similarly, integrating trauma-informed care with compassion-based interventions can address the emotional and psychological wounds that contribute to criminal behavior, fostering a deeper sense of healing and resilience.

The use of technology and digital platforms also presents exciting possibilities for future research and practice. Digital mindfulness programs, mobile apps, and virtual reality (VR) experiences can make mindfulness and compassion training more accessible and engaging for offenders. For instance, a mindfulness app could provide daily guided meditations, progress tracking, and reminders to practice, making it easier for offenders to integrate mindfulness into their daily lives. VR experiences could simulate real-life scenarios, allowing offenders to practice mindfulness and emotional regulation in a safe and controlled environment. These technological innovations can complement traditional in-person programs, providing additional support and flexibility.

Developing evidence-based guidelines for integrating Buddhist principles into justice policies is another critical area for future research. By systematically evaluating the impact of mindfulness, compassion, and ethical education on offender outcomes, researchers can generate robust data to inform policy development. Longitudinal studies that track offenders over time can provide insights into the long-term effects of these interventions on recidivism, mental health, and overall well-being. For example, a longitudinal study might follow a group of offenders who participate in a mindfulness-based rehabilitation program, assessing changes in their behavior, mental health, and recidivism rates over several years. This data can provide valuable evidence to support the adoption of Buddhist-informed practices in justice policies.

Future research should also explore the cultural adaptation of Buddhist-informed practices to ensure their relevance and effectiveness in diverse contexts. By working with communities and cultural leaders, researchers can develop programs that respect and incorporate local traditions and values. This collaborative approach can enhance the acceptance and effectiveness of these interventions, fostering a sense of ownership and empowerment among participants. For instance, a culturally adapted mindfulness program in a predominantly Indigenous community might incorporate traditional practices and teachings alongside Buddhist principles, creating a more holistic and culturally resonant approach to rehabilitation.

27.2: Benefits for Modern Criminology and Justice Systems

The benefits of integrating Buddhist principles into modern criminology and justice systems are profound and far-reaching. These benefits extend to the mental health and emotional well-being of offenders, the reduction of recidivism rates, the enhancement of public safety, and the overall fostering of a more compassionate and humane justice system. By focusing on rehabilitation, healing, and ethical living, Buddhist-informed practices offer a transformative approach that addresses the root causes of criminal behavior and supports long-term positive change for individuals and society. One of the most significant benefits of integrating Buddhist principles into criminology is the improvement in the mental health and emotional well-being of offenders. Many individuals within the criminal justice system suffer from mental health issues, trauma, and emotional dysregulation, which contribute to their criminal behavior. By incorporating mindfulness and meditation practices into rehabilitation programs, offenders can develop greater self-awareness and emotional regulation. Mindfulness meditation, a core Buddhist practice, teaches individuals to observe their thoughts and emotions without judgment, fostering a sense of inner calm and stability. This practice helps reduce symptoms of anxiety, depression, and PTSD, which are prevalent among offenders. For example, a daily mindfulness meditation session might involve guiding offenders through focused breathing exercises, body scanning, and observing their thoughts as they arise and pass. Over time, regular mindfulness practice can lead to significant improvements in mental health, supporting the overall well-being of offenders and reducing the likelihood of reoffending.

Another key benefit of integrating Buddhist principles into justice systems is the reduction in recidivism rates. Traditional punitive approaches to justice often fail to address the underlying issues that lead to criminal behavior, resulting in high rates of reoffending. In contrast, Buddhist-informed practices focus on rehabilitation and personal transformation, providing offenders with the tools and support needed to make positive changes in their lives. By addressing the root causes of criminal behavior, such as trauma, addiction, and lack of education or vocational skills, these practices help offenders develop the skills and resilience needed to avoid future criminal activity. For instance, vocational training programs that teach practical job skills and provide opportunities for community service help offenders build a sense of purpose and self-worth, reducing the likelihood of returning to criminal behavior. Research has shown that offenders who participate in mindfulness-based programs and restorative justice practices are less likely to reoffend, demonstrating the effectiveness of these approaches in promoting long-term rehabilitation.

Enhanced public safety is another significant benefit of integrating Buddhist principles into criminology and justice systems. By focusing on rehabilitation and addressing the root causes of criminal behavior, these practices contribute to a safer society. When offenders receive the support and resources needed to change their behavior and reintegrate into society, they are less likely to engage in future criminal activity. This reduction in recidivism leads to fewer crimes being committed, enhancing public safety and reducing the burden on the criminal justice system. Additionally, restorative justice practices, which involve dialogue and reconciliation between offenders and victims, help repair the harm caused by crime and restore relationships within the community. This approach fosters a sense of justice and healing, promoting a culture of empathy and understanding. For example, a restorative justice circle that includes offenders, victims, and community members can create a space for open dialogue, allowing participants to share their experiences and work towards repairing the harm caused by the crime. This process helps build trust and cohesion within the community, contributing to overall public safety.

The promotion of a more compassionate and humane justice system is another important benefit of integrating Buddhist principles into criminology. Traditional justice systems often prioritize punishment and retribution, which can perpetuate cycles of harm and fail to address the needs of offenders and victims. In contrast, Buddhist-informed practices emphasize compassion, healing, and ethical living, creating a justice system that prioritizes rehabilitation and the well-being of all individuals involved. By promoting mindfulness, compassion, and ethical education, these practices help create a more supportive and understanding environment within correctional facilities and the broader community. For example, a correctional facility that incorporates mindfulness and trauma-informed care into its daily routines and policies creates a culture of respect and empathy, where both offenders and staff feel valued and supported. This approach not only benefits offenders by providing them with the tools and support needed for personal transformation but also improves the working environment for staff, reducing stress and burnout.

The benefits of integrating Buddhist principles into criminology extend beyond individual offenders to their families and communities. By supporting the rehabilitation and reintegration of offenders, these practices help strengthen family bonds and promote a more supportive and understanding environment for reintegration. Programs that involve family members in the rehabilitation process, such as family counseling sessions and workshops on mindfulness and ethical living, help create a network of support that reinforces the offender's rehabilitation efforts. For example, a family counseling session that includes mindfulness practices and discussions on ethical living can help family members understand the offender's experiences and challenges, fostering empathy and support. This support network is crucial for the offender's long-term success, helping them maintain their rehabilitation efforts and build positive relationships within the community.

Buddhist-informed practices also contribute to systemic transformation and the development of more effective justice policies. By integrating principles such as mindfulness, compassion, and trauma-informed care into justice policies, these approaches create a more holistic and comprehensive system that addresses the complexities of criminal behavior and rehabilitation. This shift in focus from punishment to rehabilitation leads to better outcomes for individuals and communities, promoting long-term public safety and well-being. For instance, policies that mandate the inclusion of mindfulness and meditation programs in correctional facilities, support restorative justice practices, and ensure access to trauma-informed care create a more supportive environment for rehabilitation. These policies not only reduce recidivism and improve mental health outcomes but also contribute to a more just and compassionate society. Moreover, the integration of Buddhist principles into criminology supports ongoing research and innovation in the field.

The holistic and compassionate perspective offered by Buddhism provides a rich foundation for developing new theories, practices, and interventions that address the complexities of criminal behavior and rehabilitation. Researchers can explore how Buddhist principles can be applied to various aspects of criminology, from understanding the psychological and emotional dimensions of criminal behavior to developing effective rehabilitation programs and policies. This interdisciplinary approach can lead to new insights and innovations that enhance the effectiveness of the justice system and support the well-being of offenders and communities. Future research should also explore the cultural adaptation of Buddhist-informed practices to ensure their relevance and effectiveness in diverse contexts. By working with communities and cultural leaders, researchers can develop programs that respect and incorporate local traditions and values. This collaborative approach can enhance the acceptance and effectiveness of these interventions, fostering a sense of ownership and empowerment among participants. For instance, a culturally adapted mindfulness program in a predominantly Indigenous community might incorporate traditional practices and teachings alongside Buddhist principles, creating a more holistic and culturally resonant approach to rehabilitation.

27.3: Practical Applications in Future Research

Practical applications in future research for integrating Buddhist principles into justice systems are vast and multifaceted, promising to transform how we approach criminal rehabilitation and systemic justice reform. By developing and testing new mindfulness-based interventions, implementing longitudinal studies, creating evidence-based guidelines, and exploring the use of technology, researchers can significantly enhance the effectiveness of justice systems. These practical applications aim to address the root causes of criminal behavior, promote rehabilitation, and support the long-term well-being of offenders and society. One of the most promising practical applications is the development and testing of new mindfulness-based interventions specifically tailored for the justice system. While mindfulness meditation has already shown significant benefits in reducing stress, anxiety, and recidivism among offenders, future research can explore more targeted and specialized interventions. For example, researchers can develop mindfulness programs that address specific issues such as anger management, impulse control, and trauma recovery. These programs could include a combination of seated meditation, mindful movement, and compassion practices, tailored to the unique needs of different offender populations. A pilot study could be conducted to evaluate the effectiveness of these interventions, measuring outcomes such as changes in mental health, behavior, and recidivism rates. For instance, a mindfulness-based anger management program might include daily meditation sessions focused on developing awareness of anger triggers and practicing non-reactive responses. Evaluating the program's impact on participants' anger levels, aggression, and overall behavior could provide valuable insights into the potential benefits of this targeted approach.

Implementing longitudinal studies is another critical area for future research. Longitudinal studies allow researchers to assess the long-term impact of Buddhist-informed practices on offenders, providing a comprehensive understanding of their effectiveness over time. By following participants over several years, researchers can track changes in mental health, behavior, recidivism rates, and overall well-being. For example, a longitudinal study might follow a cohort of offenders who participate in a mindfulness-based rehabilitation program, assessing their progress at multiple points, such as six months, one year, and three years after program completion. This data can provide valuable insights into the sustainability of the program's benefits and identify any factors that contribute to long-term success or challenges. Additionally, longitudinal studies can help identify the optimal duration and intensity of interventions, informing the development of more effective and efficient programs.

Creating evidence-based guidelines for integrating mindfulness, compassion, and ethical education into justice policies is another important practical application. These guidelines can provide a framework for policymakers, practitioners, and correctional facilities to implement Buddhist-informed practices effectively. By systematically reviewing existing research and conducting new studies, researchers can develop comprehensive guidelines that outline best practices for various aspects of the justice system. For example, guidelines might include recommendations for incorporating mindfulness meditation into daily routines in correctional facilities, integrating compassion training into rehabilitation programs, and providing ethical education to offenders and staff. These guidelines can also address practical considerations, such as staff training, program evaluation, and resource allocation. For instance, a guideline on implementing mindfulness meditation might include detailed instructions on how to set up meditation spaces, train facilitators, and measure program outcomes. By providing clear and actionable recommendations, these guidelines can help ensure that Buddhist-informed practices are implemented effectively and consistently across different settings.

Exploring the use of technology and digital platforms is another promising area for future research. Technology can enhance the accessibility, scalability, and engagement of Buddhist-informed practices, making them more widely available to offenders and justice system personnel. Researchers can develop and test digital mindfulness programs, mobile apps, and virtual reality (VR) experiences that deliver mindfulness and meditation training in innovative and engaging ways. For example, a mobile app might offer daily guided meditations, instructional videos, and progress tracking tools, allowing users to practice mindfulness at their own pace and convenience. A VR program could provide immersive experiences that simulate real-life scenarios, helping offenders practice mindfulness and emotional regulation in a safe and controlled environment. Evaluating the effectiveness of these digital interventions through randomized controlled trials can provide valuable insights into their potential benefits and limitations. For instance, a study might compare the outcomes of participants who use a mindfulness app with those who participate in in-person meditation sessions, assessing differences in engagement, mental health, and behavior.

Developing new interventions that combine Buddhist principles with contemporary psychological therapies is another important area for future research. For example, integrating mindfulness practices with cognitive-behavioral therapy (CBT) can enhance the effectiveness of both approaches. Mindfulness can help offenders become more aware of their thought patterns, while CBT provides strategies for challenging and changing these patterns. Researchers can develop and test integrated programs that combine mindfulness meditation with CBT techniques, assessing their impact on offenders' mental health, behavior, and recidivism rates. For instance, an integrated program might include mindfulness exercises to develop awareness of negative thoughts, followed by CBT sessions that teach participants how to reframe these thoughts and develop healthier coping strategies. Evaluating the effectiveness of this combined approach can provide valuable insights into the potential benefits of integrating Buddhist principles with established psychological therapies.

In addition to developing new interventions, future research can focus on adapting existing Buddhist-informed practices to different cultural and contextual settings. By working with communities and cultural leaders, researchers can ensure that interventions are relevant and respectful of local traditions and values. For example, a mindfulness program in a predominantly Indigenous community might incorporate traditional practices and teachings alongside Buddhist principles, creating a more holistic and culturally resonant approach to rehabilitation. Researchers can conduct pilot studies to evaluate the effectiveness of these culturally adapted interventions, measuring outcomes such as engagement, satisfaction, and overall impact on participants' well-being. By tailoring interventions to specific cultural contexts, researchers can enhance their acceptance and effectiveness, fostering a sense of ownership and empowerment among participants.

Exploring the role of community engagement and public education in supporting Buddhist-informed justice practices is another important area for future research. Engaging the community in the rehabilitation process can provide additional support and reinforcement for offenders, helping them maintain their rehabilitation efforts and build positive relationships within the community. Researchers can develop and test community-based interventions, such as peer support groups, volunteer mentoring programs, and community service projects, assessing their impact on offenders' reintegration and overall well-being. For example, a peer support group might provide a space for offenders to share their experiences, challenges, and successes with others who understand their struggles, fostering a sense of camaraderie and mutual support. Evaluating the effectiveness of these community-based interventions can provide valuable insights into the potential benefits of involving the community in the rehabilitation process.

Public education and awareness campaigns can also play a crucial role in supporting Buddhist-informed justice practices. By raising awareness about the benefits of mindfulness, compassion, and ethical living, these campaigns can help build public support and reduce stigma. Researchers can develop and test different public education strategies, such as workshops, community forums, and media campaigns, assessing their impact on public attitudes and perceptions. For example, a media campaign might feature stories of individuals who have successfully transformed their lives through Buddhist-informed rehabilitation programs, demonstrating the potential for positive change and inspiring others to support these initiatives. Evaluating the effectiveness of these public education strategies can provide valuable insights into the best ways to engage the public and build a supportive community environment.

Promoting interdisciplinary research that combines insights from criminology, psychology, sociology, and Buddhist studies is another important area for future research. By integrating knowledge from different disciplines, researchers can develop a more comprehensive understanding of criminal behavior and rehabilitation. For example, combining insights from criminology and Buddhist studies can provide a deeper understanding of the ethical and philosophical dimensions of criminal behavior, while integrating knowledge from psychology and sociology can enhance our understanding of the psychological and social factors that contribute to criminal behavior. Researchers can develop and test interdisciplinary interventions that address the multifaceted nature of criminal behavior, assessing their impact on offenders' mental health, behavior, and overall well-being. For instance, an interdisciplinary intervention might combine mindfulness meditation with group therapy sessions that address social and relational issues, providing a holistic approach to rehabilitation. Evaluating the effectiveness of these interdisciplinary interventions can provide valuable insights into the potential benefits of combining knowledge from different disciplines.

Finally, securing funding and resources for ongoing research and program development is essential for the long-term success and sustainability of Buddhist-informed justice practices. Researchers can develop grant proposals and funding applications that highlight the potential benefits of these practices, demonstrating their impact on reducing recidivism, improving mental health, and enhancing public safety. Collaborating with funding agencies, community organizations, and private foundations can help secure the necessary resources to support ongoing research and program development. For example, a grant proposal might highlight the cost savings associated with reduced recidivism and improved mental health outcomes, making a compelling case for the allocation of resources to support Buddhist-informed rehabilitation programs.

27.4: Case Studies of Innovative Practices

Case studies of innovative practices in integrating Buddhist principles into justice systems provide valuable insights into how these approaches can be effectively implemented and the positive outcomes they can achieve. These case studies highlight the practical applications of mindfulness, compassion, and ethical education in diverse contexts, demonstrating their potential to transform the lives of offenders and contribute to a more humane and effective justice system. In Denmark, the Prison Phoenix Project has pioneered the integration of mindfulness and meditation into its rehabilitation programs. This initiative, launched in collaboration with local Buddhist centers, offers inmates the opportunity to participate in intensive mindfulness and meditation retreats within the prison setting. These retreats are designed to help offenders develop self-awareness, emotional regulation, and a deeper understanding of their actions. Inmates participate in daily meditation sessions, guided by experienced meditation teachers, and engage in reflective practices that encourage them to confront and understand their past behaviors. The program also includes group discussions and individual counseling sessions, providing a holistic approach to rehabilitation. Evaluations of the Prison Phoenix Project have shown significant improvements in inmates' mental health, reduced aggression, and increased positive behavior. The success of this initiative demonstrates the transformative potential of integrating mindfulness and meditation into correctional programs.

In Brazil, the "Meditation for Life" program has been implemented in several juvenile detention centers, focusing on providing young offenders with tools for emotional regulation and personal growth. This program is based on the principles of mindfulness and compassion, teaching participants to develop greater self-awareness and empathy. The program includes daily mindfulness meditation sessions, where participants practice focused breathing, body scanning, and loving-kindness meditation. Additionally, the program incorporates elements of ethical education, encouraging young offenders to reflect on their actions and the impact they have on others. The program also offers workshops on conflict resolution and emotional intelligence, helping participants develop the skills needed to navigate challenging situations. Preliminary evaluations of the "Meditation for Life" program have shown promising results, with participants reporting reduced anxiety, improved self-control, and a greater sense of responsibility for their actions.

In Germany, the "Mindfulness Behind Bars" initiative has been introduced in several prisons, aiming to support the rehabilitation of offenders through mindfulness and meditation practices. This initiative, supported by the German Mindfulness Association, provides inmates with access to mindfulness training programs that include weekly meditation sessions, mindfulness workshops, and one-on-one coaching. The program emphasizes the development of self-awareness and emotional resilience, helping participants manage stress and reduce impulsive behavior. Inmates are encouraged to integrate mindfulness practices into their daily routines, using techniques such as mindful eating and walking meditation. The program also includes training for prison staff, helping them develop mindfulness skills to support their well-being and enhance their interactions with inmates. Evaluations of the "Mindfulness Behind Bars" initiative have shown positive outcomes, including improved mental health, reduced incidents of violence, and enhanced relationships between inmates and staff.

In Canada, the "Circle of Compassion" program has been introduced in several correctional facilities, focusing on integrating mindfulness and compassion practices into the rehabilitation process. This program is based on the principles of compassion meditation, which involves generating feelings of compassion for oneself and others. Inmates participate in daily compassion meditation sessions, where they are guided to cultivate empathy and understanding for their victims, their families, and themselves. The program also includes group discussions and workshops on ethical living, encouraging participants to reflect on their actions and commit to making positive changes. Additionally, the program offers support for inmates as they prepare for reintegration into society, including vocational training and community service opportunities. Evaluations of the "Circle of Compassion" program have shown significant improvements in inmates' emotional well-being, reduced recidivism rates, and increased engagement in prosocial behavior.

In South Korea, the "Zen Meditation for Inmates" program has been implemented in collaboration with local Zen Buddhist temples. This program provides inmates with access to Zen meditation practices, helping them develop greater self-awareness and emotional regulation. Participants engage in daily meditation sessions, where they practice seated meditation, walking meditation, and mindful breathing. The program also includes teachings on Zen ethics and principles, encouraging inmates to reflect on their actions and cultivate a sense of responsibility and compassion. Additionally, the program offers individual counseling sessions with Zen teachers, providing personalized support and guidance. Evaluations of the "Zen Meditation for Inmates" program have shown positive outcomes, including reduced stress, improved mental health, and increased positive behavior among participants.

In the United States, the "Compassionate Rehabilitation" initiative has been introduced in several juvenile detention centers, focusing on integrating compassion training into the rehabilitation process. This initiative is based on the principles of compassion-focused therapy (CFT), which aims to help individuals develop self-compassion and empathy for others. Participants engage in daily compassion meditation sessions, where they practice generating feelings of compassion for themselves, their victims, and others affected by their actions. The program also includes workshops on emotional intelligence, conflict resolution, and ethical living, helping participants develop the skills needed to navigate challenging situations and make positive choices. Evaluations of the "Compassionate Rehabilitation" initiative have shown promising results, with participants reporting reduced aggression, improved self-control, and a greater sense of responsibility for their actions.

In India, the "Vipassana Meditation for Rehabilitation" program has been implemented in several prisons, providing inmates with the opportunity to participate in intensive Vipassana meditation courses. Vipassana, which means "insight" or "clear seeing," is a traditional Buddhist meditation practice that involves observing the sensations of the body and developing a deep understanding of the mind. Inmates participate in ten-day Vipassana courses, where they engage in continuous meditation practice and receive guidance from experienced teachers. The program also includes teachings on ethical living and the principles of non-violence, encouraging participants to reflect on their actions and commit to making positive changes. Evaluations of the "Vipassana Meditation for Rehabilitation" program have shown significant improvements in inmates' mental health, reduced recidivism rates, and increased positive behavior.

In Australia, the "Mindful Pathways" program has been introduced in several correctional facilities, focusing on integrating mindfulness and ethical education into the rehabilitation process. This program provides inmates with access to mindfulness training, including daily meditation sessions, mindfulness workshops, and one-on-one coaching. The program also includes teachings on ethical living, encouraging participants to reflect on their actions and cultivate a sense of responsibility and compassion. Additionally, the program offers support for inmates as they prepare for reintegration into society, including vocational training and community service opportunities. Evaluations of the "Mindful Pathways" program have shown positive outcomes, including improved mental health, reduced recidivism rates, and increased engagement in prosocial behavior.

In the Netherlands, the "Compassionate Justice" initiative has been introduced in several juvenile detention centers, focusing on integrating compassion training into the rehabilitation process. This initiative is based on the principles of compassion-focused therapy (CFT), which aims to help individuals develop self-compassion and empathy for others. Participants engage in daily compassion meditation sessions, where they practice generating feelings of compassion for themselves, their victims, and others affected by their actions. The program also includes workshops on emotional intelligence, conflict resolution, and ethical living, helping participants develop the skills needed to navigate challenging situations and make positive choices. Evaluations of the "Compassionate Justice" initiative have shown promising results, with participants reporting reduced aggression, improved self-control, and a greater sense of responsibility for their actions.

In Kenya, the "Mindfulness for Rehabilitation" program has been implemented in several correctional facilities, providing inmates with access to mindfulness and meditation practices. This program is based on the principles of mindfulness-based stress reduction (MBSR), which aims to help individuals develop greater self-awareness and emotional regulation. Participants engage in daily mindfulness meditation sessions, where they practice focused breathing, body scanning, and observing their thoughts as they arise and pass. The program also includes teachings on ethical living and the principles of non-violence, encouraging participants to reflect on their actions and commit to making positive changes. Additionally, the program offers support for inmates as they prepare for reintegration into society, including vocational training and community service opportunities. Evaluations of the "Mindfulness for Rehabilitation" program have shown significant improvements in inmates' mental health, reduced recidivism rates, and increased positive behavior.

27.5: Strategies for Continuing Research and Development

Strategies for continuing research and development in the integration of Buddhist principles into modern criminology and justice systems are vital for ensuring the sustainability and effectiveness of these innovative approaches. By establishing research partnerships, securing funding, promoting interdisciplinary research, engaging in continuous evaluation, and fostering a culture of collaboration and innovation, we can create a robust framework that supports the ongoing advancement of Buddhist-informed justice practices. Establishing research partnerships and collaborative networks is a foundational strategy for advancing Buddhist-informed justice practices. These partnerships can bring together experts from various fields, including criminology, psychology, sociology,

Buddhist studies, and public policy, to develop comprehensive and interdisciplinary approaches to criminal justice reform. Universities, research institutions, and non-governmental organizations can play a crucial role in facilitating these partnerships, providing the necessary infrastructure and resources for collaborative research projects. For example, a partnership between a university's criminology department and a local Buddhist center could lead to the development of new mindfulness-based rehabilitation programs, combining academic research with practical expertise. Additionally, international collaborations can provide opportunities for cross-cultural research and the sharing of best practices, enhancing the global impact of Buddhist-informed justice initiatives.

Securing funding and resources for ongoing research and program development is essential for the long-term success of Buddhist-informed justice practices. Researchers and practitioners can apply for grants from government agencies, private foundations, and international organizations to support their work. Developing compelling grant proposals that highlight the potential benefits of these practices, such as reduced recidivism rates, improved mental health outcomes, and enhanced public safety, can help attract funding. For example, a grant proposal might emphasize the cost savings associated with reduced recidivism, demonstrating how Buddhist-informed rehabilitation programs can provide a cost-effective alternative to traditional punitive approaches. Additionally, securing funding for pilot studies and small-scale implementations can provide valuable data to support larger-scale initiatives. Collaborating with funding agencies and stakeholders to develop strategic funding plans can ensure that resources are allocated effectively and sustainably.

Promoting interdisciplinary research that combines insights from criminology, psychology, sociology, and Buddhist studies is another critical strategy for advancing Buddhist-informed justice practices. By integrating knowledge from different disciplines, researchers can develop a more comprehensive understanding of criminal behavior and rehabilitation. For instance, combining insights from psychology and Buddhist studies can provide a deeper understanding of the psychological and emotional dimensions of criminal behavior, while integrating knowledge from sociology can enhance our understanding of the social and environmental factors that contribute to crime. Researchers can develop and test interdisciplinary interventions that address the multifaceted nature of criminal behavior, assessing their impact on offenders' mental health, behavior, and overall well-being. For example, an interdisciplinary intervention might combine mindfulness meditation with group therapy sessions that address social and relational issues, providing a holistic approach to rehabilitation. Evaluating the effectiveness of these interdisciplinary interventions can provide valuable insights into the potential benefits of combining knowledge from different disciplines.

Engaging in continuous evaluation and improvement is crucial for ensuring the long-term success and sustainability of Buddhist-informed justice practices. Regular assessment and feedback can help identify strengths and areas for improvement, allowing programs to be adjusted and refined over time. Evaluation methods might include pre- and post-assessment surveys, interviews, and focus groups with participants, staff, and volunteers, as well as quantitative measures of outcomes such as recidivism rates, mental health symptoms, and participant engagement. For example, a program might conduct pre- and post-assessment surveys to measure changes in participants' levels of anxiety, depression, and PTSD symptoms, as well as their overall sense of well-being and satisfaction with the program. Focus groups and interviews can provide qualitative insights into participants' experiences, highlighting the aspects of the program that are most beneficial and any challenges or barriers they have encountered. This feedback can be used to make data-driven improvements to the program, ensuring that it continues to meet the needs of participants and achieve its goals.

Fostering a culture of collaboration and innovation within the justice system is essential for the ongoing advancement of Buddhist-informed practices. Encouraging open communication and knowledge sharing among practitioners, researchers, and policymakers can help create a supportive environment for innovation. Regular workshops, conferences, and training sessions can provide opportunities for professionals to share their experiences, learn from each other, and develop new ideas. For example, a conference on Buddhist-informed justice practices might feature presentations on recent research findings, case studies of successful implementations, and discussions on best practices and future directions. Creating platforms for ongoing dialogue and collaboration, such as online forums and professional networks, can further support the exchange of knowledge and ideas. Additionally, fostering a culture of continuous learning and professional development can help practitioners stay up-to-date with the latest research and best practices, enhancing their ability to implement effective programs.

Developing standardized training programs for justice system personnel is another important strategy for advancing Buddhist-informed practices. These training programs can provide staff with the knowledge and skills needed to implement mindfulness, compassion, and ethical education effectively. Training might include workshops on mindfulness meditation, compassion practices, and trauma-informed care, as well as practical exercises and role-playing scenarios to help staff develop the skills and confidence needed to support offenders. For example, a training program for correctional officers might include sessions on mindfulness techniques for stress management, strategies for fostering positive relationships with inmates, and methods for creating a supportive and trauma-informed environment. By providing comprehensive and standardized training, we can ensure that justice system personnel are equipped to implement Buddhist-informed practices effectively and consistently.

Exploring the use of technology and digital platforms is another promising strategy for advancing Buddhist-informed justice practices. Technology can enhance the accessibility, scalability, and engagement of these practices, making them more widely available to offenders and justice system personnel. Researchers and practitioners can develop and test digital mindfulness programs, mobile apps, and virtual reality (VR) experiences that deliver mindfulness and meditation training in innovative and engaging ways. For example, a mobile app might offer daily guided meditations, instructional videos, and progress tracking tools, allowing users to practice mindfulness at their own pace and convenience. A VR program could provide immersive experiences that simulate real-life scenarios, helping offenders practice mindfulness and emotional regulation in a safe and controlled environment. Evaluating the effectiveness of these digital interventions through randomized controlled trials can provide valuable insights into their potential benefits and limitations. For instance, a study might compare the outcomes of participants who use a mindfulness app with those who participate in in-person meditation sessions, assessing differences in engagement, mental health, and behavior.

Promoting public awareness and education about the benefits of Buddhist-informed justice practices is essential for building community support and reducing stigma. Public workshops, community forums, and media campaigns can help raise awareness about the transformative potential of mindfulness, compassion, and ethical living in the justice system. By highlighting success stories and sharing research findings, these efforts can inspire greater acceptance and support for these approaches. Engaging the public in discussions about the benefits of rehabilitation over punishment and the importance of creating a more compassionate and just society can help shift public perceptions and build a broader base of support for policy changes and program implementation. For example, a public awareness campaign might feature stories of individuals who have successfully transformed their lives through Buddhist-informed rehabilitation programs, demonstrating the potential for change and inspiring others to support these initiatives.

Encouraging community involvement in the rehabilitation process is another important strategy for advancing Buddhist-informed justice practices. Community engagement can provide additional support and reinforcement for offenders, helping them maintain their rehabilitation efforts and build positive relationships within the community. Researchers and practitioners can develop and test community-based interventions, such as peer support groups, volunteer mentoring programs, and community service projects, assessing their impact on offenders' reintegration and overall well-being. For example, a peer support group might provide a space for offenders to share their experiences, challenges, and successes with others who understand their struggles, fostering a sense of camaraderie and mutual support. Evaluating the effectiveness of these community-based interventions can provide valuable insights into the potential benefits of involving the community in the rehabilitation process.

Integrating Buddhist principles into the design and structure of correctional facilities is another promising strategy for advancing Buddhist-informed justice practices. By creating environments that support mindfulness, compassion, and ethical living, we can enhance the effectiveness of rehabilitation programs and support the well-being of both offenders and staff. For example, correctional facilities can be designed to include quiet spaces for meditation, gardens for mindful walking, and areas for group discussions and activities. Additionally, policies and practices that promote a culture of respect, empathy, and non-violence can help create a supportive environment for rehabilitation. Researchers and practitioners can develop and test different design and structural elements, assessing their impact on the mental health, behavior, and overall well-being of offenders and staff. For example, a study might compare the outcomes of inmates in a facility with integrated mindfulness spaces and supportive policies to those in a traditional correctional facility, evaluating differences in mental health, behavior, and recidivism rates.

Finally, promoting policy advocacy and legislative change is essential for ensuring the long-term sustainability and effectiveness of Buddhist-informed justice practices. Researchers and practitioners can work with policymakers, community organizations, and advocacy groups to develop and promote policies that support the integration of mindfulness, compassion, and ethical education into the justice system. This might include advocating for funding for mindfulness-based rehabilitation programs, supporting legislation that prioritizes rehabilitation over punishment, and promoting the inclusion of trauma-informed care in justice policies. By presenting evidence-based research and compelling case studies, advocates can demonstrate the potential benefits of these practices and build support for policy changes. For example, an advocacy campaign might highlight the cost savings associated with reduced recidivism and improved mental health outcomes, making a compelling case for the allocation of resources to support Buddhist-informed rehabilitation programs.

References

- Anklesaria, F., & Lary, S. T. (1992). A New Approach To Offender Rehabilitation: Maharishi's Integrated System of Rehabilitation. Journal of Correctional Education, 43(1), 6–13. http://www.jstor.org/stable/41971899
- Awofẹsọ, O. A., & Opesanwo, O. A. (2024). The Pivotal Role of Prison Libraries as an Information Resource for Prisoner Rehabilitation: An Integrative Review of the Literature. The International Journal of Information, Diversity, & Inclusion, 8(1), 61–82. https://www.jstor.org/stable/48775520
- Braithwaite, J. (1999). Restorative Justice: Assessing Optimistic and Pessimistic Accounts. Crime and Justice, 25, 1–127. http://www.jstor.org/stable/1147608
- Chakrabarty, C. (2006). Crime and Punishment [Review of Crime and Urbanisation: Calcutta in the 19th Century, by S. Banerjee]. Economic and Political Weekly, 41(50), 5119–5121. http://www.jstor.org/stable/4419024
- Chinmay, C. (2006). Crime and Punishment [Review of Crime and Urbanisation: Calcutta in the 19th Century, by S. Banerjee]. Economic and Political Weekly, 41(50), 5119–5121. http://www.jstor.org/stable/4419024
- Conrad, J. P. (1973). Corrections and Simple Justice. The Journal of Criminal Law and Criminology (1973-), 64(2), 208–217. https://doi.org/10.2307/1142991
- Corcoran, K. E., Robbins, B., & Pettinicchio, D. (2012). Religion and the Acceptability of White-Collar Crime: A Cross-National Analysis. Journal for the Scientific Study of Religion, 51(3), 542–567. http://www.jstor.org/stable/41681810
- Ferrell, J. (1999). Cultural Criminology. Annual Review of Sociology, 25, 395–418. http://www.jstor.org/stable/223510
- GAMO, M. D. (2013). Voices Behind Prison Walls: Rehabilitation from the Perspective of Inmates. Philippine Sociological Review, 61(1), 205–227. http://www.jstor.org/stable/43486361
- Geraghty, T. F. (2004). Prisons and after Prison [Review of Shared Beginnings, Divergent Lives: Delinquent Boys to Age 70; Total Confinement, Madness and Reason in the Maximum Security Prison;

Prisoners Once Removed: The Impact of Incarceration and Reentry on Children, Families, and Communities; Gates of Injustice: The Crisis of America's Prisons, by J. H. Laub, R. J. Sampson, L. A. Rhodes, J. Travis, M. Waul, & A. Elsner]. The Journal of Criminal Law and Criminology (1973-), 94(4), 1149–1162. https://doi.org/10.2307/3491418

- Giles, J. (1993). The No-Self Theory: Hume, Buddhism, and Personal Identity. Philosophy East and West, 43(2), 175–200. https://doi.org/10.2307/1399612

- Gul, R. (2018). Our Prisons Punitive or Rehabilitative? An Analysis of Theory and Practice. Policy Perspectives, 15(3), 67–83. https://doi.org/10.13169/polipers.15.3.0067

- Haines, F., & Sutton, A. (2000). CRIMINOLOGY AS RELIGION? Profane Thoughts about Sacred Values. The British Journal of Criminology, 40(1), 146–162. http://www.jstor.org/stable/23638535

- Hargreaves, J. (2015). HALF A STORY? MISSING PERSPECTIVES IN THE CRIMINOLOGICAL ACCOUNTS OF BRITISH MUSLIM COMMUNITIES, CRIME AND THE CRIMINAL JUSTICE SYSTEM. The British Journal of Criminology, 55(1), 19–38. http://www.jstor.org/stable/43819258

- Hughes, J. J. (1987). World Buddhism and the Peace Movement. Bulletin of Peace Proposals, 18(3), 449–468. http://www.jstor.org/stable/44481451

- Kadish, S. H. (1983). Rehabilitation Revisited [Review of The Decline of the Rehabilitative Ideal: Penal Policy and Social Purpose, by F. A. Allen]. Stanford Law Review, 35(2), 363–371. https://doi.org/10.2307/1228667

- Lucken, K. (1998). CONTEMPORARY PENAL TRENDS: Modern or Postmodern? The British Journal of Criminology, 38(1), 106–123. http://www.jstor.org/stable/23638585

- Martin, R. (1990). Treatment and Rehabilitation as a Mode of Punishment. Philosophical Topics, 18(1), 101–122. http://www.jstor.org/stable/43154067

- Mascini, P., & Houtman, D. (2006). REHABILITATION AND REPRESSION: Reassessing their Ideological Embeddedness. The British Journal of Criminology, 46(5), 822–836. http://www.jstor.org/stable/23639634

- McEvoy, K., Mika, H., & Hudson, B. (2002). INTRODUCTION: Practice, Performance and Prospects for Restorative Justice. The British Journal of

Criminology, 42(3), 469–475. http://www.jstor.org/stable/23638876

- Morash, M. A., & Anderson, E. A. (1978). Liberal Thinking on Rehabilitation: A Work-Able Solution to Crime. Social Problems, 25(5), 556–563. https://doi.org/10.2307/800104
- Neigenfind, L. K. (2020). Is Nonviolence and Pacifism in Christian and Buddhist Ethics Obligatory or Supererogatory? Buddhist-Christian Studies, 40, 387–401. https://www.jstor.org/stable/48618654
- O'Brien, R. (2016). REFORMING GOALS. RSA Journal, 162(5566), 10–15. http://www.jstor.org/stable/26204495
- Olson, S. M., & Dzur, A. W. (2004). Revisiting Informal Justice: Restorative Justice and Democratic Professionalism. Law & Society Review, 38(1), 139–176. http://www.jstor.org/stable/1555115
- Phelps, M. S. (2011). Rehabilitation in the Punitive Era: The Gap Between Rhetoric and Reality in U.S. Prison Programs. Law & Society Review, 45(1), 33–68. http://www.jstor.org/stable/23011958
- Roberts, L. A. (1984). Bridewell: The World's First Attempt at Prisoner Rehabilitation Through Education. Journal of Correctional Education, 35(3), 83–85. http://www.jstor.org/stable/41970751
- Rotman, E. (1986). Do Criminal Offenders Have a Constitutional Right to Rehabilitation? The Journal of Criminal Law and Criminology (1973-), 77(4), 1023–1068. https://doi.org/10.2307/1143667
- Schipper, J. (2012). Toward a Buddhist Sociology: Theories, Methods, and Possibilities. The American Sociologist, 43(2), 203–222. http://www.jstor.org/stable/41485740
- Soontravanich, C. (2013). The Regionalization of Local Buddhist Saints: Amulets, Crime and Violence in Post-World War II Thai Society. Sojourn: Journal of Social Issues in Southeast Asia, 28(2), 179–215. http://www.jstor.org/stable/43186958
- Sykes, G. M. (1956). The Corruption of Authority and Rehabilitation. Social Forces, 34(3), 257–262. https://doi.org/10.2307/2574049

A Moment Of Gratitude

Dip Tse Chok Ling Monastery

*"The way forward lies humourously in the understanding
and synthesis of irony; the balance of contradictions."*

Writing "Transformative Justice & Tibetan Buddhism: Principles for
Restorative Offender Rehabilitation & Modern Criminology" has been a
journey of reflection and mindful exploration. As I sit here, by my work
desk, I am filled with a sense of gratitude and peace.

In this book, we have ventured into the heart of Tibetan Buddhist
principles, uncovering their timeless wisdom and their relevance to
modern justice systems. The concepts of the Middle Way, Dependent
Origination, and the Four Noble Truths are not just philosophical ideas;
they are practices that bring us closer to understanding the true nature

of our interconnectedness. They remind us that every action, every thought, and every intention shapes the world we live in. The Eightfold Path offers a gentle yet firm guide for living a life of ethical conduct, mental discipline, and wisdom. These principles are not abstract; they are practical steps we can take every day to cultivate mindfulness, compassion, and understanding. In the context of offender rehabilitation, they offer a path to healing and transformation, helping individuals to rediscover their inherent worth and potential for change.

The Bodhisattva Ideal, with its deep commitment to compassion and altruism, calls us to look beyond the surface of human behavior and see the suffering that lies beneath. It invites us to respond with kindness and understanding, to offer support and guidance rather than judgment. This approach, when applied to the justice system, has the potential to create a space where healing and reconciliation can flourish. Mindfulness and meditation are at the heart of this transformative process. They teach us to be present, to observe our thoughts and feelings without judgment, and to cultivate a sense of inner peace and stability. These practices are powerful tools for personal transformation, helping individuals to manage stress, regulate emotions, and develop a deeper sense of self-awareness. In the context of offender rehabilitation, they offer a way to break free from the cycles of suffering and create a foundation for lasting change.

As I reflect on the journey of writing this book, I am reminded of the importance of hope. Hope is not a distant dream, but a reality we can touch in each moment. It is the belief that transformation is possible, that every person has the capacity for growth and change. This hope is rooted in the practice of mindfulness, in the compassionate understanding of our interconnectedness, and in the commitment to ethical living.

Thanks for Reading!